PRAISE FOR *KNOWL* *MANAGEMENT*

'This book is really awesome and gives a strong basis for knowledge management.'
Professor Pascale Zarate, Editor-in-Chief for *International Journal of Decision Support System Technology*, **University of Toulouse, France**

'A must-read contemporary KM book, suitable for all KM practitioners, researchers and students. It intertwines knowledge management in the fields of business, organizations, human decision making, knowledge networks, information systems and technology, decision support systems and big data analytics.'
Professor Boris Delibasic, University of Belgrade, Serbia

'The book offers a rich approach to knowledge management, focusing on knowledge sharing and learning across boundaries. It also discusses how to implement KM for supporting business decision making in the context of the supply chain and globalization. All readers, from students to practitioners, will discover precious resources integrating the latest state-of-the-art research results.'
Professor Isabelle Linden, University of Namur, Belgium

'This book has many distinctive features, including an interdisciplinary approach by knitting together knowledge management and other neighbouring disciplines, and treating knowledge management as a key ingredient to building business intelligence systems. The sections on the impact of ICT technologies such as big-data analytics and Internet of Things on knowledge management were especially valuable. Providing such an overall view of the discipline does a great service to all stakeholders in the field. I recommend it to all students, researchers and practitioners interested in knowledge management and business intelligence systems.'
Professor Sean Eom, Southeast Missouri State University, USA

Knowledge Management

An interdisciplinary approach for business decisions

Shaofeng Liu

KoganPage

First published in Great Britain and the United States in 2020 by Kogan Page Limited

2nd Floor, 45 Gee Street
London
EC1V 3RS
United Kingdom

122 W 27th St, 10th Floor
New York, NY 10001
USA

4737/23 Ansari Road
Daryaganj
New Delhi 110002
India

www.koganpage.com

© Shaofeng Liu, 2020

The right of Shaofeng Liu to be identified as the author of this work has been asserted by her in accordance with the Copyright, Designs and Patents Act 1988.

ISBNs

Hardback   978 1 78966 105 7
Paperback   978 0 7494 9483 4
Ebook   978 0 7494 9687 6

British Library Cataloguing-in-Publication Data

A CIP record for this book is available from the British Library.

Library of Congress Cataloging-in-Publication Data
Names: Liu, Shaofeng (Expert in knowledge management), author.
Title: Knowledge management : an interdisciplinary approach for business
   decisions / Shaofeng Liu.
Description: London, United Kingdom ; New York, NY : Kogan Page Limited,
   2020. | Includes bibliographical references and index.
Identifiers: LCCN 2019045475 (print) | LCCN 2019045476 (ebook) | ISBN
   9781789661057 (hardback) | ISBN 9780749494834 (paperback) | ISBN
   9780749496876 (ebook)
Subjects: LCSH: Knowledge management. | Business–Decision making.
Classification: LCC HD30.2 .L584 2020 (print) | LCC HD30.2 (ebook) | DDC
   658.4/038–dc23
LC record available at https://lccn.loc.gov/2019045475
LC ebook record available at https://lccn.loc.gov/2019045476

Typeset by Integra Software Services, Pondicherry
Print production managed by Jellyfish
Printed and bound by CPI Group (UK) Ltd, Croydon, CR0 4YY

CONTENTS

PART TWO Building knowledge competence in organizations 63

PART THREE Crossing knowledge boundaries 169

LIST OF FIGURES AND TABLES

Figures

ABOUT THE AUTHOR

Professor Shaofeng Liu is an internationally recognized expert in the field of knowledge management and business decision making. She obtained her PhD degree from Loughborough University, UK, specializing in knowledge and information management for global manufacturing coordination decisions. After graduation, she worked for Bath University and Strathclyde University before joining the University of Plymouth Business School. She has undertaken a great number of influential collaborative research projects, with a total value of over €40 million, funded by various research councils, including the European Commission, UK ESRC, EPSRC and Innovate UK. She is currently Principal Investigator and Co-Investigator for five EU projects, four of which are funded by the Horizon 2020 programme and one by the Erasmus Plus scheme. She is a very productive and successful supervisor for PhD research and postgraduate students. She has published over 160 research papers in peer-reviewed, high-quality books, journals and conference proceedings. She was Senior Editor for *Cogent Business & Management* (2013–2018) and Associate Editor for *Journal of Decision Systems* (2013–2017), and has been Associate Editor for *International Journal of Decision Support System Technology* since 2015. She was lead guest-editor for the Special Issue on 'Knowledge-based decision systems' with *Journal of Decision Systems* (2014) and the Special Issue on 'Sustainable knowledge-based decision support systems for business performance improvement in real industrial environment' with *Industrial Management & Data Systems* (2017). She has been a co-guest editor for six books in the Decision Support Systems (I–VI) series published by Springer, among which book IV is dedicated to 'Information and Knowledge Management in Decision Process'. She has been a Management Board member for the Euro Working Group on Decision Support Systems (EWG-DSS) since 2011. Through her research and teaching over the past 20 years, Professor Liu has obtained considerable insights and developed her own views on knowledge management, especially in how knowledge management can contribute to achieving better business decisions.

PREFACE

Knowledge management is important, exciting and challenging

Regarded as one of the most crucial assets in all businesses, knowledge is extremely important to individuals, organizations and communities nation-wide. This importance has been highlighted by many well-known phrases and statements, including 'knowledge is power', 'knowledge-based view' (ie knowledge is the source of sustainable competitive advantage for organiza-tions) and the 'knowledge economy' (ie the whole economy is driven by knowledge intangibles). Because of this high level of importance, knowledge management (KM) has become a hot topic for academics, researchers, engi-neers, practitioners, business leaders, managers and other professionals who endeavour to improve the process and lifecycle of the creation, holding, mo-bilization and utilization of knowledge. Efficient and effective management of knowledge not only helps to achieve excellent business performance but also catalyses the innovation of new products and services, which is the key to business prosperity and sustainability in the long term.

KM is exciting because it fundamentally influences business decisions at all levels, strategic or operational, and from individual, group, and organization to the supply chain. Without support from the right knowledge, business lead-ers and managers cannot reach the right judgement on business problems and make the most appropriate choice. KM has brought much excitement to busi-ness, because it is KM that channels the right knowledge to the right people (as decision makers) at the right time in the right place. From an organiza-tional perspective, the right business decisions based on the right knowledge can help organizations to grab the most precious business opportunities in advance of competitors. Incorrect business decisions resulting from poor judgement based on the wrong knowledge could result in severe business fail-ures. In short, knowledge and KM play a dominant role in making or break-ing a business. From a people and career development perspective, making the right business decisions supported by the right knowledge can be the mark of promotable and successful business leaders and managers. Such a high level of impact on business decisions makes the topic of KM very exciting.

There is no doubt that KM is challenging. There are a number of main reasons. First, knowledge is mostly tacit and intangible. For managing tangible entities such as products or machines in an organization, people can attach visible artefacts such as a label or a handbook to help the management process. However, such visible artefacts will not work for managing tacit knowledge. Converting tacit knowledge into explicit knowledge has long been considered a challenge. Second, in many businesses, KM is not recognized as one of the core business functions, such as accounting and finance, marketing and sales, human resource management and leadership, operations and supply chain management. Business leaders and managers are often appointed for those core business functions, but chief knowledge officers may not be appointed. Sometimes KM seems nowhere to be seen, while the truth is that knowledge is actually everywhere in businesses. KM is not restricted only to the creation and delivery of products and services through operations and supply chain management, but also involves, for example, marketing and sales knowledge. Furthermore, KM needs to consider the links among all core business functions, which requires deep understanding of the whole business from a higher level, so that knowledge can be transformed into organizational competence. KM becomes even more challenging when the KM activities need to cross knowledge boundaries, such as knowledge sharing across different stages of a supply chain. Various types of boundaries can be erected, such as syntactic, semantic or political barriers. Crossing each of those boundaries has been proven to be not easy at all. Finally, KM and decision making (DM) have been traditionally treated as two subject areas in an isolated manner. The need to integrate KM and DM has been recognized; however, it is still quite a challenge to transform knowledge assets to implementable inputs into decision processes. This book explores various means to establish a bridge between KM and business DM.

Distinctive features of this book

This book provides an integrative and logical path to KM together with an understanding of KM support for business decision making. The discussion on KM progresses through four parts. Part One (Chapters 1–3) introduces key concepts of knowledge and KM, tacit and explicit knowledge conversion, and KM process and lifecycle models. Then Part Two (Chapters 4–6) focuses on building knowledge competence for organizations, covering key topics of organizational learning, learning organization and how organizational culture impacts on KM. Part Three (Chapters 7–10) looks at knowledge and learning activities beyond the scope of an organization and emphasizes knowledge mobilization crossing boundaries. The four chapters in this Part of the book discuss some of the most popular topics in contemporary KM, including communities of practice, knowledge boundaries and boundary-spanning mechanisms, knowledge networks, and ICT-enabled KM, including the Internet of Things and big data analytics. The final Part of the book (Chapters 11–13) integrates knowledge and KM into business decision making, starting with a chapter on the business decision context; then the human decision-making process is examined and the need for knowledge support established. The last chapter of the book introduces knowledge-based decision support systems, following discussion on technologies for knowledge modelling and knowledge reasoning. This book has many distinctive features that make the book stand out from the crowed, including:

- An interdisciplinary approach. KM is discussed in this book through a holistic framework integrating four perspectives: people (ie as carrier for tacit knowledge, key enabler for KM process, key driver behind organizational learning, decision maker, entities to form communities of practice and knowledge social networks), technology (eg ICT, Internet of Things, big data analytics, knowledge modelling and reasoning, knowledge-based decision support systems), process (including KM process, learning process and DM process) and business environment (such as organizational culture and business context). Therefore, this book takes an interdisciplinary approach by knitting together knowledge from business management, information systems, psychology, computer science, decision support systems, process modelling, artificial intelligence, organizational studies and so on.

- Establishing linkage between KM and business DM. The power of knowledge and KM is more evident when properly managed knowledge can be channelled to value-added utilization, in the business context, to influence business decisions and actions and subsequently to help achieve excellent business performance. This book provides insights into establishing the bridges between KM and business DM.

- Crossing knowledge boundaries. Besides introducing classic and modern theories for KM within organizations, this book puts great emphasis on discussion of knowledge mobilization and learning crossing boundaries.

Part Three of the book is dedicated to crossing knowledge boundaries by addressing communities of practice, boundary-spanning mechanisms, knowledge networks and ICT technologies such as the Internet of Things and big data analytics.

- Research-led and research-informed learning. This book consolidates classic and advanced KM theories with the most up-to-date, fresh new knowledge generated from state-of-the-art research, so that readers can get a good view of current research trends and their learning of KM theories can be truly research-led and research-informed.

- Critical thinking and evaluation. Throughout the book, valuable debate and constructive critique are offered on both classic KM theories and state-of-the-art research findings, many of which are often taken for granted. As an experienced researcher, the author believes that readers can learn much more based on critical analysis and assessment than by blindly accepting information, concepts and ideas.

Who can benefit from reading this book?

Anyone who is interested in KM and business DM, whether they are students, academics, researchers, practitioners or other business professionals. In particular:

- Postgraduates on taught programmes in business schools and management schools, as future business leaders and managers, can use the book as a core text for KM-related modules. Students in wider areas such as social science, computer science, information systems, decision support systems, product development, innovation, engineering and technology can use the book as a reference and select their preferred chapters to complement their learning about managing knowledge and making decisions.

- Postgraduate researchers, including PhD students, can use the book as a core reference to enhance their knowledge and expertise for their research related to KM, DM and decision support systems. The state-of-the-art research findings embedded in the book will provide research students with a quick catch-up on current research trends in KM and DM.

- MBA students will find the book's discussion on organizations' practical business decisions particularly interesting, including organizational learning, organizational culture, the learning organization, communities of practice, the business decision environment, structures and typology. The practical examples and business cases should provide insights for MBA students' in-class and after-class discussion.

- Undergraduates in business studies, management studies, computer science and information systems can all benefit from the book, by learning classic KM and DM theories to build their confidence in the topics. Part One, Part Two and Chapters 11–12 of Part Four are particularly useful to undergraduates who wish to establish a solid foundation for their knowledge and expertise in KM and business DM.

- Researchers, academics and business practitioners can read the book to consolidate their knowledge and expertise for KM and business DM, either to expand their general knowledge or to focus on selected topics for more in-depth exploration.

ACKNOWLEDGEMENTS

My special thanks go to my husband, Tim. I would like to thank him for his patience and tolerance of my many absences from family duties, as well as his encouragement and support throughout the writing period. His expertise in ICT technologies has been very handy, and I have greatly benefited from his expertise and learned so much from him over every day's casual conversations at the dinner table and relaxation walk in the Central Park. He is wonderful! I also would like to thank my daughter, Jenny. She has been an absolute inspiration to me. I highly appreciate all the medical knowledge she has taught me and shared with me, so that I have been able to write all the case studies related to medicine and the healthcare industry. She is my sunshine which has brought all the positive energy to me, especially when I was writing late into the evenings and during long weekends.

A great number of people at Kogan Page have greatly helped with this book project right from its inception. First, I would like to thank Amy Minshull, our Commissioning Editor. Through all the e-mail exchanges and telephone conversations, Amy helped me to set the vision of the book and clarify the scope of the chapters. Without Amy's considerable help, this book would not have materialized so soon. Thank you, Amy, your professional approach has paved a smooth way for this book! Second, I would like to express my gratitude to Adam Cox, our Development Editor. Adam has been fantastic all the way through the book project. He has not only read all 13 chapters of the book and offered constructive comments about my writing, but has also shown excellent project management skills to keep me on track all the time. Your help is highly appreciated, Adam. You have been a delight to work with!

Special acknowledgement goes to my fellow colleagues in many universities and in the Society of Euro Working Group on Decision Support Systems. As experienced book authors, Professor Kerry Howell and Professor Pascale Zarate have offered the most precious advice about planning this book project. Professor Boris Delibasic, Professor Isabelle Linden, Dr Festus Oderantie, Dr Uchitha Jayawickrama and Dr Femi Olan have used their expertise in knowledge management and decision making to provide their feedback on the book. I owe my gratitude to my research team, including my research fellows and PhD students who have contributed their hard work researching on relevant topics, in particular Aira Ong, Ali Alkhuraiji, Biljana Boshkoska, Bin Gao, Guoqing Zhao, Huilan Chen, Jiang Pan, Karim Soliman, Sulaiman Alfadhel and Xuemuge Wang. Most state-of-the-art research contributions from them have been reflected in this book.

Finally, I would like to thank the anonymous reviewers who read specific draft chapters of this book and offered valuable comments. I believe that their comments have made this book better.

LIST OF ABBREVIATIONS/ ACRONYMS

AI	Artificial Intelligence
ATM	Automated Teller Machine
BDA	Big Data Analytics
BN	Bayesian Network
CAD/CAM	Computer Aided Design/Computer Aided Manufacturing
CERP	Cluster of European Research Projects
CIO	Chief Information Officer
CKO	Chief Knowledge Officer
CoP	Community of Practice
CVF	Competing Values Framework
DAML	DARPA Agent Markup Language
DLOQ	Dimensions of Learning Organization Questionnaire
DM	Decision Making
DSS	Decision Support System
FDI	Foreign Direct Investment
GDSS	Group Decision Support System
GMO	Genetically Modified Organism
HRD	Human Resource Development
ICT	Information and Communication Technology
IoT	Internet of Things
IP	Internet Protocol
IPR	Intellectual Property Rights
ITU	International Telecommunications Union
KB-DSS	Knowledge-Based Decision Support System
KBS	Knowledge-Based System
KBV	Knowledge-Based View
K/DM	Knowledge and Decision Making
KM	Knowledge Management
KMS	Knowledge Management System
LAN	Local Area Network
LO	Learning Organization

MBV	Market-Based View
MCDA	Multi-Criteria Decision Analysis
MNC	Multinational Corporation
MIT	Massachusetts Institute of Technology
NGO	Non-Governmental Organization
OECD	Organization for Economic Co-operation and Development
OC	Organizational Culture
OEM	Original Equipment Manufacturer
OIL	Ontology Inference Layer
OL	Organizational Learning
OM	Organizational Memory
OWL	Ontology Web Language
PM	Project Management
RBR	Rule-Based Reasoning
RBV	Resource-Based View
R&D	Research and Innovation
RDF	Resource Description Framework
RFID	Radio Frequency Identification
SECI	Socialization, Externalization, Combination, Internalization
SME	Small- and Medium-sized Enterprise

GUIDE TO THE BOOK

Critical thinking and reflection: pause and reflect on the material being discussed. These sections are written to develop your critical thinking skills and deepen your understanding of the theories and practices of knowledge management and decision making.

Short illustrations: short, snappy illustrations are carefully selected from research and the business world, illustrating the concepts discussed in the chapter, with accompanying questions to prompt you to analyse the knowledge-management and decision-making practices of a range of organizations and application scenarios.

Case studies: longer, more comprehensive case studies at the end of sections or chapters provide further opportunities for you to analyse how the knowledge you have learned from the section or chapter can be applied to practical business cases. Accompanying case study questions can facilitate reflection and discussion.

PART ONE
Knowledge management – key concepts and models

This first part of the book lays the foundation for knowledge management and business decisions. Part One consists of three chapters:

- Chapter 1 includes definitions of knowledge and knowledge management, why knowledge and knowledge management are important to individuals, organizations and the economy, some well-known knowledge management approaches, and the multidisciplinary perspectives of knowledge management.

- Chapter 2 classifies knowledge into categories. Great attention has been paid to the concepts of tacit and explicit knowledge. This chapter also discusses the four knowledge processes for conversion between tacit and explicit knowledge, known as the SECI model (Socialization, Externalization, Combination and Internalization). Knowledge 'Ba' theory, which provides knowledge spaces for knowledge conversion, is discussed.

- In Chapter 3, knowledge management processes are analysed first, including the knowledge building stage, knowledge holding stage, knowledge mobilization stage and knowledge utilization stage. Following the discussion of the four main stages of the knowledge management process, knowledge lifecycle models are examined in detail.

Introduction to knowledge management

01

1.1 What is knowledge and knowledge management?

As a relatively young subject, knowledge management (KM) has gained enormous popularity in the post-industrial era. In order to facilitate the discussion of KM, it is essential to have some understanding of what knowledge is. Hence, this section starts with the definition of knowledge.

Knowledge definition

Drucker (1988) identified that knowledge was the most important resource for individuals, businesses, governments, nations and society at large, but knowledge is complex by nature. While knowledge is increasingly being viewed as a valuable commodity or intellectual asset, that is, embedded in businesses, delivered in the form of products (especially high-technology products) and embodied in highly mobile employees, there are some paradoxical characteristics of knowledge that are radically different from other value products. This is the very reason why KM can stand as a distinctive subject in its own right, rather than a sub-topic of product development such as design, manufacture or management. These knowledge characteristics include (Dalkir, 2017):

- Using knowledge does not consume it.
- Sharing and transferring knowledge does not result in losing it.
- Knowledge is abundant, but the ability to use knowledge is scarce.
- Much of an organization's valuable knowledge walks out of the door at the end of the day.

Despite the popularity KM has gained, there has been so far no consensus on what knowledge is. Many definitions have been provided over the years, and a few of them are given here:

> Knowledge can be defined as 'justified true belief related to human actions'. (Nonaka and Takeuchi, 1995)
>
> Knowledge consists of truths and beliefs, perspectives and concepts, judgements and expectations, methodologies and know-how. It is possessed by humans, agents or other active entities, and is used to receive information and to recognize and identify; analyse, interpret, and evaluate; synthesize and decide; plan, implement, monitor and adapt – that is, to act more or less intelligently. In other words, knowledge is used to determine what a specific situation means and how to handle it. (Wiig, 1999: 179–202)
>
> Knowledge is 'a fluid mixture of framed experience, values, contextual information and expert's insight that provides a framework for evaluating and incorporating new experience and information. It originates and is applied in the mind of knowers. In organizations, it often becomes embedded not only in documents or repositories but also in organizational routines, processes, practices and norms'. (Davenport and Prusak, 1998: 5)
>
> Knowledge is a high value form of information that is ready to apply to decisions and actions. (Davenport and Prusak, 2000)
>
> Knowledge could be considered as 'actionable information'. (Jashapara, 2011: 18).
>
> Knowledge in an area is defined as 'justified beliefs about relationships among concepts relevant to that particular area'. (Becerra-Fernandez and Sabherwal, 2015: 18)

Knowledge refers to 'the understanding of people about relationships among phenomena. It is embodied in routines for the performance of activities, in organizational structures and processes and in embedded beliefs and behaviour. Knowledge implies an ability to relate inputs to outputs, to observe regularities in information, to codify, explain and ultimately to predict'. (North and Kumta, 2018: 36)

Even though these definitions of knowledge look quite different in expression, there are some commonalities that we can get from the interpretation and implications below the surface:

- Knowledge is closely related to human 'action', 'judgements', 'activities' and 'prediction', which positively suggest decision making.

- People are a key element of knowledge because it is related to 'human' action, the understanding of 'people', and possessed by 'humans, agents or other entities'. This view makes it comfortable for people who are decision makers to make good use of knowledge for making better decisions.

- Knowledge is contextualized because it has 'a specific situation' and is in 'a particular area' and 'organizational structures'. This fits well with the point that decisions are made within a specific culture, situation and environment.

- Knowledge is related to, but more valuable than, information in supporting decision making, because knowledge is 'justified', 'truths', 'actionable' and 'ability'. This point has support from the well-known 'data–information–knowledge ladder' (North and Kumta, 2018: 35), but this book extends the ladder from knowledge to decisions by closing the gap through KM and business decision making, as illustrated in Figure 1.1.

Figure 1.1 Extending the 'data–information–knowledge ladder' to decisions

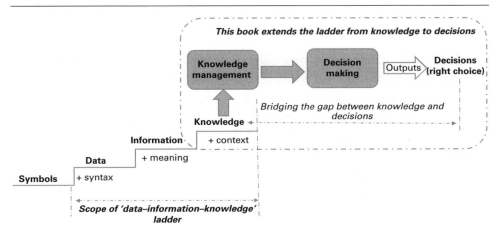

Starting from the bottom of the ladder, the most basic form for people to use to communicate is symbols. Symbols can be numbers (such as 1, 3 and 5), letters (such as a, b and c) or signs (such as +, – and £). These symbols can only be interpreted if there are clear rules of understanding (ie syntax). When symbols are combined with syntax, they become data.

 Illustration
Data–information–knowledge

Combining 1, 3, 5 and £ together with the plus sign transforms symbols into the data '+ £135'. When data are given meaning, they become information. For example, if we talk about a bank statement, '+ £135' could mean the balance one has in the bank, which is not negative. If we talk about a wage slip, '+ £135' could mean income per week from work, which is not very high. Hence, information is organized data adding meaning to a message. However, information can be interpreted differently depending on context. For example, if we need to use the £135 to buy food to feed a family, it depends on how many people there are in the family, what they already have in the fridge and how many days the food needs to last. In such situations, a person's experience and expectations of the family will come into play in terms of what and why to buy using the £135 (ie knowledge). Most likely, a person with sufficient know-how will be able to buy the right types and amounts of food, using the money to feed the family for the required period of time; in other words, they will be able to make the right decisions. The data–information–knowledge–decision ladder illustrates the important role of knowledge in the sense that knowledge has more value than information and data, which can help people to make the right decisions.

Question

In this example of buying food for a family using £135, what other knowledge can you think of that could help with the food-buying decisions, and why?

In other words, data refer to bare facts or observations void of meaning, context and intent, information is structured data with meaning, and knowledge refers to the understanding of relationships among concepts relevant to a particular context that can enable action and decisions. In other words, data without context or reference point analysis have no meaning, but they are essential for the creation of information. Humans give data meaning by adding context and reference points that are relevant and purposeful for communicating new information to a receiver. Knowledge connects the stuff in the mind and the stuff of the world. It is not a recorded thing (data or information), or at least, it is not just that (Bumblauskas *et al*, 2017). Let us consider two more examples of what can be considered to be data, information and knowledge.

Example 1: numbers 0, 1, 2, 3, 4, 5, 6, 7, 8 and 9 can be considered raw data. If we organize numbers using a structure and put the organized data stream in a phone book, such as 0044 (0)1752 585 000, it becomes information that represents a phone number in Plymouth, United Kingdom. Many people may be indifferent to the phone number. However, an example of knowledge includes recognizing that it is the phone number of a very important client from whom the company can usually get big orders, so the person knows that they need to use the number to call the client to give updates on new products and offer after-sale services regularly.

Example 2: a sales order at a café may include one beef burger and two ham sandwiches. Here one (beef burger) and two (ham sandwiches) are data. At the end of the day, all sales are added up, which becomes information for the café manager. An example of knowledge would be to be aware of the relationships among the total number of beef burgers sold, the cost of the sold burgers and the profit from selling beef burgers. If there is a good profit from selling the burgers, a sensible decision would be that beef burgers should be kept on the menu. Another example of knowledge would be realizing the relationships among the number of burgers sold on the day, the number of burgers still in stock and the number of burgers expected to be sold the next day, hence enabling the decision of how many burgers should be ordered for the next day.

It is apparent that technologies such as ICT and social networks are immensely important in supporting the transformation from data to information to knowledge and finally to decisions.

Critical thinking and reflection
Knowledge, information and data

In your opinion, is it possible to draw clear boundaries between knowledge, information and data? Is there a need on some occasions to draw clear boundaries between them, or would you be happy to take a 'fuzzy' approach without searching for clear boundaries? Use some real-life examples to support your argument.

Figure 1.2 The four key dimensions of knowledge and business decision making (K/DM)

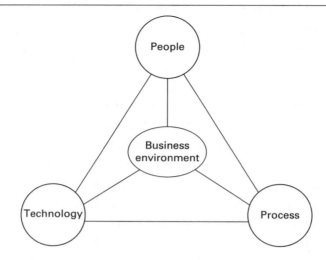

To summarize, we can see four dimensions of knowledge: people, process, technology and business environment, as shown in Figure 1.2. These four dimensions will also form the key constructs for decision making: 1) people (not machines) make decisions; 2) important business decisions need to follow systematic and scientific processes (rather than gut feelings); 3) advanced technologies such as Internet 4.0 and Industry 4.0 are useful in supporting decision making to overcome human limitations; and 4) business decision making has to take account of the specific environment where business decisions are made, such as organizational structures and culture.

In this book, these four dimensions will be used as the threads to guide the integration of KM and business decision making (DM) across chapters.

KM definition

Most scholars agree that the late 1980s saw the phrase 'knowledge management' entering popular usage (eg conferences in KM began appearing and the term KM started to be seen in business-oriented journals), but the mid-1990s could be considered the starting point of KM as a distinctive discipline and a field of practice (ie the systematic study and deliberate leveraging of knowledge assets, illustrated by a large number of international conferences and consortia being developed, more books being published and definitions of KM emerging). In fact, KM-related activities were around long before the 1980s, for example those undertaken by librarians, philosophers, teachers and writers who had been making use of many of the same techniques as we currently use in KM. For historic reasons, KM has roots in many different disciplines, including information science, cognitive science, sociology, organizational behaviour and business management. Because of the interdisciplinary nature of this emerging field, it is not surprising that a variety of KM definitions have been proposed and that they come from different perspectives. It is claimed that there are over 100 published definitions of KM (Dalkir, 2017). Table 1.1 summarizes some of the well-known KM definitions which can be related to the four dimensions of K/DM. Some of the definitions show integration of two or more dimensions. These definitions are presented in the order of their publication year in order to show the pattern of KM evolution.

Table 1.1 Representative sample of KM definitions

Author/s, year	Definition	Link to the four dimensions of K/DM
Grey, 1996	KM is a collaborative and integrated approach to the creation, capture, organization, access and use of the enterprise's intellectual assets.	Process
Broadbent, 1997	KM is understanding the organization's information flows and implementing organizational learning practices which make explicit key aspects of its knowledge base. It is about enhancing the use of organizational knowledge through sound practices of information management and organizational learning.	Technology
Brooking, 1999	KM is the process by which we manage human-centred assets. The function of KM is to guard and grow knowledge owned by individuals, and where possible, transfer the asset into a form in which it can be more readily shared by other employees in the company.	Process + People
Davenport and Prusak, 2000	KM draws from existing resources that your organization may already have in place – good information systems management, organizational change management, and human resources management practices.	Technology

(continued)

Table 1.1 (Continued)

Author/s, year	Definition	Link to the four dimensions of K/DM
Mertins, Heisig and Vorbeck, 2000	Methods, instruments and tools that in a holistic approach contribute to the promotion of core knowledge processes.	Technology
Abell and Oxbrow, 2001	The creation and subsequent management of an environment that encourages knowledge to be created, shared, learnt, enhanced, organized and utilized for the benefit of the organization and its customers.	Process
Groff and Jones, 2003	Tools, techniques and strategies to retain, analyse, organize, improve and share business expertise.	Technology
Yew and Aspinwall, 2004	KM deals with the management of knowledge-related activities such as creating, organizing, sharing and using knowledge in order to create value for an organization. It is promoted as an essential cornerstone for companies to develop sustainable competitive advantage to remain at the forefront of excellence in a level playing-field market.	Process + Business environment
Alavi, Kayworth and Leidner, 2005–6	A systemic and organizationally specified process for acquiring, organizing and communicating both tacit and explicit knowledge of employees that other employees may make use of to be more effective and productive in their work	Process + Business environment
Slagter, 2007	Knowledge management focuses on ways of sharing, storing and maintaining knowledge, as a means of improving efficiency, speed, and competency of individuals within an organization, and therefore increasing the profitability, flexibility and adaptability.	Process + Business environment
Feghali and El-Den, 2008	The set of activities which focus on the initiation, creation, capture, transformation, retention, and access of opinions and ideas imbedded in a group's memory and intellect satisfying a set of predefined goals and objectives.	Process + People + Business environment

(continued)

Table 1.1 (Continued)

Author/s, year	Definition	Link to the four dimensions of K/DM
Newell et al, 2009	Improving the ways in which firms facing highly turbulent environments can mobilize their knowledge base (or leverage their knowledge assets) in order to ensure continuous innovation.	Process + Business environment
Payne and Britton, 2010	A systematic approach to managing the use of information in order to provide a continuous flow of knowledge to the right people at the right time enabling efficient and effective decision making in their everyday business.	Process + Technology + Business environment
O'Dell and Hubert, 2011	A conscious strategy of getting the right knowledge to the right people at the right time and helping people share and put information into action in ways that strive to improve organizational performance	All
Becerra-Fernandez and Sabherwal, 2015	KM may simply be defined as doing what is needed to get the most of out of knowledge resources.	All
Dalkir, 2017	KM is the deliberate and systematic coordination of an organization's people, technology, process and organizational structure in order to add value through reuse and innovation. This is achieved through the promotion of creating, sharing and applying knowledge as well as through the feeding of valuable lessons learned and best practices into corporate memory in order to foster continued organizational learning.	All
North and Kumta, 2018	KM enables individuals, teams and entire organizations as well as networks, regions and nations to collectively and systematically create, share and apply knowledge to achieve their strategic and operational objectives. KM contributes to increase the efficiency and effectiveness of operations on the one hand and to change the quality of competition (innovation) on the other by developing a learning organization.	All

One pattern emerging from the KM definitions is that earlier definitions are more focused on the process and technology aspects of KM, while later definitions pay more attention to the people aspect, including the central role people play in KM activities and in innovating technologies for KM, as well as managing intellectual assets. Furthermore, KM is no longer seen as something to be done separately from work, but as fully integrated in business processes and the decision environment.

The vast diversity of KM definitions may cause confusion and difficulties to learners or novice decision makers. However, it is a reality we must deal with. The lack of agreement on one universal formulation of a definition for KM may result from its interdisciplinary nature, and that KM is still a fast-evolving area. Hence it is advised that a decision maker or a group of decision makers can exercise their analytical capability, techniques and skills to arrive at a 'working' or 'operational' definition for their decision situations. For example, concept analysis is recommended as a useful technique that allows people in both research and practice to develop a clear description of KM that can be adapted to a particular decision context (Dalkir, 2017).

1.2 The value in knowledge and knowledge management

From the previous section, we have already learned that data can be transformed into information and that information can be transformed into knowledge. In terms of supporting decision making, raw data have zero or low value and information has greater value, even though different types of information might have differing values (Becerra-Fernandez and Sabherwal, 2015: 20). It is widely accepted that knowledge itself has value, and KM adds value for business and decision making (North and Kumta, 2018). This section looks at the value dimension of KM at three different but related levels: individual, organization and economy. The discussion is based on three tremendously popular expressions: 'knowledge is power', 'knowledge-based view' and 'knowledge economy'.

Knowledge is power

There may be different interpretations of the famous quote 'knowledge is power'. In the context of business decision making, it can be understood as meaning that a person of knowledge, as an individual, may have more decision power and influence in the group, organization or community. This point has support from the viewpoint that knowledge is part of intangible assets (ie an identifiable non-monetary asset without physical substance) and has economic value. That is why many scholars and practitioners like to use the phrase 'intellectual capital'. Typically, the Organization for Economic Co-operation and Development (OECD) defined intellectual capital as 'knowledge that can be converted into value or as resource utilized in future value creation without a physical embodiment' (OECD, 2008).

Intellectual capital, alongside financial capital, is considered a key part of the market value of a company (Skandia, 1998; Dalkir, 2017). Intellectual capital is traditionally divided into three categories: human capital, organizational capital and customer capital.

Human capital comprises the competencies of the workforce (human knowledge, expertise and experience) and their motivation as well as relations and values (North and Kumta, 2018: 53). Many scholars emphasize that the success of any business lies in the development and optimal utilization of its core competence rather than its products or services or current markets (Hamel and Prahalad, 1994). However, Jashapara (2011) argues that a human capital approach needs to take three considerations into account. First, economic theory has not adequately dealt with the problem of knowledge creation. Second, human capital flows and their transformation are predominantly discussed from an individual and organizational learning perspective. Lastly, human capital, as human embodied knowledge, should be distinguished from non-embodied knowledge (organizational capital). Human capital departs with employees when they leave work at the end of their working day.

Organizational capital has been seen as an extension of human capital, as it contains both organizational and behavioural variables (Reinhardt *et al*, 2001). It is based on knowledge sharing, cooperative effort and conflict resolution within organizations (Jashapara, 2011). Some people further divide organizational capital into process capital, innovation capital and culture (North and Kumta, 2018: 53). While process capital and culture have been well understood, innovation capital is less often discussed; it can be considered as the renewal strength of an organization. In fact, innovation capital may be evident in protected property such as patents, licences, brand names and the intangible virtues that enable future cash flows. It contains, for example, a valuation of creativity (Skandia, 1998). In other words, organizational capital is what employees leave in the office at the end of their working day.

Customer capital represents the value of a business's relationship with customers, comprising the depth (penetration), width (coverage) and attachment (loyalty) of the customer base (Bontis, 1996; North and Kumta, 2018).

Another type of intellectual capital is social capital (Jashapara, 2011). This concept emerged from the more recent phenomenon of knowledge sharing crossing organizational boundaries to form communities of practice. It places more emphasis on the connections and networks essential for cooperation and collaboration in business globalization and is useful for facilitating distributed and collaborative decision making.

When more and more types of intellectual capital are emerging, there is a need to develop a structure to frame the different types of intellectual capital to help learners get an overall picture of the topic, especially how much a business is worth and how its value is composed. Figure 1.3 illustrates a typology of a business's market value.

A key issue of the value and power of knowledge (intellectual capital) is the useful lifespan of a piece of knowledge – when is knowledge of no value or use, and what about knowledge that never loses its value? To answer these questions, we approach KM with a fresh lens. It is no longer advisable simply to discard knowledge items that may look past their sell-by date. Instead, more advanced techniques such as content analysis and cost–benefit analysis

Figure 1.3 A typology of intellectual capital

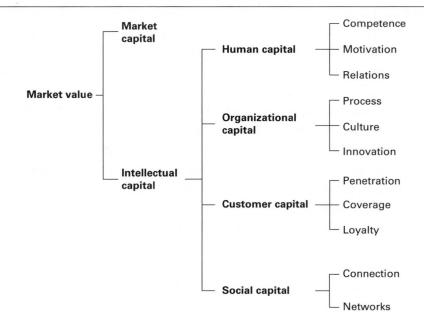

are needed in order to manage valuable knowledge for better decision making in business. KM provides benefits to individual employees to enhance their power in the organization and their decision power, so that they can do their jobs better and save time in decision making and problem solving.

Knowledge-based view

Knowledge that is embedded within the employees, systems and business processes of an organization can result in sustainable competitive advantage for a company (Afiouni, 2007). In the knowledge-based view (KBV), companies exist because they are in a position to transform individual knowledge into collective knowledge and employ that knowledge for business purposes (Castro, Saez, and Verde, 2011). KBV is the evolution of two earlier views: the market-based view (MBV) and the resource-based view (RBV).

MBV was developed in the 1980s and is typically represented by Porter's value model (Porter, 1985). MBV advocates that some companies are ahead of their competitors because they recognize market opportunities earlier than their competitors. This view is very much about the environment of a business. If a company has corresponding competencies, it will convert market opportunities into business faster than others, hence the company will enter the market first. The criticism of MBV is that with this type of competition it is difficult to build long-lasting competitive advantage (Selen, 2000).

Following wider acknowledgement of MBV, some scholars argue that companies achieve competitive advantage by being different from their competitors and acting differently from them, which is the core idea of RBV (Barney, 1992). RBV states that companies with crucial resources that are valuable to customers, rarely found in their rivals, imperfectly imitable (owing to unique historical conditions, causal ambiguity or social complexity) and non-substitutable will differentiate themselves from their competitors (Selen, 2000). As opposed to MBV, RBV enables continuous differentiation between companies.

KBV extends RBV by stressing that it is knowledge, intangible assets and intellectual capital rather than tangible physical resources that give companies unique, long-lasting competitive advantage (Jashapara, 2011; North and Kumta, 2018). Tangible resources are sources of competitive advantage only when they are applied with certain types of knowledge and they are hard to imitate. Intangible assets such as intellectual capital will create greater obstacles in attempts to imitate or substitute a company's core competence. For example, intellectual capital such as patents and brands is legally protected.

In addition, intangible assets are usually difficult to accumulate and hence more difficult to imitate. Furthermore, intangible assets such as knowledge can be used simultaneously in more than one place and its value will not decrease with increased use, which is a key advantage compared with tangible resources. There has been growing recognition that the development and deployment of knowledge is a principal source of a firm's competitive advantage (Phelps, Heidl and Wadhwa, 2012).

 Critical thinking and reflection
KBV, MBV and RBV

What do you think are the major contributions to business decisions and the limitations of the three theories (knowledge-based view, market-based view and resource-based view)? Find some examples to back up your views.

Knowledge economy

The term 'knowledge economy' evolved from the concept of the post-industrial society in the last quarter of the 20th century, typically advocated by Daniel Bell (1973). Bell suggests that industrial society and post-industrial society differ in the types of work that employees do and the types of outputs from their work: specifically, industrial workers worked manually in fabrication and manufacturing, which mainly produced goods. Comparatively, in the post-industrial society, more employees were engaged in knowledge work using their heads rather than their hands, which produced services (ideas, information and knowledge) and added value rather than simply producing goods. Bell's view has been challenged by many scholars. Some argue that service work may or may not necessarily suggest knowledge work. For example, service work such as consultancy, research, managerial and many types of professional work certainly are knowledge intensive. However, some types of service work, such as office cleaning, security and fast food restaurants, are relatively low skilled, repetitive and routine (Hislop, Bosua and Helms, 2018).

Most scholars believe that revolutionary changes did not actually occur until the early 2000s. These changes were significant and affected not only the types of products and services produced and the nature of work, but also the role of knowledge in work. Hislop, Bosua and Helms (2018) further emphasized that knowledge work relates not just to technical knowledge, such as may be used in R&D processes, but also to the application and use of such knowledge, for example in the formulation of government policy, architecture, medicine and software design, which significantly increases the impact of knowledge on productivity and economic growth at large scale. This view was supported by UK statistics showing that in 2006 knowledge workers accounted for 42 per cent of all employment in the UK (Brinkley, 2006). The concept of the 'knowledge economy' has emerged to represent this new economy driven by knowledge intangibles rather than physical capital, natural resources or low-skilled labour (Jashapara, 2011).

An early definition of the knowledge economy was given by the DTI (1998), which stated that, in the knowledge economy, the generation and exploitation of knowledge have come to play the predominant part in the creation of wealth, and that it is not simply about pushing back the frontiers of knowledge, but also about the most effective use and exploitation of all types of knowledge in all manner of economic activity (DTI 1998 cited in Jashapara, 2011). In 2005, the UK Economic and Social Research Council articulated that economic success was increasingly based upon the effective utilization of intangible assets such as knowledge, skills and innovative potential as the key resources for competitive advantage. The term 'knowledge economy' has been used since then to describe this emerging economic structure (Brinkley, 2006).

1.3 Knowledge management approaches

As seen from previous sections, both knowledge itself and KM have many different definitions. Subsequently, various KM approaches have been proposed. A comprehensive review of KM approaches was undertaken by Lloria (2008) and a critical review by Ragab and Arisha (2013). This section will discuss two well-known models closely related to business management: one as a representative of the Western view (Europe) and one of the Eastern view (Japan). Both models will be mapped onto the four dimensions of the K/DM framework, as defined in Figure 1.2.

Alvesson and Karreman's four KM orientations

In their article published in the *Journal of Management Studies*, Alvesson and Karreman (2001) identified four distinctive KM orientations that prevail in theory and practice. These four orientations can be organized along two

Figure 1.4 Mapping the four KM orientations from Alvesson and Karreman (2001) to the four-dimensional K/DM framework in this book

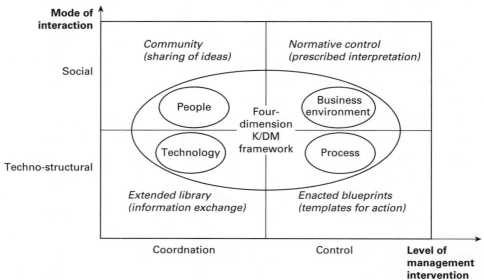

axes: mode of interaction (ie social or techno-structural) and level of management intervention (ie coordination or control), as shown in Figure 1.4.

In the figure, the four KM orientations, according to the mode of interaction (the vertical axis) and level of management intervention (the horizontal axis), are defined. These are termed 'extended library', 'community', 'normative control' and 'enacted blueprints'. In the middle of the figure is the four-dimensional K/DM framework. The mapping between the KM orientations and the K/DM dimensions is illustrated.

If the mode of interaction is techo-structural and the level of management intervention is through coordination (ie 'weak' management), the KM orientation is 'extended library', which involves extensive use of the available technologies, such as databases, search systems and communication systems, to support information and knowledge change. In this case, KM must blend a business's internal and external information and turn it into actionable knowledge through a technology platform. This KM orientation very much reflects the 'technology' dimension in the K/DM framework.

When the mode of interaction is social rather than technological and management intervention is mainly about coordination, KM is viewed as sharing ideas within a community. In this case, the community is recognized as a fundamental context for sharing knowledge, with trust as an enabler (Lloria,

2008). This KM orientation can be mapped to the 'people' dimension of the K/DM framework, because this approach highlights interest in human capital; that is, knowledge needs to be shared through social activities rather than merely accessing information or knowledge systems via technologies.

Staying with the social interaction mode while management intervention moves to the 'control' level (ie 'strong' management), KM can be viewed as an attempt by management to exercise normative control. In this case, management will stress the creation of organizational culture, such as shared values, beliefs and even regulations to impose knowledge sharing, hence this KM orientation is also considered prescribed interpretations. Organizational culture is a very important part of the business and decision environment (Oyemomi *et al*, 2019).

Lastly, with a 'techno-structural' mode of interaction and a control level of management intervention, KM takes a much more orchestrated approach, and management will attempt to engineer and control individuals so that they move closer to the behavioural level the business wishes to see. In this case, KM will explore extracting individual knowledge and converting it into organizational knowledge, storing it in knowledge bases. The stored knowledge will provide templates for thinking, decision making and action. This KM approach reflects the 'process' dimension of the K/DM framework, which emphasizes efficiency and de-skilling through classic scientific management.

Alvesson and Karreman's model has been widely cited by other KM researchers and practitioners, because the two axes used to classify the four orientations, the mode of interaction and the level of management intervention, are novel and original, offering a wide-reaching and thorough vision of the KM concept. Hislop, Bosua and helms (2018) suggest that organizations are unlikely to use one orientation to KM exclusively but are likely to use a combination of the four orientations simultaneously. This classification proves even more enriching in business management because of its links to the four dimensions of the K/DM framework proposed in this book.

Takeuchi's three KM category model

As one of the most influential scholars in the KM field, Hirotaka Takeuchi's (2001) contribution to KM approaches has been well received worldwide. In his research, Takeuchi observed that different geographic areas had taken different directions in KM: typically, European research and practice had been concerned with measuring knowledge, the United States had been more focused on the management of knowledge by maximizing the use of IT systems, and the Japanese had centred on creating new organizational knowledge. The three categories are shown in the left-hand side of Figure 1.5.

In Europe, researchers and practitioners have taken the lead in developing systems to measure knowledge, especially in how to measure intangible assets such as human capital, the combined knowledge, skills and capacity that are essential to business innovation, values and culture. Based on case studies with a number of Scandinavian companies such as Skandia AFS and PLS-Consultant, indicators have been defined to measure intangible knowledge, including employees in IT as a percentage of total cost, and the percentage of employees who work directly with customers (Ragab and Arisha, 2013).

Comparatively, Takeuchi believes that Americans have taken the lead in managing knowledge effectively by using information technologies. Knowledge managers are responsible for coding knowledge and storing it in organizational knowledge bases, and for providing knowledge users with advanced information systems, KM systems, expert systems and decision support systems to make the knowledge more readily accessible. This point was challenged by other researchers later, as people argued that even though information technologies are important in managing knowledge effectively, human factors cannot be ignored (Lloria, 2008).

While European and American scholars and practitioners focused on measuring and managing knowledge in a mechanistic, systematic way, the Japanese perspective, influenced by the work of Nonaka and his advocates, concluded

Figure 1.5 Mapping Takeuchi's KM category model to the four-dimensional K/DM framework in this book

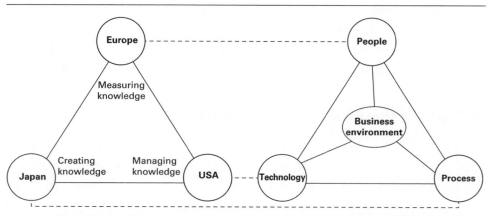

Takeuchi's three KM categories   Author's four-dimension K/DM framework

that KM has moved into a new era: that is, knowledge and knowledge creation should be distinguished. While KM is treated as working with existing knowledge, knowledge creation can only be realized through the interaction between intangible knowledge and codified knowledge forming a spiral of continuous process. This point will be extended later via the famous SECI (socialization, Externalization, Combination and Internalization) model in Chapter 2.

The above three KM categories can be directly mapped onto the author's four K/DM dimensions, as shown in Figure 1.5. That is, the European approach is more concerned with human capital, the *people* dimension, the American approach with the *technology*, and the Japanese more with the *process* (creating new knowledge and conversion between intangible knowledge and codified knowledge). However, in the past two decades, more and more researchers have realized that the three distinctive KM categories are not necessarily exclusive. For example, European companies have moved beyond measuring knowledge to looking to better apply knowledge through technologies, Americans have realized the limitations of the IT-driven approach and are considering human factors in KM, and the Japanese have been incorporating knowledge and expert systems with intangible knowledge. The three KM categories have started to come together to form a universal foundation (Lloria, 2008).

> **Critical thinking and reflection**
> The four K/DM dimensions: people, process, technology, decision/business environment
>
> If you were asked to simplify the K/DM framework by removing one of the four dimensions, which dimension would you take off, and why? If you would like to add another dimension to the four-dimensional framework, what would be that fifth dimension, and why?

1.4 Knowledge management – an interdisciplinary framework

The four-dimensional K/DM framework proposed in this book indicates that KM cannot be approached from one single discipline but needs integration of multiple disciplines. Table 1.2 summarizes all the relevant disciplines that

Table 1.2 K/DM dimensions, topics and associated disciplines

Dimensions	Key KM topics	Associated disciplines
People	• Intellectual capital (Chapter 1) • Tacit knowledge (Chapter 2) • Organizational learning (Chapter 4) • Community of practice (Chapter 7) • Knowledge networks (Chapter 9)	• Human resource management • Sociology • Cognitive science
Technology	• Explicit knowledge (Chapter 2) • Boundary-spanning mechanisms (Chapter 8) • ICT-enabled KM (Chapter 10) • Knowledge-based decision support systems (Chapter 13)	• Information systems • Computer science • Artificial intelligence
Process	• KM lifecycle models (Chapter 3) • SECI model (Chapter 2) • Organizational learning (Chapter 4) • Decision-making process (Chapter 12)	• Management science • Process management/ operations management
Business/ decision environment	• Organizational culture (Chapter 6) • Learning organization (Chapter 5) • Business decision context (Chapter 11)	• Organization studies • Performance management • Strategic management • Supply chain management

need to be involved and how these disciplines are associated with relevant topics discussed in the book.

To address the *people* dimension, the book highlights intellectual capital in this chapter and will discuss tacit knowledge in more detail in Chapter 2. How people in an organization can interact and learn will be discussed in Chapter 4. Chapter 7 will explore the sharing of knowledge in a community through social activities via the physical knowledge space or the use of knowledge networks (Chapter 9). A number of disciplines will be involved, including human resource management, sociology and cognitive science.

The *technology* dimension covers various topics, including the management of codified or explicit knowledge (Chapter 2), crossing knowledge boundaries using various mechanisms (Chapter 8), ICT-enabled KM using technologies such as the Internet of Things and big data analytics (Chapter 10), and knowledge-based decision support systems (Chapter 13). To tackle these topics, knowledge from ICT-related disciplines such as information systems, computer science and artificial intelligence will be required.

Topics on the *process* dimension include KM lifecycle models (Chapter 3), the SECI model (Chapter 2), organizational learning (Chapter 4) and the decision-making process (Chapter 12). Disciplines that can provide relevant knowledge on these topics are management science, process management and operations management.

Finally, to address the *business/decision environment*, the book will discuss important topics including knowledge sharing culture (Chapter 6), the learning organization (Chapter 5) and the business decision context (Chapter 11). Relevant disciplines are organization studies, performance management, strategic management and supply chain management.

It can be concluded that KM is truly a complex area, which requires an interdisciplinary framework to support it (Hislop, Bosua and Helms, 2018; North and Kumta, 2018). The four dimensions of people, technology, process and business/decision environment will become more obvious in the following chapters.

Illustration
A knowledge-based view of business-to-business internationalization

In their study of knowledge-intensive SME internationalization in developing economies in the context of B2B, Mejri, MacVaugh and Tsagdis (2018) identified three types of knowledge and five knowledge sources where different types of knowledge are accessed and used.

The three types of knowledge are technological knowledge, market knowledge and internationalization knowledge. Technological knowledge confers firm-specific advantages in developing products and services that are transferrable across borders, and also includes organizational awareness of technological change across the broader market and the relative position of competitors, thus informing positioning. Market knowledge is specific to each host market, including knowledge of potential customers, distribution channels, institutions, legal and regulatory conditions, and risks. Internationalization knowledge is a firm-specific ability to understand and pursue multiple international opportunities.

The five knowledge sources are direct experience, vicarious experience, grafted experience, external search and internal information. Direct experience tends to originate from the SME owner's or senior management team's previous international career, education or business venture. Vicarious knowledge acquisition refers to learning from the experience of others, for example through networking, licensing or joining clubs. Grafting knowledge involves recruiting experienced professionals or acquiring overseas business units through foreign direct investment (FDI). Externally searched knowledge is acquired from codified sources found by scanning the external environment. Such sources are crucial for internationalizing firms with limited experience. Internal information is to be found within the boundaries of a firm, for example residing in and/or developed by its staff and systems.

Mejri, MacVaugh and Tsagdis collected empirical data through semi-structured interviews from 22 SMEs in the ICT industry in Tunisia, and mapped out exactly what types of knowledge were used and accessed through which knowledge sources during the firms' internationalization process. They concluded that the SMEs accessed four out of the five sources – only internal information was not used as a source for any type of knowledge. The most frequently accessed sources were direct and vicarious experiences. In terms of knowledge types, technological knowledge was the most frequently occurring type of knowledge in the study's sample. Market knowledge was also widely sought.

Questions

Using an SME that you are familiar with, either in ICT or in other industries that have developed internationalization:

1   Find out which knowledge sources were most frequently used for acquiring which knowledge types.

2   If your findings are different from those of Mejri, MacVaugh and Tsagdis (2018), what do you think are the main reasons causing the differences?

Key learning points

- Knowledge is universally recognized as one of the critical organizational assets that differentiates the 'best' from the 'rest'. Knowledge is more complex than data and information. Knowledge can often be subjective, based on experience and highly contextual.

- KM is not necessarily something completely new but has been practised in a wide variety of settings for some time now – albeit under different monikers.

- There is no single, generally accepted definition of KM, but most practitioners and professionals concur that KM treats knowledge with the objective of supporting decision making and adding value to the organization.

- Each organization should define KM in terms of its own business objectives.

- Knowledge and decision making include four key dimensions: people, process, technology and business/decision environment.

- There have been a great number of KM approaches developed over the past three decades.

- Alvesson and Karreman defined four KM orientations based on mode of interaction and level of management intervention: extended library, community, normative control and enacted blueprints.

- Takeuchi proposed three KM categories: European focus on measuring knowledge, American focus on IT systems and Japanese focus on knowledge creation.

- KM has its roots in a variety of disciplines and requires an interdisciplinary approach.

Review questions

- How important is knowledge as against physical assets for the success of a business?

- 'Knowledge management is nothing new.' Would you argue that this statement is largely true or false, and why? Use historical antecedents to justify your arguments.

- Customer service in a call centre is typically highly controlled, routine and repetitive. It also involves the use of computers and a significant amount of interaction with customers. To what extent can such work be regarded as more skilled and knowledge intensive than less skilled or semi-skilled factory work?

- What are the strengths and weaknesses of Alvesson and Karreman's four KM orientation framework?

- What are the strengths and weaknesses of Takeuchi's three KM category model?

- Why do we need an interdisciplinary approach to KM?

References

Abell, A and Oxbrow, N (2001) *Competing with Knowledge: The information professional in the knowledge management age*, Library Association Publishing, London

Afiouni, F (2007) Human resource management and knowledge management: a road map toward improving organizational performance, *Journal of American Academy of Business*, **11**, pp 124–31

Alavi, M, Kayworth, T R and Leidner, D E (2005–6) An empirical examination of the influence of organizational culture on knowledge management practices, *Journal of Management Information Systems*, **22** (3), pp 191–224

Alvesson, M and Karreman, D (2001) Odd couple: making sense of the curious concept of knowledge management, *Journal of Management Studies*, **38** (7), pp 995–1018

Barney, J (1992) Integrating organizational behaviour and strategy formulation research, *Advances in Strategic Management*, **8**, pp 39–61

Becerra-Fernandez, I and Sabherwal, R (2015) *Knowledge Management: Systems and processes*, 2nd edn, Routledge, Abingdon

Bell, D (1973) *The Coming of Post-Industrial Society*, Penguin, Harmondsworth

Bontis, N (1996) There is a price on your head: managing intellectual capital strategically, *Business Quarterly*, **60** (4), pp 40–47

Brinkley, I (2006) *Defining the Knowledge Economy*, The Work Foundation, London

Broadbent, M (1997) The emerging phenomenon of knowledge management, *Australian Library Journal*, **46** (1), pp 6–24

Brooking, A (1999) *Corporate Memory: Strategies for knowledge management*, International Thomson Business Press, London

Bumblauskas, D *et al* (2017) Big data analytics: transforming data to action, *Business Process Management Journal*, **23** (3), pp 703–20

Castro, G M, Saez, P L and Verde, M D (2011) Towards a knowledge-based view of firm innovation, *Journal of Knowledge Management*, **15** (6), pp 871–74

Dalkir, K (2017) *Knowledge Management in Theory and Practice*, 3rd edn, MIT Press, Cambridge, MA

Davenport, T H and Prusak, L (1998) *Working Knowledge: How organizations manage what they know*, Harvard Business School Press, Boston, MA

Davenport, T H and Prusak, L (2000) *Working Knowledge: How organizations manage what they know*, 2nd edn, Harvard Business School Press, Boston, MA.

Drucker, P (1988) The coming of the new organization, *Harvard Business Review*, **66** (1), pp 45–53

DTI (1998) Building the Knowledge Driven Economy: Competitiveness White Paper, Department of Trade and Industry, London

Feghali, T and El-Den, J (2008) Knowledge transformation among virtually co-operating group members, *Journal of Knowledge Management*, **12** (1), pp 92–105

Grey, D (1996) What is knowledge management? The Knowledge Management Forum, March

Groff, T and Jones, T (2003) *Introduction to Knowledge Management: KM in business*, Butterworth-Heinemann, Burlington, MA

Hamel, G and Prahalad, C K (1994) *Competing for the Future*, Harvard Business School Press, Boston, MA

Hislop, D, Bosua, R and Helms, R (2018) *Knowledge Management in Organizations: A critical introduction*, 4th edn, Oxford University Press, Oxford

Jashapara, A (2011) *Knowledge Management: An integrated approach*, 2nd edn, Pearson Education, Harlow

Lloria, M B (2008) A review of the main approaches to knowledge management, *Knowledge Management Research and Practice*, **6**, pp 77–89

Mejri, K, MacVaugh, J A and Tsagdis, M (2018) Knowledge configurations of small and medium-sized knowledge-intensive firms in a developing economy: a knowledge-based view of business-to-business internationalization, *Industrial Marketing Management*, **71**, pp 160–70

Mertins, K, Heisig, P and Vorbeck, J (2000) *Knowledge Management: Best practices in Europe*, Springer-Verlag, New York

Newell, S *et al* (2009) *Managing Knowledge Work and Innovation*, Palgrave Macmillan, Basingstoke

Nonaka, I and Takeuchi, H (1995) *The Knowledge Creating Company*, Oxford University Press, Oxford

North, K and Kumta, G (2018) *Knowledge Management: Value creation through organizational learning*, 2nd edn, Springer, Cham, Switzerland

O'Dell, C and Hubert, C (2011) *The New Edge in Knowledge: How knowledge management is changing the way we do business*, Wiley, Hoboken, NJ

OECD (2008) [accessed 3 September 2019] Intellectual Assets and Value Creation, Synthesis Report, Paris, *OECD* [Online] www.oecd.org/sti/inno/40637101.pdf (archived at https://perma.cc/M398-MGMW)

Oyemomi, O *et al* (2019) How cultural impact on knowledge sharing contributes to organizational performance: using the fsQCA approach, *Journal of Business Research*, **94**, pp 313–19

Payne, B and Britton, M (2010) [accessed 3 September 2019] Knowledge Management, Southern California SPIN Meeting, Northrop Grumman Park, Redondo Beach, CA, 5 November, *Lnoco stories* [Online] www.nickmilton.com/2016/03/knowledge-management-at-northrop.html (archived at https://perma.cc/X96Q-XKAG)

Phelps, C, Heidl, R and Wadhwa, A (2012) Knowledge, networks and knowledge networks: a review and research agenda, *Journal of Management*, **38** (4), pp 1115–66

Porter, M (1985) *Competitive Advantage*, The Free Press, New York

Ragab, M A F and Arisha, A (2013) Knowledge management and measurement: a critical review, *Journal of Knowledge Management*, **17** (6), pp 873–901

Reinhardt, R *et al* (2001) Intellectual capital and knowledge management: perspectives on measuring knowledge, in *Handbook of Organizational Learning and Knowledge*, ed M Dierkes *et al*, Oxford University Press, Oxford

Selen, W (2000) Knowledge management in resource-based competitive environments: a roadmap for building learning organizations, *Journal of Knowledge Management*, **4** (6), pp 346–53

Skandia (1998) Human Capital in Transformation (Intellectual Capital Prototype Report), Skandia, Stockholm

Slagter, F (2007) Knowledge management among the older workforce, *Journal of Knowledge Management*, **11** (4), pp 82–96

Takeuchi, H (2001) Towards a universal management concept of knowledge, in *Managing Industrial Knowledge: Creation, transfer and utilization*, ed I Nonaka and D J Teece, pp 315–29, Sage, London

Wiig, K (1999) Introducing knowledge management into the enterprises, in *Knowledge Management Handbook*, ed J Liebowitz, CRC Press, Boca Raton, FL

Yew, K W and Aspinwall, E (2004) Characterising knowledge management in the small business environment, *Journal of Knowledge Management*, **8** (3), pp 44–61

Tacit and explicit knowledge   02

Learning outcomes

After completing this chapter, the reader will be able to:

- understand the subjective and objective views of knowledge;
- distinguish between tacit and explicit knowledge;
- examine the four processes for conversion between tacit and explicit knowledge (SECI model);
- link types of knowledge space to relevant knowledge conversion processes.

2.1 Knowledge classification

Knowledge has been classified and characterized in many different ways in the literature. One recent review of knowledge classification is available in Sudhindrea, Ganesh and Arshinder (2014). Some of the well-known classification schemes include:

- Knowledge has been categorized as individual, group, collective and organizational depending on the number of people involved (Jashapara, 2011; North and Kumta, 2018).
- There is also distinction between procedural and declarative knowledge. Procedural knowledge focuses on beliefs relating sequences of steps or actions to desired (or undesired) outcomes. In contrast, declarative knowledge focuses on beliefs about relationships among variables (Becerra-Fernandez and Sabherwal, 2015).
- Depending on the types of relationship that knowledge represents, there can be causal, conditional, relational and pragmatic knowledge (Alavi and Leider, 2001).

- According to its use, knowledge can be classified as utility knowledge, action knowledge and goal knowledge (Akerkar and Sajja, 2010).

- Knowledge can also be classified as general or specific knowledge depending on whether it is possessed widely or narrowly (Sabherwal and Becerra-Fernandez, 2005). General knowledge is possessed by a large number of individuals and can be transferred easily across individuals, while specific knowledge is possessed by a limited number of individuals and is expensive to transfer.

- Specific knowledge can be further classified into technically specific knowledge, context-specific knowledge and expertise (Becerra-Fernandez and Sabherwal, 2015). Technically, specific knowledge is deep knowledge about a specific area, for example knowledge about the tools and techniques that may be used to address problems in that area. Context-specific knowledge refers to the knowledge of particular circumstances of time and place in which work is performed. Expertise is knowledge of higher quality which addresses the degree of knowledge. That is, those with expertise are able to perform a task much better than those without expertise.

- Knowledge can also be classified as operational, tactical or strategic knowledge depending on whether it is facilitating decisions on everyday operations, or short-term or long-term positioning of the organization (Probst, Buchel and Raub, 1998; Dalkir, 2017).

It can be quite perplexing for readers when there are too many different classification schemes. It seems important that knowledge should be understood via a more philosophical approach that can 'unite' the majority of the classification schemes to support the management of knowledge effectively, so that knowledge can be better exploited as a business asset. This brought the discussion back to the classic 'objective' and 'subjective' views of knowledge, which is widely supported in the literature (Jashapara, 2011; Becerra-Fernandez and Sabherwal, 2015; Hislop, Bosua, and Helms, 2018).

The subjective view sees knowledge from two possible perspectives: as a state of mind or as a practice. Even though the foci of the two perspectives are slightly different, that is, the first one focuses on human minds and the second focuses on beliefs implicit to actions or practice, they both stress that reality is socially constructed through interactions with individuals, hence knowledge is dynamic (ie continuously emerging) and cannot be placed in one single location. In other words, knowledge cannot be separated from social practice or human experience (North and Kumta, 2018).

The objective view sees knowledge as an object or a capability (Dalkir, 2017). This view stresses that reality is independent of human perceptions that can be stored, transferred and manipulated, hence knowledge can exist in a variety of locations such as knowledge artefacts, for example repositories, technologies and systems. Furthermore, knowledge as a capability, that is, a set of beliefs about relationships of concepts relevant to a particular situation, can be applied to influence actions through decisions.

The key differences between the objective and subjective views of knowledge are summarized in Table 2.1.

The objective and subjective views of knowledge lead us to a largely ubiquitous classification of knowledge, that is, knowledge can be either tacit or explicit, despite the number of people who possess the knowledge or the types of decision that knowledge can facilitate (Groff and Jones, 2003; Hislop, Bosua, and Helms, 2018). Explicit knowledge is synonymous with the objective view of knowledge, and tacit knowledge is synonymous with the subjective view of knowledge.

Table 2.1 Subjective and objective views of knowledge

Different views	Knowledge seen as	Location of knowledge	Key features
Subjective	State of mind	Embodied in people (individual)	• Reality is socially constructed through interactions with individuals
	Practice	Embedded in practice (individual, group or organization)	• Dynamic, continuously emerging • Cannot be separated from social practice or human experience
Objective	Object	Artefacts (repositories, technologies, systems)	• Reality is independent of human perceptions • Static unless updated regularly
	Capability	Artefacts (repositories, technologies, systems)	• Can be separately stored, transferred and manipulated

Subsequently, suffice it to say that tacit knowledge represents knowledge that people possess: for example, intuitions, unarticulated mental models and embodied technical skills (Nonaka, Umemoto and Sasaki, 1998; Dalkir, 2017). The main characteristics of tacit knowledge therefore are that it is personal and that it is difficult, if not impossible, to disembody or codify. This is because tacit knowledge may not only be difficult to articulate, but it may even be subconscious. Examples of work-related tacit knowledge include how to create an effective marketing advert, how to deliver an excellent speech and how to be an effective and inspiring leader. On the other hand, explicit knowledge is impersonal, context independent and can be easily codified and stored in tangible forms such as books, reports or drawings. Figure 2.1 illustrates the main comparisons between tacit and explicit knowledge. Many scholars believe that, in business, the majority of knowledge is tacit rather than explicit, which presents a great challenge to organizations in terms of KM; that is, how to convert tacit into explicit knowledge in order for it to be shared across individuals, groups, organizations and communities (Nonaka, 1994; Feghali and El-Den, 2008). In addition, tacit knowledge can be easily lost when an employee with expertise leaves a company. Furthermore, tacit

Figure 2.1 Tacit vs explicit knowledge

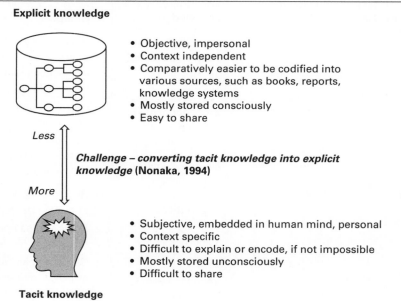

Explicit knowledge

- Objective, impersonal
- Context independent
- Comparatively easier to be codified into various sources, such as books, reports, knowledge systems
- Mostly stored consciously
- Easy to share

Less

Challenge – converting tacit knowledge into explicit knowledge (Nonaka, 1994)

More

- Subjective, embedded in human mind, personal
- Context specific
- Difficult to explain or encode, if not impossible
- Mostly stored unconsciously
- Difficult to share

Tacit knowledge

knowledge is extremely important to an organization's R&D and innovation, hence long-term prosperity and the sustainability of the business (Roy and Mitra, 2018). Section 2.2 will discuss tacit and explicit knowledge conversion in detail.

One key criticism of classifying knowledge into tacit and explicit is its simplicity and extremism. In other words, the tacit and explicit dimensions are not mutually exclusive. Instead, these two dimensions are simply different to various degrees and constitute a knowledge spectrum (Yang and Yen, 2007). Perhaps the introduction of explicitness is more appropriate, which reflects the extent to which knowledge exists in an explicit form so that it can be stored and shared with others (Nonaka and von Krogh, 2009). Explicitness indicates that rather than simply classifying knowledge as either explicit or tacit, it would be more appropriate to view explicitness as a continuous scale, that is, the two types of knowledge are at the two ends of the continuum, with explicit knowledge being high in explicitness and tacit knowledge being low in this regard (Wang, Libaers and Park, 2017). Any other types of knowledge would then be somewhere along this continuum of explicitness. This concept of explicitness may be the one that can 'unite' the different classification schemes existing in the KM literature.

 Illustration
Knowledge tacitness and explicitness embedded in product and patenting experience

Wang, Libaers and Park (2017) discussed knowledge tacitness and explicitness in detail. The research was set within a weak IPR (Intellectual Property Rights) context. Research focuses on how a focal firm's knowledge tacitness and protectiveness (ie explicitness) embedded in their product and patenting experience affects their external R&D sourcing.

The study defines product experience as the degree to which a firm has experience in managing products in its product portfolio targeted at specific product markets, and patenting experience as the cumulative stock of patents the firm has in its patent portfolio.

The research finds that product and patenting experience exert opposing influences on a focal firm's R&D outsourcing. On the one hand, a focal firm's product experience encourages external partners to seek access to the focal firm's tacit knowledge. On the other, a focal firm's patenting experience discourages external partners from providing R&D services to the focal firm.

Questions

1 Why do you think a focal firm's product experience is positively associated with external R&D sourcing?

2 Why do you think a focal firm's patenting experience is negatively associated with external R&D sourcing?

If we link this concept of explicitness back to the four dimensions in the K/DM framework (ie people, process, technology and business/decision environment), and place them onto the tacit–explicit continuum in terms of their relations to knowledge, then people would be mostly related to personal knowledge, that is, to be very much towards the tacit end. At the other end, it would be technology that can be an artefact for the storage of explicit knowledge. The business/decision environment, as the context, would be slightly towards the tacit side, while process would be towards the explicit side. This can be illustrated in Figure 2.2.

Figure 2.2 The explicitness of knowledge

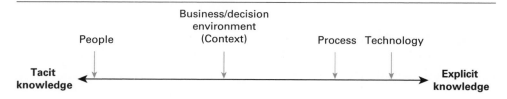

Critical thinking and reflection
Tacit and explicit knowledge or explicitness

Which statement do you support and why?

1 There should be clear distinction between tacit and explicit knowledge.

2 Knowledge explicitness is a more appropriate concept than tacit and explicit knowledge.

2.2 SECI model (tacit and explicit knowledge conversion)

It has been established that the majority of knowledge is tacit, resides in human minds and is difficult to codify or share. However, from the management point of view in an organization, it is important that tacit knowledge can be converted into explicit form so that it can be stored in repositories and accessed organization-wide rather than held by a few individuals (Dalkir, 2017). It is equally important that explicit knowledge can be converted into tacit knowledge, so that individuals can practise what they have learned from repositories, hone their skills and improve their work performance. To enable conversion between tacit and explicit knowledge, considerable research has been undertaken, and one of the most widely cited research outputs is probably the SECI model (Nonaka and Takeuchi, 1995). The SECI model introduces four processes that can enable conversion between tacit and explicit knowledge. It is also considered a model for knowledge creation because when knowledge conversion happens, usually there is new knowledge being generated. The four processes are socialization, externalization, combination and internalization. Table 2.2 summarizes the four knowledge conversion processes, the knowledge type changes (ie from one type to the other) and the occurrence of new knowledge creation.

Socialization: this is the process through which individual tacit knowledge can be converted into common/shared tacit knowledge; in other words, when individuals socialize and interact with each other, they share experiences and create common unarticulated beliefs or embodied skills. A typical example of this is the traditional master–apprentice relationship or mentoring interactions, where a young apprentice works with a master craftsman, thereby acquiring technical

Table 2.2 SECI model: conversion processes, knowledge type changes and new knowledge creation

| Conversion process | Change of knowledge type | | New knowledge creation possible during the process? |
	From	To	
Socialization	Tacit	Tacit	Yes
Externalization	Tacit	Explicit	Yes
Combination	Explicit	Explicit	Yes
Internalization	Explicit	Tacit	Yes

skills through everyday observation, imitation and practice. Another example of socialization is informal processes such as chatting with each other, brainstorming to come up with new ideas, off-site 'knowledge days', 'knowledge cafés' and 'knowledge jams', to understand each other's value to create common tacit knowledge such as a shared mental model and mutual trust. During socialization, tacit knowledge stays in tacit form, which is rarely captured, noted or written down anywhere; in other words, it remains in the minds of the original participants (Dalkir, 2017), but the process can help to create the invisible bonds of community (Nonaka, Umemoto and Sasaki, 1998).

Externalization: this process gives a visible form to tacit knowledge, that is, articulates tacit knowledge into explicit knowledge; subsequently the knowledge can be represented in tangible forms, saved, and stored in repositories such as tools, systems and technologies. The resulting explicit knowledge can then be shared by employees in an organization and may become part of its organizational memory (North and Kumta, 2018). In this case, the explicit knowledge can be retained; even if the people in whom the tacit knowledge resided leave the organization, the knowledge loss will be less severe. That is why the externalization process is very important from the management point of view. Possible means for tacit knowledge to become explicit are through the use of metaphors, analogies, concepts, hypotheses or models (Feghali and El-Den, 2008). However, the metaphors and analogies, as a language to express the essence of tacit knowledge, are often inadequate, inconsistent and insufficient. That is why, as mentioned earlier, converting tacit into explicit knowledge has been seen as a great challenge in KM. Before tacit knowledge can be written down, taped, drawn, made tangible or concrete in some manner, an intermediary is usually needed. For example, a knowledge journalist can interview knowledgeable individuals in order to extract, model and synthesize knowledge in a more professional way (such as format, length, level of detail) in order to increase its scope, so that a wider audience can understand and apply the knowledge content later (Dalkir, 2017).

Combination: this is the process of assembling discrete pieces of explicit knowledge into systematic explicit knowledge. Some examples would be a synthesis in the form of a review report, a trend analysis, a brief executive summary or a new database to organize content. In other words, combination happens when concepts are sorted and systematized in a knowledge system (Dalkir, 2017). Generally, it is considered for situations where individuals' explicit knowledge is accumulated to form an organization's knowledge base;

however, this knowledge combination process does not actually expand the organization's knowledge base (Jashapara, 2011). For example, a company's management team collects explicit knowledge from different departments, such as knowledge about marketing, knowledge about product and service design, knowledge about finance and accounting, knowledge about human resource management and knowledge about supply chain management. By synthesizing all the knowledge, the management team can then produce systematic knowledge about how to organize the company's resources effectively (people, finance, materials, distribution facilities etc) to create products and services that can meet customers' needs. Accordingly, a strategy and an operational plan can be in place to make sure that the demand-side requirement can be met by the supply-side capabilities.

Internalization: is the process of converting explicit knowledge into tacit operational knowledge such as know-how. Internalization occurs through the diffusion and embedding of newly acquired behaviour and newly understood or revised mental models. If novice workers can have access to explicit knowledge documented in text, audio and video forms that has been externalized from experienced workers, the novice workers can internalize the explicit knowledge through 'learning by doing', to expand their scope of indirect experience, reflect on the experience, and perhaps increase their tacit knowledge during the process (Feghali and El-Den, 2008). Once new knowledge has been internalized, employees can broaden it, extend it and reframe it within their own existing tacit knowledge bases. They understand, learn and buy into the new knowledge and then may do their jobs and tasks differently (Dalkir, 2017).

It needs to be emphasized that the above four knowledge conversion/creation processes are not just a one-off occurrence, but rather together they form a knowledge spiral for continuous improvement; thus it is an iterative process. Theoretically, the knowledge spiral can start from any point, but it is generally believed that it starts from the socialization process. Another point that needs emphasizing is that new knowledge is not only created during the processes that change the knowledge type, such as in externalization, where knowledge is converted from tacit to explicit, and internationalization, where knowledge is converted from explicit to tacit. Knowledge creation can also happen even when the knowledge type does not change, for example during the socialization process (ie from tacit to tacit) and combination process (ie from explicit to explicit). Hence new knowledge can be created during all four conversion processes. The SECI model has proven to be one of the most robust in the field of KM and it continues to be applied in a variety of settings. The model focuses on the knowledge transformations between tacit and explicit knowledge, but the model does not address larger issues of how decision making takes place by leveraging both these forms of knowledge (Dalkir, 2017).

Critical thinking and reflection
Socialization, Externalization, Combination, Internalization

Research relevant literature and find a list of (eg three to five) criticisms of the SECI model. Which criticism do you agree with the most, and why?

2.3 Ba theory (knowledge space)

For the SECI model to be elaborated, the concept of 'Ba' was proposed, which emphasized the importance of providing knowledge space for knowledge transformation and creation processes. 'Ba' is a Japanese word, meaning 'space' (Nonaka and Konno, 1998). It is argued that it is of paramount importance to provide shared physical, virtual, mental space or any combination of them, so that the socialization, externalization, combination and internalization processes have the environment to take place. Examples of physical space are rooms, offices or workshops. Virtual space can be an IT platform, internet or intranet, and other social networks such as WhatsApp and Twitter. Mental space includes shared experiences, ideas and concepts. Ba is considered to be a shared space that serves as a foundation for knowledge conversion and creation (Choo and Alvarenga Neto, 2010). It means that knowledge, especially tacit knowledge, is embedded in Ba (ie the shared spaces), where it is then acquired through an individual's own experience or reflections on the experiences of others. If tacit knowledge is separated from Ba, it turns into explicit knowledge, which can then be communicated independently of the Ba. Explicit knowledge is tangible and can reside in media and networks, for example. In contrast, tacit knowledge is intangible and can only reside in Ba (Oyemomi *et al*, 2019).

There are four types of Ba that correspond to the four knowledge conversion processes of the SECI model, with each type of Ba suited to each of the conversion processes. The four types of Ba are named 'originating Ba', 'interacting Ba', 'cyber Ba' and 'exercising Ba'. Together, they offer platforms to support the whole knowledge spiral process. Table 2.3 shows the mapping of the four types of Ba to the SECI model's four knowledge conversion processes.

Table 2.3 Mapping between SECI model processes and types of knowledge space in Ba theory

Ba theory – types of knowledge space	Originating Ba	Interacting Ba	Cyber Ba	Exercising Ba
SECI model – conversion processes	Socialization	Externalization	Combination	Internalization

Originating Ba is the physical knowledge space from which the knowledge creation process begins and corresponds to the socialization process in the SECI model. In this Ba, individuals can share feelings, emotions, experiences and mental models. Individuals sympathize or further empathize with each other, removing barriers among them. The shared space provides a basis for tacit knowledge conversion and creation through face-to-face interaction (Nonaka and Konno, 1998; Choudhary *et al*, 2013; Oyemomi, 2016). From originating Ba emerge care, love, trust and commitment. Organizational issues that are closely related to the originating Ba are knowledge vision and culture. A stress on open organizational designs and customer interfaces provides strong ecological stimuli through direct encounter between individuals (Nonaka and Konno, 1998).

Interacting Ba is the place where tacit knowledge is made explicit, thus it represents the externalization process in the SECI model. This knowledge space is more consciously constructed, as compared to originating Ba (Choo and Alvarenga Neto, 2010). Dialogue is key for the knowledge conversion, which is why some call this knowledge space 'dialogue Ba'. Selecting people with the right mix of specific knowledge and capabilities for a project team, taskforce or cross-functional team is critical. Through dialogue, individuals' mental models and skills are converted into common terms and concepts. During the externalization process happening in this Ba, individuals not only share the mental models of others, but also reflect and analyse their own. Interacting Ba for collective reflection is institutionalized in many companies' culture, such as Honda and 3M (Nonaka and Konno, 1998).

Cyber Ba is a knowledge space for interaction in a virtual world instead of physical space and time, and it represents the combination process in the SECI model. The combination of explicit knowledge is most efficiently supported in collaborative environments utilizing information technology. Virtual elements such as software, databases, repositories and online communication systems are particularly involved in converting one type of explicit knowledge to another in order to create new explicit knowledge. The use of online networks, groupware and internet and web-based technologies has been growing rapidly over the past decade, enhancing the knowledge conversion process (Nonaka and Konno, 1998; Oyemomi, 2016).

Exercising Ba provides the space for the internalization process where explicit knowledge is converted to tacit knowledge. This Ba facilitates continuous learning and self-improvement through workplace training, mentoring and individual participation. Focused training with senior mentors and colleagues consists primarily of continued exercises that stress certain patterns and the working out of such patterns. Rather than teaching based on analysis, learning by continuous self-refinement through active participation is emphasized. Thus the internalization of knowledge is continuously enhanced by the use of formal, explicit knowledge in real life or in simulated applications. In contrast to cyber Ba, exercising Ba is purely personal or subjective, which relies on the learner's attitude and belief (Nonaka and Konno, 1998; Oyemomi, 2016).

It can be concluded that the four types of Ba possess the dynamism to continuously create knowledge through a cycle of converting tacit into explicit knowledge and then reconverting it into tacit knowledge. The intangible knowledge embedded in the Ba can be acquired through one's own experience when organizational members share and exchange in the 'shared space'. A survey conducted in 23 international firms found that management of 'Ba' and the enabling conditions can better support innovation, sharing, learning, collaborative problem solving and tolerance of honest mistakes rather than management of knowledge itself (Choo and Alvarenga Neto, 2010). In other words, managing knowledge can be achieved through managing an enabling context in terms of Ba or shared space (Oyemomi, 2016).

Critical thinking and reflection
Ba theory

What are the main contributions of the 'Ba' theory? What do you think are the implications for knowledge managers, CIOs/CKOs or management teams who make decisions for KM in an organization?

Key learning points

- Generally speaking, knowledge can be classified into two types: tacit and explicit knowledge. Tacit knowledge is usually considered as more valuable because it is hard to replicate and there is hardly an obvious substitute. The management of tacit knowledge is incredibly challenging owing to its inherent human nature.

- The concept of explicitness is introduced to highlight the point that tacit and explicit knowledge cannot be separated in a 'black and white' manner.

- The SECI model by Nonaka and Takeuchi focuses on knowledge spirals that explain the conversion between tacit and explicit knowledge as the basis for individual, group and organizational innovation and learning.

- The four processes defined in the SECI model are socialization, externalization, combination and internalization.

- Four types of knowledge space (ie Ba in Japanese) for tacit and explicit knowledge transformation are originating Ba, interacting Ba, cyber Ba and exercising Ba.

Review questions

- Think about an example of partially explicit knowledge you are familiar with, for example a set of instructions on how to conduct a certain task. What tacit knowledge is necessary for you to make sense of them? What does this say about the inseparability of tacit and explicit knowledge?

- Describe how the two types of knowledge, that is, tacit and explicit, are transformed in the SECI model by Nonaka and Takeuchi. Use a concrete example to make your points:

  a. Which transformation(s) would prove to be the most difficult, and why?

  b. Which transformation(s) would prove to be fairly easy, and why?

  c. What other factors would influence how well the knowledge spiral model works within a given organization?

- What are the strengths and weaknesses of the SECI model by Nonaka and Takeuchi? Use an example to make your points.

- Think about interactions you have had with people from different nationalities. Have there been examples from these interactions where people's contrasting understandings of the same phenomenon have revealed the socially constructed and culturally embedded nature of knowledge?

References

Akerkar, R A and Sajja, P S (2010) *Knowledge-Based Systems*, Jones and Bartlett, London

Alavi, M and Leider, D (2001) Knowledge management and knowledge management systems: conceptual foundations and research issues, *MIS Quarterly*, **25** (1), p 107

Becerra-Fernandez, I and Sabherwal, R (2015) *Knowledge Management: Systems and processes*, 2nd edn, Routledge, Abingdon

Choo, C W A and Alvarenga Neto, R C D (2010) Beyond the Ba: managing enabling contexts in knowledge organizations, *Journal of Knowledge Management*, **14** (4), 592–610

Choudhary, A K *et al* (2013) Knowledge management and supporting tools for collaborative networked organizations, *International Journal of Production Research*, **51** (7), pp 1953–57

Dalkir, K (2017) *Knowledge Management in Theory and Practice*, 3rd edn, MIT Press, Cambridge, MA

Feghali, T and El-Den, J (2008) Knowledge transformation among virtually co-operating group members, *Journal of Knowledge Management*, **12** (1), pp 92–105

Groff, T and Jones, T (2003) *Introduction to Knowledge Management: KM in business*, Butterworth-Heinemann, Burlington, MA

Hislop, D, Bosua, R and Helms, R (2018) *Knowledge Management in Organizations: A critical introduction*, 4th edn, Oxford University Press, Oxford

Jashapara, A (2011) *Knowledge Management: An integrated approach*, 2nd edn, Pearson Education, Harlow

Nonaka, I (1994) A dynamic theory of organizational knowledge creation, *Organizational Science*, **5** (1), pp 14–37

Nonaka, I and Konno, N (1998) The concept of 'Ba': building a foundation for knowledge creation, *California Management Review*, **40** (3), pp 40–54

Nonaka, I and Takeuchi, H (1995) *The Knowledge Creating Company*, Oxford University Press, Oxford

Nonaka, I, Umemoto, K and Sasaki, K (1998) Three tales of knowledge-creating companies, in *Knowing In Firms: Understanding, managing and measuring knowledge*, ed G von Krogh, J Roos and D Kleine, pp 240–52, Sage, London

Nonaka, I and von Krogh, G (2009) Tacit knowledge and knowledge conversion: controversy and advancement in organizational knowledge creation theory, *Organization Science*, **20** (3), pp 635–52

North, K and Kumta, G (2018) *Knowledge Management – Value Creation Through Organizational Learning*, 2nd edn, Springer, Cham, Switzerland

Oyemomi, O (2016) The Impact of Organizational Factors on Knowledge Sharing Performance, PhD Thesis, University of Plymouth, UK

Oyemomi, O *et al* (2019) How cultural impact on knowledge sharing contributes to organizational performance: using the fsQCA approach, *Journal of Business Research*, **94**, pp 313–19

Probst, G, Buchel, B and Raub, S (1998) Knowledge as a strategic resource, in *Knowing in Firms: Understanding, managing and measuring knowledge*, ed G von Krogh, J Roos and D Kleine, pp 240–52, Sage, London

Roy, S and Mitra, J (2018) Tacit and explicit knowledge and assessment of quality performance of public R and D in emerging economies: an Indian perspective, *Journal of Organizational Change Management*, **31** (1), pp 188–214

Sabherwal, R and Becerra-Fernandez, I (2005) Integrating specific knowledge: insights from Kennedy Space Centre, *IEEE Transactions on Engineering Management*, **52** (3), pp 301–315

Sudhindrea, S, Ganesh, L S and Arshinder, K (2014) Classification of supply chain knowledge: a morphological approach, *Journal of Knowledge Management*, **18** (4), pp 812–23

Wang, T, Libaers, D and Park, H D (2017) The paradox of openness: how product and patenting experience affect R&D sourcing in China, *Journal of Product Innovation Management*, **34** (3), pp 250–68

Yang, C and Yen, H C (2007) A viable systems perspective to knowledge management, *Kybernetes*, **36** (5–6), 636–51

Knowledge management process and lifecycle models

03

Learning outcomes

After completing this chapter, the reader will be able to:

- describe the major stages in a knowledge management process;
- compare various knowledge management lifecycle models.

This chapter starts with the main stages usually considered in the KM process, then looks at how these process stages are arranged in different KM lifecycle models. Feedback loops are introduced.

3.1 Key knowledge management process stages

As was the case without a generally accepted definition of KM (Section 1.1), a lack of consensus exists with respect to KM process stages.

Effective KM requires individual, group, organization and community to capture the benefits of knowledge that provides a strategic advantage. There have been hundreds of KM processes discussed in the literature. Heisig (2009) undertook a comprehensive review of the topic and compared 160 KM frameworks. He found that a wide range of terms were used. This section will discuss some widely accepted process stages based on the following criteria:

- The process stage is used in multiple KM processes developed from different times (longitudinally).

- A detailed description of the process stage is available, which can be comprehended without ambiguity.

- It is implemented and validated in real-world settings.

By using the above criteria, despite the diversity of KM frameworks and use of terms, there are some common underlying stages for KM processes. We divide a KM process into four key stages, shown in Figure 3.1:

- Knowledge building stage: this includes knowledge activities happening in the early stage of KM, such as knowledge creation, capture and acquisition (Dalkir, 2017). One key feature of this stage is the increase in amount of knowledge, such as from zero to existence through creation or capture, and from low volume to higher volume through acquisition.

- Knowledge holding stage: this stage is about keeping knowledge for later use. The inventory of knowledge is a crucial factor in assessing the intellectual capital of an organization. During this stage, the inventory level of total knowledge may not change but knowledge is likely to be sorted, structured or indexed for easy retrieval when needed (Becerra-Fernandez and Sabherwal, 2015).

- Knowledge mobilization stage: at this stage, knowledge flows from one place, person or ownership to another through knowledge sharing, transfer or dissemination activities. In this sense, it is a dynamic phase in which people needing knowledge for specific tasks can be efficiently matched with counter-parties possessing that knowledge (Venkitachalam and Bosua, 2014).

Figure 3.1 Key stages in a KM process

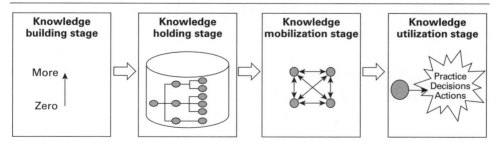

- Knowledge utilization stage: this is where knowledge is used, reused or applied in practice through decision making, actions and problem-solving activities (Nesheim, Olsen and Tobiassen, 2011).

Knowledge building stage – knowledge creation/ acquisition/capture

Knowledge creation, capture, and acquisition are terms usually used in the early stage of the KM process. They have similar meanings but do have differences as well. Knowledge creation is the development of new knowledge, typically in the form of ideas, practices, research papers, technical inventions or products – innovations that did not have a previous existence within an organization (Phelps, Heidl and Wadhwa, 2012; Dalkir, 2017). Knowledge acquisition emphasizes accepting knowledge from the external environment and turning it into a commodity that can be used within the organization (Holsapple and Joshi, 2002). Knowledge capture refers to the identification and subsequent codification of existing (usually previously unnoticed) internal knowledge within the organization or external knowledge from the environment (Dalkir, 2017).

Knowledge creation is regarded as the main source for innovation that leads to financial, market and organizational performance improvement, hence it is of paramount importance to stimulate knowledge creation activity (Ferraris, Santoro and Dezi, 2017). Knowledge creation may occur in a number of ways:

- through the conversion of tacit and explicit knowledge in socialization, externalization, combination and internalization (Nonaka and Takeuchi, 1995);

- through R&D projects, innovations by individuals to improve the way they perform their tasks, experimentation, reasoning with existing knowledge, and hiring new people (Wiig, 1993; Dalkir, 2017);

- through value-adding activities such as sharing tacit knowledge, creating concepts, justifying concepts, building a prototype and cross-levelling knowledge (Shongwe, 2017);

- through importing, for example eliciting knowledge from experts, from procedure manuals, by a joint venture to obtain technology or by transferring people between departments and organizations (Wiig, 1993; Dalkir, 2017);

- through the organization's prototyping, interviewing experts, competence and process mapping, and information workflow analysis (Evans, Dalkir and Bidian, 2015);

- through observing the real world, for example site visits, observing processes after the introduction of a change (Wiig, 1993; Dalkir, 2017).

Different from knowledge creation, knowledge acquisition comprises several steps, such as locating, accessing, capturing and collecting knowledge from customers, competitors, suppliers and other knowledge sources (Shongwe, 2017). Knowledge acquisition can be also achieved in different ways:

- Organizations can acquire knowledge by searching, grafting, congenial learning, vicarious learning and experiential learning (Huber 1991; Shongwe, 2017).

- Externally searched knowledge can usually be acquired from codified sources found by scanning the external environment (Mejri, MacVaugh and Tsagdis, 2018).

- Grafting knowledge acquisition through recruiting experienced profess-ionals or acquiring business units such as via foreign direct investment. However, it should be pointed out that experienced managers are usually costly and not readily available (Mejri, MacVaugh and Tsagdis, 2018).

- Vicarious knowledge acquisition through learning from the experience of others, for example via networking, licensing or joining expert clubs (Mejri, MacVaugh and Tsagdis, 2018).

- By extracting, interpreting and transferring knowledge to improve existing organizational knowledge (Pacharapha and Ractham, 2012).

- Through knowledge contextualization, that is, knowledge can be acquired from repositories, learning from others and learning from experiences (Dalkir, 2017).

 Critical thinking and reflection
Knowledge creation

Can you think of any real-life examples where new knowledge is created, and how is the new knowledge created?

Knowledge holding stage – knowledge storage/retention

The knowledge holding stage is important because knowledge can be easily lost, especially if it is still tacit and held by knowers. When they leave an organization, they take knowledge with them, hence knowledge needs to be held within the organization for future use. This stage refers to the storage and retention of knowledge for retrieval when needed. Knowledge is stored and kept for many purposes, such as operational and reporting reasons, for strategic decision making or for organizational learning. Knowledge that needs to be retained includes both tacit and explicit knowledge, and these may need different approaches.

Tacit knowledge retention, also known as knowledge continuity, is a relatively less researched area compared with explicit knowledge holding (Levy, 2011). It is usually achieved by proper management of human resources, so that important human capital will stay with the organization (Roy and Mitra, 2018). Knowledge retention tackles the situation in which an expert's most valuable knowledge has to become an organizational asset in a limited period of time (ie before they leave the organization). Knowledge retention has been linked to organization capability (Candra, 2014). It is argued that an organization's capability is dependent on the knowledge it retains for innovation and new knowledge generation (Jayawickrama et al, 2019). The knowledge retention process normally includes three (high-level) tasks: 1) decision making – whether or at what level vertical knowledge transfer is required; 2) planning – defining the knowledge to be retained and how; and 3) practical implementation of the plan (Levy, 2011).

Explicit knowledge can be stored manually or electronically. Manually, knowledge can be stored in manuals, meeting minutes, reports, policies and many other physical organizational documents. Electronically, explicit knowledge can be stored in organizational memories, knowledge bases, data warehouses, portals and the Internet of Things (Jashapara, 2011; Becerra-Fernandez and Sabherwal, 2015).

Knowledge mobilization stage – knowledge sharing/transfer

This stage is about how to mobilize knowledge effectively from one place, person, organization or community to another. A number of terms have been coined, for example knowledge sharing (Oyemomi et al, 2019), knowledge transfer (Guechtouli, Rouchier and Orillard, 2013), knowledge dissemination

(Lages *et al*, 2013), knowledge exchange (Sedighi *et al*, 2018), knowledge diffusion (Appleyard and Kalsow, 1999) and knowledge flow (Bhosale, Kant and Shankar, 2018). These terms can all be considered as forms of mobilizing knowledge. Some differences have been observed by some researchers. For example, Oyemomi (2016) compares knowledge sharing with knowledge transfer, and concludes that in knowledge transfer the transmission of knowledge is in one direction, from knowledge owner to knowledge receiver, while knowledge sharing is a bi-directional process. The term knowledge dissemination implies that the speed of knowledge transmission is important, especially while talking about transmitting knowledge to large and mass audiences (Lages *et al*, 2013). Knowledge diffusion is often used when referring to the movement of multiple types of knowledge between organizations, especially in relation to integrating knowledge for innovation (Appleyard and Kalsow, 1999). Knowledge flow is particularly appropriate in the context where there are more than two parties involved in the knowledge-sharing activities, such as in supply chain management (Liu *et al*, 2014; Bhosale, Kant and Shankar, 2018).

The term 'knowledge mobilization' is used in this book to highlight that for knowledge to be mobilized, especially in crossing-boundary situations, a significant effort is required from both sides involved in the knowledge activities. On the one hand, effort is required from the knowledge senders, such as representing knowledge in an easy-to-understand form or providing a more appropriate knowledge space so that knowledge activities can take place more efficiently. On the other, effort is required from the knowledge receivers' side, for example through active and deep learning in order to digest and reflect upon the knowledge received. Through the effort from both sides, knowledge is not only mobilized, but also improved and renewed. This way, the knowledge spiral effect suggested by the SECI model can actually materialize, even in knowledge boundary situations. Furthermore, besides knowledge senders and knowledge receivers, effort can also come from third parties. For example, in an organizational context, chief knowledge officers and top management teams may invest significant resources in mobilizing knowledge among different individuals, groups and functional units so that it can be of benefit to everyone in the organization. In the case of crossing organization boundaries, knowledge spanners will be one of the main forces to close cognitive gaps between knowledge senders and receivers. The concept of knowledge spanners will be discussed in detail in Chapter 8. For these reasons, knowledge mobilization is considered to be more suitable terminology in this book.

> **Critical thinking and reflection**
> Knowledge mobilization
>
> Which do you think is a better concept, knowledge mobilization or knowledge flow?
> Use examples to support your opinion. What would be the main barriers to
> knowledge mobilization crossing organizational boundaries?

Despite the use of different terminologies, some common characteristics can be established for knowledge mobilization, as illustrated in Figure 3.2.

For knowledge mobilization to take place, there has to be a transmission process. Some form of supporting resources is required, such as the media or carrier where knowledge is embedded, or people in the case of tacit knowledge mobilization. As already discussed in the previous chapter, knowledge space has to be provided as well. For tacit knowledge mobilization, *originating Ba* and *interacting Ba* such as social networks are commonly used. Technological networks such as online platforms are mainly used for explicit knowledge mobilization. Social and technological networks will be discussed in detail later, in Chapters 9 and 10. The top of the diagram shows that trust and mutual respect are important factors for knowledge mobilization.

Knowledge mobilization can be initiated in two ways. The first is by knowledge owners, who voluntarily donate knowledge to the workplace or

Figure 3.2 Key constructs of knowledge mobilization

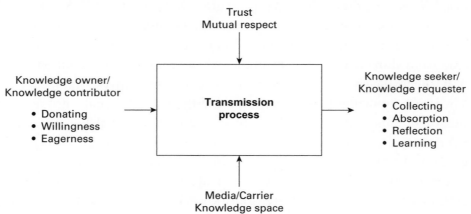

community for sharing. In this case, knowledge seekers can collect and gather knowledge from knowledge owners. In the second case, knowledge may be requested by knowledge seekers, and if knowledge contributors are willing to share their knowledge, the knowledge mobilization process will occur (Jashapara, 2011). However, knowledge mobilization should not be interpreted as a straightforward process simply passing knowledge from one person or organization to another. It requires knowledge seekers or requesters to put significant effort and commitment into absorbing the knowledge and exercising their learning and reflection, so that knowledge is not only received by the knowledge seeker but also improved, and new knowledge can even be created (Phelps, Heidl and Wadhwa, 2012; Oyemomi, 2016).

Illustration
Multi-level knowledge sharing

In contrast to the majority of studies in the literature that focus on only one level of knowledge sharing, Sedighi *et al* (2018) explored knowledge sharing at multiple levels and analysed the benefits of participation at different levels. Their paper defines three levels of knowledge sharing: private knowledge sharing between two participants, group knowledge sharing for few-to-few communication between a group of participants, and public knowledge sharing for many-to-many sharing between all members of organizations or communities. Three categories of perceived benefits are presented by the authors: intrinsic benefits, internalized extrinsic benefits and external regulation.

Intrinsic benefits include altruism – the value of gratification in helping others by sharing knowledge, and knowledge self-efficacy – the value of a person's competency to provide/share knowledge to/with others. Internalized extrinsic benefits include reciprocity, that is, the participant's perception of the value of receiving knowledge in return. External regulation includes: material rewards – a range of monetary and non-monetary incentives, the latter including job promotion, job security, flexible work hours and sabbaticals; and reputation – the value of enhancing one's respect or earning prestige through participation in knowledge sharing.

Question

Using your own experience in participating in knowledge sharing or examples you are familiar with, what perceived benefits do you think are important at which level of knowledge sharing?

Knowledge utilization stage – knowledge use/application

Knowledge utilization represents the next logical stage after knowledge mobilization in the KM process. It is not enough to share or disseminate knowledge. Rather, knowledge needs to be used to support decision making, influence actions or change behaviour. For example, best practices and similar knowledge elements are of limited value if they are not applied in business units in which a given practice is relevant. It is argued that the key point of KM is the extent to which the receivers acquire useful knowledge and use that knowledge in their operations (Nesheim, Olsen and Tobiassen, 2011). However, despite the fact that much research has been devoted to 'knowledge movement', focusing on different aspects of knowledge sharing and transfer, there has been less attention paid to knowledge utilization. The knowledge utilization stage is where tacit and explicit knowledge captured and stored in organizational knowledge bases or human heads is actually used. During this stage, knowledge may be applied in innovation, product and service design, production and delivery to customers, decision making, problem solving or any other tasks.

There have been several definitions of knowledge application. Song, van der Bij and Weggeman (2005) defined it as an organization's timely response to technological change by utilizing the knowledge and technology generated to produce new products and services. Later, Nesheim, Olsen and Tobiassen (2011) defined it as the extent to which knowledge acquired from other employees or units has been applied in a beneficial manner in a given organizational unit. Gottschalk summarizes it as applying knowledge in organizational processes and routines (Gottschalk, 2007). The knowledge-based view emphasizes that the real source of a company's competitive advantage lies in the application of knowledge, when knowledge adds value to business processes (Castro, Lopez-Saez and Delgado-Verde, 2011; Shongwe, 2017).

During the knowledge utilization stage, context plays an important role. For example, does the knowledge user have sufficient business context to utilize the knowledge that has been created, acquired, shared and stored? Context also includes rules about copyright, confidentiality and other restrictions that may apply (Dalkir, 2017). This stage is where knowledge really demonstrates its value to business, such as through decision-making or problem-solving processes, where knowledge is transformed into business assets (North and Kumta, 2018). Different business decisions may be approached differently at this stage. Decisions on routine and standard tasks are typically made using compiled knowledge that decision makers can readily access and use almost unconsciously or automatically, such as most decisions at operational level. However, difficult decisions are usually made in a more deliberate and conscious manner, as decision makers cannot use automated knowledge in unanticipated situations, such as strategic decisions and emergent decisions (Dalkir, 2017). Knowledge support for business decision making will be discussed in great detail in Part Four of the book, that is, Chapters 11 to 13.

Critical thinking and reflection
Knowledge reuse

Most precious knowledge is not used just once and then discarded, but reused again and again. What do you think are the main benefits of knowledge reuse? What management implications are there for knowledge reuse?

3.2 Knowledge management lifecycle models

Based on the understanding of the key KM process stages, this section links KM stages sequentially or in parallel to form KM processes, and discusses in particular the feedback loops that distinguish a KM lifecycle from a linear KM process. Some well-known KM lifecycle models are introduced and annotated against the four KM stages discussed in Section 3.1. Most of them have the four major stages discussed above, even though slightly different terms may have been used. Some models include additional stages or steps.

Wiig's KM lifecycle model

One of the earliest KM lifecycle models was proposed by Wiig (1993) and was widely cited in the 1990s. It specifies four stages – build knowledge, hold knowledge, pool knowledge and use knowledge, as shown in Figure 3.3. Knowledge can be built from personal experience, formal education and training, intelligence sources, media, books and peers. Knowledge can be held in people (tacit knowledge) or in tangible forms such as books and organizational memories (explicit knowledge). Knowledge may be used in work contexts and embedded in work processes.

Figure 3.3 Annotation of Wiig's model

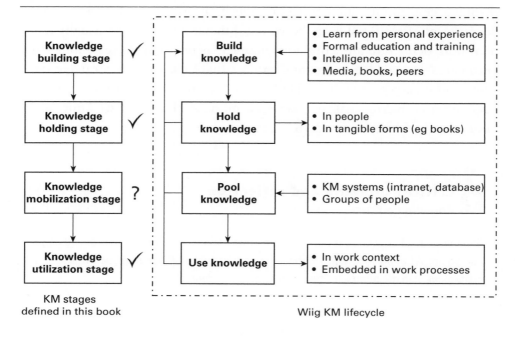

As can be seen from the diagram, three stages of Wiig's model are the same as those defined in this book. One stage is different: Wiig uses 'pool knowledge' rather than knowledge mobilization. Organizations may pool knowledge in a variety of ways. Apparently, explicit knowledge can be pooled from KM systems such as intranets and databases, and tacit knowledge can be pooled from groups of people, for example through brainstorming. An employee may realize that he or she does not have the necessary knowledge to make a decision or solve a particular problem. The individual can contact others in the organization who have faced similar problems by finding an expert through the expertise locator network. Hence, in this stage, Wiig emphasizes the coordination of knowledge, which typically requires the formation of collaborative teams to work with particular content in order to create the 'who knows what' network (Dalkir, 2017).

It is important that feedback loops are possible whenever there is a need to cycle back to repeat functions and activities that may have been performed earlier but now with a different emphasis and/or level of detail. For example, during the 'hold knowledge' stage, it is necessary to validate the knowledge content obtained from the 'build knowledge' stage, to make sure that only potentially useful/valuable knowledge is accumulated and stored in the organizational memory and repositories. It may be necessary to go back to the previous stage to obtain 'extra' knowledge in order to conduct the organization's business (eg creating the right products and services for customers). Similarly, when the organization uses 'pool knowledge' from KM systems and encounters unexpected difficulty resulting from poor codification and structuring, or cannot retrieve the required knowledge from the repositories, there may be a need to cycle back to the previous stages to improve the knowledge sorting, organization and indexing. Progressing from a simplified, linear KM process to a lifecycle model allows iterative and continuous improvement in KM, so that knowledge, initially perceived as a resource as in the resource-based view, can enable employees to work smarter. Thus knowledge becomes part of individual and organizational ability to approach tasks and businesses more intelligently, to really become an organization's competitive advantage as advocated by the knowledge-based view (Castro, Lopez-Saez and Delgado-Verde, 2011).

Bukowitz and Williams' KM lifecycle model

Bukowitz and Williams' (2000) lifecycle model was developed at the dawn of the new millennium. It is shown in Figure 3.4 surrounded by the dashed rectangle. As can be seen from the diagram, Bukowitz and Williams structured KM in two distinctive cycles: one on a tactical/operational level (the left-hand cycle) and the other on a strategic level (the right-hand cycle). They think that the *get–use–learn–contribute* cycle is more tactical/operational in nature, which means that it is triggered by market-driven opportunities or demands and typically results in short-term or day-to-day use of knowledge to respond to these demands. The *assess–build–sustain* or *divest* cycle is more strategic in nature, triggered by shifts in the macro environment, which focuses on the more long-term process of matching intellectual capital to strategic requirements (Dalkir, 2017).

It is apparent that the *build–sustain* stages in the strategic cycle are the same as defined in this book ('knowledge building' and 'knowledge holding'). The *use* stage in the tactical/operational cycle also matches 'knowledge utilization'. The *get* stage consists of seeking out knowledge needed in order to make decisions, solve problems or innovate, which can be considered as part of the 'knowledge mobilization' (as defined in this book) or 'pool knowledge' stage (as in Wiig's model). An interesting *learn* stage is explicitly defined.

Figure 3.4 Annotation of Bukowitz and Williams' model

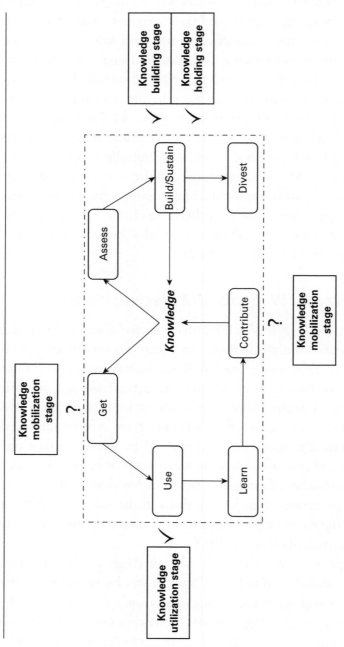

Bukowitz and Williams (2000) argue that learning in an organization is important because it represents the transition step between the application of ideas and the generation of new ones. Equally important is getting employees to share what they have learned and *contribute* to the communal knowledge base. These two stages make great sense when dealing with successful and failed knowledge activities such as best practices and lessons learned. In this sense, *contribute* can be seen as part of 'knowledge mobilization'.

It is worth mentioning two other stages in the strategic cycle, *assess* and *divest*. The *assess* stage refers to the evaluation of intellectual capital to ensure that it is relevant, accurate, useful and up to date. This requires an organization to define mission-critical knowledge and map current intellectual capital against future knowledge needs (Dalkir, 2017). The organization must also develop metrics to demonstrate that it is growing its knowledge base and profiting from its investment in intellectual capital (Oyemomi *et al*, 2019). The final stage in the Bukowitz and Williams KM cycle model is *divest*. An organization should not hold on to assets if they are no longer creating value. During this stage, organizations need to examine their intellectual capital in terms of the resources required to maintain it and consider whether these resources would be better spent elsewhere. This involves understanding the why, when, where and how of formally divesting part of its knowledge base. Traditional divesture decisions include obtaining patents, spinning off companies, outsourcing work, terminating a training programme and/or employees, replacing/upgrading technologies, and ending partnerships, alliances or contracts. The aim is to discriminate between forms of knowledge that can be leveraged and those that are of limited use. Knowledge that is a drain on resources should be divested if it cannot be converted into value.

Because Bukowitz and Williams' model clearly distinguishes between strategic and tactical/operational cycles for KM, and by introducing a number of innovative stages such as learning, contributing, assessing and divesting, the model has been considered more comprehensive than Wiig's model and has been widely cited.

 Critical thinking and reflection
Bukowitz and Williams' KM cycle model (2000)

What is your view on Bukowitz and Williams' KM lifecycle model in terms of having two cycles (one strategic and one tactical/operational)?

Evans, Dalkir and Bidian's KM lifecycle

A more recent KM lifecycle model developed by Evans, Dalkir and Bidian (2015) includes seven stages, as shown in the dashed rectangle of Figure 3.5.

As can be seen from the diagram, four stages of the KM lifecycle map well to the four stages defined in this book (represented by a tick in the diagram). They are *create*, which can be mapped to the 'knowledge building stage', *store* mapped to the 'knowledge holding stage', *share* mapped to the 'knowledge mobilization stage', and *use* mapped to the 'knowledge utilization' stage. The model includes three more stages: *identify*, *learn* and *improve*, which can be considered the major contributions of the model.

The first stage in the KM lifecycle, *identify*, is to determine whether the knowledge exists or needs to be created. If some knowledge already exists in the organizational memory, the organization should not waste resources by reinventing the wheel. In many KM processes, *learn* is often overlooked. Evans, Dalkir and Bidian's lifecycle model refers to double loop learning, which is a much more holistic review of knowledge than single

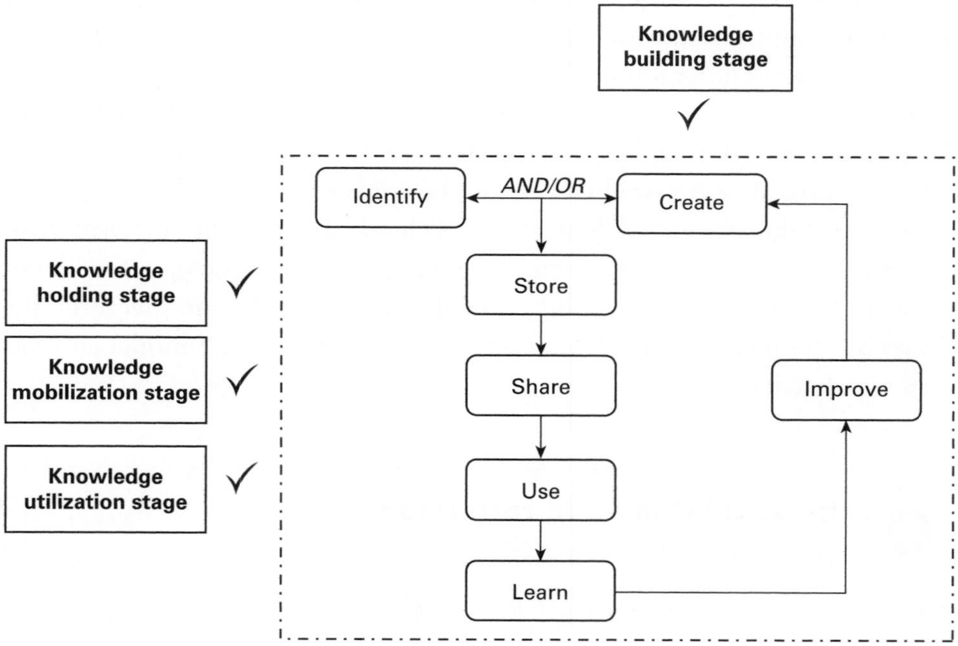

Figure 3.5 Annotation of Evans, Dalkir and Bidian's KM lifecycle

loop learning (ie incremental improvements). The *learn* and *improve* stages serve to document metadata, update, refine and, as needed, correct existing knowledge, add to it and extend it. Improvements are then fed back into the KM cycle.

This section discussed three comprehensive KM lifecycle models, as representatives selected from different times: the Wiig model from the early 1990s, the Bukowitz and Williams model from the dawn of new millennium, and the more recent Evans, Dalkir and Bidian model. A significant number of KM lifecycle models have been developed over the years. A synthesis of seven KM lifecycle models is provided by Dalkir (2017). In Jayawickrama's PhD thesis, he compared 16 KM lifecycle models and found that the number of stages ranged from three to seven (Jayawickrama, 2015), but the common stages featured in most of the models support the four stages defined in this book, as detailed in Section 3.1.

 Critical thinking and reflection
KM lifecycle model: learn

How important do you think it is that a KM lifecycle model should include a 'learn' step?

Key learning points

- There are hundreds of KM processes defined in the literature. Different KM processes suit different businesses (products and services created and delivered to customers), environments or business contexts, and the resources available (technology and people to implement KM).

- Different KM processes may include a varied number of steps. Some common stages can be identified. They are knowledge building, knowledge holding, knowledge mobilization and knowledge utilization.

- KM processes should not be interpreted as simple, straightforward, linear activities. Often some stages and steps may occur in parallel rather than sequentially. Moreover, feedback loops should be added to form KM lifecycle models.

- There are different KM lifecycle models, such as those by Wiig, Bukowitz and Williams, and Evans, Dalkir and Bidian.

- Besides the four key KM process stages, the KM lifecycle should consider/ evaluate/assess the worth of content based on organizational business goals, contextualize content in order to better match it with a variety of users, and continuously learn and improve/update/modify as required, to further decide whether to retain, keep or divest is most appropriate.

Review questions

- KM activities such as create, store, share and apply are central to many KM processes and lifecycle models. However, if you look at the business process descriptions of an organization (such as sales, marketing, production, distribution, retailing), there is no mention of these KM activities. What do you think can explain this omission of KM activities in business process descriptions?

- Imagine that you were appointed to take charge of a KM programme and had a number of people (with a mixture of computer science and business management graduates) on your KM team. You need to allocate job tasks and select sub-team leaders for each stage of the KM process. Would you select a computer science or business management graduate to lead a specific stage of the KM process, and why?

- What are the main barriers to knowledge mobilization within an organization and across organizations?

- What do you think are the key benefits and shortcomings of reusing knowledge?

- Provide an example of how each of the following KM process stages can add value to knowledge and increase the strategic worth of the knowledge asset:

  a. create

  b. codify

  c. share

  d. apply

- What is the main difference between a KM process and a KM lifecycle?

- Where are the go/no-go decisions in a KM life cycle? What information would you need in order to decide whether specific knowledge content would be needed or not in the next step of the cycle?

References

Appleyard, M M and Kalsow, G A (1999) Knowledge diffusion in the semiconductor industry, *Journal of Knowledge Management*, **3** (4), pp 288–95

Becerra-Fernandez, I and Sabherwal, R (2015) *Knowledge Management: Systems and processes*, 2nd edn, Routledge, Abingdon

Bhosale, V A, Kant, R and Shankar, R (2018) Investigating the impact of knowledge flow enablers on SC performance in Indian manufacturing organizations, *Benchmarking: An International Journal*, **25** (2), pp 426–39

Bukowitz, W and Williams, R (2000) *The Knowledge Management Field-book*, Prentice Hall, London

Candra, S (2014) Knowledge management and enterprise resource planning implementation: a conceptual model, *Journal of Computer Science*, **10** (3), pp 499–507

Castro, G, Lopez-Saez, P and Delgado-Verde, M (2011) Towards a knowledge-based view of firm innovation, *Journal of Knowledge Management*, **15** (6), 871–74

Dalkir, K (2017) *Knowledge Management in Theory and Practice*, 3rd edn, MIT Press, Cambridge, MA

Evans, M, Dalkir, K and Bidian, C (2015) A holistic view of the knowledge life cycle: the knowledge management cycle (KMC) model, in *Leading Issues in Knowledge Management*, ed K Grant and J Dumay, vol 2, pp 85–97, Academic References and Publishing International, Reading

Ferraris, A, Santoro, G and Dezi, L (2017) How MNC's subsidiaries may improve their innovative performance? The role of external sources and knowledge management capabilities, *Journal of Knowledge Management*, **21** (3), pp 540–52

Gottschalk, P (2007) Predictors of police investigation performance: an empirical study of Norwegian police as value shop, *International Journal of Information Management*, **27** (1), pp 36–48

Guechtouli, W, Rouchier, J and Orillard, M (2013) Structuring knowledge transfer from experts to newcomers, *Journal of Knowledge Management*, **17** (1), pp 47–68

Heisig, P (2009) Harmonization of knowledge management – comparing 160 KM frameworks around the globe, *Journal of Knowledge Management*, **13** (4), pp 4–31

Holsapple, C W and Joshi, K D (2002) Knowledge management: a threefold framework, *The Information Society*, **18**, pp 47–64

Huber, G P (1991) Organizational learning: the contributing processes and the literatures, *Organizational Science*, **12** (1), pp 88–115

Jashapara, A (2011) *Knowledge Management: An integrated approach*, 2nd edn, Pearson Education, Harlow

Jayawickrama, U (2015) Knowledge management competence for ERP implementation success, PhD thesis, University of Plymouth, UK

Jayawickrama, U *et al* (2019) Knowledge retention in ERP implementations: the context of UK SMEs, *Production Planning and Control*, **30** (10-12), pp 1032–47

Lages, C R *et al* (2013) Knowledge dissemination in the global service marketing community, *Managing Service Quality: An International Journal*, **23** (4), pp 272–90

Levy, M (2011) Knowledge retention: minimising organizational business loss, *Journal of Knowledge Management*, **15** (4), pp 582–600

Liu, S *et al* (2014) A knowledge chain management framework for global supply chain integration decisions, *Production Planning and Control*, **25** (8), pp 639–49

Mejri, K, MacVaugh, J A and Tsagdis, M (2018) Knowledge configurations of small and medium-sized knowledge-intensive firms in a developing economy: a knowledge-based view of business-to-business internationalization, *Industrial Marketing Management*, **71**, pp 160–70

Nesheim, T, Olsen, K M and Tobiassen, A E (2011) Knowledge communities in matrix-like organizations: managing knowledge towards application, *Journal of Knowledge Management*, **15** (5), pp 836–50

Nonaka, I and Takeuchi, H (1995) *The Knowledge Creating Company*, Oxford University Press, New York

North, K and Kumta, G (2018) *Knowledge Management: Value creation through organizational learning*, 2nd edn, Springer, Cham, Switzerland

Oyemomi, O (2016) The Impact of Organizational Factors on Knowledge Sharing Performance, PhD Thesis, University of Plymouth, UK

Oyemomi, O *et al* (2019) How cultural impact on knowledge sharing contributes to organizational performance: using the fsQCA approach, *Journal of Business Research*, **94**, pp 313–19

Pacharapha, T and Ractham, V (2012) Knowledge acquisition: the roles of perceived value of knowledge content and source, *Journal of Knowledge Management*, **16** (5), pp 724–39

Phelps, C, Heidl, R and Wadhwa, A (2012) Knowledge, networks and knowledge networks: a review and research agenda, *Journal of Management*, **38** (4), pp 1115–66

Roy, S and Mitra, J (2018) Tacit and explicit knowledge and assessment of quality performance of public R&D in emerging economies: an Indian perspective, *Journal of Organizational Change Management*, **31** (1), pp 188–214

Sedighi, M *et al* (2018) Multi-level knowledge sharing: the role of perceived benefits in different visibility levels of knowledge exchange, *Journal of Knowledge Management*, **22** (6), pp 1264–87

Shongwe, M (2017) An analysis of knowledge management lifecycle frameworks: towards a unified framework, *The Electronic Journal of Knowledge Management*, **14** (3), pp 140–53

Song, M, van der Bij, H and Weggeman, M (2005) Determinants of the level of knowledge application: a knowledge-based and information-processing perspective, *Journal of Product Innovation Management*, **22**, pp 430–44

Venkitachalam, K and Bosua, B (2014) Roles enabling the mobilization of organizational knowledge, *Journal of Knowledge Management*, **18** (2), pp 396–410

Wiig, K (1993) *Knowledge Management Foundations*, Schema Press, Arlington, TX

PART TWO
Building knowledge competence in organizations

This part focuses on building competence through KM at organizational level, in order to understand how knowledge-based activities can contribute to business overall performance. This part will discuss in detail three important topics in three separate chapters. Chapter 4 is dedicated to organizational learning, which is considered as the key to renew knowledge for organizations. An ideal outcome from organizational learning would be a learning organization, which is the central topic for Chapter 5. Chapter 6 is dedicated to organizational culture, which is widely recognized and accepted as a key enabler of or barrier to knowledge management (especially knowledge sharing) and organizational learning.

Organizational learning

04

Learning outcomes

After completing this chapter, the reader will be able to:

- understand the links between individual, group and organizational learning;
- analyse major frameworks for organizational learning;
- describe the key features of single, double and triple loop learning;
- appreciate the importance of organizational memory in organizational learning.

In the organizational learning (OL) literature, there is an underlying assumption that learning will change the status of knowledge and improve an organization's performance. As seen from previous chapters, there are many ways to define the categories of knowledge and many approaches that can be taken to manage knowledge through different KM process and lifecycle models. One important purpose of KM is to build organizational competence by embedding knowledge into organizational processes and routines, so that the organization can continuously improve its practices and behaviours to achieve its goals. From this perspective, organizational learning is believed to be one of the most important ways in which an organization can sustainably improve over time by learning from its successes (best practices and innovations) and failures (lessons learned), hence building long-lasting competence, especially in an uncertain and changing business environment. In order to be able to learn, an organization must be able to capture and document milestone events and relevant knowledge, in the form of either best practices or lessons learned, and 'remember' them through access to organizational memory.

Scholars have found that organizational learning positively influences knowledge creation (leading to innovation) and organizational performance

(Abubakar *et al*, 2019), hence it is important to have a dedicated chapter to discuss the topic. This chapter starts with the learning flow, from individual learning through group/team learning to organizational learning, then looks at some widely cited frameworks for organizational learning, followed by various types of loops for learning, and finishes with the management of organizational memory.

4.1 From individual through group/team to organizational learning

Because knowledge can exist in the mind of an individual, be shared among participants in a work group/team and be recognized and used by a whole organization, learning can subsequently take place on these three different levels as well. Figure 4.1 illustrates the links from individual learning through group/team learning to organizational learning, and back to individual learning.

Of course, knowledge obtained from individual learning can be applied directly to performing individual tasks; however, the knowledge can also be shared with others in a group/team, while at the same time receiving knowledge from co-workers/team members, for example through socialization processes as defined in the SECI model (Nonaka and Takeuchi, 1995) or by using knowledge spaces as defined in the 'Ba' theory (Nonaka and Konno, 1998). On the group/team learning level, knowledge held in common can be applied to perform tasks in a coordinated manner. Various types of knowledge can be produced as an output from group/team learning, for example knowledge that can help the group/team to perform tasks better (know-how), help generate new capabilities and justifications for decisions (know-why) or create new ideas or new things the group can do (know-what). When different groups interact with each other, organizational learning occurs, which then produces integrated knowledge that can help generate a coherent vision for the whole organization, aimed at achieving organizational goals.

Individual learning

Individuals are the decision makers and actors in an organization and it is their learning outcome that becomes part of how decisions are made and how things are done in the organization; therefore, it is essential to understand

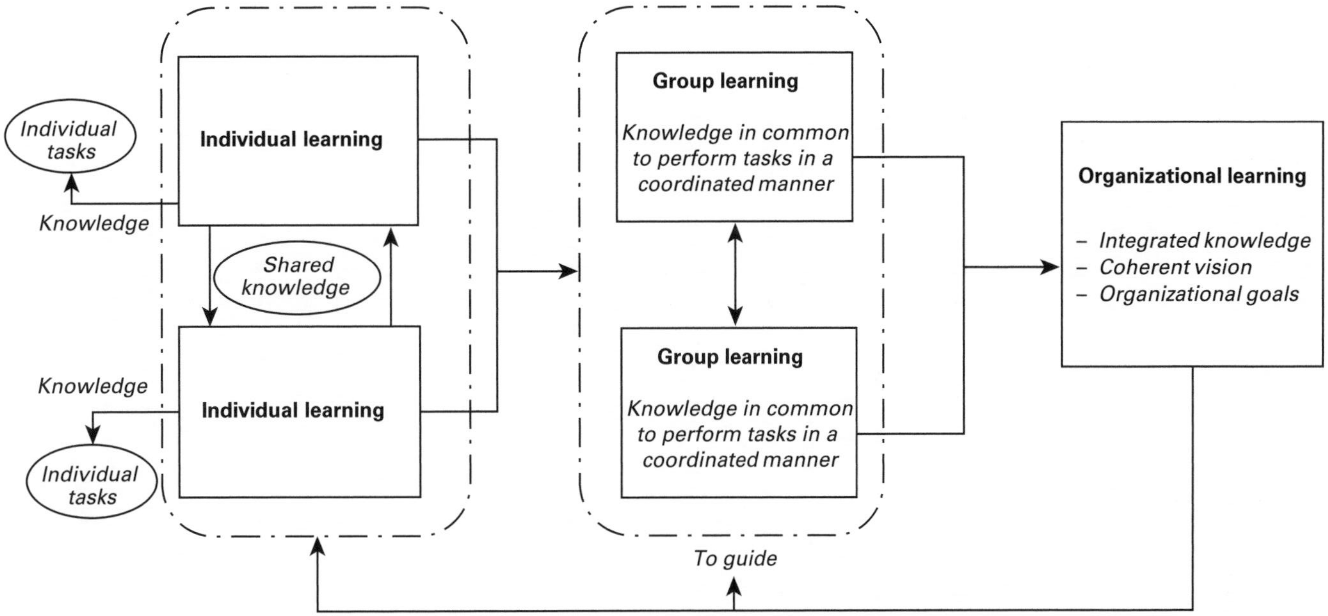

Figure 4.1 Links between individual, group/team and organizational learning

how an individual learns as the starting point for a group/team's collective learning and organizational learning.

Individual learning can be defined as 'increasing one's capacity to take effective action' (Kim, 1993). The current theories of individual learning come from three main branches: behaviourism, information processing and social learning.

Behaviourist theories state that individual learning is based on a stimulus–response model of behaviour. For example, positive reinforcement such as praise and reward are likely to result in the desired behavioural outcome to encourage learning. Negative reinforcement such as punishment can weaken certain behaviour to discourage learning. Research shows that this stimulus–response model tends to work in the short term (Jashapara, 2011).

A second branch of learning theory came from information processing, which sees learning as a change in states of knowledge rather than a change in the probability of response. This perspective emphasizes understanding the different levels of experience, meaning and insights within individuals, and led to wide acceptance of computer modelling and simulation of learning process (Dalkir, 2017).

From a constructivist perspective, learning occurs when individuals engage in social activity and conversations around shared tasks and problems. Social learning theory explains human behaviour as continuous interaction between cognitive, behavioural and environmental factors. Some scholars even extend this theory by arguing that all learning is situated in activity, context and culture (Medama, Wals and Adamowski, 2014; Doyle, Kelliher and Harrington, 2016).

In parallel to these three branches of learning theories, three learning mechanisms have been widely studied in the literature: learning via formal education and training, learning via the use of interventions in work processes, and learning that is embedded in day-to-day work activities (Hislop, Bosua and Helms, 2018). First, learning is closely linked to formal education and training, that is, learning occurs and is facilitated via workers attending and participating in formal processes of training and education, such as through professional certification training courses and executive education programmes (Zhou, Hu and Shi, 2015). Second, learning can also occur in a range of practices, values and activities via intentional interventions in work processes. Many of these can be enabled and supported by advanced ICT technologies; for example, learning can be facilitated through the use of web-based systems (such as the Internet of Things) to create a 'learning culture' and 'insert' learning opportunities into business processes (Hortovanyi and Ferincz, 2015). Finally, the practice-based view, which is compatible with the social learning theory, sees learning as occurring via day-to-day work practices. This learning mechanism is often referred to as 'learning by doing', or more widely known as 'experiential learning', which is predominantly related to individuals' tacit knowledge (Kolb, 1984).

 Critical thinking
Individual learning

Learners' motivation to learn is extremely important. Without motivation, or 'fire in the belly', it is unlikely that an individual will have much incentive to learn. How do you think an organization can ignite the fire in individuals to foster learning?

Group/team learning

Group/team learning can be viewed as the capacity of a group/team to engage appropriately and learn from each other, for example by sharing knowledge with others in the group/team they work in and receive knowledge from their co-workers. Some key features of effective group/team learning that distinguish it from individual learning include (Sanchez, 2003; Jashapara, 2011):

- collective intelligence of the group/team;
- group decision making and coordinated action;
- shared knowledge and practices.

Some common mechanisms to facilitate group/team members' effective engagement and promote group/team learning are dialogue and discussion. In an organization, the biggest barrier to group/team learning is defensive routines. Table 4.1 summarizes some of the main characteristics of the enhancers and barriers and the consequences for group/team learning (Jashapara, 2011; Doyle, Kelliher and Harrington, 2016).

Learning is the process that results in changes in knowledge. First, group/team members must have some shared knowledge (knowledge in common) in order to perform group tasks in a coordinated manner, but they may also add to that knowledge. In performing group tasks, they may learn by doing

Table 4.1 Enhancers and barriers to group/team learning

	Mechanisms	Consequences	How did it happen?
Enhancer	Dialogue	Divergent thinking	• Suspending one's own view and assumptions • Listening to group/team members • Playing with different ideas
	Discussion	Convergent thinking	• Different views presented and defended • Search for best view and arguments • Reach consensus and group decisions
	Collaborative activity	Collaborative practice	• Using artefacts, routines, stories • Sense-making the 'here and now' • Socially construct meaning and understanding
Barrier	Defensive routines	Block effective learning	• Causing group/team conflict • Leading to entrenched views • Blocking energy flow in a group/team

or learn by analysing. The outputs from group/team learning can be various forms of knowledge:

- 'Know-how': knowledge of how to perform a task consistently that is created by practical and hands-on experience through learning by doing. Routine-based know-how is essential for improving a group's work efficiency, for example doing more of the same thing in a more coherent, consistent, predictable way (Zhou, Hu and Shi, 2015).

- 'Know-why': understanding why doing certain things developed through learning by analysis. Know-why knowledge is essential for justifying decisions on when to do new things or why to do familiar things in new ways.

- 'Know-what': knowledge of what resources are available to the group/team and any constraints they face in getting the tasks done, what needs to be done first based on group/team preferences, and what new things can be done when the situation changes (Oh, 2019).

- 'Know-who': knowledge gained by engagement in group/team dialogue and discussion, to have a clear idea of who has what skills, expertise and experience in order to allocate the right resources to the right tasks and complement each other's strengths and weaknesses in group work.

Organizational learning

For learning experienced at individual level to have wider impact, the learning must flow and the knowledge gained must transfer beyond the individual to group/team level. Similarly, a group/team must communicate their know-how, know-why and know-what knowledge gained from group/team learning to other groups, in order to acquire other resources or support in order to put their own knowledge into action. In this sense, knowledge moves upwards through flow between multiple levels of learning. The knowledge of individuals becomes understood and adopted by their work group, then the knowledge of one group/team is shared with other groups, and is finally evaluated, selected and integrated within an organization; this is where organizational learning occurs (Hislop, Bosua, and Helms, 2018; Oh, 2019). During this process, managers occupy a privileged position that gives them significant influence in deciding which knowledge will ultimately be accepted, adopted and embedded in the organization's business process. However, it should be noted that organizational learning is not the exclusive concern of top managers in an organization, but rather a process in which work groups and even key individuals outside top management may play a role (Park and Kim, 2018).

The organizational learning literature has been fragmented, which has resulted in different definitions. Table 4.2 provides some examples of definitions from different times, as well as implications for management.

Table 4.2 Examples of definitions of organizational learning

Source	Definitions	Implications for management
Huber, 1991	An entity learns if, through its processing of information, the range of its potential behaviours is changed	Organizational learning leads to *change.*
Crossan, Lane and White, 1999	A principal means of achieving the strategic renewal of an enterprise.	Organizational learning leads to *renewal* at *strategic* level.
Schwandt and Marquardt, 2000	A system of actions, actors, symbols and processes that enables an organization to transform information into new knowledge which in turn increases its long-run adaptive capacity.	Organizational learning leads to *new knowledge* and *capacity* to cope with *change.*

(continued)

Table 4.2 (Continued)

Source	Definitions	Implications for management
Garvin, Edmondson and Gino, 2008	An organization can be said to learn when its actions have been modified as a result of reflection on new knowledge or insight	Organizational learning results in *new knowledge* and *changed* actions.
Jashapara, 2011	The process of improving actions through better knowledge and understanding	Organizational learning contributes to *knowledge* and leads to *improvement*.
Zhou, Hu and Shi, 2015	The capability of an organization to adapt to its environment	Organizational learning should include *change* and cope with an *uncertain* business environment.
Guinot, Chiva and Tarter 2016	A critical intervention to gain and maintain a sustainable competitive advantage for organizations	Organizational learning plays a significant role in acquiring, disseminating and using *knowledge* to adapt to a *changing* external environment.
Dalkir, 2017	Learning what worked and what did not work from the past and transferring this experiential learned knowledge effectively to present-day and future knowledge workers	According to this view, the primary by-products of organizational learning are the *best practices* and the *lessons learned*. The main purpose of organizational learning is therefore for an organization to *improve* over time, by making use of the best practices that have proven to be working well and available for reuse, and preventing mistakes happening again or redoing work that has been already done.
Oh, 2019	As organizational capability denoting how an organization deals with a dynamic environment	Organizational learning should develop *capability* that can adapt to a *dynamic* environment.

Despite the exponential growth of the literature studying organizational learning, there is little agreement on the definition of the term or clear research-based guidelines for managers. This has led to conceptual divergence, uncertainty about the term and difficulty in translating it into a measurable construct (Zhou, Hu and Shi, 2015; Oh, 2019). In short, the concept is highly elusive even though it is extremely popular.

There have been three main approaches to organizational learning: behavioural, cognitive and practice based. The behavioural approach does not look into the 'black box' of organizational learning directly but rather into its antecedents, such as its structures, routines, systems and technologies. The focal interest of this approach is on how environmental changes affect an organization's strategies, processes and structures (Jashapara, 2011; Hislop, Bosua, and Helms, 2018). In contrast, the cognitive approach is more interested in the 'black box' of organizational learning. The emphasis is on how organizations reflect on their assumptions and values, which affect individual and collective learning (Hislop, Bosua, and Helms, 2018). The practice-based approach expresses what managers need to do, such as being open to discordant information and avoiding losing critical knowledge, but there is less guidance on how managers can actually achieve these ambitions (Jashapara, 2011).

It is clear that learning in organizations is a continuous process and can be characterized as involving a dynamic reciprocity and interdependence between individual, group/team and organizational levels (Amman, 2012). Organizations cannot 'think', 'behave' or 'learn' independently of the people who work within them, as individuals and as groups/teams. Instead, organizations learn through the embedding of individual and group/team learning in organizational processes, routines, structures and systems. In other words, organizational learning occurs when insights developed by individuals and groups/teams impact on organizational-level processes and structures, subsequently resulting in systematic transformation of the organization's work practices and values. Scholars have stressed that organizational learning is not the simple sum of the individual and group/team learning processes.

Critical thinking and reflection
Learning flow between individual, group and organization

1 The literature has extensively discussed the feed-forward learning flow from the individual through the group/team to organizational level. What do you think is the nature of feedback flow from organizational learning through group/team learning to individual learning?

2 To what extent do you agree with the statement 'Organizations cannot think, behave or learn independently of people who work within them', and why? Use examples that you are familiar with to support your arguments.

4.2 Organizational learning frameworks

A number of frameworks for organizational learning have been proposed over the past few decades. Each has a different focus with a different perspective. A comprehensive review of learning frameworks developed from the 1970s up to the mid-1990s is available in Crossan, Lane and White (1999). Based on their critical review, Crossan et al concluded that the existing frameworks failed to address how organizational learning could be conceived of as a principal means of achieving an organization's strategic renewal. Furthermore, few existing frameworks had illustrated the tension between exploration (assimilating new learning) and exploitation (using what has been learned) that was at the heart of strategic renewal. Subsequently, Crossan and her colleagues developed a new organizational learning framework to address the phenomenon of renewal: the 4I framework (Crossan, Lane and White, 1999; Crossan, Maurer and White, 2011). The 4I framework has since become one of the most widely cited frameworks in organizational learning.

The framework conceptualizes four sequential learning processes as represented by the 4Is, shown on the left-hand side of Figure 4.2: intuiting, interpreting, integrating and institutionalizing.

Figure 4.2   The four learning processes, three learning levels, two learning flows and learning stocks

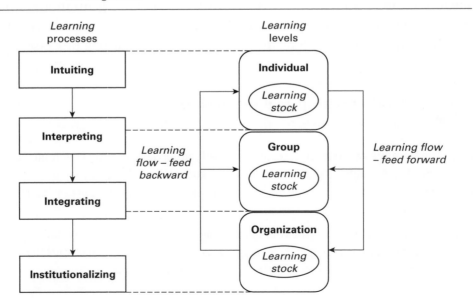

Intuiting is the beginning of new learning. It is largely a subconscious process. There are many definitions of intuiting and most of them involve some sort of pattern recognition. The two views most closely aligned with the 4I framework are expert intuiting and entrepreneurial intuiting (Crossan, Lane and White, 1999; Jashapara, 2011). The expert view of intuiting is a process of (past) pattern recognition. Experts, based on their many years of experience and acquisition of sufficient knowledge, can often perceive patterns that novices cannot. Having been in the same or similar situations many times before, an expert recognizes the pattern almost instantaneously and knows what to do without thinking consciously about actions. In this sense, the intuiting has become tacit knowledge. If asked to explain their actions, experts may be unable to do so. Whereas expert intuiting provides insights into the process of pattern recognition, entrepreneurial intuiting has more to do with innovation and change. Strictly speaking, in reality no two situations are the same, hence patterns can be similar but are never identical. You can argue that what is more important than pattern recognition is actually the ability to make novel connections between the situations and to discern possibilities. Entrepreneurial intuiting enables people to make these novel connections, perceive new and emergent relationships, and discern possibilities that have not been identified previously. In summary, expert intuiting is more past pattern oriented, while entrepreneurial intuiting is future possibility oriented (Crossan, Lane and White, 1999).

Interpreting begins to pick up on the conscious elements of the individual learning process (Doyle, Kelliher and Harrington, 2016). Individuals develop their own cognitive maps about various domains and can interpret the same stimulus differently thanks to the cognitive maps. Language plays a pivotal role in the development of cognitive maps, as language enables individuals to name things, make explicit connections among things, and explain what were once simply feelings, hunches and sensations. In a group/team situation, interpreting is also a social activity that creates and refines common language, clarifies images and creates shared meaning and understanding (Crossan, Lane and White, 1999). It is possible that in a group/team situation, multiple and even potentially conflicting interpretations can arise about the domain and the best course of action (Jashapara, 2011).

Integrating focuses on coordinated, coherent collective actions. Through continuous conversations among members of an organization, a community and even a society, shared understanding and collective minds develop, mutual interests are negotiated and adjustments are made, and then shared practice takes place (Hislop, Bosua, and Helms, 2018). During the learning process, conversations are used not only to convey established meaning but also to evolve new meaning. Through continuous conversations, the group/team, community or society can evolve new and deeper shared meaning. This shared meaning can cause those who participated to more or less spontaneously make mutual adjustment to their actions and practices (Nugroho, 2018). Scholars have observed that actual practice is not what is specified in manuals or necessarily what is taught in classrooms. Rather, it is captured and promulgated by stories told by members in an organization, a community or society. Hence storytelling plays a significant part in the learning process.

Institutionalizing sets organizational learning apart from individual and group/team learning. This learning process ensures that successful actions become embedded in organizational routines, procedures and processes. Such routines, procedures and processes will, over time, have an effect on an organization's systems, structures, strategies, values and norms. Structures, systems and processes provide a context for interactions. Over time, spontaneous individual learning and ad hoc group/team learning become less prevalent, as prior learning becomes embedded in the organization and begins to guide actions and practices (Crossan, Maurer and White, 2011). One characteristic of institutionalization is that behaviour and culture endure over a period of time. Organizations naturally outgrow their ability to use spontaneous and ad hoc interactions exclusively to interpret, integrate and take coherent actions. Over time, when coherent actions are achieved through formalized systems, and if the actions produce favourable outcomes, the routines become 'best practice', which should be stored in the organizational memory (Dalkir, 2017).

The four learning processes defined in the 4I framework – intuiting, interpreting, integrating and institutionalizing – can be mapped onto the three learning levels defined in Figure 4.1: individual, group and organizational. Intuiting and interpreting mainly occur at the individual level, interpreting and integrating occur at the group level, and integrating and institutionalizing occur at the organizational level. It should be noted that learning processes such as interpreting and integrating take place at more than one level. The three learning levels define the structure through which organizational learning takes place, and the processes form the glue to bind the structure together. This interdependence between the learning processes and levels is illustrated in Figure 4.2.

In order to highlight the learning outcomes from learning processes, the terms 'learning stocks' and 'learning flows' have been defined (Oh, 2019). Learning stocks are distinguished from learning flows in that they are the form of knowledge, explicit or tacit, accumulated by learners through their interaction within a distinct context on each level, while learning flow refers to the dynamic process amplifying or reifying the meaning of knowledge by sharing and assessing it (Prieto and Revilla, 2006). There are two types of learning flow: feed-forward and feedback. Feed-forward learning occurs in the process of transferring knowledge from individual to group to organizational level, which is the innovative organizational capability to continuously investigate new possibilities, hence associated with the exploration aspect of learning. Feedback learning, most associated with exploitation, is the capability to improve existing competence by selection, adaptation and refinement, which takes place when an organization distributes its accumulated knowledge to group and individual levels (Oh, 2019). Figure 4.2 provides an overall picture of the interdependent relationships among the four learning processes (intuiting, interpreting, integrating and institutionalizing), the three learning levels (individual, group and organizational), the two types of learning flow (feed-forward and feedback), and learning stocks.

When the 4I framework proposed by Crossan, Lane and White (1999) became increasingly popular, many scholars examined the framework by comparing it with other relevant frameworks. One such is also called the 4I framework, which was proposed by Alan Mumford. Mumford's 4I model (Mumford, 1991) was developed earlier and is a well-known model in action learning. The 4Is in Mumford's model represent interaction, integration, implementation and iteration. There seem to be clear links between the two 4I models. Interaction in Mumford's model and interpreting in Crossan, Lane and White's model are similar. Integration is present in both models. Iteration could be seen as a form of feedback loop leading to institutionalization.

Some scholars think that Crossan, Lane and White's 4I framework is an extension from another organizational learning model previously developed by Huber (1991). In Huber's model, there are also four constructs of organizational learning: knowledge acquisition, information distribution, information interpretation and organizational memory. Knowledge acquisition is related to learning from experience, observation and grafting. Information distribution focuses on how organizational units share information from a wide range of sources to enable the creation of new information or understanding, so that the units that need the information and the information sources can find each other quickly (McClory, Read and Labib, 2017). Information interpretation is the organizational process through which information is given meaning, through cognitive maps and framing, but also considering conditions of overload and unlearning. Organizational memory is related to storing and retrieving information and making decisions at the organizational level supported by technological processes (Park and Kim, 2018). It is clear that Huber's model takes a more information-processing perspective of organizational learning, but Crossan, Lane and White's model takes a combination of the process-oriented and organizational structure perspectives.

It can be seen that both Mumford's and Huber's models were developed before Crossan, Lane and White's 4I framework. Since Crossan, Lane and White's 4I framework was published at the end of the last century, it has been widely accepted in the research community and has been cited over 5,000 times. Because of this extraordinary achievement, 10 years later the Academy of Management Review instituted the 'Decade Award' to recognize the contribution of the 4I framework. Crossan and White, together with Maurer, took the opportunity to reflect on the 4I framework, including the 4I processes, multiple levels and the strategic renewal of interest in organizational learning (Crossan, Maurer and White, 2011). They concluded that while some of the subsequent research has added value to the original work, the challenge of developing an accepted organizational learning theory remains unrealized, hence it continues to be called the 4I framework. Maybe because of its wide influence, there has been little mention of new organizational learning frameworks being developed until very recently.

Aiming to link organizational learning to organizational performance, Zhou, Hu and Shi (2015) proposed a new organizational learning framework with three building blocks: learning orientation, learning process and learning leadership.

Learning orientation refers to the organization-wide activity of creating and using knowledge to enhance competitive advantage. It helps to build up a supportive environment in the organization. Three components of learning orientation are: *openness to new ideas*, *psychological safety* and *team orientation*. First, learning is not simply about problem solving or correcting mistakes. It should also be about crafting novel approaches, taking risks and exploring the unknown and untested (Garvin, Edmondson, and Gino, 2008). Second, employees should feel psychologically safe in disagreeing with peers or authority figures, asking naïve questions, owning up to mistakes or presenting minority viewpoints (Haight and Marquardt, 2018). Lastly, teams need to allow for innovative problem solving and for the development of synergy, whether to bring collective knowledge and skills to bear on problems or to develop new and innovative ideas. Team orientation can be defined as the degree to which employees stress collaboration and cooperation in performing activities and making decisions. All three components are essential to innovation and the organization's continuous improvement. An organization with a strong learning orientation is not simply a collector or storehouse of knowledge but a processor of it. For example, feedback from customers, sales channels and competitors must be used to develop core competence. Hence learning orientation positively influences the degree to which organizations are likely to promote generative learning as long-lasting core competence and innovation capability (Zhou, Hu and Shi, 2015).

The **learning process** defined by Zhou, Hu and Shi (2015) concerning experiential learning consists of four sub-processes: *information collection, knowledge sharing and integration, education and training*, and *experimentation*. Information collection is the first step towards learning about customers, competitors and regulators so that an organization can stand a better chance of detecting and acting upon events and trends in the marketplace. Knowledge sharing and integration are two closely linked activities that occur simultaneously. Knowledge sharing refers to exchanging knowledge through fluid communication, dialogue and debate (Oyemomi, 2016). Knowledge integration leads to the creation of a collective corpus of knowledge rooted in the work processes and organizational culture, which contributes to organizational memory (Nugroho, 2018). Education and training is believed to be positively related to employees' and the organization's performance. Hence organizations with higher learning abilities place great store on education and training for employees. Experimentation, as an essential aspect of generative learning, implies the process of searching for innovative, flexible solutions to current and future problems. Organizational learning should encourage and reward employees for testing new knowledge and also individual initiatives to try new methods of work and problem solving, thus employees can be more creative and learn from mistakes. It is important for organizations to ensure that mistakes and failures as a result of experimentation are not punished but are used as lessons learned (Dalkir, 2017).

Leadership strongly fosters organizational learning, because when leaders demonstrate their willingness to accommodate different viewpoints, employees are encouraged to offer new ideas and suggest alternative options (Oh,

2019). If leaders signal the importance of learning processes, these activities are likely to flourish and employees are encouraged to learn. Evidence has shown that transformational leadership has a positive effect on organizational learning (Park and Kim, 2018).

The comparisons between Crossan, Lane and White's 4I framework and Zhou, Hu and Shi's three building blocks framework are summarized in Table 4.3. Both frameworks include a learning process, even though the actual learning activities specified in each framework are different. Crossan, Lane and White's 4I framework focuses on the learning process across multiple levels of an organization, while Zhou, Hu and Shi's framework does not explicitly discuss the different learning levels, but stresses the importance of leadership and learning orientation in organizational learning.

The organizational learning frameworks discussed in this section provides us with an overall picture of various dimensions that organizational learning involves: learning processes, learning flows and feedback at multiple learning levels. The next section will provide some in-depth discussion on the importance of learning feedback and how different learning loops have been developed based on feedback.

Table 4.3 Comparisons between the 4I framework proposed by Crossan, Lane and White and the three building blocks framework by Zhou, Hu and Shi

	The 4I framework by Crossan, Lane and White	The three building blocks framework by Zhou, Hu and Shi
Learning orientation	No	Yes • Openness to new ideas • Psychological safety • Team orientation
Learning process	Yes • Intuiting • Interpreting • Integrating • Institutionalizing	Yes • Information collection • Knowledge sharing and integration • Education and training • Experimentation
Learning leadership	No	Yes
Multi-level	Yes • Individual level • Group level • Organization level	No

4.3 Learning cycles – single, double and triple loop learning

Organizational learning has been conceptualized as a multi-level (ie the breadth of learning) and iterative process of examining actions, assumptions, values, rules and hypotheses. This iterative process with feedback loops is often called a learning cycle (Medama, Wals and Adamowski, 2014). This section looks at the depth of learning, that is, the degree of learning an organization achieves at the end of each learning cycle, and focuses on multi-loop learning, involving single loop, double loop and triple loop learning.

Single loop learning

Single loop learning is the learning cycle in which errors are tracked down and corrected within the existing set of rules and norms but without questioning or altering the underlying values of the system (Argyris, 1978, 1999). Subsequently, single loop learning is the result of repetition and routine. This means that, given any set of problems, an organization is likely to act in the same traditional ways and follow the same patterns. Successful examples of this type of learning include decision-making rules. Pre-defined decision rules can be very useful for many operational-level repetitive, routine situations in which organizations can control the operations environment well. Although it may have far-reaching consequences, single loop learning primarily concentrates on a specific activity with a direct or short-term effect. Because single loop learning lacks analysis of the underlying causes of the problems and errors in the entire organizational context, it is an isolated problem-solving cycle based on knowledge of simple problems, acquired in the past, and the change in behaviour in future, similar situations. Single loop learning is considered as adaptive learning, where individuals adapt to the work to be performed (McClory, Read and Labib, 2017). The appropriate lessons learned can be documented and stored in organizational memory for future reuse.

Let's look at an example of single loop learning for quality improvement in a business management context, illustrated in Figure 4.3. As can be seen from the diagram, there are four steps. The cycle starts with assessing quality performance (outputs of the production system, such as the number of defective products on a production line in a factory or telephone response time in a call centre), then compares actual performance with specified quality

Figure 4.3 Example of single loop learning cycle for quality management

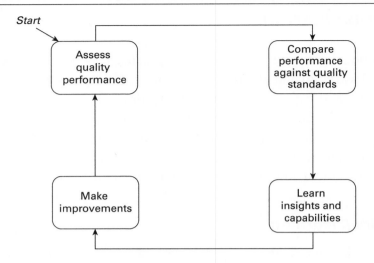

standards. If the actual performance deviates from the required standards (in the case of a production line, if the widely known six sigma quality standards are adopted, it means that the number of defects should be fewer than 3.4 in one million opportunities), new insights and capabilities are learned. These will be used to make improvements, such as by altering input conditions, for example by imposing stricter control of supplier quality, manufacturing consistency and staff training, with the intention of improving the quality of outputs. Every time a quality problem is detected, it is corrected or solved, and more is learned about the process. However, this cycle occurs without questioning or altering the underlying values and objectives of the process, which can, over time, create an inertia that prevents it from adapting to a changing environment (Medama, Wals and Adamowski, 2014).

 Critical thinking and reflection
Single loop learning

If you were asked to create a process diagram to illustrate a single loop learning cycle for project management, how many steps would you include in your diagram, and why? If your diagram includes more or fewer than four steps, do you think the cycle you designed is fundamentally similar to or different from the cycle for quality management illustrated in Figure 4.3?

Double loop learning

Double loop learning refers to the reflective learning process in which an organization continuously learns and evolves as a whole by using collective experiences, failures and successes through consistent correction of its basic governing variables (Matties and Coners, 2018). This means that learned lessons are used not just for future problem solving in similar situations, but also for the re-evaluation and modification of the underlying standards, policies, procedures and objectives of the whole organization (Kantamara and Vathanophas, 2014). In other words, individuals and groups/teams reflect not only on whether deviations have occurred and how to correct them, but also on whether 'rules' should be changed. If necessary, 'breaking the rules' may be needed to ensure that a problem or an issue will not recur by refining or fixing the framework that governs the actions. Hence, double loop learning is considered more suitable than single loop learning for delving deeply and gaining new knowledge and skills for an organization. During double loop learning, organizational norms and assumptions are questioned, hence such organizations do not continue with their age-old patterns but establish a new set of norms and values, which often leads to new ways of working and acting. Thinking outside the box, creativity and critical reflection are important in double loop learning. This type of learning cycle is also referred to as generative learning. It occurs by revisiting and reshaping underlying assumptions and patterns of thinking and behaviour, that is, reframing the organizational values and systems (Medama, Wals and Adamowski, 2014). Compared with single loop learning, during which a key question often asked is 'Are we doing things right?', in double loop learning the key question that should be asked is 'Are we doing the right things?' Double loop learning generally has longer-term effects compared with single loop learning. The context for double loop learning is much more complex and unclear. In reality, crisis situations often lead to (opportunities for) double loop learning.

Let's have a look at an example. If an organization's sales of a particular product are drastically decreasing while its competitor's sales for the same or similar products are not decreasing or are even increasing, a simple reaction would be to assume that the marketing and sales department is not doing their jobs right or not working hard enough. Subsequent decisions could be to put more resources into marketing and sales or to punish their sales forces by reducing their pay or even laying off employees. This would be falling into the trap of single loop learning. A double loop learning approach would be to analyse the drop in sales and discover the underlying reasons for it. It might be found that the real reasons lie in product design, such as an outdated, unappealing look or insufficient functions, or the product is overpriced – not value for money in customers' eyes, compared with the competitor's offerings. By discovering the real reasons behind the product design and pricing strategy, appropriate decisions should be to improve the product design or pricing strategy, for example by engaging potential customers from the early stages of the product development process. This is the current 'sense and response' strategy (ie engaging customers early to sense the market and make the right products that customers would be willing to pay for) rather than the old 'make and sell' strategy (Jashapara, 2011). Figure 4.4 is an illustration of double loop learning for the product sales example. It can be seen from the diagram that the double loop learning comprises two loops. Loop 1 consists of four steps similar to those in single loop learning. There is an additional Loop 2 which demonstrates the cycle of questioning the relevance of existing performance objectives (ie sales target in this example) and setting new rules and performance objectives.

Figure 4.4 Double loop learning for product sales example

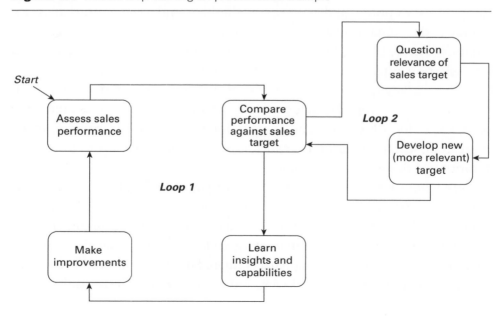

> ⭘ **Critical thinking and reflection**
> Double loop learning
>
> **1** What are the key differences between double loop learning and single loop learning? Use examples to help articulate your answers.
>
> **2** In reality, power and politics may hinder an organization's learning. Double loop learning especially can be considered too disruptive by management. How do you think an organization can balance power and politics with learning?

Triple loop learning

Triple loop learning is generally seen as an elaboration/extension/reconfiguration of the twin concepts of single loop learning and double loop learning (Flood and Romm, 2018). As seen from the previous sections, single loop learning entails adaptations and corrective actions, and double loop learning entails reframing issues and problems. Triple loop learning entails developing new processes and methodologies to make the reframing possible. Therefore, triple loop learning involves reflexivity about the single and double loop learning process, that is, learn about the learning, such as how to learn, why individuals and groups/teams learn the way they learn, and what norms, values and paradigms guide their learning (McClory, Read and Labib, 2017). Triple loop learning may involve a process of transformation by creating a shift in context or perspective. Ultimately, this kind of learning may lead to redesigning the existing governance norms, protocols, institutional structures and decision-making procedures (Medama, Wals and Adamowski, 2014).

The divergent concepts of triple loop learning have been provided by a literature review from Tosey, Visser and Saunders (2011). They classified the concepts in three categories:

1 Triple loop learning is beyond and superior to double loop learning and single loop learning.

2 It is a third level of learning inspired by Paul Bateson's learning levels. In total, four levels of learning were defined by Bateson (2006). Level I is change in specificity of response by correction of errors or by making a choice within a set of alternatives. Level II is change in the process of Level

I, for example a corrective change in the set of alternatives from which choice is made, or a change in how the sequence of experience is punctuated. Level III is change in the process of Level II, for example a corrective change in the system of sets of alternatives from which choice is made. Level IV would be change in Level III, but probably does not occur in any adult living organism on this earth.

3 It is the equivalent of 'deuteron-learning' (Argyris and Schön, 1996), which can be presented in a process of inventing and co-inventing. Inventing is creating ways of coming up with new structures of thought and actions suitable for particular occasions, and monitoring the effects of these frames. Co-inventing is creating collective mindfulness, where members discover where they and their predecessors have facilitated or inhibited learning and produce new structures and strategies for learning.

A number of examples of triple loop learning can be found in the literature. Arevalo, Ljung and Sriskandarajah (2010) identified triple loop learning within a land management action research project conducted in the Upper Amazon region of Peru. The triple loop learning concept was explored for the potential of NGO participants to reflect on values and assumptions underlying their work. Medama, Wals and Adamowski (2014) discussed triple loop learning for sustainable land and water governance, involving a process of managing change by engaging members in a social-ecological system. McClory, Read and Labib (2017) developed a triple loop learning framework for project management by conceptualizing lessons learned (refer to the 'Single, double and triple loop learning in project management' case study for details).

To summarize, single, double and triple loop learning are important learning processes to form multi-loop learning in organizations. Even though double loop learning is considered a higher-level learning than single loop learning, and triple loop learning is considered a higher-level learning than double loop learning, triple loop learning needs double loop learning as its foundation, and similarly, double loop learning needs single loop learning as its foundation. This leads to the conclusion that higher-level learning such as triple/double loop learning can only co-exist with its lower level(s) of learning. Triple, double and single loop learning do have their own characteristics. Table 4.4 provides an overall comparison among the three types of learning.

Table 4.4 Comparisons between single, double and triple loop learning

	Single loop learning	Double loop learning	Triple loop learning
Definition	Incremental learning focusing on correcting errors and mistakes	Facilitating error corrections by examining underlying values and policies within an organization system	Meta-learning designing norms and protocols that govern single and double loop learning
Nature of change resulted in	Change routine behaviour	Change rules and assumptions	Change institutional structures and decision-making processes
Impact level	Adaptive	Generative	Transformative, creative
Thinking behind the learning	Are we doing things right?	Are we doing the right things?	How do we decide what is right?
Key references	Argyris, 1978, 1999	Kantamara and Vathanophas, 2014; Matties and Coners, 2018	Medama, Wals and Adamowski, 2014; McClory, Read and Labib, 2017; Flood and Romm, 2018

CASE STUDY   Single, double and triple loop learning in project management

Project management (PM) is important in business management because all managers will, at some point, get involved with managing projects. The market requires a specified time, quality and cost for a project, and the organization's operations need to deliver the project on time, on specification and to the budget. The recipe for PM success has yet to be found, and there will probably be no single best solution. Solutions can depend on many factors that may be different from project to project and from organization to organization. In business operations management terms, a project has low volume and high variety. For example, large-scale projects are very complex and undertaking them consumes a large amount of resources, takes a long time to complete (can be months or years) and typically involves interactions between different parts of an organization. In addition, a project can be unique, which means that there may not be much existing knowledge or experience from similar cases that a manager or organization can borrow and reuse to make decisions and solve problems. Hence, it is essential that individuals, project teams and even the whole organization can learn effectively in order to gain new knowledge in the fast-changing environment.

Lessons learned have been the central interest of many organizations in terms of knowledge management and learning. Most PM professionals work on a three-stage process to maintain a lessons-learned knowledge bank by:

- accessing previous lessons during project planning and delivery phases;
- keeping project logs to record lessons throughout the project's duration; and
- writing lessons-learned reports both during the project and at project closure.

In McClory, Read and Labib (2017), the authors presented a learning framework including all three types of learning: single, double and triple loop learning. The learning framework enables the capture and reuse of lessons between projects to support decision making on three different levels: individual, process and organization.

Six steps are defined in each loop of project learning: act, measure, evaluate, decide, react and learn. The activities in the first three steps (act, measure and evaluate) are similar, but the last three steps (decide, react and learn) are quite different in the processes of single loop learning, double loop learning and triple loop learning. Table 4.5 provides an overview of all steps in the three learning loops.

In single loop learning, the project is managed with outcomes measured at project milestones, gates or regular time intervals. Outcome evaluation takes place, where lessons learned are recorded throughout the project's duration in daily or weekly logs, and in a closing project report. Comparison of outcome against project parameters allows decisions to be made to determine the required actions to keep the project on track or bring it back on track. As can be seen from the table, single loop learning adjusts project actions to meet targets as much as possible, while leaving the project parameters unchanged. This process helps to track project progress, provide accurate forecasts for cash flow and staff allocation for resource managers, and keep stakeholders abreast of

Table 4.5 An overview of all steps in the three learning loops

	Act	Measure	Evaluate	*Decide*	*React*	*Learn*
Single loop learning	PM	Outcome	Lessons learned log/report	*Compare with project parameters*	*Adjust project action to meet targets*	*Personal learning = experience*
Double loop learning	PM	Outcome	Lessons learned log/report	*Review project process and parameters*	*Update process and parameters*	*Project learning = process*
Triple loop learning	PM	Outcome	Lessons learned log/report	*Develop learning action plans*	*Set learning targets and culture*	*Organizational learning = ethos*

important changes or issues. By measuring project output, making adjustments and re-running the loop, project managers learn many of their skills through their experience at personal level. The process continues looping for every period of measurement determined in the project plan until the closure of the project.

In double loop learning, the evaluation step is broadened to analyse both the measured outcome and the value against which it is measured. Decisions made now include the assessment of parameters and processes to ensure that the decisions fulfil the higher-level goals of both project and organization. Actions are taken to change project-level parameters and update the organization's policies. It should be noted that when project parameters are changed, the project requires re-assessment of the measured outcomes against the updated parameter values, which is concurrent with single loop learning. This is where the underlying assumptions determined for the project come into play; they are neither measured values nor governing variables, but their value can affect the outcome of either or both of these data sets. Learning within the double loop occurs at project level rather than the personal level, where learning is embedded within organizational processes.

Triple loop learning includes the organization's cultural values and goals in terms of a learning organization. The evaluation step provides the project management office with its role definitions at multiple levels. At project level, performance data, closing reports and lessons-learned logs are gathered for review and reporting. At process level, project targets are revised with sponsors and procedures are updated if necessary, while at the organizational level, learning action plans for new projects are generated and information passed to board level.

Question

Closely examine the last three steps (decide, react and learn) in the three learning loops. Through this project management case, what differences can you find among triple, double and single loop learning in terms of the depth of learning?

4.4 Management of organizational memory

Even though individuals and groups/teams learn on behalf of organizations, over time an organization 'remembers' and builds its own institutional or corporate memory. This 'organizational memory' (OM) can be viewed as a large repository of all of an organization's archived experiences, decisions, actions, routines and processes as well as knowledge embedded in human minds (Hislop, Bosua, and Helms, 2018). Employees cannot benefit from the accumulated experience of an organization unless that valuable experiential learning has been captured, coded and made accessible through the

Figure 4.5 Position of OM and OL in KM process

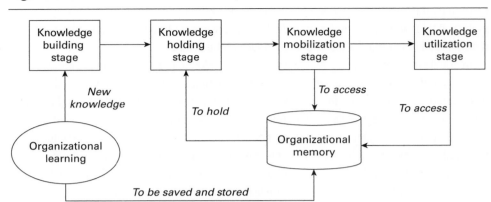

organizational memory. Organizational learning and organizational memory are therefore integral components of knowledge management to facilitate the access, use and reuse of valuable knowledge resources (Dalkir, 2017).

Figure 4.5 shows the position of organizational memory and organizational learning in the KM process (defined in Section 3.1). OM holds knowledge for an organization (facilitating the 'knowledge holding stage' in the KM process), so that it can be accessed during the 'knowledge mobilization stage' and 'knowledge utilization stage'. New knowledge gained through OL is saved and stored in the OM. The figure demonstrates the close relationships among OL, OM and KM. This is why we need to include OL and OM when discussing KM.

Organizational memory is essentially a technological container holding what has worked and what has not worked in an organization; these are the by-products of organizational learning, primarily the best practices and lessons learned. The role of an OM is multifaceted. First, OM is a facility for accumulating and preserving valuable knowledge for wider or future access and reuse. Second, OM is a facility for knowledge sharing. As knowledge in OM is made explicit, it augments the organization's intellectual power, becoming a basis for communication and learning. For example, best practices can be shared to avoid reinventing the wheel and lessons learned can be shared to avoid repeating mistakes. In this sense, OM is a means by which organizational knowledge is transferred from one employee to many. Third, knowledge extracted from experienced employees when they leave the organization can be reused by new hires who join the organization. OM is thus also considered as the means by which organizational knowledge is transferred from the past to the present and future (Dalkir, 2017).

Content of organizational memory

Plenty of KM literature has discussed the broad processes required to both populate an OM and to retrieve valuable knowledge for reuse from OM. Even though many forms of knowledge can be put in OM, the most common contents of OM are the key successes (often called best practices) and key failures (lessons learned) that have a sufficient degree of generalization. If a particular success, innovation or failure is too specific, this content will typically reside in a group memory, either in a project database or a community of practice archive. However, organizational best practices and lessons learned have broader applicability – they are not limited to a particular context or particular event, which can offer reuse potential to an organization-wide audience (Dalkir, 2017).

Some scholars clearly distinguish best practices from lessons learned (Perrin, Rolland and Stanley, 2007). The term 'best practices' is associated with positive experiences such as a success, an innovative discovery or a tried-and-tested method for accomplishing a task, while the term 'lessons learned' often implies negative experiences, for example a critical mistake or failure, that can be used to avoid repeating them (Herbst, 2017). However, many scholars often use lessons learned to represent both positive and negative experiences, illustrated through following definitions of lessons learned:

- Lessons learned can be defined as the knowledge acquired from an innovation or an adverse experience that causes a worker or an organization to improve a process or activity to work safer, more efficiently or with higher quality (Kitimbo, 2015).

- Lessons learned are knowledge or understanding gained by experience. The experience may be positive, as in a successful test or mission, or negative, as in a mishap or failure. Successes are also considered as sources of lessons learned (Becerra-Fernandez and Sabherwal, 2015).

Despite the different views from different scholars on the definition of lessons learned, there is a degree of agreement that lessons learned must represent something new, not encountered before, in either a positive or negative way. If everything went according to plan, lessons learned are likely to be classified as best practices. If something unanticipated occurred, then, despite the consequences, there is one bright side: the individuals, the group/team and the organization can learn from the surprising event. By following the lessons-learned process, it is possible to analyse what happened, why it happened, and what people can do differently next time (Herbst, 2017).

Some key attributes of lessons learned can be summarized as (Dalkir, 2017; Herbst, 2017):

- They can be learned from both successful and unsuccessful events.
- They need to be validated in some way to ensure their usefulness.
- They can be at operational, tactical and strategic levels.
- They need to be applied by people who were not involved in the original event.
- They must be significant enough to pass a cost–benefit analysis. In other words, they should have sufficient impact on the organization to warrant the effort of documenting and sharing them.

In general, there are two basic types of problem from which lessons may be learned: new problems (alpha-problems) and problems already known to someone else in the organization (beta-problems) (Herbst, 2017). New knowledge is often generated when alpha-problems occur and are dealt with. If the organization has a formal lessons-learned process in place, the lessons learned can then be incorporated into the organizational procedures to avoid alpha-problems from resurfacing as beta-problems in the future (Kloss-Grote and Moss, 2008).

Lessons-learned process

Strictly speaking, lessons learned are essentially a type of new knowledge generated through organizational learning that is worth being stored in OM. Therefore, lessons-learned processes should be guided by the generic KM process defined in Chapter 3. However, because of the importance of lessons learned to organizations, many dedicated processes have been put forward, which consist of various numbers of stages.

A four-stage process was proposed by the United States General Accounting Office (US GAO, 2002), which is quite similar to a generic KM process. The four stages are:

1 Collect: involves collecting the lessons (ie the content) that will be incorporated into the OM. There are six possible lesson collection approaches (Becerra-Fernandez and Sabherwal, 2015):

   a. Passive collection: contributors submit lessons through a paper or web-based form.

b. Reactive collection: contributors are interviewed by a third party to obtain lessons. The third party will submit the lessons on behalf of the contributors.

c. Active collection: a computer-based system may scan documents to identify lessons through specific keywords or phrases.

d. Proactive collection: lessons are automatically collected by an expert system, which may suggest that a lesson exists based on analysis of specific content.

e. Interactive collection: a computer-based system collaborates with the lesson's author to generate clear and relevant lessons.

f. After-action collection: lessons are collected during a mission debriefing, for example as in military organizations.

2 Verify: lessons are verified to ensure that they are valid and applicable. Typically, a team of domain experts verify the content for correctness, redundancy, consistency and relevance. The verification stage is critically important, but sometimes introduces a significant bottleneck in the inclusion of lessons into OM, since it is very time consuming.

3 Store: this stage relates to the representation of the lessons, including the tasks of formatting the lessons, indexing them and incorporating them into the OM. Once approved, lessons are stored in the OM in a format to allow easy search and retrieval later. Besides text format, relevant multi-media such as audio and video may be useful to help illustrate important lessons.

4 Disseminate: relates to how lessons learned can be shared to promote their reuse. There are a number of dissemination approaches based on the degree of activeness or passiveness (Becerra-Fernandez and Sabherwal, 2015), including:

a. Passive dissemination: where users looking for lessons access the OM and retrieve them.

b. Reactive dissemination: when users request lessons, a response will be produced. For example, when a user asks for help, a lessons-earned system launches a Help function in the context of specific software.

c. Active dissemination: users are alerted to relevant lessons in the context of their work, for example by a software help wizard that alerts a user of related automated assistance.

d. Active casting: lessons are transmitted to users who have specified relevant profiles for that particular lesson.

e. Proactive dissemination: a system anticipates events used to predict when the user will require the assistance provided by the lesson.

f. Broadcasting: lessons are disseminated throughout an organization.

A key criticism of this four-stage process is that it finishes at the dissemination stage, which does not necessarily guarantee that lessons learned are applied. Lessons are of little benefit unless they are shared, accessed and reused. This limitation of US GAO's process seems to be overcome by Weber, Aha and Becerra-Fernandez (2001), who defined a five-stage process:

1 Collect the lessons.

2 Verify the lessons.

3 Store the lessons.

4 Disseminate the lessons.

5 Apply the lessons.

By having a fifth stage on applying the lessons learned, Weber *et al*'s process extends US GAO's process to complete a full circle, from collecting through verifying, storing, disseminating to utilization, hence the lessons learned are not just being put in the OM for the sake of capturing and storing, but they are used and reused to make an impact on the organization's behaviour through decisions and actions.

Another way to extend the US GAO's process is to add new stages at the beginning, that is, before collecting lessons. In this line, Milton proposed a five-stage process (Milton, 2010). The five stages of the lessons-learned process are quite different from the generic KM process. The five stages are:

1 Reflect on the experience and discuss what has happened.

2 Identify key learning themes (positive and negative).

3 Analyse and try to ascertain the root causes of any divergence in the event compared to what was originally planned.

4 Generalize from this analysis, that is, ask the question – can it apply to other situations in the organization?

5 Apply the lessons learned to change a decision, a guideline or a procedure.

Milton's process includes an important stage of reflection and a stage of identifying key learning themes, meaning that the process needs to assess and re-assess the action and experience for improvement, in order to make sure that the lessons to be collected are associated with key learning themes for future indexing and reuse. These stages can be considered as having a similar function to the 'verification' stage in US GAO's process. One possible criticism of Milton's process would be that the technical side of 'storing' lessons in OM is not explicitly addressed. Further, it is not clear whether Milton's process is restricted to dealing with lessons learned from one single event. In a more recent process, the question is clearly answered by the US Center for Army Lessons Learned (CALL, cited by Dalkir, 2017), which also contains five stages:

1 Collection

2 Repository

3 Transfer process

4 Implementation

5 Analysis and data mining.

The first four stages of the process are similar to those of US GAO and Weber *et al*. However, the fifth stage makes an important contribution by including second-order analysis, which means aggregating a number of events and analysing them as a whole in order to identify patterns that would not be apparent otherwise. The data mining technique allows finding trends across organization units over time and ultimately identifying any gaps in the knowledge as learning opportunities.

Barriers to managing organizational memory

Despite the clear benefits of managing lessons learned and the widespread practice of using OM in organizations, OM still faces many obstacles, which can be classified into two main categories: technical and cultural.

The main technical barriers include:

- how to make the knowledge capture process easier or more transparent;

- how to make knowledge retrieval and reuse easier and more transparent;

- how to ensure the relevance and intelligibility (ie through sufficient context) of retrieved knowledge;

- how to make knowledge sharing easier and more transparent.

The main cultural barriers include:

- a cultural emphasis on artefacts and results, to the exclusion of process;
- resistance to knowledge capture because of the huge effort required and the fear of litigation;
- resistance to knowledge sharing and the fear of loss of job security;
- resistance to knowledge reuse because of the effort required and the low likelihood of finding relevant knowledge.

Because of the high importance and complexity of the technical and cultural factors to knowledge sharing, these issues will be discussed in more depth later in the book. Chapter 6 will be dedicated to organizational culture and its impact on knowledge sharing and organizational learning, and Chapter 10 will look at technological support for knowledge sharing crossing boundaries.

Critical thinking and reflection
Organizational memory

1 Using an example from an organization that you have worked for or studied with, what do you think are the top two technical obstacles to developing and managing organizational memory and how would you address them?

2 Using an example from an organization that you have worked for or studied with, what do you think are the top two cultural obstacles to developing and managing organizational memory and how would you address them?

Key learning points

- Organizational learning is the key process of building long-lasting organizational competence by generating new knowledge and embedding that knowledge into the organization's business processes, procedures and routines, so that the organization can continuously improve its practices and performance.

- In an organization, learning can occur on multiple levels: individual, group/team and organizational.

- Three types of learning loop have been widely acknowledged in organizational learning literature. Single loop learning is an adaptive learning process focusing on tracking down and correcting errors within the existing set of rules and norms but without questioning or altering the underlying values of the system. Double loop learning is the reflective, generative learning process through which an organization continuously learns and evolves by re-evaluating and modifying the underlying standards, policies, procedures and objectives of the whole organization. Triple loop learning is the transformative, creative learning process that entails developing new processes and methodologies that make double loop learning and single loop learning possible, that is, learning about learning.

- Even though double loop learning starts from a learner's mental model, defined by base norms, values, strategies and assumptions, it usually suggests critical reflection in order to challenge, invalidate or confirm the 'theory-in-use' (ie the base norms, values, strategies and assumptions). Double loop learning also encourages genuine inquiry into, and testing of, one's actions and requires self-criticism, that is, the capacity for questioning one's 'theory-in-use' and openness to changing as a function of learning. The result of reflection, inquiry, testing and self-criticism should lead to reframing one's norms and values and restructuring one's strategies and assumptions according to the new settings.

- The 4I framework proposed by Crossan, Lane and White (1999) conceptualizes four learning processes: intuiting, interpreting, integrating and institutionalizing.

- More recently, Zhou, Hu and Shi (2015) proposed a new organizational learning framework with three building blocks: learning orientation, learning processes and leadership. Compared with the 4I framework by Crossan, Lane and White, the framework by Zhou, Hu and Shi highlights the importance of leadership in learning, which is a key factor in developing a supportive organizational culture to foster knowledge sharing and learning.

- Two types of learning flow can be defined: feed-forward flow and feedback flow. Feed-forward flow occurs in the process of transferring knowledge from individual to group to organization level, which is associated with the exploration aspect of learning. Feedback flow takes place when an organization distributes its accumulated knowledge to group and individual levels, which is most associated with the exploitation aspect of learning.

- Organizational memory systems are containers that serve to identify, preserve and make available valuable lessons learned and best practices. Lessons learned and best practices are flip sides of the same coin – they represent the accumulated results and learning from trial-and-error experiences that an organization has accumulated.

- A lessons-learned process has a number of stages in which lessons are identified, collected, analysed, selected and preserved in organizational memory for access and utilization. An important prerequisite to learning is that employees must be aware that lessons exist, and that they actively seek them out and learn from them.

- Some major challenges for organizational learning are motivating people to participate, getting management to support them, and transforming tacit experiential knowledge into an explicit form that can be easily found and reused.

Review questions

- What are the differences and links among knowledge management, organizational learning and organizational memory?

- Conduct a literature review of organizational learning theories (such as models and frameworks). Compare and contrast a number of theories. Why do you think there are so many theories but with little intersection – what do you think may have caused this fragmentation? How would you go about trying to put the various pieces together in order to better understand organizational learning?

- Most individual learning theories tend to focus on how we can change the external environment to promote greater learning. How could we synthesize cognitive and behavioural approaches to better understand our internal learning mechanisms?

- In group/team learning, some members are naturally more argumentative whereas others are more reflective and deeper thinkers. How can we manage group/team learning without developing defensive routines in specific circumstances where discussion and dialogue are required?

- Using an organization you have worked for or studied with as an example, in terms of the depth of learning, which type(s) of learning cycle (single loop, double loop or triple loop learning) can you identify from the organization, and what kinds of evidence are there to support your findings?

- What criteria can be used to identify a lesson learned or best practice that is worthy of being preserved in organizational memory?
- Discuss how you can learn from an unsuccessful project.
- What are the key stages of a lessons learned process?
- If you were tasked with initiating an organization-wide programme for surfacing people's mistakes and learning from them, how would you instigate such an 'error-harvesting' programme where mistakes could be surfaced and errors could be discussed for 'lessons learned'? What main difficulties would you anticipate in implementing such a programme?

References

Abubakar, A M *et al* (2019) Knowledge management, decision making style and organizational performance, *Journal of Innovation and Knowledge*, **4**, pp 104–14

Amman, E (2012) Organizational learning cycles by means of knowledge dynamics, in *Proceedings of the International Multi-conference of Engineers and Computer Scientists (IMECS)*, vol 1, pp 14–16, March, Hong Kong, China

Arevalo, K M, Ljung, M and Sriskandarajah, N (2010) Learning through feedback in the field: reflective learning in a NGO in the Peruvian Amazon, *Action Research*, **8** (1), pp 29–51

Argyris, C (1978) *Organizational Learning: A theory of action perspective*, Addison-Wesley, Reading, MA

Argyris, C (1999) *On Organizational Learning*, 2nd edn, Blackwell, Oxford

Argyris, C and Schön, D A (1996) *Organizational Learning II: Theory, method and practice*, Addison-Wesley, Reading, MA

Bateson, P (2006) Bateson's levels of learning: a framework for transformative learning? Universities' Forum for Human Resource Development conference, University of Tilburg, May

Becerra-Fernandez, I and Sabherwal, R (2015) *Knowledge Management: Systems and processes*, 2nd edn, Routledge, Abingdon

Crossan, M M, Lane, H W and White, R E (1999) An organizational learning framework: from intuition to institution, *Academy of Management Review*, **24** (3), pp 522–37

Crossan, M M, Maurer, C C and White, R E (2011) Reflections on the 2009 AMR decade award: do we have a theory of organizational learning? *Academy of Management Review*, **36** (3), pp 446–60

Dalkir, K (2017) *Knowledge Management in Theory and Practice*, 3rd edn, MIT Press, Cambridge, MA

Doyle, L, Kelliher, F and Harrington, D (2016) How multi-levels of individual and team learning interact in a public healthcare organization: a conceptual framework, *Action Learning: Research and Practice*, **13** (1), pp 10–22

Flood, R L and Romm, N R A (2018) A systemic approach to processes of power in learning organizations: part 1 – literature, theory and methodology of triple loop learning, *The Learning Organization*, **25** (4), pp 260–72

Garvin, D A, Edmondson, A C and Gino, F (2008) Is yours a learning organization? *Harvard Business Review*, **86** (3), pp 109–16

Guinot, J, Chiva, R and Tarter, C J (2016) Linking altruism and organizational learning capability: a study from excellent human resources management organizations in Spain, *Journal of Business Ethics*, **138** (2), pp 349–64

Haight, V D and Marquardt, M J (2018) How chief learning officers build learning organizations, *The Learning Organization*, **25** (5), pp 331–43

Herbst, A S (2017) Capturing knowledge from lessons learned at the work package level in project engineering teams, *Journal of Knowledge Management*, **21** (4), pp 765–78

Hislop, D, Bosua, R and Helms, R (2018) *Knowledge Management in Organizations: A critical introduction*, 4th edn, Oxford University Press, Oxford

Hortovanyi, L and Ferincz, A (2015) The impact of ICT on learning on-the-job, *The Learning Organization*, **22** (1), pp 2–13

Huber, G (1991) Organizational learning: the contributing processes and a review of the literature, *Organizational Science*, **2** (1), pp 88–115

Jashapara, A (2011) *Knowledge Management: An integrated approach*, 2nd edn, Pearson Education, Harlow

Kantamara, P and Vathanophas, V (2014) Single loop and double loop learning: an obstacle or a success factor for organizational learning, *International Journal of Education and Research*, **2** (7), pp 55–62

Kim, D H (1993) The link between individual and organizational learning, *Sloan Management Review*, Fall, pp 37–50

Kitimbo, I (2015) Lessons learned: theory and practice, in *Utilizing Evidenced-Based Lessons Learned for Enhanced Organizational Innovation and Change*, ed S McIntyre *et al*, pp 1–23, IGI Global, Hershey, PA

Kloss-Grote, B and Moss, M A (2008) How to measure the effectiveness of risk management in engineering design projects? Presentation of RMPASS: a new method for assessing risk management performance and the impact of knowledge management – including a few results, *Research in Engineering Design*, **19** (2–3), pp 71–100

Kolb, D A (1984) *Experiential Learning: Experience as the source of learning and development*, Prentice Hall, Englewood Cliffs, NJ

Matties, B and Coners, A (2018) Double loop learning in project environments: an implementation approach, *Expert Systems With Applications*, **96**, pp 330–46

McClory, S, Read, M and Labib, A (2017) Conceptualizing the lessons-learned process in project management: towards a triple-loop learning framework, *International Journal of Project Management*, **35**, pp 1322–35

Medama, W, Wals, A and Adamowski, J (2014) Multi-loop social learning for sustainable land and water governance: towards a research agenda on the potential virtual learning platforms, *NJAS – Wageningen Journal of Life Sciences*, **69**, pp 23–38

Milton, N (2010) *The Lessons Learned Handbook: Practical approaches to learning from experience*, Elsevier Science and Technology, Oxford

Mumford, A (1991) Learning in action, *Personnel Management*, July, pp 34–37

Nonaka, I and Konno, N (1998) The concept of 'Ba': building a foundation for knowledge creation, California Management Review, 40(3), pp 40–54

Nonaka, I and Takeuchi, H (1995) *The Knowledge Creating Company*, Oxford University Press, New York

Nugroho, M A (2018) The effects of collaborative cultures and knowledge sharing on organizational learning, *Journal of Organizational Change Management*, **31** (5), pp 1138–52

Oh, S Y (2019) Effects of organizational learning on performance: the moderating roles of trust in leaders and organizational justice, *Journal of Knowledge Management*, **23** (2), pp 313–31

Oyemomi, O (2016) The Impact of Organizational Factors on Knowledge Sharing Performance, PhD Thesis, University of Plymouth, UK

Park, S and Kim, E J (2018) Fostering organizational learning through leadership and knowledge sharing, *Journal of Knowledge Management*, **22** (6), pp 1408–23

Perrin, A, Rolland, N and Stanley, T (2007) Achieving best practices transfer across countries, *Journal of Knowledge Management*, **11** (3), pp 156–66

Prieto, I M and Revilla, E (2006) Learning capability and business performance: a non-financial and financial assessment, *The Learning Organization*, **13** (2), pp 299–331

Sanchez, R (2003) Managing knowledge into competence: the five learning cycles of the competent organization, in *Knowledge Management and Organizational Competence*, ed R Sanchez', pp 3–37, Oxford University Press. Oxford

Schwandt, D R and Marquardt, M J (2000) Organizational Learning: from World-class Theories to Global Best Practices, CRC Press, Boca Raton, FL

Tosey, P, Visser, M and Saunders, M N K (2011) The origins and conceptualizations of 'triple-loop' learning: a critical review, *Management Learning*, **43** (3), pp 291–307

United States General Accounting Office (US GAO) (2002) [accessed 3 September 2019] NASA: Better Mechanisms Needed for Sharing Lessons Learned, *GAO-02-195* [Online] www.gao.gov/new.items/d02195.pdf (archived at https://perma.cc/VXT9-B9YL)

Weber, R, Aha, D W and Becerra-Fernandez, I (2001) Intelligent lessons learned systems, *Expert Systems Research and Applications*, **20** (1), pp 17–34

Zhou, W, Hu, H and Shi, X (2015) Does organizational learning lead to higher firm performance? An investigation of Chinese listing companies, *The Learning Organization*, **22** (5), pp 271–88

The learning organization

05

Learning outcomes

After completing this chapter, the reader will be able to:

- understand the concept of the learning organization;
- compare and contrast different theoretical models of learning organization developed in the United States and the UK;
- identify key cross-cutting themes across different theoretical models of learning organization;
- explain the relationships among learning organization, organizational learning and knowledge management.

Since the publication of Peter Senge's seminal book *The Fifth Discipline: The art and practice of the learning organization* (1990), research on the learning organization (LO) has proliferated. Definitions of LO and models for creating an LO have also flourished. A dedicated journal, *Learning Organization*, has been publishing research on the topic for 25 years, since 1994. A number of comprehensive review papers on LO are available, representing the high level of maturity of the research on the topic (Thomas and Allen, 2006; Santa, 2015). This chapter starts with definitions of LO, then discusses various theoretical LO models developed in the United States and the UK, followed by the identification of key cross-cutting themes across different LO models, and finishes on the links among LO, OL and KM.

5.1 Definitions of a learning organization

A learning organization is a type of organization that has successfully implemented the process of organizational learning (OL). In this sense, LO can be considered as a product or end state of the OL. It is believed that LO provides organizations with a winning advantage in an ever-changing and globalized business environment (Reese and Sidani, 2018). A great number of definitions exist in the literature. In a recent review paper, a total of 29 definitions of LO are listed (Santa, 2015). Here we select a number of definitions that are widely cited, some of which are included in Santa's review:

- LO are organizations where people *continually* expand their *capacity* to create the results they truly desire, where new and expansive patterns of thinking are nurtured, where collective aspiration is set free, and where people are continually *learning* to see the *whole organization together* (Senge, 1990).

- LO is a vision of what might be possible. It is not brought about simply by training individuals. It can only happen as a result of *learning* at the *whole organization level*. An LO is an organization that facilitates the learning of *all its members* and *continuously transforms* itself (Pedler, Burgoyne and Boydell, 1991).

- An LO is an organization skilled at creating, acquiring, interpreting, transferring and retaining *knowledge*, and at purposefully *modifying* its behaviour to reflect *new knowledge* and insights (Garvin, 2000).

- LO is a living organism that uses *learning* to *improve* organizational *performance* (Marsick and Watkins, 2003).

- LO is the product or result of a critical combination of internal *change* mechanisms concerned with structure, process and human *capability* allied to *continuous* environmental *reviews* intended to maintain or *improve* performance (Thomas and Allen, 2006).

- An LO is an organization that *learns* effectively and collectively and *continually transforms* itself for better management and use of *knowledge*, empowers people within and outside the organization to *learn* as they work, utilizes technology to maximize *learning* and production (Marquardt, 2011).

- An LO is a *continuously adaptive* enterprise that *aligns* itself to the environment by focusing its *learning* on the major *competitive forces* at a given time (Jashapara, 2011).

- LO is an organization that possesses *continuous learning* characteristics or mechanisms to meet its ever-*changing* needs (Ali, 2012).

- Learning as an *entire* organization at *all levels* to *adapt* and succeed with the environment that *continually changes* (Reese and Sidani, 2018).

Despite the lack of a unified definition, we can see that there are a number of common features that these definitions emphasize, including:

- Learning feature: an LO can learn at multiple levels (organizational, group and individual), using both types of flow (feedback and feed-forward), with different levels of depth (triple loop learning, double loop learning and single loop learning).

- Results feature: in an LO, new knowledge and insights resulting from the learning process are generated, integrated, applied to the development and delivery of products and services (either through lessons learned or best practice), and the organization's learning capacity, capability, competitiveness and performance are increased.

- Changing feature: an LO should allow appropriate levels of changes, and adapt, adjust and transform itself so that it is aligned with its internal business requirements and external business environment.

- Strategic feature: LOs learning and change focus on the strategic level for the whole organization, that is, for all members in the organization, rather than at individual or group/team level. An LO should have a vision for long-term benefits and continuous improvement of the organization. Ideally, LO should not be seen as just an end state of learning but as a continuous journey to the Holy Grail.

- Culture feature: to build an LO, all people in the organization should be encouraged to learn and not to be afraid of making mistakes during changes. Employees value knowledge sharing and deep learning to prevent a blaming culture. Lessons can be freely exposed, analysed and learned. The development of a learning culture should be rewarded.

These definitions also show that the concept of LO is closely linked to other concepts discussed in previous chapters: organizational learning – the intentional use of learning processes to continuously transform the organization, and knowledge creation – knowledge is the core asset representing an organization's competitive advantage as advocated by the knowledge-based view (Castro, Saez and Verde, 2011). In today's knowledge economy, the pace of change has accelerated, which is demonstrated by the fact that, in less than 10 years, half of the companies listed as members of the Fortune 500 can disappear from the list (Thomas and Allen, 2006). Thus, organizations must operate amid continual and disruptive changes. In order to thrive in the new dynamic environment, organizations' vision and strategy are shifting their focus from seeing people and other resources as tangible resources to be moved, replaced and eliminated as business needs dictate, to seeing the organization as a set of knowledge assets deployed through people, process and technology. The capacity to accelerate the cycle of 'organizational learning–knowledge management–learning organization' has become extremely important. As pointed out earlier, tacit knowledge is mainly embodied in people, even though it can be articulated and made explicit on some occasions, but rarely without losing a good deal of its richness and applicability.

 Critical thinking and reflection
Definitions of LO

1 Most definitions of LO highlight the 'changing' feature. What do you think are the main reasons for the authors to have highlighted the 'changing' feature?

2 What is your understanding of the links among learning organization, organizational learning and knowledge management?

The next section will introduce different LO models developed in the United States and the UK at different times. It should be noted that the contexts and culture in which knowledge management and organizational learning take place may differ.

5.2 Theoretical models for developing learning organizations

This section will examine a number of influential models of LO. The theoretical models have been mainly developed in Western countries, especially the United States and the UK, but their applications have been worldwide. By analysing the models from different culture and business contexts, different views can be compared and contrasted so that a more comprehensive picture of LO theories and practices can be provided.

LO models – US contributions

Along with developing scientific definitions for LO, many US scholars have researched developing LO models to help guide organizations moving towards utopia. A great number of scholars and their representative work have become known worldwide in the LO and OL fields, including:

- Peter Senge for his book *The Fifth Discipline: The art and practice of the learning organization* (Senge, 1990);
- Karen Watkins and Victoria Marsick for their 'Dimensions of the Learning Organization Questionnaire' (Marsick and Watkins, 2003);
- David Garvin, Amy Edmondson and Francesco Gino's three building blocks of a learning organization (Garvin, 2000; Garvin, Edmondson and Gino, 2008); and
- Michael Marquardt and his work *Building the Learning Organization* with systems thinking theory (Marquardt, 2011).

Because of the wide influence of these works, this section will discuss the four models in detail.

The Five Disciplines

Peter Senge's book *The Fifth Discipline* (1990) was widely seen as one of the most influential works in the 1990s in the learning organization field (Reese and Sidani, 2018). In this book, Senge explicitly defined five key disciplines of a learning organization: personal mastery, team learning, systems thinking, mental models and shared vision. Table 5.1 summarizes the meanings of the five disciplines and the main reasons why they are included in the model.

Table 5.1 Five disciplines of a learning organization

Constructs	Meaning	Reasons for inclusion
Personal mastery	Developing capacity to clarify what is important to individuals and the organization in terms of personal vision and purpose.	To highlight a 'creative intension' between current reality and future vision, and also to emphasize the important relationship between individuals' commitment to their own growth and a supportive environment in the organization.
Team learning	Developing capacity for team conversation to balance dialogue (engaging team members for divergent thinking) and discussion (engaging team members for convergent thinking).	To discover new views within the team and for team members to be receptive to new and different views and willing to change their own view in order to achieve consensus.

(continued)

Table 5.1 (Continued)

Constructs	Meaning	Reasons for inclusion
Systems thinking	Developing capacity for putting pieces together and seeing the whole organization rather than disparate parts.	To provide incentives and means to integrate disciplines to recognize the whole, in order to understand complex and dynamic systems and processes in the organization.
Mental models	Developing capacity to reflect on internal pictures, such as using scenario planning to force managers to examine how they would manage different situations in the future.	To balance skills of inquiry and advocacy as well as understanding how mental models influence actions.
Shared vision	Building a sense of agreement in an organization on what people really would like to create together. This shared vision should reflect personal vision and team vision.	To align personal goals with organizational goals.

These five disciplines should not be seen as isolated components of a learning organization but as interrelated. Linking back to the three levels in an organization (individual level, group/team level and organizational level), the relationships between the five disciplines can be interpreted as shown in Figure 5.1. Good *personal mastery* at individual level will make a contribution to *team learning* at group/team level, which in turn contributes to creating a *shared vision* at organizational level. *Systems thinking* can be used as a philosophy to guide these three disciplines at all three levels. *Mental models* can provide a means to support capacity building at the three levels.

Senge's Five Disciplines Model covers all three levels of an organization. The model highlights the importance of individuals' commitment and team learning in creating an organization's shared vision, which is considered as a clear contribution to LO theory. The model also recognizes the importance of systems thinking in understanding an organization's complex and dynamic situations resulting from the organization's structure, process and systems. The model laid a solid foundation for the LO field and influenced many other scholars, including Michael Marquardt who was able to extend Senge's work later.

Figure 5.1 Linking the five disciplines together

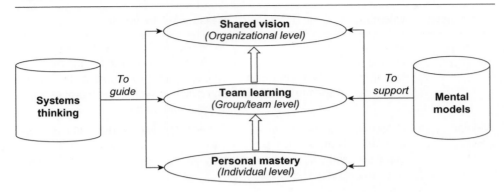

However, there have been a number of criticisms of the Five Disciplines Model. The criticisms are mainly of the justification of the five disciplines (why these five only and no other disciplines as well?) and the practicality of the model (the model seems to be conceptual and prescriptive without concrete support from real case studies). Some critics consider the five disciplines to be too abstract, hence organizations have struggled to identify them empirically (Chai and Dirani, 2018). Others argue that one of the biggest problems with Peter Senge's approach has nothing to do with the rightness of the theory nor the way it is presented, but that the people to whom the idea is addressed do not have the mindset to engage with it. This is largely a philosophical and cultural issue (Elkin, Cone and Liao, 2009).

 Critical thinking and reflection
Senge's Five Disciplines Model of LO

If you were to extend Peter Senge's Five Disciplines Model for LO, what other disciplines would be at the top of your priority list that you would like to add, and why?

To overcome the shortcomings of Senge's Five Disciplines Model, later work in the United States on developing LO models paid more attention to the measurement instruments for implementation in management practice. Some of the best-known efforts are the Dimensions of the Learning Organization Questionnaire (DLOQ), the Three Building Blocks of LO and the Systems Thinking LO Model, which are discussed below.

Dimensions of the Learning Organization Questionnaire

It is widely accepted that Karen Watkins and Victor Marsick (Watkins and Marsick, 1993; Watkins, Yang and Marsick, 1997; Marsick and Watkins, 2003; Watkins and Dirani, 2013) have been the pioneers who have championed the work of the DLOQ (Kim, Egan and Tolson, 2015). As early as 1993, Watkins and Marsick published their book *Sculpting the Learning Organization: Lessons in the art and science of systemic change* (Watkins and Marsick, 1993). In this book, they suggested six imperatives for the design of an LO:

1 empowering people towards a collective vision;

2 promoting inquiry and dialogue;

3 encouraging collaboration and team learning;

4 creating continuous learning opportunities;

5 connecting the organization to the environment;

6 establishing systems to capture and share learning.

In the book, leadership for learning was originally ruled out from the action imperatives; instead, the underlying role of leaders was highlighted through the metaphor of 'a sculptor' of the LO. According to Watkins and Marsick (1993), a leader, as sculptor, plays the pivotal role by empowering people with a vision and engaging in a dialogue that shapes the emerging product. Three years later, this emphasis on the critical role of leaders in the LO led to the inclusion of leadership as the seventh imperative (Phillips, Watkins and Marsick, 1996).

These seven imperatives are expected to occur at four different levels for an organization to have the capacity for continuous learning and change: individual, group/team, organizational and societal (connection to the environment). Figure 5.2 illustrates the links between the seven imperatives and the four different levels associated with an organization.

It can be seen that most of the imperatives are required for more than one level. *Inquiry* is extremely important at individual level, but *dialogue* is more targeted at group level. Investment in technology *systems to capture learning* is essential at both group and organizational levels. Similarly, *leadership* for learning is a must not only for the group and organizational levels, but also for the societal level. The purpose of Figure 5.2 is not to provide prescriptions about the links between imperatives and levels associated with an organization, but to illustrate the complex and overlapping

Figure 5.2 The seven imperatives and four levels associated with an organization

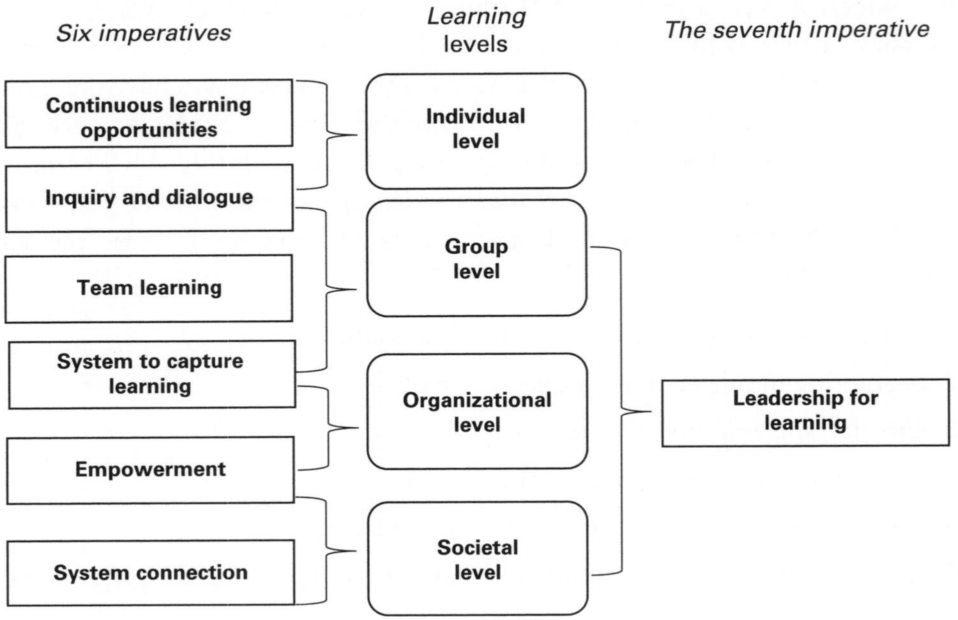

Six imperatives

Learning levels

The seventh imperative

- Continuous learning opportunities
- Inquiry and dialogue
- Team learning
- System to capture learning
- Empowerment
- System connection

- Individual level
- Group level
- Organizational level
- Societal level

- Leadership for learning

relationships between them, in the sense that there is no simple one-to-one relationship but that there are often many-to-one and one-to-many bidirectional relationships.

 Critical thinking and reflection
Seven imperatives of LO by Watkins and Marsick

Do you think it is a good idea to include 'leadership for learning' as the seventh imperative, or would you rather exclude it from the imperatives list? Why do you think so?

Based on the seven action imperatives from their previous work, Watkins, Yang and Marsick (1997) published the DLOQ by constructing seven dimensions from the seven imperatives. The DLOQ was designed to measure the presumed seven dimensions of the LO, formally termed *continuous learning*, *dialogue and inquiry*, *team learning*, *empowerment*, *system to capture learning*, *system connection*, and *leadership for learning*. Initially, their

Likert-type instrument consisted of 42 items in total, with six items for each dimension. Later, Marsick and Watkins (2003) separated one item in the *continuous learning* scale into two items, which resulted in a 43-item version of the DLOQ. They also used the 43-item version of the DLOQ to demonstrate the value of an organization's learning culture (Marsick and Watkins, 2003). They further presented two shorter versions of the DLOQ: DLOQ-A with 21 items (3 items for each dimension/scale) and a 7-item version for organizational study (Yang, Watkins and Marsick, 2004). All three versions have been validated in different cultural contexts beyond the Western culture in which the DLOQ was developed. For example, validation of the 43-item version of DLOQ is reported in Dirani (2013) and the testing of the 21-item and 7-item versions of the DLOQ is presented in Chai and Dirani (2018), both in Lebanese culture.

Since its publication, the DLOQ has been widely deployed in many different cultures across all major continents, including Africa, Asia, Europe, North America, South America and Oceania (Watkins and Dirani, 2013). In practice, the DLOQ has been adapted for non-profit organizations, higher education, government and the army (Watkins and O'Neil, 2013). This wide application itself demonstrates the satisfactory validity of the DLOQ as a whole instrument. Its contribution is not only to the LO-related research and theory building, but also to the framing and assessment of human resource development (HRD) practices (Marsick, 2013).

The criticisms of the DLOQ are mainly of its statistical limitations regarding the construct validity of the DLOQ (in both the full and shortened versions), such as multi-collinearity and single factor extraction (Kim, Egan and Tolson, 2015). Another debate is centred around whether the inclusion of leadership as a seventh dimension is a good idea. In Watkins and Marsick's early work, leadership was not included in the six imperatives for an organization to evolve into an LO. Rather, leadership for learning was assumed as an underlying characteristic, which supports the overall learning culture in an organization. It implies that leadership for learning is an overarching construct that may include the other six dimensions of the DLOQ, or as the key driver of the remaining six imperatives. That is, leadership promotes continuous learning opportunities, dialogue and inquiry, team learning, empowerment, system to capture learning, and system connection. In this way, leadership seems to be able to provide the links among the other six dimensions. By moving leadership into a seventh dimension, which is in parallel to other six dimensions, it has actually removed the multidimensional feature of the LO framework.

The three building blocks of a learning organization

Also aiming to address the difficulty in implementing LO models published earlier because of a lack of standards and tools for managers to assess how individuals' and teams' learnings were contributing to the organization as a whole, Garvin, Edmondson and Gino (2008) developed a comprehensive, concrete survey instrument that can be used as a tool to rate and assess how well a company learns and adeptly refine the organization's strategies and processes.

Their survey instrument is structured around three building blocks: a supportive learning environment, concrete learning processes and practices, and leadership behaviour that provides reinforcement. Each building block has its discrete components. The building blocks and their components, though vital to the whole, are independent and can be measured separately, which allows organizations to assess their learning proficiencies with great granularity and flexibility. For example, organizations that do not perform consistently across the three blocks or across all components within each block can still be measured. Figure 5.3 shows the three building blocks and their corresponding components.

Building block 1, a supportive **learning environment,** is about creating a culture for learning. It has four distinguished characteristics:

Figure 5.3 Three building blocks and their components in an LO

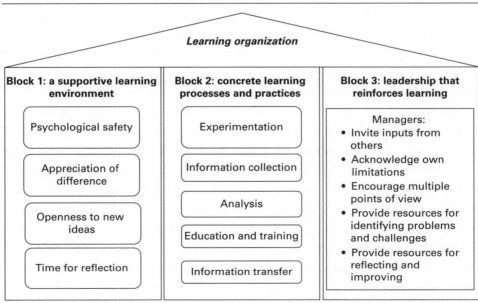

- Psychological safety: employees feel safe and comfortable expressing their thoughts, including disagreeing with peers or authority figures, asking naïve questions, owning up to mistakes or presenting a minority viewpoint.

- Appreciation of differences: learning occurs when people value opposing ideas and competing functional outlooks. Alternative views increase energy and spark fresh thinking.

- Openness to new ideas: employees should be encouraged to take risks and explore the untested and unknown.

- Time for reflection: a supportive learning environment allows time for a pause in the action and encourages thoughtful review and reflection.

Building block 2, concrete **learning processes** and practices, covers five important aspects:

- Experimentation: experimenting frequently with new ways of working, new products and service offerings, new ideas, prototyping and simulation.

- Information collection: systematically collecting information on customers, competitors, technological trends, economic and social trends, and comparing the organization's own performance with that of competitors and best-in-class organizations.

- Analysis: frequently identifying and evaluating underlying assumptions that affect key decisions.

- Education and training: periodic education and training updates, providing education and training to new employees, to experienced employees when switching to new positions, and when new initiatives are launched.

- Information transfer: providing access to a network of experts, and sharing information and knowledge for learning from all stakeholders.

Building block 3, **leadership** that reinforces learning, is used to assess how well leaders do in strengthen learning in an organization. Managers with leadership qualities such as openness have the ability to inspire others and instil confidence. There are a variety of things leaders can do, including:

- invite inputs from others;
- acknowledge their own limitations;
- encourage multiple points of view;
- provide resources for identifying problems and challenges;
- provide resources for reflecting and improving.

Even though the three building blocks of a learning organization are defined independently and with agility, in fact they reinforce each other and, to some extent, overlap. Leadership behaviours (block 3) help create and sustain a supportive learning environment (block 1), and such an environment makes it easier for managers and employees to execute concrete learning processes and practices (block 2) smoothly and efficiently.

Because of its practicality, the Three Building Block Model of LO has been applied in various contexts. Outside the United States, Borge *et al* (2018) successfully enacted the model in four Norwegian police districts at an early stage of reform implementation. There had been specific calls for the police force to become an LO. One of the objectives of the reform was to develop the police towards being more knowledge based and have the ability to learn and change to be adaptive to the dynamic economic and social environment. The work explored how hierarchical positions and organizational size affected the perception of LO. Based on empirical data from a large-scale survey with over 750 respondents, Borge *et al* find that managers at higher levels are more positive about the idea of an LO than middle managers, and that middle managers are more positive than ordinary employees. The study also shows that respondents across hierarchical levels in large police districts give their organization a higher rating for learning than those in small ones. Hence it can be concluded that hierarchical positions and organizational size do have an impact on the three building blocks and their corresponding components of a learning organization.

Systems Thinking Model

Marquardt spent about 20 years on developing his Systems Thinking Model (Marquardt, 2011). His definition of LO originated from his work at George Washington University, beginning in 1991. At the University, he worked with David Schwandt, a famous scholar on organizational learning. After almost 10 years, they published their co-authored book *Organizational Learning: From world-class theories to global best practices* (Schwandt and Marquardt, 2000). After starting from some general theories and Schwandt's work on OL, Marquardt began to build from a review of existing literature focusing on LO. He learned from Senge's Five Disciplines Model about the importance of systems thinking. He also knew Victoria Marsick and Karen Watkins from the Academy of Human Resource Development, and were familiar with their work 'Dimensions of the Learning Organization Questionnaire', which Marquardt thought was a useful tool that organizations could utilize to evaluate themselves. Based on the inspirations from these colleagues' work and his own background from extensive consultancy work for companies, Marquardt was able to extend their work into a broader context, focusing on developing an LO model that can be used as a tool to help organizations understand the capabilities of the few best-in-class organizations (Reese and Sidani, 2018). Finally, in 2011 he published his famous Systems Thinking Model.

Marquardt's Systems Thinking Model comprises five subsystems: learning dynamics, organization transformation, people empowerment, knowledge management and technology application (Marquardt, 2011). These five subsystems together can be used as a tool for management to create a learning organization profile to evaluate their organization against an established list of best-in-class activities. Marquardt had a clear view that using a best-in-class structure would create a goal and the assessment would create the targeted gap area. Using the gaps, management teams could define the next steps. Hence, the model could help organizational leaders in their evolution towards building a learning organization.

The **learning dynamics** subsystem emphasizes that learning is ultimately a social phenomenon; it means that an organization's ability to learn, and the quality and openness of its relationships, determine what employees know and how fast the organization can learn. The learning dynamics consists of three aspects:

- multi-levels of learning: individual, group/team, and organizational learning;
- various types of learning: adaptive (single loop), generative (double loop) and transformative and creative (triple loop) learning;
- critical OL skills: systems thinking and mental models.

The **organization transformation** subsystem refers to the necessary setting and body in which learning occurs in order to bring about the transformation of the organization into a learning organization. This subsystem includes four key dimensions: vision, culture, structure and strategy:

- Vision: a solid foundation of a shared vision about learning which provides the focus and energy for learning.
- Culture: a successful learning culture has a system of values that is supportive to learning. Taking risks, trying new approaches and sharing knowledge are encouraged.

- Structure: the structural characteristics of an LO are based on the need to learn. The driving principle is to put the necessary freedom, support and resources in the hands of the people who need them. The structure should help to avoid rigid boundaries, bulky size, disjointedness of projects and tasks, and bureaucratic restriction.

- Strategy: top management support for becoming a learning organization and making learning a part of the organization's policies and procedures.

The **people empowerment** subsystem is about empowering all people in the organization and in the value chain to enable them to learn, including employees, managers and leaders, customers, business partners and the community:

- Empowering employees: treat employees as mature and capable workers and learners; encourage employee freedom, energy and enthusiasm; involve employees in the decision-making processes; strike a balance between organizational needs and individuals' productivity and happiness.

- Empowering managers and leaders: provide skills to enable management to move from controlling to empowering, from being a commander to being a steward, from acting as a transactional manager to being a transformational leader.

- Empowering customers: engage customers through pre-market conversations, not only to gather information and intelligence from customers, but also to use customers' knowledge and expertise in the early stages of product and service design and planning in order to create and deliver the best customer experience.

- Empowering business partners: in the current business globalization environment, an organization's success is to a large extent dependent on the success of its entire value chain rather than the organization alone, hence it is important to include business partners in the empowering plan.

The **knowledge management** subsystem refers to the effective management of acquired and generated knowledge to support effective decision making for the organization. Marquardt's KM subsystem has six stages: acquisition, creation, storage, analysis (data mining), transfer/dissemination and application/validation. As knowledge acquisition, creation, storage, transfer/ dissemination and application/validation were discussed extensively in Chapter 3, this section will not repeat the explanation of these stages but rather focus on the knowledge analysis stage, which is new in Marquardt's model for LO. As mentioned earlier, Marquardt spent significant effort on case studies with companies during his consultancy work and obtained a clear vision of moving knowledge from bench scientists to the entire organization to achieve the target of building a learning organization. Benefiting from his case studies, such as that with 3M which excelled at moving knowledge from scientific research to management practice, Marquardt was able to see the importance of technology in helping to convert tacit knowledge to explicit knowledge for organization-wide learning, and also to articulate the importance of analysis through advanced technologies such as data mining in helping to generate further business insights from the acquired/created initial knowledge. For example, data mining can help generate business intelligence such as market trends and sales patterns, which would be a lot more valuable in supporting higher-level decision making than the initial customer/market knowledge or product sales knowledge. The strength of knowledge analysis through data mining comes through large scale, such as at organizational level, which is able to provide a sufficient amount of initial knowledge, information and data for the mining process, and hence it fits well with the context of LO discussed in this chapter. This is why in Chapter 3, when discussing the generic KM process, knowledge analysis is not explicitly listed as a stand-alone stage.

The **technology application** subsystem concerns the supporting and enabling technological networks and tools that facilitate learning and KM, including technical processes, systems and structures for collaboration, coaching, coordination and decision support. In the past few decades, technology leaps and revolutions have been dramatic, which greatly changed the business environment, and an organization's reaction to its environment has necessitated the application of technology advancements to improve the organization's learning and KM (Sanz-Valle *et al*, 2011; Tseng, 2017). Key components within this subsystem include IT technology, technology-based learning and knowledge-based decision support systems:

- IT technology: as one of the fastest-growing technologies, IT technology such as internet and web technologies has transformed almost every aspect of organizations, not only by providing tools and systems for communication among people, between people and machines, and among organizations, to enable unprecedented capacity for knowledge capture, access, storage, analysis and transfer/dissemination, but also to provide powerful analytical support for decision making. By using state-of-the-art IT technology, the conversion of individual employees' tacit knowledge to explicit knowledge for building organizational memory and organizational learning has greatly advanced.

- Technology-based learning: today, multimedia training using video, audio and e-learning platforms are everywhere, for the delivery and sharing of knowledge, experience, expertise and skills. All people in an organization can use technology-based learning to reach a higher level of skills in order to be more flexible and adaptive in highly dynamic and fast-changing working positions. When jobs get more complex, technology-based learning can equip all people to gain more module-based, multisensory, portable and transferable knowledge and skills.

- Knowledge-based decision support systems (KB-DSS): a KB-DSS is a computer-based interactive system that aims to support decision making with a knowledge base and inferring, reasoning and learning mechanisms. The knowledge base can be a type of organizational memory that stores explicit knowledge which can be accessed and utilized by all people in an organization. A knowledge base is built upon domain knowledge from experts with a high-level quality of advice and recommendations for complex decision making and problem solving. A KB-DSS coherently integrates organizational memory, such as a knowledge base, decision analysis, such as big data analytics and data mining, and human–computer interfaces, such as visual dashboards, within human decision-making processes. As a result, organization-wide decisions can be made to realize the overall aim of the organization. KB-DSS will be discussed in detail in Chapter 13.

The five subsystems are required to work together to build a learning organization. Haight and Marquardt further explored how organizations could better exploit the Systems Thinking Model, lead the change and build a learning organization through appointing a chief learning officer in organizations (Haight and Marquardt, 2018). There are a number of key contributions from Marquardt's LO model. First, he built his model from his consulting work with organizations and adapted his model as he saw organizations succeeding and failing in becoming a learning organization. His model is not purely a theory but is implementable in practice. Second, Marquardt's model emphasizes the importance of people and leadership in learning. It is people who are at the centre of any organization, whether in establishing organizational value and culture for learning or creating a shared vision for strategy, structure and systems. Leadership is of paramount importance for an organization's direction and vision (Lee, Shiue and Chen, 2016; Tseng, 2017). Without strong leadership, internal learning enthusiasm and energy cannot be channelled into collective power for change and transformation, and the external environment for change can be quickly overlooked or not synthesized into learning. Third, Marquardt's model incorporates two very important subsystems – technology application and KM in supporting learning. Technology is recognized as a medium for learning to occur across all organizational levels and as a platform for KM. The linkages from knowledge acquisition to application are established via technology. His model greatly expanded the emphasis on technology and the interplay with KM. Finally, the impact of Marquardt's model is unprecedented in the field. There have been over 2,000 citations of *Building the Learning Organization* (Reese and Sidani, 2018) within a short period of eight years (since publication of the model in 2011 until 2019 when this book was written). The Systems Thinking Model has been used as a tool in organizations with various cultural contexts, not only in Western cultures such as United States and Europe but also in Eastern cultures, including Singapore (Retna and Jones, 2013), Indonesia and China (Reese and Sidani, 2018). This wide impact demonstrates not only the usefulness of the model but also its ease of use, which allows organizations to implement it quite quickly and at multiple levels.

By using Marquardt's model, a learning organization profile can be built from each of the five subsystems. Each subsystem contains a series of 10 questions, and in total 50 questions are available for all five subsystems. Each question is rated from 1 to 4, where 1 represents little or no extent and 4 represents total applicability. Hence, the maximum score within each subsystem is 40 and the maximum score across all five subsystems is 200, which indicates a perfect learning organization.

Critical thinking and reflection
Marquardt's LO model

One of the critical comments on Marquardt's Systems Thinking Model for LO is that the relationships among the five subsystems are not specified. What other limitations or weaknesses do you perceive when critiquing the model?

LO models – UK contributions

Almost at the same time as researchers in the United States were investigating the concept of LO and developing relevant models for practice, in the UK research on the topic attracted many scholars. This section will discuss some of the most significant contributions from the UK on developing LO models over the past three decades, including the Three-Level Hierarchy Model by Garratt (1987, 1999), the Quality of Experimentation Model (Easterby-Smith, 1990) and the Learning Company Model (Pedler, Burgoyne and Boydell, 1991; Pedler and Burgoyne, 2017).

Bob Garratt was among the earliest researchers to have major influence in the field. His early representative work is his **Three-Level Hierarchy Model** (Garratt, 1987). He classified organizational learning into three levels: policy level, strategy level and operations level. The model highlights the importance of double loop learning with multiple feedback loops from information flow, direction giving and monitoring environmental changes. Garrat was influenced by the principles of action learning but was critical of the 'action-fixated non-learning cycle' found in many organizations (Jashapara, 2011). For Garratt, the reflection phase is the key to learning, which he branded as thinking smarter rather than working harder. Over 10 years later, Garratt reflected on his journey in research on LO and improved his initial Three-Level Hierarchy Model by addressing the dynamic interplay of learning at the policy, strategy and operations levels of an organization, which led to his triple loop learning model of LO: policy formulation/strategic thinking and integration/operational learning (Garratt, 1999). Then he concluded that LO was more an inspiration for a continuous process rather than a single product. It is inspiration that can energize people for a very long period of time. It is vision that motivates, stretches and leverages the organization for the long term.

Approaching from a different perspective, Easterby-Smith's **Quality of Experimentation Model** highly values the role of experimentation (Easterby-Smith, 1990) in organizational learning. The model suggested a number of ways to promote experimentation, including:

- experimenting in *people* to generate creativity and innovation;
- experimenting in *organizational structure* to introduce flexibility;
- experimenting in *reward systems* so that risk takers are not disadvantaged;
- experimenting in *information systems* by focusing on unusual variations.

Whether the experimentation is successful or not, there is no doubt that new learning materials can be generated either in the form of best practice or as lessons learned. When conditions allow, especially financial resources and time, experimenting should be encouraged. The practical difficulty is that experimentation can be costly, especially when it does not lead to any clear signs of creativity or innovation. In that case, the lessons learned may not be passed around the organization, hence the effort invested will be lost to the organizational learning process.

Critical thinking and reflection
Quality of Experimentation Model for LO

Despite wide acceptance of the Quality of Experimentation (QoE) Model for LO in theory, it has been argued that experimentation is expensive and risky in practice. What is your view on the QoE Model? To what extent would you support or be against implementing the model in your organization if you were the top manager in charge?

One of the most well-known UK contributions to LO is probably the **Learning Company Model** developed by Mike Pedler and his colleagues. They viewed the learning company as a vision of what might be possible, which cannot be brought about simply by training individuals but can only happen as a result of learning at the whole organizational level (Pedler, Burgoyne and Boydell, 1991). A learning company's collective aim should be organizational transformation, which is concerned with the production of corporate identity through a lifecycle spiral – the progression of identity through lifecycle stages is never ending, as the stages are just repeated at a higher level. The model defined five key components for a learning company:

1 *Strategy*: a learning approach to strategy with small-scale experiments and feedback loops to enable continuous improvement and participative policy making.

2 *Structure*: a flexible structure to allow for experimentation, adaptation and growth.

3 *Looking in*: this component includes using technology such as IT systems to help individuals understand what is going on, using formal mechanisms, processes and systems to assist learning. It also includes developing an environment of collaboration among groups, teams, departments and

functional units. By looking in internal systems, processes and mechanisms, the whole organization can be integrated as a whole with one corporate identity.

4 *Looking out*: regularly examining and reviewing the external environment, developing joint learning with other stakeholders, including competitors, for a 'win–win' learning situation. Environment fit is extremely important, especially when applying LO theories developed from Western cultures in a different culture and context. This view is strongly supported by Elkin, Cone and Liao (2009).

5 *Learning opportunities*: a climate of continuous improvement where mistakes are allowed and learning is encouraged, together with self-development opportunities for all in the organization.

In their book, Pedler, Burgoyne and Boydell (1991) explicitly presented 11 characteristics of a learning company. These characteristics include not only 'soft' human components but also 'hard' elements such as IT systems, accounting and marketing systems.

In order to glue the various components together to achieve a company's readiness for organizational transformation, Pedler *et al* (1991) further proposed an energy-flow model (shortened to e-flow model). Energy flows through an organization on four dimensions: individual and collective, inner and outer. All of these four dimensions are connected through double loop learning. In their recent publication, Pedler and Burgoyne (2017) reflected on their work on the e-flow model and the 11 characteristics of the learning company. Based on their more recent survey findings, they concluded that similar characteristics were revealed and that many managers are still very excited about the ideas. The paper recommended directions for further study, including the relationships between learning orientation and organizational performance, which require support from more empirical evidence, and how an LO makes use of what has been learned from OL, KM and dynamic capabilities.

5.3 Cross-cutting themes across different learning organization models

In Section 5.2, seven LO models have been discussed separately in detail. This section will synthesize them together in order to identify cross-cutting themes. The seven models discussed in the previous section include four models from the United States and three models from the UK. The four US models are Senge's (1990) Five Disciplines, the DLOQ proposed by Marsick and Watkins (2003), the Three Building Blocks by Garvin, Edmondson and Gino (2008) and Marquardt's Systems Thinking Model (Marquardt, 2011). The three models from the UK are Garratt's (1987) Three-Level Hierarchy Model, the Quality of Experimentation Model proposed by Easterby-Smith (1990) and the Learning Company (Pedler, Burgoyne and Boydell, 1991; Pedler and Burgoyne, 2017). We can see some similarities and differences when comparing these models. Table 5.2 summarizes the cross-cutting themes among the seven models.

Table 5.2 Cross-cutting themes among the seven LO models

Model	Source	Content
Three-Level Hierarchy Model	Garratt, 1987	Policy, Strategy, Operations
Five Disciplines	Senge, 1990	Shared vision, Systems thinking, Team learning, Personal mastery, Mental model
Quality of Experimentation	Easterby-Smith, 1990	People, Organizational structure, Reward systems, Information system
Learning Company	Pedler, Burgoyne and Boydell, 1991	Strategy, Structure, Looking in, Looking out, Learning opportunities
DLOQ (Seven imperatives)	Watkins and Marsick, 2003	Continuous learning opportunities, Inquiry and dialogue, Team learning, System to capture learning, Empowerment, System connection, Leadership for learning
Three Building Blocks	Garvin, Edmondson and Gino, 2008	Supportive learning environment, Learning process, Leadership
Systems Thinking (Five subsystems)	Marquardt, 2011	Learning dynamics, Organization transformation, People empowerment, Knowledge management, Technology application

These models may have different numbers of key components, or even use slightly different terms for the same or similar meaning, but there are some cross-cutting themes among them:

- Theme 1 – shared vision, strategy, systems thinking and organization transformation: these are measures of organizations at a high level which are included in four out of the seven models.

- Theme 2 – people, empowerment and leadership: these are important factors concerning people committing to, mastering and leading learning in organizations. Five out of the seven models include these factors.

- Theme 3 – structure, systems and technology: these are infrastructures and platforms that are required to facilitate learning. Five out of the seven models include these factors.

- Theme 4 – learning environment and learning opportunities: three models (the Learning Company, the DLOQ and the Three Building Blocks) emphasize these factors concerning creating opportunities and providing an environment for learning.

Other factors may not be able to form cross-cutting themes, but they demonstrate overlapping between particular models. For example, both the Five Disciplines and the DLOQ have *team learning*. Also, some models use different terms to mean similar things. For example, learning dynamics is used in Marquardt's Systems Thinking Model to represent various types of learning but also critical thinking, for example by using *mental models*, and mental model is identified as a key discipline in Senge's Five Disciplines. There are only a small number of factors that are unique to one model alone: for example, *knowledge management* is a subsystem exclusively belonging to the Systems Thinking Model.

 Critical thinking and reflection
Cross-cutting themes of LO models

Cross-cutting themes can be identified when various LO models are analysed together. As an example, four themes have been identified from the synthesis of seven LO models, as shown in this section. If you conduct a comprehensive literature review of LO models, analyse for example over 10 LO models together, then it is likely that you will be able to identify new themes. Which new themes will emerge depends on the LO models you include in your synthesis. Discuss which new themes you have identified, how they have emerged and from which LO models they have been identified.

Chapter summary

A number of patterns can be observed from LO's evolution over the past three decades:

1 LO has traditionally been seen as outcomes (ie solely the product of learning processes), but more recently it has been seen more as a combination of strategy, structure, people, process, technology and environment for learning. The popularization of various LO models shifts the focus onto the change, reconstruction and best practices of organizations. Even though the literature shows differences concerning what constitutes an LO and whether LOs can be compared across cultures and sectors, there seems to be general agreement on the core constructs (such as the cross-cutting themes) at the heart of an LO.

2 Even though LO theories were mainly developed in the United States and the UK, the application of LO models has been worldwide, in countries such as China (Elkin, Cone and Liao, 2009), Finland (Moilanen, 2005), Iran (Vatankhah *et al*, 2011), Jordan (Khadra and Rawabdeh, 2006), Lebanon (Chai and Dirani, 2018), Malaysia (Ali, 2012), Norway (Borge *et al*, 2018) and Singapore (Retna and Jones, 2013). Over the period of application, it has been gradually realized that broader and more culturally sensitive perspectives must be adopted in order to recognize the limitations and biases inherent in this Euro/American-centric concept and its practices. Some scholars even have gone beyond the 'cross-cultural approach' and argued that the issue is not only that of culturally appropriate implementation, but of recognizing that LO theory has been developed in a Western context and requires rethinking beyond that context (Retna and Jones, 2013).

3 A learning organization should not be a teaching organization. When members of management teams such as managers, leaders or chief learning officers champion learning programmes in an organization aiming for an LO, it is very important to avoid slipping into a teaching organization, where managers, leaders and chief learning officers become 'teachers'. Learning should be for all employees at all levels engaging with all types of learning. It should be not the responsibility of senior managers, organizational strategists or the human resources department. The energy of learning should be channelled to flow both ways, top-down and bottom-up, not just about operational employees following instructions from the top management team. A static teaching organization is not an LO. An LO can only be achieved through dynamic learning, which is always emphasized in the literature (Senge, 1990; Garvin, Edmondson and Gino, 2008; Marquardt, 2011).

4 LO is a long-term ambition and should not be interpreted as a quick fix for organizations. Skills involving fundamental new ways of thinking and interacting take years to master. New sensibilities and perceptions of the business world are a by-product of long-term growth and change. Deep beliefs and assumptions are not like light switches that can be turned on and off in a second (Gorelick, 2005). LO is more an inspiration for a continuous process rather than a single product. It is an inspiration that energizes people for a long period of time. It is a vision that motivates, stretches and leverages organizations for the long term (Garratt, 1999).

5 LO, OL and KM interplay and enhance each other. Organizational learning, the learning organization and knowledge management should co-exist with each other. The LO concept is about building learning and knowledge-creating capacity not just in individuals and groups but also enabling the effective dissemination of this knowledge through the whole organization. In essence, LO is the result of a critical combination of internal change mechanisms concerned with structure, process and human capacity allied to continuous environment reviews intended to maintain and improve performance (Thomas and Allen, 2006). Fundamentally, for a learning organization to be effective, there is a need for deep learning cycles and recognition that it will take time. Deep learning facilitates a learning organization to continuously generate new knowledge, which in turn improves the organization's competitiveness over time. It is a win–win–win situation among LO, OL and KM.

Key learning points

- Even though there has not been an agreed definition of a learning organization, there is agreement that a learning organization can continuously learn at multiple levels of the organization, using both feedback and feed-forward flows, possibly with a mixture of single loop, double loop and triple loop learning cycles. As a result, new knowledge and insights can be generated, integrated and applied to business processes and systems, which allows an appropriate level of changes, adaptation, adjustment and transformation of an organization.

- The five disciplines of a learning organization highlighted by Peter Senge are: personal mastery, team learning, systems thinking, mental models and shared vision.

- The Dimensions of Learning Organization Questionnaire (DLOQ) developed by Watkins and Marsick is a useful tool for organizations to assess and evaluate their readiness to become an LO. Leadership for learning is included as a key dimension, together with empowering people towards a collective vision, promoting inquiry and dialogue, encouraging collaboration and team learning, creating continuous learning opportunities, connecting the organization to the environment and establishing systems to capture and share learning. The full version of the DLOQ has 43 items.

- Garvin, Edmondson and Gino's three building blocks of an LO include a supportive learning environment, concrete learning processes and practices, and leadership for learning. Each building block is comprised of a number of key components.

- The Systems Thinking Model proposed by Marquardt, based on his extensive experience in consultancy with companies, has five subsystems. Besides learning dynamics, organization transformation and people empowerment, the other two subsystems are knowledge management and technology application.

- The Learning Company Model developed in the UK by Pedler, Burgoyne and Boydell stresses the importance of both 'looking in' and 'looking out', together with strategy, structure and learning opportunities.

- A learning organization is not a teaching organization.

- A learning organization is a long-term ambition and should not be interpreted as a quick fix for organizations.

- Learning organization, organizational learning and knowledge management are interrelated concepts which interplay with and enhance each other.

Review questions

- What are the main differences and links among learning organization, organizational learning and knowledge management?

- Learning organization is a topic that has produced an enormous amount of debate and heated arguments among consultants, practitioners and academics. Those engaged in the debate can be broadly classified into two camps: the advocates and the sceptics. Which camp would you be likely to join, and why?

- How can an idealized notion of learning organization help organizations succeed in reality?

- Select three definitions of the learning organization outlined in the chapter and compare them. Which one do you most agree with, and why?

- If you were asked to examine Peter Senge's Five Disciplines Model within the context of a university or college you have studied with, to what extent would you conclude that the university or college has the characteristics of a learning organization? Among the five disciplines, which discipline(s) would be evaluated as 'high performer(s)' and which discipline(s) would be evaluated as the 'worst performer(s)' in your opinion, and what evidence have you used to reach your conclusions?

- What do you think are the strengths and limitations of the Dimensions of the Learning Organization Questionnaire (DLOQ) designed by Watkins and Marsick?

- To what degree would you support Marquardt's decision to have included 'knowledge management' as one of the five subsystems in his Systems Thinking Model for the learning organization?

- How important do you think it is to include 'looking in' and 'looking out' as two important components in the Learning Company Model?

- Most models of the learning organization, such as those discussed in this chapter, were developed in Western culture (the United States and the UK). When these models are applied to Eastern cultural contexts, what difficulties do you think there might be?

- What are the advantages and drawbacks of a prescriptive approach to the learning organization?

- How can a shared vision in organizations be achieved?

References

Ali, A K (2012) Academic staff's perceptions of characteristics of learning organization in a higher learning institution, *International Journal of Educational Management*, **26** (1), pp 55–82

Borge, B H *et al* (2018) Diverging assessments of learning organizations during reform implementation, *The Learning Organization*, **25** (6), pp 399–409

Castro, G M, Saez, P L and Verde, M D (2011) Towards a knowledge-based view of firm innovation, *Journal of Knowledge Management*, **15** (6), pp 871–74

Chai, D S and Dirani, K (2018) The dimensions of the learning organization questionnaire (DLOQ): a validation study in the Lebanese context, *The Learning Organization*, **25** (5), pp 320–30

Dirani, K (2013) Does theory travel? Dimensions of the learning organization culture relevant to the Lebanese culture, *Advances in Developing Human Resources*, **15** (2), pp 177–92

Easterby-Smith, M (1990) Creating a learning organization, *Personnel Review*, **19** (5), pp 24–28

Elkin, G, Cone, M H and Liao, J (2009) Chinese pragmatism and the learning organization, *The Learning Organization*, **16** (1), pp 69–83

Garratt, B (1987) *The Learning Organization*, Gower, Aldershot

Garratt, B (1999) The learning organization 15 years on: some personal reflections, *The Learning Organization*, **6** (5), pp 202–06

Garvin, D A (2000) *Learning in Action: A guide to putting the learning organization to work*, Harvard Business Press, Boston, MA

Garvin, D A, Edmondson, A C and Gino, F (2008) Is yours a learning organization? *Harvard Business Review*, **86** (3), pp 109–116

Gorelick, C (2005) Organizational learning vs the learning organization: a conversation with a practitioner, *The Learning Organization*, **12** (4), pp 383–88

Haight, V D and Marquardt, M J (2018) How chief learning officers build learning organizations, *The Learning Organization*, **25** (5), pp 331–43

Jashapara, A (2011) *Knowledge Management: An integrated approach*, 2nd edn, Pearson Education, Harlow

Khadra, M F A and Rawabdeh, I A (2006) Assessment of development of the learning organization concept in Jordanian industrial companies, *The Learning Organization*, **13** (5), pp 455–74

Kim, J, Egan, T and Tolson, H (2015) Examining the dimensions of the learning organization questionnaire: a review and critique of research utilising the DLOQ, *Human Resource Development Review*, **14** (1), pp 1–22

Lee, J C, Shiue, Y C and Chen, C Y (2016) Examining the impacts of organizational culture and top management support of knowledge sharing on the success of software process improvement, *Computers in Human Behaviour*, **54**, pp 462–74

Marquardt, M J (2011) *Building the Learning Organization: Achieving strategic advantage through a commitment to learning*, 3rd edn, Nicholas Brealey, Boston, MA

Marsick, V J (2013) The dimensions of a learning organizations questionnaire (DLOQ): introduction to the special issue examining DLOQ use over a decade, *Advances in Developing Human Resources*, **15**, pp 127–32

Marsick, V J and Watkins, K E (2003) Demonstrating the value of an organization's learning culture: the dimensions of the learning organization questionnaire, *Advances in Developing Human Resources*, **5** (2), pp 132–51

Moilanen, R (2005) Diagnosing and measuring learning organizations, *The Learning Organization*, **12** (1), pp 71–89

Pedler, M, Burgoyne, J and Boydell, T (1991) *The Learning Company: A strategy for sustainable development*, McGraw-Hill, London

Pedler, M and Burgoyne, J (2017) Is the learning organization still alive? *The Learning Organization*, **24** (2), pp 119–26

Phillips, J J, Watkins, K E and Marsick, V J (1996) *Action Creating the Learning Organization*, vol 1, ASTD, Alexandria, VA

Reese, S and Sidani, Y (2018) A view of the learning organization from a practical perspective: interview with Michael Marquardt, *The Learning Organization*, **25** (5), pp 353–61

Retna, K S and Jones, D (2013) The learning organization and Singapore culture, *The Learning Organization*, **20** (4–5), pp 338–51

Santa, M (2015) Learning organization review: a 'good' theory perspective, *The Learning Organization*, **22** (5), pp 242–70

Sanz-Valle, R *et al* (2011) Linking organizational learning with technical innovation and organizational culture, *Journal of Knowledge Management*, **15** (6), pp 997–1015

Schwandt, D R and Marquardt, M J (2000) *Organizational Learning: From world-class theories to global best practices*, CRC Press, Boca Raton, FL

Senge, P M (1990) *The Fifth Discipline: The art and practice of the learning organization*, Doubleday Currency, New York

Thomas, K and Allen, S (2006) The learning organization: a meta-analysis of themes in literature, *The Learning Organization*, **13** (2), pp 123–39

Tseng, S M (2017) Investigating the moderating effects of organizational culture and leadership style on IT: adoption and knowledge sharing intention, *Journal of Enterprise Information Management*, **30** (4), pp 583–604

Vatankhah, M *et al* (2011) Surveying of learning organization indices and academic quality improvement in Islamic Azad universities, *Interdisciplinary Journal of Contemporary Research in Business*, **3** (5), pp 861–75

Watkins, K E and Dirani, K M (2013) A meta-analysis of the dimensions of a learning organization questionnaire: looking across cultures, ranks and industries, *Advances in Developing Human Resources*, **15** (2), pp 148–62

Watkins, K E and Marsick, V J (1993) *Sculpting the Learning Organization: Lessons in the art and science of systemic change*, Jossey-Bass, San Francisco, CA

Watkins, K E and O'Neil, J (2013) The dimensions of the learning organization questionnaire (the DLOQ): a nontechnical manual, *Advances in Developing Human Resources*, **15** (2), pp 133–47

Watkins, K E, Yang, B and Marsick, V J (1997) Measuring dimensions of the learning organization, in *1997 Conference Proceedings of the Academy of Human Resource Development*, ed R J Torraco, pp 543–46, The AHRD, Baton Rouge, LA

Yang, B, Watkins, K E and Marsick, V J (2004) The construct of the learning organization: dimensions, measurement and validation, *Human Resource Development Quarterly*, **15**, pp 31–55

Organizational culture for knowledge sharing and learning

06

Learning outcomes

After completing this chapter, the reader will be able to:

- understand the concept of organizational culture;
- compare different types of organizational culture;
- analyse the impact of organizational culture on knowledge sharing and learning;
- appreciate approaches to creating an organizational culture to foster knowledge sharing and learning.

Culture exists in many types of context depending on the unit of analysis. When a group of individuals with a shared objective work together, they may create a unique 'group culture'. If culture occurs at the country or state level, it is called 'national culture'. At an ethnic level, there is 'ethnic culture'. Culture can also be observed or developed on the professional level, namely 'occupational culture', where each profession creates certain behaviours that are demonstrated by those who practise it. This chapter uses 'organization' as the unit of analysis, hence discusses 'organizational culture'.

Organizational culture (OC) can encourage or discourage knowledge sharing and learning activities, hence organizations must create and sustain a desirable culture in order to enable or accommodate KM and learning to succeed; that is, to be innovative and transformative, further to build or maintain their competitive advantage in the market. This chapter first defines and discusses various types of organizational culture. Then, how organizational culture impacts on knowledge sharing and learning is identified. Finally, the chapter explores how to create a supportive organizational culture to facilitate knowledge sharing and learning.

6.1 Concept of organizational culture

Culture, which is about patterns of human interaction and is often deeply ingrained, has been called the DNA of an organization (Dalkir, 2017). In particular, culture is likely to influence top-down knowledge-sharing activities in terms of both the degree and the content of knowledge-sharing processes. Following this, organizational culture may exert a powerful influence on knowledge-related behaviours, especially when it comes to investigating organizational learning (Cavaliere and Lombardi, 2015). A challenging question that needs answering is how to create and/or manage organizational culture for the purpose of knowledge sharing and learning.

Organizational culture generally refers to the underlying values, beliefs and codes of practice that make an organization what it is (Dalkir, 2017). Culture has long been on the agenda of management theorists (Lee, Shiue and Chen, 2016; Oyemomi *et al*, 2019). Culture change means changing the corporate ethos, the images and values that inform decisions, actions and management processes. Not surprisingly, there have been many definitions of organizational culture:

- Corporate culture is the set of understandings (often unstated) that members in the organization share in common. Shared understandings consist of norms, values, attitudes, beliefs and paradigms (Sathe, 1985).

- Organizational culture can be defined as a system of shared values and norms that define appropriate attitudes and behaviours for its members (Tushman and O'Reilly, 2002). Similarly, organizational culture is a pattern of norms, values, beliefs, assumptions and attitudes that influences behaviour within an organization (Kassem *et al*, 2019).

- Organizational culture has been defined as a pattern of shared basic assumptions that was learned by a group as it solved its problems of external adaptation and internal integration, that has worked well enough to be considered valid and, therefore, to be taught to new members as the correct way to perceive, think, and feel in relation to those problems (Schein, 2004).

- Organizational culture is a set of shared values among the members of an organization that sets the standards and rules of the way of working (Ortiz and Arnborg, 2005).

- Organizational culture consists of four dynamic and cyclic elements: assumptions, values, artefacts and symbols (Alavi, Kayworth and Leidner, 2005–6).

- Organizational culture is a pattern of basic assumptions invented, discovered or developed by a given group as it learns to cope with its problems of external adaptation and internal integration, thus serves the leader through nurturing the value system to serve incoming members (Rasmussen and Hall, 2016).

- Organizational culture can be defined as a manifest pattern of behaviour, cross-individual behavioural consistencies, or the way we do things around here (Dalkir, 2017).

From the large number of definitions of organizational culture, we can summarize a number of central aspects of OC (Alavi, Kayworth, and Leidner, 2005–6; Jashapara, 2011; Dalkir, 2017; Hislop, Bosua and Helms, 2018; Oyemomi *et al*, 2019):

1 The evaluative aspect: involving social expectations, standards, values and beliefs that people hold central and that bind organizational units together.

2 The material/artefacts aspect: These include not only the signs, metaphors, symbols and images that an organization is recognized by, but also events, behaviours and social interactions.

3 The outcomes aspect: OC can be taught to new members of the organization as the 'correct' or accepted way to think, perceive and feel with respect to organizational work, problems and so forth.

4 The process aspect: the consistent ways in which an organization perform their tasks, solve problems, resolve conflicts, treat customers and treat employees.

5 The social aspect: climate and feelings evoked by the way people interact with each other.

As can be seen from the above, the very breadth of organizational culture, including the wide range of definitions and multi-aspects of the concept, understandably causes great challenges for managers to make sense of the construct. Some of the aspects, such as the artefacts of OC, can be relatively easily sensed; other aspects, such as the core of the OC, values, are difficult to sense (Alavi, Kayworth, and Leidner, 2005–6). Values, defined as 'broad, non-specific feelings of good and evil, beautiful and ugly, normal and abnormal, rational and irrational', are often unconscious and rarely discussable (Hofstede *et al*, 1990: 291). On the one hand, the very richness of this construct provides organizational researchers with a multitude of ways to explain social group behaviours. On the other, this same richness often leads to much confusion and misunderstanding in organizational culture research (Alavi, Kayworth, and Leidner, 2005–6). To put some boundary around this concept without sacrificing its richness, Schein (2004) approaches this issue through a three-level structure to understand OC, as illustrated in Figure 6.1: underlying assumptions at the bottom, stated values in the middle, and visible artefacts on the surface. Assumptions are basic and abstract or unconscious, taken for granted, beliefs, perceptions, thoughts and feelings that form the foundational level of organizational culture. The essential meanings of the basic assumptions can be expressed by values in the middle level. Values are often imposed by management in a number of forms, such as strategy, goals, philosophies and justifications. On the surface are the visible artefacts, such as norms, behaviour, logos, organizational structures and processes.

Figure 6.1 Three levels of organizational culture

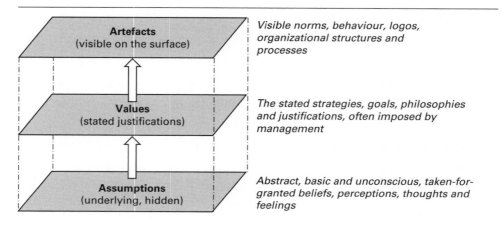

To summarize, organizational culture has a number of functions, including (Dalkir, 2017):

- establishing a set of roles with social identities;

- establishing a set of expectations, such as traits, competencies and values associated with each identity;

- establishing the status or value/worth to the reference group of each identity;

- providing values, cognitive schema and mental models to influence how individuals behave with respect to the various groups and communities of which they find themselves a member (micro-cultures) as well as with respect to the organizational culture as a whole.

Finally, organizational culture is not easy to understand by having one agreed definition, because it is not so much a discrete 'thing' or static object that can be pointed to. Instead, organizational culture should be envisaged more as a medium that an organization resides in. This medium is not only complex but also dynamic; in other words, it is constantly in the process of changing, hence it is a moving target. Furthermore, there can be a series of micro-cultures that are typical of different working groups or functional units within a given organization. Hence organizational culture is a complex, dynamic and changing entity (Dalkir, 2017).

Critical thinking and reflection
Organizational culture in your eyes

Culture is often described as 'how we do things here' (Jashapara, 2011: 266). Examining an organization you have worked for or studied with:

- How would you describe the culture of the organization?

- Is it a uniform, homogeneous culture for the whole organization, or are you aware of subcultures that exist within the organization in different units, functional areas and job ranks?

- Have you observed any significant changes in your organizational culture over the past few years? Do you think the changes have had positive or negative effects on the organization's performance, and why?

- What were the driving forces for the changes and how effective were these changes in your opinion?

6.2 Classification of organizational culture

Although an organization as a whole may be characterized as having a particular type of culture, there will be in fact many different types of culture or subculture in evidence. One way of exploring OC is to classify them into different types based on appropriate criteria/dimensions. Table 6.1 provides an overview of seven well-known classifications of OC in the literature. Details of each of the seven classification schemes and relevant types of culture are discussed in this section.

Table 6.1 An overview of seven classifications of organizational culture

Source	Criteria/ dimensions	Number of culture types	Content
(Deal and Kennedy, 1982)	Risk level and speed of feedback	4	Tough-guy, macho culture; work-hard, play-hard culture; bet-your-company culture; process culture
(Handy, 1985)	Level of rigidity/ autonomy	4	Power culture; role culture; task culture; person culture
(Denison and Mishra, 1995)	Flexibility–stability, internal–external focus	4	Mission culture; adaptability culture; involvement culture; consistency culture
(Goffee and Jones, 2000)	Sociality, solidarity	4	Communal culture; networked culture; mercenary culture; fragmented culture
(Cameron and Quinn, 2011)	Flexibility–stability, internal–external focus	4	Adhocracy culture; clan culture; market culture; hierarchy culture
(Chang and Lin, 2015)	Orientation, control level, openness	10 (5 pairs)	Tightly controlled, loosely controlled; closed system, open system; process oriented, results oriented; job oriented, employee oriented; professional culture, parochial culture
(Cavaliere and Lombardi, 2015)	Flexibility of process, internal–external orientation	4	Community culture; innovative culture; competitive culture; bureaucratic culture

OC classification based on degree of risk and speed of feedback

One of the earliest organizational culture classifications was proposed by Deal and Kennedy (1982), who used two main criteria: the degree of risk in company activities and the speed of feedback on decisions and actions. The four types of organizational culture are called: tough-guy, macho culture; work-hard, play-hard culture; bet-your-company culture; and process culture. The key features of the four types of organizational culture along the two criteria are summarized in Table 6.2.

Table 6.2 Classification of organizational culture based on level of risk and speed of feedback

		Speed of feedback	
		Low	**High**
Degree of risks	High	**Bet-your-company culture** • High risk but low speed • Greater tendency towards cooperative endeavours and producing innovations	**Tough-guy, macho culture** • High risk and fast feedback • Predominantly uncooperative and can lead to high turnover
	Low	**Process culture** • Low risk and slow feedback • Organizations are characterized by procedures, rules and hierarchies • Unable to respond quickly and can be threatening in highly changeable environments	**Work-hard, play-hard culture** • Low risk and quick feedback • Can be fun and action oriented • May suffer from quick-fix solutions and lack of reflection

Critical thinking and reflection
Deal and Kennedy's classification of OC

Examine the key characteristics of the four types of organizational culture proposed by Deal and Kennedy (1982). Using an organization and business that you are familiar with as an example, explain what type of organizational culture is adopted in the particular organization and business, and why the culture suits the organization and business.

OC classification based on level of rigidity/autonomy of organizing people

Shortly after the publication of Deal and Kennedy's four types of OC, Handy (1985) also classified OC in four types by analysing the level of rigidity/autonomy of how people are organized to get tasks done in an organization. The four types of culture are illustrated in Figure 6.2.

Figure 6.2 Illustration of power–role–task–people cultures

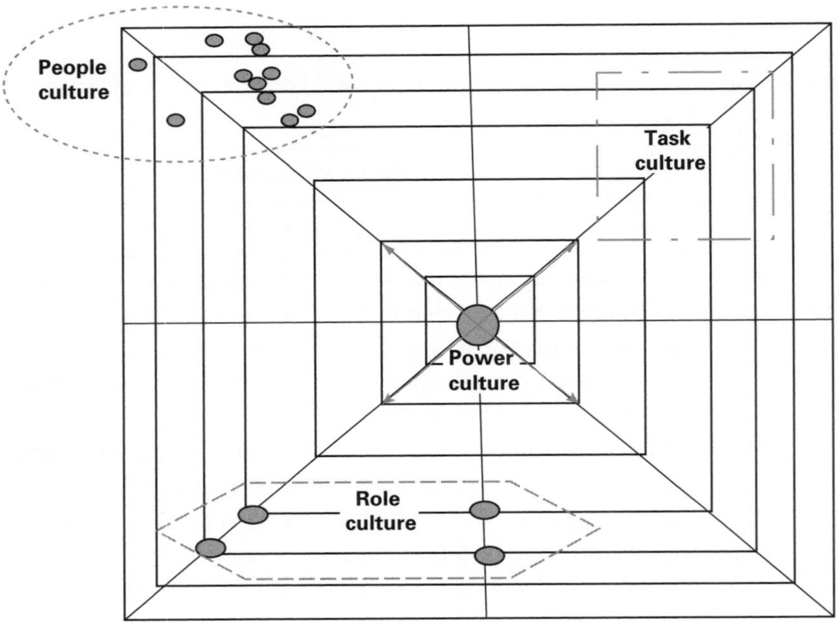

They are defined as follows:

- **Power culture**: characterized as a web of power with the most powerful decision makers sitting in the centre and other people around them. There are few rules written down and people with decision power can make rules where appropriate. This type of culture can respond fast in a changing business environment. People far away from the power centre can be discouraged from knowledge sharing and learning, and may suffer from high turnover when the managers/leaders are too powerful and take autocratic approaches.

- **Role culture**: people are assigned clearly defined roles in the organization where rules, procedures and job descriptions tend to predominate. This type of culture can work very well in a stable business environment. However, organizations may have difficulties in adapting to a more turbulent environment.

- **Task culture**: this type of culture is characterized by project or matrix organizations. They bring together the appropriate resources and competence required for effective team functioning to get tasks done. Mutual respect is based on an individual's ability rather than their position, status, power or role. This type of culture can be highly effective for innovative projects but may be less successful in cost rationalization and economies of scale.

- **People culture**: this type of culture gives people the highest level of autonomy. Collective actions are based on fulfilling individual employees' self-interest while contributing to the group objectives and overall organizational goal. Individuals are given great flexibility in allocating their time and way of working. Typical examples of people working in this type of culture are academics and barristers.

OC classification according to flexibility and stability

Denison and Mishra (1995) built an organizational culture model based on four characteristics that can help companies improve their business excellence: mission, adaptability, involvement and consistency. These are grouped primarily by internal or external focus, and also by flexibility or stability. Adaptability and involvement are focused on flexibility, while mission and consistency are focused towards stability.

- **Mission culture**: a mission culture covers establishing strategic direction and intent, and setting strategic objectives, goals and a vision for the organization. An organization with a mission culture has a robust sense of organizational direction, a clear vision and goals. Organizations having a strong mission culture will be able to handle their external environment to achieve stability. Mission culture consists of three indices: 1) strategic direction – the mission is accompanied by a long-term vision and explained clearly to all employees; 2) goals and objectives – the leaders of the organization agree on a set of challenging but achievable goals directly linked to its mission and purpose, and there is a mechanism to measure progress towards the goals on an ongoing basis; 3) vision – leaders and employees agree on their view of the future and the vision is able to enthuse and inspire employees.

- **Adaptability culture**: an adaptability culture requires the ability to perceive and detect signs from the external environment, and react to the external environment by changing or restructuring their internal behaviour and processes to allow adaptation, more improvement and growth. The external environment focuses on clients, customers and competitors. The organization should also react to the needs of their employees, who are considered to be 'internal customers' (Denison, Nieminen and Kotrba, 2014). Three key indices for adaptability culture are: 1) creating changes – the organization should demonstrate its clear ability to forecast future scenarios, analyse the industry environment and take fast actions to deal with the situation; 2) customer focus – take care of customers by listening to and understanding their expectations and requirements, and use feedback from customers to make necessary changes; (3) organizational learning – inspire innovation and support initiatives to acquire organizational knowledge and encourage employees to commit to and take risks in learning.

- **Involvement culture**: this type of culture encourages employees to be more involved in their work and with their colleagues, and to take on more responsibilities with a sense of ownership. Employees are willing to do more work on a voluntary basis. Organizations believe that decision making should be a collective process and carried out with participation from employees. There is very little bureaucracy. Three key indices for an involvement culture include empowerment, team orientation and capability building.

- **Consistency culture**: the consistency attribute includes values, agreement, coordination and integration. Employees who work within a consistency culture have clear instructions on how to work, with well-defined roles, clear guidance and a code of conduct. When employees meet unfamiliar conditions, they respond in predictable ways. Organizations with this type of culture usually have an internal focus and provide stability for their workforce. A consistency culture consists of three key indices: a high level of coordination and integration, agreement and consensus, and core values that establish an organization's clear identity (Fey and Denison, 2003).

Denison and Mishra's model suggests that the best-performing organizations are those that show a complete and balanced profile, or high levels of all four traits. In particular, top-achieving organizations found ways to empower and involve their employees, enable harmonized activities and endorse consistent behaviours that show commitment to the main organizational values. These organizations have the ability to respond to changes in the business environment and to provide a clear vision and future direction for employees. This model is different from other organizational culture models. Most OC models are based on culture effectiveness theory, but Denison and Mishra's model is based on field theory, which has been used to describe different behaviours at the organizational level (Kassem *et al*, 2019).

OC classification according to sociability and solidarity

Goffee and Jones (2000) also used two criteria and identified four types of OC. The two criteria are sociability and solidarity. Sociability is a measure of friendliness. A highly social culture indicates that people within the culture tend to be friendly towards each other. Solidarity measures task orientation. High solidarity means that people can work together towards common goals very well, even if they may have personal disputes and conflicts. The four types of OC following the two criteria are communal culture (high sociability–high solidarity), networked culture (high sociability–low solidarity), mercenary culture (low sociability–high solidarity) and fragmented culture (low sociability–low solidarity), as illustrated in Figure 6.3.

The advantages and disadvantages of the four types of OC are summarized in Table 6.3.

Figure 6.3 Four types of organizational culture based on sociability and solidarity

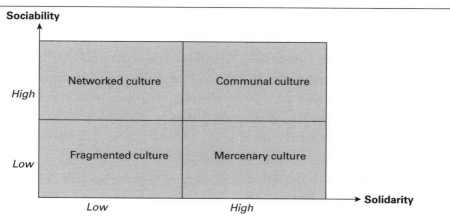

Table 6.3 Advantages and disadvantages of the four types of OC based on sociability and solidarity

Types of OC	Advantages	Disadvantages
Communal culture	• Members have sense of belonging • Task driven	• Leaders exert too much influence and other members are rarely heard from
Networked culture	• Members are friendly to each other and willing to share knowledge	• Members are reluctant to point out and criticize poor performance
Mercenary culture	• Focus on strict goals and get job done quickly	• Poor performance may be treated inhumanly
Fragmented culture	• Weak sense of belonging and organization identity	• Lack of cooperation

OC classification – Competing Values Framework

One of the most widely acknowledged and extended OC classifications is probably the Competing Values Framework (CVF) defined by Cameron and Quinn (2011). The four types of culture in Cameron and Quinn's CVF are adhocracy culture, clan culture, market culture and hierarchy culture. These four types of culture are based on two dimensions: the level of flexibility and discretion/stability and control, and internal–external focus:

- **Adhocracy culture:** high flexibility and externally oriented. The key values of this type of culture are creativity, entrepreneurship and risk taking. It is a highly dynamic culture and has a higher ability to assume risks and encourage employees' initiative and innovation.

- **Clan culture:** also emphasizes flexibility but is internally oriented. This type of culture encourages teamwork, employee involvement and the organization's commitment to employees; in other words, this type of culture is about people and sharing between individuals. Because of its emphasis on teamwork, loyalty, commitment and the participation of employees, the culture helps human resource development.

- **Market culture:** low flexibility and external orientation. The core values of this type of culture are goal achievement, consistency and competitiveness through focusing on the management of external affairs. It is regarded as a results-oriented and customer-based culture. It contributes to organizational effectiveness and operates as a market (Fong and Kwok, 2009).

- **Hierarchy culture:** focuses on the internal issues of the organization and intends to build a stable environment to increase productivity, or to generate efficient and reliable products/services by setting up rules, policy or specialization for tight control. Efficiency, coordination, predictability and close adherence to norms, rules and regulations are its main characteristics. This type of culture is considered to be the earliest approach that evolved, recognized by a formalized and structured workplace.

☉ Critical thinking and reflection
Competing Values Framework of OC

1 Compare the four types of organizational culture in the CVF (adhocracy culture, clan culture, market culture and hierarchy culture) with those in the OC classification proposed by Handy (1985) and Deal and Kennedy (1982). Can you find any links between these four types of culture and any types of the culture in the other two classification schemes?

2 In what ways could the development of 'care among employees', such as in a clan culture, be detrimental to an organization?

OC classification using flexibility of processes and internal-external orientation

More recently, Cavaliere and Lombardi (2015) proposed four types of OC using two criteria. One is the flexibility of organizational processes (organic or mechanistic). The other is whether the organization focuses more on the internal work environment (such as integration and smoothing activities) or on positioning itself in the external environment (eg competition and differentiation). These two criteria are quite similar to the two dimensions used by Cameron and Quinn (2011). The four types of culture are community culture, innovative culture, competitive culture and bureaucratic culture. The links between these four types of culture and other types of culture are illustrated in Figure 6.4.

Figure 6.4 Four types of culture based on process flexibility and internal–external orientation and their links to other cultures

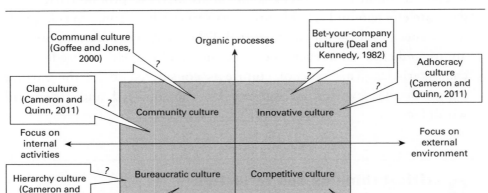

They are defined as follows:

- **Community culture**: characterized by a high level of process flexibility and discretion, together with a focus mainly on internal work integration and smoothing activities rather than external orientation. It emphasizes employees' cohesiveness and participation in decision making. In this type of culture, great attention is paid to employees' work satisfaction and their loyalty to the organization, as well as trust and mutual respect between employer and employees. Is this similar to the 'communal culture' in Goffee and Jones (2000) and the 'clan culture' in Cameron and Quinn (2011)?

- **Innovative culture**: this type of culture is also characterized by organic processes but with a focus on the external environment, that is, on competition and differentiation. The culture encourages entrepreneurship, creativity and the need for the organization to find new opportunities for new growth. Employees' risk orientation and rapid adaptability to change are central to this type of organizational culture. Culturally innovative firms are more likely to support social interaction and to encourage knowledge sharing and stimulate learning. This type of culture shares many features with the 'bet-your-company' culture (Deal and Kennedy, 1982) and the 'adhocracy culture' (Cameron and Quinn, 2011).

- **Competitive culture**: emphasizes more mechanistic and rational approaches to gain competitive advantages over rivals. In this type of culture, work practices and task scheduling are designed to stimulate employees to work hard to achieve the organization's market superiority. This is similar to the 'market culture' in Cameron and Quinn (2011).

- **Bureaucratic culture**: characterized by mechanistic processes and internal orientation, that is, focuses on procedures and rules, hence resulting in slow and long decision-making processes. It usually emphasizes the use of hierarchical systems to coordinate decisions and actions. The culture would suit organizations that pursue stability, efficiency and formalization. This type of culture is somewhat similar to Deal and Kennedy's 'process culture' (Deal and Kennedy, 1982) and the 'hierarchy culture' in Cameron and Quinn (2011).

OC classification using five dimensions

As it can be seen from the above, it is commonly accepted that organizational culture has multifaceted dimensions rather than a single dimension (Hofstede *et al*, 1990; Eaves, 2014). Chang and Lin (2015) further extended the OC classification by using five dimensions, which resulted in ten types (five pairs) of organizational culture: process-oriented versus results-oriented culture, job-oriented versus employee-oriented culture, loosely controlled versus tightly controlled culture, closed-system versus open-system culture, and professional versus parochial culture. Key characteristics of the 10 types of culture are contrasted in Table 6.4.

To summarize, many types of organizational culture have been identified. Each culture has its own features and suitability. Every organization culture is organization specific, resulting from the organization's experience and history, and evolves over time to shape the organization's identity. Diagnosing organizational culture effectively can help explain otherwise unexpected employee behaviour patterns. Furthermore, scholars have revealed that organizational performance can depend on how employees accept and share the organization's cultural values, in particular that a strong culture has been associated with organizational learning and knowledge sharing (Cavaliere and Lombardi, 2015; Evans, Wensley and Frissen, 2015). In general, organizations with more open and supportive value orientations are predisposed towards constructive knowledge behaviours. Value orientations such as trust and collaboration will lead to greater willingness to share insights and expertise with each other.

Table 6.4 Contrast of 10 types of culture based on five dimensions

Process-oriented culture	**Results-oriented culture**
• Focus on method and process of how work is accomplished	• Emphasizing accomplishing goals
• Conform to rules and regulations	• Encouraging adventures to get things done
• Risk aversion	• Willing to be innovative and face challenges
• Mechanistic and stable organizations	• Organic and flexible organizations

Job-oriented culture	**Employee-oriented culture**
• Focuses on work performance	• Considerable concern for individual welfare, including care, family, trust, love and spirit of mutual support
• Emphasis on work flow optimization and productivity	• Decisions tend to be made by committees and individuals
• Limited concern for employees' personal or family welfare	
• Ignoring individual feelings	

Loosely controlled culture	**Tightly controlled culture**
• Having few written or unwritten codes of behaviour	• Having strict written and unwritten policies
• Casual attitude towards deadlines and cost	• Placing more importance on cost-consciousness and punctuality
• Less formal and restrained control of individuals	• Controls individuals in a restrained and official way
	• Adhering to rules, laws
	• Emphasis on precise, serious and joke-free attitude

Closed system culture	**Open system culture**
• Secretive	• Emphasis on clear communication channels
• Suspicious of outsiders and insiders	• Open to outsiders and new employees
• Selected few become 'inner circle'	• Encouraging employee interaction
• Long time for new employees to settle in	

Professional culture	**Parochial culture**
• Shaping a community by ensuring that members think and behave as the profession requires	• Individuals obtain identity from the company they work for, whose social values, beliefs and norms are similar to their own
• Individuals obtain sense of identity from the type of work (ie profession such as doctors, lawyers, teachers) they do	• Tending to recruit new employees with personalities and beliefs compatible with the organizational culture
• When recruiting, emphasis on individual's professional ability	

Critical thinking and reflection
Analysis across different OC classification schemes

Figure 6.4 provides an analysis across four different OC classification schemes. Compare the types of culture that are grouped in the same area of the coordinate system; for example, in the top left-hand corner are communal culture and clan culture. What further insights can you obtain through your comparison analysis? Do the comparisons for the types of culture in each of the four areas.

In contrast, value systems that emphasize individual power and competition among firm members will lead to knowledge hiding (this refers to a dyadic relationship between one individual requesting knowledge from another, who in response withholds that knowledge) and knowledge hoarding (the simple withholding of knowledge which has not been requested by any specific individual) (Holten *et al*, 2016). Consequently, organizations should seek to reinforce and mould those culture values most consistent with knowledge-sharing and learning behaviours (Alavi, Kayworth, and Leidner, 2005–6).

 Illustration
Organizational culture – integration and differentiation

One of the major debates on organizational culture has been on whether organizations have one uniform, dominant corporate culture driving KM decisions, practices and outcomes, or whether there could be multiple local cultures at work, each with its own distinctive values.

Alavi, Kayworth, and Leidner (2005–6) provide an overview of arguments from both sides of the debate, represented by *integration* and *differentiation* perspectives. The key characteristics, benefits and drawbacks of both perspectives are contrasted in the table.

Questions

1 Which perspective, integration or differentiation, can you mostly agree on, and why?

2 Why do you think that in large complex organizations, a differentiation perspective of organizational culture would be more realistic?

	Integration perspective	Differentiation perspective
Main characteristics	• Regards organizational culture as a homogeneous collection of values that acts as an integrating mechanism or social or normative glue that holds together a potentially diverse group of organizational members. • Characterized by consistency across cultural manifestations, consensus among cultural members and usually a focus on leaders as cultural creators.	• Portrays organizational culture as a mix of various local cultures, each with their own distinctive values. • Although there may be an underlying dominant organizational culture, various other cultures may exist within the firm. • This view may be more realistic, particularly in large, complex organizations.
Benefits	• Efforts centre on developing strategies to create unifying organizational cultures where people will be motivated to share a common basis for action. • Culture is something that can and should be managed.	• Organizations are umbrellas for collections of subcultures. • Leaders are not the only ones who generate values. Joint force can come from, for example, the task and technology used by employees, the constraints of the organization's stage in its lifecycle, or external factors such as major changes in the business environment.
Drawbacks	• Inability to explain cultural conflict and ambiguity in values. • Organizational values are valid only to the extent that they are widely shared across the organization.	• Organizations as mini-societies, each with distinctive values, could potentially lead to competing or even conflicting local cultures formed along functional lines, shared fate, professional occupation, ethnic background or job rank. • More difficult to manage at organizational level.

6.3 Impact of organizational culture on knowledge sharing and organizational learning

Although much work has been done on defining and classifying organizational culture over the past four decades or so, exploration of the impact of organizational culture on knowledge-based activities and processes has taken place much later (Al-Alawi, Al-Marzooqi and Mohammed, 2007; Sackmann and Friesl, 2007); in particular, empirical study highlighting the influence of organizational culture on knowledge-sharing and learning behaviours has been mostly conducted in more recent years (Oyemomi *et al*, 2019).

OC impact on knowledge sharing

Knowledge sharing has received immense attention owing to the recognition of its value in organizational learning and innovation (Casimir, Lee and Loon, 2012). Employees sharing knowledge with each other is a key driver for competitiveness. However, a fundamental problem faced by organizations is that employees may lack the desire to share their knowledge with other members of the organization, depending on the type of organizational culture and its impact. In order to create an organizational culture that can foster knowledge sharing, this section looks at how different types of organizational culture and cultural factors impact on knowledge sharing.

By taking the four types of culture defined in the CVF – adhocracy, clan, market and hierarchy culture (Cameron and Quinn, 2011), Fong and Kwok (2009) studied how the cultures impacted on knowledge flow and sharing in organizations. The context of their work is with contracting firms in the construction sector. Among the four types of culture, clan culture is found to be the most effective in knowledge sharing at both project and organization levels, which means that the culture of contracting firms very much depends on honest communication, respect for people, trust, and cohesive relationships. This finding shows that teamwork and networks/people are important to contracting firms. It also emphasizes that the construction industry, besides being a project-based industry, is also a people-based one. This finding about clan culture's impact on knowledge sharing is supported by Lee, Shiue and Chen (2016), who reveal that clan culture and hierarchy culture have positive impacts on knowledge sharing, while there is less knowledge shared among employees in organizations with market and adhocracy cultures. Fong and Kwok (2009) further concluded that senior management and other factors of organizational culture should be taken into consideration when establishing a knowledge management system and the implementation of KM solutions, especially for knowledge sharing between projects through the use of organizational memory.

Cavaliere and Lombardi (2015) conducted a study with 389 employees from six manufacturing subsidiaries of MNCs. Their study shows that the four types of culture (community culture, innovative culture, competitive culture and bureaucratic culture) all play important roles in knowledge-based processes. The research further reveals that community, innovative and bureaucratic cultures positively affect knowledge donating, but competitive culture negatively affects employees' orientation towards knowledge donating, while both bureaucratic culture and competitive culture positively affect knowledge collecting. Moreover, strong top management support is particularly critical to both knowledge-donating and knowledge-collecting behaviours. One of the key contributions from Cavaliere and Lombardi's work is that the study addresses both sides of knowledge sharing (ie knowledge donating from the knowledge sender's perspective and knowledge collecting from the knowledge receiver's perspective).

Based on Chang and Lin's (2015) study, the impact of specific types of organizational culture on knowledge sharing is also evident. The findings are drawn from a survey with 326 valid questionnaires conducted with 15 IT companies in Taiwan. Table 6.5 summarizes their findings on how different types of organizational culture impact knowledge transfer and sharing. This table should be read from left to right. For example, a results-oriented culture has a more positive effect on individuals' knowledge-sharing intention than in a process-oriented culture. Note that the survey was not able to provide sufficient evidence to support the last two statements in the table about the comparative level of impact between closed-system and open-system cultures, and between professional and parochial cultures in terms of knowledge-sharing intention.

The positive relationship between a collaborative culture and the effectiveness of knowledge sharing is also supported by Yang (2007). Positive relationships have also been found between certain organizational/cultural factors and knowledge sharing. These factors include trust, communication, top management support, adoption of information systems, rewards and

Table 6.5 Comparative nature of the impact of types of organizational culture on knowledge sharing

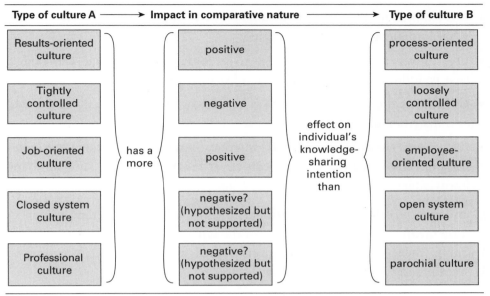

leadership style (Al-Alawi, Al-Marzooqi and Mohammed, 2007). Park, Ribiere and Schulte (2004) identified and ranked a total of 44 organizational culture attributes that support KM and stimulate knowledge sharing. In summary, organizational culture not only influences the willingness and behaviour of knowledge owners to share their knowledge with other organizational members (Javenpaa and Staples, 2003), but a learning-encouraging culture also provides an environment to ease and facilitate knowledge sharing with technological support and social interaction (Chang, Liao and Wu, 2017; Tseng, 2017).

OC impact on organizational learning

Research has shown that culture is a key element in organizational learning processes because culture strongly influences the behaviour of employees. Thus organizational culture can facilitate learning or be a major barrier to learning, depending on the values it encourages in the organization (Sanz-Valle *et al*, 2011). In general, there has been agreement in the literature about the need for a culture that emphasizes the desire to improve and learn.

Organizational culture can affect organizational learning in four main ways (De Long and Fahey, 2000; Lee and Chen, 2005):

- OC shapes employees' assumptions on how important knowledge is and what knowledge is worth managing.
- OC allows individual knowledge to become organizational knowledge, that is, influences the organizational learning process.
- OC shapes the processes by which new knowledge is created, legitimated and distributed.
- OC creates the context for social interaction which ultimately determines how effective an organization can be at creating, sharing and applying knowledge.

Consequently, different organizational cultures will have different influences on organizational learning. In terms of the impact of specific culture types on learning, there have been conclusions drawn from research. According to Cameron and Quinn (2011):

- Adhocracy culture *positively* impacts on organizational learning.
- Clan culture *positively* impacts on organizational learning.
- Market culture *negatively* impacts on organizational learning.
- Hierarchy culture *negatively* impacts on organizational learning.

 Critical thinking and reflection
Organizational culture and organizational learning

Linking organizational culture (the topic of this chapter) and organizational learning (the topic of Chapter 4), do you think double loop learning is asking for cultural change when its tenet is to question the underlying assumptions and values in the organization?

While the impact of organizational culture on knowledge sharing and learning is understood, organizations should create and maintain the right culture so that knowledge sharing and learning becomes a natural activity in employees' daily work (Tseng, 2017).

6.4 Creating organizational culture to foster knowledge sharing and organizational learning

Although every organization has its culture, strong or weak, many organizations do not consciously create their culture for knowledge sharing and learning. Instead, culture may be created and ingrained into people's life and work unconsciously. Unless special effort is taken, people will not recognize that the attitude, belief and vision they have always taken for granted are actually standardized assumptions that they may pass on to the future generations.

Organizations must create and manage their culture so as to become and remain innovative and competitive. In particular, organizational culture can encourage or discourage knowledge sharing and learning activities. For example, certain cultural symptoms such as failure apprehension, knowledge hoarding and the 'not invented here' stance can severely inhibit knowledge sharing and learning in organizations (Lyu and Zhang, 2017). One of the fundamental prerequisites for business success is to create an organizational culture that fosters knowledge sharing and learning rather than hinders these activities. A culture that favours knowledge sharing and learning will allow organizations to adapt to their surrounding environment (Lyu and Zhang, 2017; Tseng, 2017). As discussed in previous sections, there have been dozens of organizational and cultural factors identified in the literature. This section will focus on a number of factors that are highly ranked and widely acknowledged in order to create the desired organizational culture for knowledge sharing and learning.

Creating an organizational culture with trust

Trust has been recognized as one of the most important factors in creating a learning culture for knowledge sharing, especially in terms of social transactions (Park, Ribiere and Schulte, 2004). It is clear that trust is a prerequisite to both knowledge donating from the knowledge owners' side and knowledge collecting at the receivers' side (Oyemomi, 2016). A critical aspect of creating a knowledge-sharing culture is interpersonal trust, which refers to the extent to which a person is confident in and willing to act on the basis of the words, decisions and actions of another; in other words, the trust that exists between people (Casimir, Lee and Loon, 2012). There are other types of trust used in the literature but they are out of the scope of this section, such as inter-organizational trust (trust between organizations) and trust between organizations and customers (Dietz and Hartog, 2006).

Interpersonal trust can be conceptualized into two dimensions: cognition-based trust and affective trust. Cognition-based trust is built on the available knowledge, competence and responsibility of the individuals in an organization. Affective trust is based on emotional bonds between individuals, which is more relevant to voluntary knowledge sharing because it reduces feelings of vulnerability and mitigates the fear that the other party will be exploitative or opportunistic (Madjar and Ortiz-Walters, 2009).

Numerous studies have reported the positive relationship between trust and knowledge sharing (Holste and Fields, 2010; Holten *et al*, 2016; Rutten, Blaas-Franken and Martin, 2016). For example, Lucas (2005) finds that interpersonal trust between co-workers and the reputation of co-workers has separate effects on employee experiences in transferring knowledge within an organization. Smedlund (2008) suggests that tacit knowledge sharing is facilitated by a social network within organizations characterized by ties based on both interpersonal relationships and longstanding working relationships where reciprocity among co-workers is the norm. Holste and Fields (2010) explored the effects of both cognition-based and affect-based trust on the willingness of employees to share and use tacit knowledge. Research findings reveal that tacit knowledge sharing and use depends on the formation of both affect-based and cognition-based trust among co-workers. This suggests that diagnosis of organizational knowledge exchange processes should carefully consider the types and levels of trust between employees. The work further finds that affect-based trust has a greater influence on willingness to share tacit knowledge, while cognition-based trust has a larger influence on willingness to use tacit knowledge.

In Levin and Cross (2004), the significant positive effect of cognition-based trust on knowledge sharing is confirmed. One reason of this positive effect could be because professionals see the tacit knowledge they have accumulated in work as a valuable asset, hence they are willing to share only with colleagues who have a good reputation for solid performance (ie cognition-based trust) (Rutten, Blaas-Franken and Martin, 2016). The recommendation for tacit knowledge sharing is that social relationships built on affect-based trust may be the most important and can be facilitated by intrinsic motivation such as sociability and friendships (Yang and Farn, 2009).

In terms of sharing explicit knowledge, Bakker *et al* (2006) found a significant negative effect of cognition-based trust on knowledge sharing in a team. A possible reason could be that a high level of cognition-based trust means that a co-worker is believed to be competent in the area and already possesses a lot of knowledge. As a result, colleagues will be reluctant to share their knowledge with the believed-to-be-competent colleague because they feel that the knowledge would be redundant. Thus a conclusion can be drawn that a high level of cognition-based trust discourages knowledge sharing. In contrast, Swift and Hwang (2012) found a positive but not significant effect of cognition-based trust on sharing explicit knowledge. Ko (2010) also did not find a significant effect for cognition-based trust. To summarize, research on the effect of cognition-based trust on explicit knowledge sharing is inconclusive.

When individuals have positive regard for their colleagues based on trust, it is less likely that they view their colleagues from an economic perspective but more from a social transaction perspective, thus they will be more willing to share knowledge (Casimir, Lee and Loon, 2012).

Creating an organizational culture with top management support

Top management support has been widely regarded as one of the most relevant influences on employees' willingness to share knowledge with colleagues, hence it is a key success factor for knowledge sharing and learning (Ke and Wei, 2008; Cavaliere and Lombardi, 2015; Jayawickrama, 2015). In this context, top management support can be defined as the degree of support provided by the top management level to encourage employees to share their knowledge and stimulate learning (Park, Ribiere and Schulte, 2004). Top management support can be understood from four different levels:

- Top managers think that encouraging knowledge sharing with colleagues and learning is beneficial.

- Top managers always support and encourage employees to share their knowledge with colleagues and learn from each other.

- Top managers provide most of the necessary help and resources to enable employees to share knowledge and learn.

- Top managers are keen to see that employees are happy to share knowledge with colleagues and learn from each other.

Of course, top management support should be encouraging rather than coercive, that is, employees should receive suggestions and feedback from their superior about what to share and how to do it within the organization to improve their involvement in the organizational activities and their motivation to contribute to the organization's performance (Cavaliere and Lombardi, 2015). Based on the analysis of data collected from academics and industrial specialists using a questionnaire survey in the context of software process improvement, Park, Ribiere and Schulte's (2004) work revealed an important finding: top management support has a positive influence on knowledge sharing and learning. Other research also agrees with this finding (Hung *et al*, 2012; Cavaliere and Lombardi, 2015).

Top management is typically responsible for setting the vision and willing to allocate valuable resources to nurture organizational culture. Accordingly, a number of suggestions can be made (Park, Ribiere and Schulte, 2004; Lin, 2007; Jayawickrama, 2015):

- In terms of knowledge donation, top management needs to value and reward employees not only for the accomplishment of their work but also for donating knowledge to work and participating in learning.

- Top management should periodically hold award ceremonies to recognize and compensate those employees who enthusiastically participate in knowledge sharing and learning.

- Top management should create opportunities for knowledge sharing through educational avenues such as conferences, seminars and workshops.

- Top management should act as role models to exemplify the desired behaviour of active knowledge sharing and learning.

- In terms of knowledge collection and acceptance, it is usually not easy for employees to accept and collect different knowledge, so top management must lead by example to accept new knowledge and the opinions of others as well as to avoid groupthink.

Dalkir (2017) argues that it is not enough for top management merely to provide support; instead they must build strong cultures for knowledge sharing and learning. It is immensely important for top management to construct the social reality of the organization, shape values and help create and attain the vision of the organization.

Creating an organizational culture with motivation and incentives

Incentives are essential in developing a culture that favours knowledge-sharing activities and organizational learning. Organizations need to design and provide incentives to induce workers to actively participate in knowledge sharing and learning, so as to nurture the right types of organizational culture (Lyu and Zhang, 2017).

Individual motivational drivers for knowledge sharing and learning can be classified into two categories: intrinsic motivation and extrinsic motivation (Lee and Ahn, 2007). Intrinsic motivation includes self-efficacy and altruism. Individuals can be intrinsically motivated when they seek enjoyment, interest, satisfaction or self-expression in the knowledge-sharing and learning processes. Common extrinsic incentives include monetary rewards, recognition and promotion. Because intrinsic motivation is more difficult to change and has a more uncertain outcome, these inherent shortcomings often discourage management teams from implementing intrinsic motivation in practice. That is why extrinsic incentives are more widely accepted.

The effectiveness of using incentives in knowledge sharing depends on the form of knowledge: codified or personalized. Codified knowledge stored in organizational memory is more easily accessed for sharing, while personalized knowledge is closely tied to its creator and is shared mainly through person-to-person socialization processes. Research has indicated that extrinsic incentives, such as monetary reward systems based on individual knowledge-sharing behaviour, are best suited to codified knowledge (Bartol and Srivastava, 2002). Extrinsic incentives for personalized knowledge sharing may not be as effective as for codified knowledge sharing, because recording and measuring the knowledge shared among individuals as prerequisites of intrinsic incentives are not easy with personalized knowledge. However, intrinsic motivation is most appropriate for influencing knowledge sharing within a community of practice (Lee and Ahn, 2007).

Lee and Ahn (2007) researched how to design incentive systems for effective, intra-organizational knowledge sharing. The context for their work is codified, explicit knowledge sharing through formal organizational memory. They discussed two types of reward systems: an individual-based reward system and a group-based system. They note that it can be costly to reward each knowledge worker on an individual basis according to their contribution to knowledge sharing. If performance at group level is rewarded, individuals are likely to think that the knowledge they share will improve the performance of others, which in turn will increase the reward for individuals. Therefore, individuals are likely to have a higher motivation to share knowledge. In this way, a company can base the reward on the performance of the whole group or the whole organization. The findings from Lee and Ahn's (2007) research indicate that, in general, group-based reward is inferior to individual reward in terms of the effectiveness of sharing codified knowledge. With codified knowledge, an organization can capitalize efficiently on the knowledge assets by implementing a simple linear reward system based on the amount and productivity of knowledge sharing. However, for personalized knowledge, measurement of individual contributions would be difficult, so reward systems based on the performance of the whole group would be more practical. Furthermore, the findings show that workers with more productive knowledge may not share their knowledge under a group-based reward system. However, they suggest that this potential problem may be mitigated by establishing an organizational ownership norm.

An interesting implication from Lee and Ahn's (2007) work is that reward systems can be complemented by other organizational factors, such as the presence of job security, trust, care and organizational citizenship behaviour. Similarly, investment in IT systems can also complement rewards in facilitating knowledge sharing. This suggestion was taken by Lyu and Zhang (2017) and supported by Tseng (2017). These researchers further investigated the combined impact of incentives and information technology on knowledge sharing and learning. Their work draws conclusions on seven effects:

- An incentive for knowledge sharing motivates knowledge workers to share their knowledge voluntarily with their fellow workers.
- Shared knowledge will be captured by knowledge management systems and stored in organizational memory (ie knowledge base), augmenting its volume.
- The larger the volume of the knowledge base, the higher the probability of culturally unfit workers obtaining their desired knowledge to facilitate learning.
- Learning from the knowledge base enables culturally unfit workers to become culturally fit, thus increasing the overall level of organizational cultural fit (the total number of culturally fit workers).
- More workers will engage in knowledge sharing to increase the volume of the knowledge base when an organization has a higher level of cultural fit.

- Information technology provides useful tools for workers to share their valuable knowledge more easily.

- Information technology makes it easier for workers to search the knowledge base and find the knowledge they desire to learn from.

Creating an organizational culture with good leadership and communication

Leadership style usually determines communication style within a team and organization, hence it is essential to have the most appropriate leadership with good communication in order to create an agreeable culture for fostering and cultivating knowledge sharing and learning (Tseng, 2017). Leadership refers to individual behaviour when orchestrating a group of people to accomplish tasks. It is about interpersonal influence utilized through communication processes leading to a particular objective or goal (Ke and Wei, 2008). Some leaders can receive support and commitment from their followers, but some cannot. The difference results from their different leadership styles.

There are four commonly recognized leadership styles: charismatic leadership, transactional leadership, transformational leadership and servant leadership (Ghazali, Ahmad and Zakaria, 2015; Tseng, 2017):

- Charismatic leadership: encouraging others through optimistic statements about the future and what should be achieved, inspiring positive feelings about the group's common objective among followers.

- Transactional leadership: giving rewards and punishment, encouraging followers through processes of communication with, for example, rewards or preferences being given when a task is accomplished.

- Transformational leadership: using communication and interactions with followers to build organizational collectivity, gaining understanding of followers' needs with regard to achieving their goals. Transformational leaders are usually more flexible when it comes to achieving the desired goals and more open to change when necessary.

- Servant leadership: desiring to serve others and meet their needs, wishes and interests, using altruistic attitudes to influence followers' willingness to make sacrifices for the organization or others.

The literature shows that there are direct and indirect influences of different leadership styles on knowledge sharing (Li *et al*, 2014; Bai, Lin and Li, 2016).

In particular, Tseng (2017) finds that there is correlation between leadership styles and the knowledge-sharing intentions of the staff within an organization. The significance of the influence of different leadership styles, from high to low, is as follows: servant leadership, charismatic leadership, transformational leadership, transactional leadership. Tseng further investigates the relationships between four different types of culture (adhocracy culture, clan culture, market culture and hierarchy culture) and knowledge sharing. The findings show that the significance of cultural influence, from high to low, is clan culture, hierarchy culture, market culture and adhocracy culture. Based on these findings, the study derives a matrix table to illustrate the important roles of types of organizational culture and leadership in knowledge sharing. The work concludes that organizations should adopt servant leadership within clan culture in order to have the strongest effect on knowledge sharing. In contrast, organizations should avoid the combination of transactional leadership with adhocracy culture, which has the weakest effect on knowledge-sharing intention (Tseng, 2017).

 Critical thinking and reflection
Organizational culture in practice

Reflect on situations where knowledge sharing is needed but you have had cultural misunderstandings or conflicts among colleagues at work or among fellow students at university/college. How did you manage those situations and what lessons have you learned? How could some of those misunderstandings and conflicts have been potentially avoided and better cultural understanding be promoted in your organization for knowledge sharing and learning?

Chapter summary

It is important to point out that research on the impact of organizational culture, especially specific types of OC and specific factors of OC, on knowledge sharing and organizational learning is still in its infancy. Existing research has covered neither all identified types of culture nor all identified OC factors for their effect on knowledge sharing or wider KM. Furthermore, the business environment is highly dynamic and can change very fast, so it should be expected that new types of culture and new OC factors could emerge at any time. The main purpose of this chapter is not to try to provide an exhaustive list of culture types or to prescribe all possible relationships between OC types and knowledge sharing and organizational learning. The purpose is to use some examples to illustrate that there is a close link among some organizational cultures, knowledge management and organizational learning. One critical thought should be for learners who are interested in the topic to watch out for the state of the art, using this chapter as a foundation knowledge base. It is also important to keep in mind that different, or even conflicting, findings may be reported on the nature of the OC impact on knowledge sharing and learning, because all existing research has its own specific context (such as industry, geographic origin, research method, sample size constraints and the culture background of the respondents). Interpretation of the relationships needs to take account of the specific context. Application of existing findings, especially to a different culture context, needs careful consideration.

Key learning points

- Culture penetrates to the essence of an organization – it is almost analogous with the concept of personality in relation to an individual, and this acute sense of what an organization is (including its mission and core values) seems to have become a necessary asset of a modern company.

- Organizational culture is concerned with a system of understanding of values, norms, beliefs and artefacts that is shared by the members of an organization. Organizational culture sets the standards and rules of the way of working for existing employees and for nurturing new employees.

- There have been plenty of definitions of organizational culture. These definitions may emerge from different contexts and cover different aspects, such as the evaluative aspect, the material/artefacts aspect, the outcome aspect, the process aspect and the social aspect.

- Organizational culture can be understood using a three-level structure: assumptions on the foundation level, stated values in the middle level and visible artefacts on the surface level.

- There have been various classification schemes in the literature which have defined a great many types of organizational culture. Many classification schemes use their own criteria and dimensions, and as a result the defined types of culture are termed very differently. Despite the terminology and the wide range of criteria used, there are some overlaps among many of the organizational culture types. An interesting observation is that the majority of the classification schemes use two criteria/dimensions, subsequently resulting in four types of organizational culture.

- Based on one single criterion – that is, the level of rigidity/autonomy of how people are organized in an organization to complete tasks – four types of culture are defined: power culture, role culture, task culture and people culture.

- By using two criteria – the degree of risk and speed of feedback – organizational culture is classified as a tough-guy, macho culture, a bet-your-company culture, a work-hard, play-hard culture and a process culture.

- The Competing Values Framework classified organizational culture as adhocracy culture, clan culture, market culture and hierarchy culture.

- Sociability and solidarity are the criteria behind the communal culture, networked culture, mercenary culture and fragmented culture.

- By examining culture using two dimensions – the level of flexibility of processes and the organization's orientation (on internal or external environment), OC can be classified as innovative culture, community culture, competitive culture and bureaucratic culture.

- By using multiple dimensions, culture can be classified into contrasting pairs: process oriented versus results oriented, job oriented versus employee oriented, loosely controlled versus tightly controlled, closed-system culture versus open-system culture, and professional culture versus parochial culture.

- Organizational culture can encourage or discourage knowledge sharing and organizational learning. The nature of the impact (positive or negative) and the level of impact (significant or small) depend on specific types of culture and the types of knowledge (tacit or explicit) to be shared.

- Many factors play crucial roles in creating a supportive culture to foster knowledge sharing and learning, including trust, top management support, motivation and incentives, and leadership and communication.

Review questions

- Why is organizational culture important for knowledge management, especially knowledge sharing?

- Does organizational culture have a direct or indirect impact on learning, and why do you think so?

- In your opinion, is organizational culture visible or invisible?

- If you examine the six OC classification schemes (ie those that have specified culture into four types) discussed in this chapter together, what patterns or trends do you observe?

- In manufacturing industry, business processes are usually classified into five types, depending on the volume and variety of products to be produced. The five types are (in the ascending order of volume and descending order of variety): project process, jobbing process, batch process, mass process and continuous process. What type(s) of organizational culture would you recommend for the organizations using the five manufacturing processes, and why?

- In service industry, business processes are usually classified into three types depending on the volume and variety of services provided. They are professional services (high level of contact with customers with a high level of customization, that is, high variety and low volume), service shops and mass service. What type(s) of organizational culture would you prefer to create if you were running an organization that provides these different types of service, and why?

- What type(s) of culture would be appropriate for SMEs or start-up companies? What are the advantages and disadvantages of having the type(s) of culture in SMEs or start-up companies? How can such a culture be created and maintained?

- Some companies are market leaders and some are followers. What type(s) of culture would benefit market leaders, and why? What type(s) of culture would benefit followers, and why do you think so?

- Why is it important to build an organizational culture with a high level of trust among workers for knowledge sharing and organizational learning?

- How effective are incentives in fostering knowledge sharing and learning? Using examples you are familiar with, either from your work experience, something you have read in the media or something you have heard from somewhere, are those incentives working well or not in encouraging knowledge sharing and learning? If not, what recommendations would you make to improve the situation?

- Based on your own experience, have you found trust to be an important factor underpinning attitudes to knowledge sharing and learning? Have you had any experiences where a lack of trust has inhibited knowledge sharing and learning, or where the existence of trust has facilitated it?

- Research the impact of organizational culture on knowledge sharing. Try to find some conflicting conclusions in the literature; for example, some may claim that cognition-based trust has a positive relationship with knowledge sharing, and some may claim a negative relationship between them. When you get conflicting or contradictory conclusions from different publications, what would you do?

- In what type(s) of organizational culture does leadership play a big role? In what type(s) of culture will leadership have only a very limited effect?

- Do a literature review on leadership styles and their relationships with knowledge sharing and learning. Does most of the literature fundamentally agree with each other, or are they mainly in disagreement?

- Based on your own experience, what has been the attitude of work colleagues to sharing knowledge? Have you found them to be willing to share, or has knowledge hiding or knowledge hoarding been more typical? What do you think are the main reasons for your colleagues to share, hide or hoard knowledge?

- If you were appointed as a knowledge officer in a multinational corporation to promote knowledge sharing, what difficulties would you perceive for people coming from different cultures to share knowledge? From a management point of view, what, if anything, can management in multinationals do to address such problems?

References

Al-Alawi, A I, Al-Marzooqi, N Y and Mohammed, Y F (2007) Organizational culture and knowledge sharing: critical success factors, *Journal of Knowledge Management*, **11** (2), pp 2–42

Alavi, M, Kayworth, T R and Leidner, D E (2005–6) An empirical examination of the influence of organizational culture on knowledge management practices, *Journal of Management Information Systems*, **22** (3), pp 191–224

Bai, Y, Lin, L and Li, P P (2016) How to enable employee creativity in a team context: a cross-level mediating process of transformational leadership, *Journal of Business Research*, **69** (9), pp 3240–50

Bakker, M *et al* (2006) Is trust really social capital? Knowledge sharing in product development projects, *The Learning Organization*, **13** (6), pp 594–605

Bartol, K M and Srivastava, A (2002) Encouraging knowledge sharing: the role of organizational reward systems, *Journal of Leadership and Organization Studies*, 9 (1), pp 64–76

Cameron, K and Quinn, R (2011) *Diagnosing and Changing Organizational Culture: Based on the Competing Values Framework*, 3rd edn, Addison-Wesley, Boston, MA

Casimir, G, Lee, K and Loon, M (2012) Knowledge sharing: influences of trust, commitment and cost, *Journal of Knowledge Management*, 16 (5), pp 740–53

Cavaliere, V and Lombardi, S (2015) Exploring different cultural configurations: how do they affect subsidiaries' knowledge sharing behaviours? *Journal of Knowledge Management*, 19 (2), pp 141–63

Chang, C L and Lin, T C (2015) The role of organizational culture in the knowledge management process, *Journal of Knowledge Management*, 19 (3), pp 433–55

Chang, W J, Liao, S H and Wu, T T (2017) Relationships among organizational culture, knowledge sharing and innovation capacity, *Knowledge Management Research and Practice*, 15, pp 47–90

Dalkir, K (2017) *Knowledge Management in Theory and Practice*, 3rd edn, MIT Press, Cambridge, MA

Deal, T E and Kennedy, A A (1982) *Corporate Culture: The rites and rituals of corporate life*, Addison-Wesley, Reading, MA

De Long, D and Fahey, L (2000) Diagnosing cultural barriers to knowledge management, *Academy of Management Executive*, 14 (4), pp 113–27

Denison, D R and Mishra, A K (1995) Toward a theory of organizational culture and effectiveness, *Organization Science*, 6 (2), pp 204–23

Denison, D R, Nieminen, L and Kotrba, L (2014) Diagnosing organizational cultures: a conceptual and empirical review of culture effectiveness surveys, *European Journal of Work and Organizational Psychology*, 23 (1), pp 145–61

Dietz, G and Hartog, D J D (2006) Measuring trust inside organizations, *Personnel Review*, 35 (5), pp 557–88

Eaves, S (2014) Middle management knowledge by possession and position: a panoptic examination of individual knowledge sharing influences, *Electronic Journal of Knowledge Management*, 12 (1), pp 6–86

Evans, M M, Wensley, A K P and Frissen, I (2015) The mediating effects of trustworthiness on social-cognitive factors and knowledge sharing in a large professional service firm, *Electronic Journal of Knowledge Management*, 13 (3), pp 240–54

Fey, C F and Denison, D R (2003) Organizational culture and effectiveness: can American theory be applied in Russia? *Organization Science*, 14 (6), pp 686–706

Fong, P S W and Kwok, C W C (2009) Organizational culture and knowledge management success at project and organizational levels in contracting firms, *Journal of Construction Engineering and Management*, 135 (12), pp 1348–56

Ghazali, R, Ahmad, M N and Zakaria, N H (2015) The mediating role of knowledge integration in effect of leadership styles on enterprise systems success: the post-implementation stage, *Journal of Enterprise Information Management*, 28 (4), pp 531–55

Goffee, R and Jones, G (2000) *The Character of a Corporation: How your company's culture can make or break your business*, Harper Business, New York

Handy, C B (1985) *Understanding Organizations*, Penguin, Harmondsworth

Hislop, D, Bosua, R and Helms, R (2018) *Knowledge Management in Organizations: A critical introduction*, 4th edn, Oxford University Press, Oxford

Hofstede, G *et al* (1990) Measuring organization cultures: a qualitative and quantitative study across twenty cases, *Administrative Science Quarterly*, **35**, pp 286–316

Holste, J S and Fields, D (2010) Trust and tacit knowledge sharing and use, *Journal of Knowledge Management*, **14** (1), pp 128–40

Holten, A L *et al* (2016) Knowledge hoarding: antecedent or consequent of negative acts? The mediating role of trust and justice, *Journal of Knowledge Management*, **20** (2), pp 215–29

Hung, W H *et al* (2012) Relationship bonding for a better knowledge transfer climate: an ERP implementation research, *Decision Support Systems*, **52**, pp 406–14

Jashapara, A (2011) *Knowledge Management: An integrated approach*, 2nd edn, Pearson Education, Harlow

Javenpaa, S L and Staples, S D (2003) Exploring perceptions of organizational ownership of information and expertise, *Journal of Management Information Systems*, **18** (1), pp 151–83

Jayawickrama, U (2015) Knowledge management competence for ERP implementation success, PhD thesis, University of Plymouth, UK

Kassem, R *et al* (2019) Assessing the impact of organizational culture on achieving business excellence with a moderating role of ICT: an SEM approach, *Benchmarking: An International Journal*, **26** (1), pp 117–46

Ke, W and Wei, K K (2008) Organizational culture and leadership in ERP implementation, *Decision Support Systems*, **45** (2), pp 208–18

Ko, D G (2010) Consultant competence trust doesn't pay off, but benevolent trust does! Managing knowledge with care, *Journal of Knowledge Management*, **14** (2), pp 202–13

Lee, C and Chen, W J (2005) The effects of internal marketing and organizational culture on knowledge management in the information technology industry, *International Journal of Management*, **22** (4), pp 661–72

Lee, D J and Ahn, J H (2007) Reward systems for intra-organizational knowledge sharing, *European Journal of Operational Research*, **180**, pp 938–56

Lee, J C, Shiue, Y C and Chen, C Y (2016) Examining the impacts of organizational culture and top management support of knowledge sharing on the success of software process improvement, *Computers in Human Behaviour*, **54**, pp 462–74

Levin, D Z and Cross, R (2004) The strengths of weak ties you can trust: the mediating role of trust in effective knowledge transfer, *Management Science*, **59** (11), pp 1477–90

Li, G *et al* (2014) Differentiated transformational leadership and knowledge sharing: a cross-level investigation, *European Management Journal*, **32** (4), pp 554–63

Lin, H F (2007) Effects of intrinsic and extrinsic motivation on employee knowledge sharing intentions, *Journal of Information Sciences*, **33** (2), pp 135–49

Lucas, L (2005) The impact of trust and reputation on the transfer of best practices, *Journal of Knowledge Management*, **9** (4), pp 8–101

Lyu, H and Zhang, Z (2017) Incentives of knowledge sharing: impact of organizational culture and information technology, *Enterprise Information Systems*, **11** (9), pp 1416–35

Madjar, N and Ortiz-Walters, R (2009) Trust in supervisors and trust in customers: their independent, relative and joint effects on employee performance and creativity, *Human Performance*, **22**, pp 128–42

Ortiz, J P and Arnborg, L (2005) Making high performance last: reflections on involvement, culture and power in organizations, *Performance Improvement*, **44** (6), pp 31–37

Oyemomi, O (2016). The Impact of Organizational Factors on Knowledge Sharing Performance, PhD Thesis, University of Plymouth, UK

Oyemomi, O *et al* (2019) How cultural impact on knowledge sharing contributes to organizational performance: using the fsQCA approach, *Journal of Business Research*, **94**, pp 313–19

Park, H, Ribiere, V and Schulte, J W D (2004) Critical attributes of organizational culture that promote knowledge management technology implementation success, *Journal of Knowledge Management*, **8** (3), pp 106–17

Rasmussen, L and Hall, H (2016) The adoption process in management innovation: a knowledge management case study, *Journal of Information Science*, **42** (3), pp 356–68

Rutten, W, Blaas-Franken, J and Martin, H (2016) The impact of (low) trust on knowledge sharing, *Journal of Knowledge Management*, **20** (2), pp 199–214

Sackmann S A and Friesl, M (2007) Exploring cultural impacts on knowledge sharing behaviour in project teams: results from a simulation study, *Journal of Knowledge Management*, **11** (6), pp 142–56

Sanz-Valle, R *et al* (2011) Linking organizational learning with technical innovation and organizational culture, *Journal of Knowledge Management*, **15** (6), pp 997–1015

Sathe, V (1985) *Culture and Related Corporate Realities*, 1st edn, Richard D. Irwin, Homewood, IL

Schein, E H (2004) *Organizational Culture and Leadership*, 3rd edn, Jossey-Bass, San Francisco, CA

Smedlund, A (2008) The knowledge system of a firm: social capital for explicit, tacit and potential knowledge, *Journal of Knowledge Management*, **12** (10), pp 63–77

Swift, P E and Hwang, A (2012) The impact of affective and cognitive trust on knowledge sharing and organizational learning, *The Learning Organization*, **20** (1), pp 20–37

Tseng, S M (2017) Investigating the moderating effects of organizational culture and leadership style on IT: adoption and knowledge sharing intention, *Journal of Enterprise Information Management*, **30** (4), pp 583–604

Tushman, M L and O'Reilly, C A (2002) *Winning through Innovation: A practical guide to learning organizational change and renewal*, Harvard Business School Press, Cambridge, MA

Yang, S C and Farn, C K (2009) Social capital, behavioural control and tacit knowledge sharing: a multi-informant design, *International Journal of Information Management*, **29** (3), pp 210–18

Yang, J T (2007) Knowledge sharing: investigate appropriate leadership roles and collaborative culture, *Tourism Management*, **28** (2), pp 530–43

PART THREE
Crossing knowledge boundaries

This part extends the discussion of KM to crossing knowledge boundaries rather than KM within a single organization. The part is comprised of four chapters.

A community of practice focusing on tacit knowledge sharing can span organizational boundaries, hence it is included in this part as Chapter 7. Another reason for not including community of practice in Part Two, which is focused on organizational structures for KM and learning, is that, in communities of practice individuals choose other individuals to 'practise' with outside formal organizational structures and ties (ie departments, divisions etc), thus creating informal networks that may or may not overlap with formal ones. By taking account of both the boundary and level of informality of a community of practice, it was decided that the best place to position Chapter 7 is in Part Three rather than in Part Two.

Chapter 8 first discusses, in depth, different types of knowledge boundaries that may exist in and beyond formal organizational structures. Then, some well-established and emerging boundary-crossing mechanisms are explained, so that readers can examine the mechanisms and use them to cross the types of knowledge boundaries they may encounter. Finally, the chapter presents various industrial cases where boundary-crossing knowledge activities take place.

Chapters 9 and 10 discuss important enablers to knowledge sharing and learning across boundaries with a different focus. Chapter 9 is dedicated to knowledge networks that enable boundary-spanning knowledge activities from a mainly social perspective, and Chapter 10 mainly from an ICT technology perspective. Chapter 9 is more concerned with tacit knowledge sharing and learning through social interaction using knowledge networks, while Chapter 10 is more concerned with explicit knowledge using technologies such as the Internet of Things and big data analytics. As tacit and explicit knowledge often cannot be distinctively separated (as pointed out in Chapter 2, the word 'explicitness' is probably more appropriate for discussing this knowledge feature), Chapters 9 and 10 should not be interpreted as two totally isolated perspectives. Instead, they should be seen as two sides of the same coin, hence these two chapters should be studied together, taking a holistic view.

Communities of practice 07

It is generally acknowledged that a community of practice (CoP) can facilitate knowledge sharing and learning, especially in terms of tacit knowledge sharing and learning through social interaction, because CoP provides a type of 'Ba', that is, a knowledge space where people can socialize and interact through practice/work to enable knowledge sharing. This chapter starts with the definitions of CoP and its key features, then looks at different types of CoP. Because CoP is often informal and interpersonal, knowledge activities and learning within CoP may be different from that within formal project teams, business units or organizational learning. This chapter will ask the question of whether CoP can be managed. Finally, the chapter discusses what a successful CoP looks like and how to create one.

7.1 Definitions, features and lifecycle of communities of practice

Definitions

The term 'community of practice' (CoP) was introduced by cognitive anthropologists Jean Lave and Etienne Wenger at the beginning of the 1990s as a part of a broader conceptual framework for reflecting about learning in its social dimensions (Lave and Wenger, 1991). At the time, Lave and Wenger were studying apprenticeships as a way to share knowledge. They noticed that learning was not just a one-to-one relationship between an apprentice and a master, but a relationship with a whole community of people, and among apprentices at different levels. One of the main conclusions drawn from their studies is that learning is a social factor fostered by involvement and participation in practice. In fact, this type of collaborative group has existed for as long as people have been learning and sharing their experiences through activities not only in apprenticeship but also in mentoring and even storytelling (Mabery, Gibbs-Scharf and Bara, 2013). The notion of CoP has gained popularity and found extensive use in many fields, such as business (Corso, Giacobbe and Martini, 2009), innovation (Pattinson and Preece, 2014), product development (Pohjola and Puusa, 2016) and public health (Barbour *et al*, 2018). Since the 1990s, there have been a great number of definitions, for example:

- A Community of Practice is defined as a group of individuals who share a common interest, a set of problems or a passion about a topic and seek to deepen their knowledge and expertise through ongoing interactions (Wenger *et al*, 2002).

- Communities of Practice are informal, self-selecting groups consisting of like-minded individuals who share similar interests, problems and outlooks (Jashapara, 2011).

- A group of people who have a particular activity in common, and as a consequence, have some common knowledge, a sense of community identity, and some element of a shared language and overlapping values (Hislop, Bosua and Helms, 2018).

Similar to many other KM concepts, it is difficult to have a unified definition for CoP. However, there has been some degree of agreement on the characterization of the three main elements making up a CoP (Corso, Giacobbe and Martini, 2009; Bolisani and Scarso, 2014):

1   A domain: an area of interest that creates a common base among members and allows them to develop a group identity. The area of interest brings the group together.

2   A community: a group of people to whom the domain is relevant, the relationships among them and the boundaries. It is a social learning

factory where a group of people interact with each other and learn together, build relationships and develop a sense of membership and reciprocal commitment.

3   Practice: a shared repository of competences and common resources; that is, a body of knowledge, routines, methods, tools, styles, documents, symbols and languages that members have developed together. The knowledge created and shared in the past allows for future learning, for trusted relationships and for circulation of explicit and tacit knowledge.

Each CoP can be seen as a different combination of these three fundamental elements, which evolve according to the context in which a community exists through a process of continuous redefinition led by its members (Corso, Giacobbe and Martini, 2009). Community groups are usually self-organized on a voluntary basis, but they can sometimes be initiated and facilitated by sponsoring organizations, hence are built intentionally (Mabery, Gibbs-Scharf and Bara, 2013). Once formed, these groups may meet in physical environments such as around coffee machines and in canteens. They can also meet virtually, for example through forums on the internet to discuss their shared problems or practice. The interactions found in communities of practice tend to encourage novel practice rather than simply reworking everyday processes. CoP can be very powerful in creating socially embedded tacit knowledge and making it 'sticky', that is, making it very difficult for competitors to replicate such socially embedded knowledge. The most important way to access this type of knowledge is to join the community and gradually gain access to the knowledge and learn from the community through practice. Derived from social learning theory, CoP has been seen by some scholars as the ideal environment for the generation and sharing of knowledge (Adams and Freeman, 2000).

 Critical thinking and reflection
Definitions of CoP

What do you think are the main differences between an informal community of practice and a formal organizational work group/team, in terms of their formation, structure, membership, focus of effort, governance, management and time frame?

Key features

A number of key features of CoP have been identified (Lave and Wenger, 1991; Wenger *et al*, 2002; Bolisani and Scarso, 2014; Schiavone and Borzillo, 2014; Hislop, Bosua and Helms, 2018):

- Common activity or mutual engagement: members build 'the community' and 'the practice' by conducting practice-related interactions with each other on a regular basis.
- Shared knowledge: developed and possessed by members of a community.
- Shared values and attitudes: developed within a community, in other words, a CoP has its own culture or micro-culture.
- Shared identity: possessed by the members of a community.
- Dynamic roles of leaders and learners: in order to manage CoP activities, new organizational roles have been proposed, such as community leaders, champions, facilitators and learners. These roles are not appointed as in typical organizational settings such as formal departments and bureaucratic structures, operational teams and project teams. The scope of a CoP is to expand organizational knowledge and enable the mechanisms of knowledge sharing and learning by individuals; the roles in a community are in part voluntarily self-selected on the basis of their expertise, passions or commitment in a domain/topic area. The boundaries of a CoP are generally more fluid and can evolve organically, hence the roles in a CoP such as leaders, champions and facilitators are dynamic and can change easily.
- Legitimate access: this recalls the importance of the 'space' where knowledge is created and the learning processes occur. Ongoing knowledge-based interaction results in member relationship reciprocity, shared understanding and a sense of commitment. The membership is legitimized by sustained participation rather than official status.
- Peripheral participation: to grow individually and to contribute their knowledge to the rest of the community, newcomers or more generally members who are distant from the 'core group' must be legitimately involved in the community. According to Wenger *et al* (2002), four main levels of community participation can be identified: core group, active, peripheral and outsider. A small core group forms the heart of the community, participates proactively in discussions and debates, usually leads the community and assists coordination of the community. The second-level participants form an active group who do not work with the same

regularity and intensity as the core group. The third group is at the outer periphery. Its members do not often participate in community activities but they are an essential dimension of the CoP. The fourth group consists of people around the community who are not members of the CoP but are interested in the CoP's subject matter and its mission. This group may include customers or suppliers of a core business.

These features underpin the taken-for-granted assumptions and values of a CoP. Furthermore, the existence of these features is likely to foster trust-based relations, creating social conditions that are conducive to knowledge sharing and learning (Hislop, Bosua and Helms, 2018). Successful CoPs generally demonstrate a transparent, non-judgemental sharing of challenges, failures and successes to build the trust, openness and cooperation necessary for members to ask challenging questions and deal with disagreement as they tackle tough issues (Wenger *et al*, 2002).

Benefits of participating in a CoP

The benefits of participating in a CoP are both tangible and intangible. Tangible benefits can be resolving problems by learning from what other members in the CoP have done already, whether in the form of best practice or lessons learned. Intangible benefits include experiencing a sense of belonging through identification with a cohort of people who are dealing with similar issues. The benefits of a CoP exist at multiple levels: individual level, organizational level and community level (O'Dell and Hubert 2011; Mabery, Gibbs-Scharf and Bara, 2013). Specifically, benefits to individual members include:

- helping people form relationships that provide social support, excitement and personal validation;
- continual learning and professional development;
- access to expertise;
- improved communication with peers;
- increased productivity and quality of work;
- networking for staying current in the field;
- sense of professional identity;
- enhanced professional reputation;

- members collaborate, use one another as sounding boards, teach each other and strike out together to explore relevant subject matter.

Benefits to organizations include:

- provide the means to translate local know-how into global, collective knowledge;
- help employees exchange ideas, collaborate and learn from each other, hence with faster, less costly retrieval of knowledge and reduced learning curves;
- knowledge sharing and distribution transcending boundaries created by workflow, business functions, geography and time;
- coordination, standardization and synergy across organizational units;
- reduced rework and reinvention;
- enable the speed and innovation needed for marketplace leadership;
- benchmarking against and influencing industry standards;
- can integrate into the fabric of an organization's core work and value chains;
- alliance building;
- can successfully align with formal governance structures.

Benefits to the CoP domain include:

- help reveal and refine best practice in the community;
- consistent communication and reporting;
- improved analytical capability;
- promotion of standards;
- support and promotion of key national and international initiatives;
- advancement of domain-specific capabilities;
- links among geographically dispersed practitioners;
- increased government efficiency.

At the community level, participating in a CoP also provides professionals working in a field with a unified, enhanced and more influential voice for engaging with other groups and stakeholders. Research done by Mabery, Gibbs-Scharf and Bara (2013) has further revealed that the impact of a CoP is greatest when members initiate the CoP's formation and collectively identify the scope, focus and work of the CoP, because members feel empowered to choose their work, learning and tackling key issues in their domains. Conversely, CoPs formed by an organization to focus and work on a topic deemed significant by that organization struggle to build the necessary relationships and connect around work they believed to be important. Such CoPs require an inordinate amount of support to achieve any ongoing benefits to individuals and their organizations (Mabery, Gibbs-Scharf and Bara, 2013).

 Critical thinking and reflection
Critical perspectives on CoPs

Much of the literature on communities of practice takes a positive perspective, suggesting that in relation to knowledge processes it is largely or exclusively beneficial for individuals, organizations and the community domain. Do you have any critical comments on CoPs, for example about the ambiguity, problems, difficulties, hostility or blindness to ideas generated outside of a CoP?

Lifecycle stages of a CoP

Although communities of practice continually evolve over time, it is possible to observe a CoP's lifecycle, consisting of birth, growth and death. Corso, Giacobbe and Martini (2009) presented five stages of a community's development: potential, coalescing, maturing, stewardship and transformation. Corso, Giacobbe and Martini's (2009) five-stage model can be seen as an adaptation and evolution of Wenger's work, which defined five similar stages of CoP development: potential, coalescing, active, dispersed and memorable (Wenger, 1998; Wenger *et al*, 2002). Table 7.1 provides an overview of the five stages of community development together with the main activities undertaken at each stage (Wenger, 1998; Wenger *et al*, 2002; Pohjola and Puusa, 2016).

As can be seen from the table, each stage of CoP development is characterized by different levels of interaction among the members and the various types of activities.

Community development typically starts with loose social networks, which usually attract an informal group of people who start networking, that hold the potential for people to become more connected and thus a more important influence in an organization, industry or business sector.

Table 7.1 Five stages of CoP development

Number	Stage	Meaning	Typical activities
1	Potential	People face similar situations without the benefit of shared practice	Finding each other, discovering commonalities
2	Coalescing	People come together and recognize the group's potential	Exploring connectedness, defining joint enterprise, negotiating community
3	Active	Members engage in developing a practice	Engaging in joint activities, creating artefacts, adapting to changing circumstances, renewing interests, commitment and relationships
4	Dispersed	Members no longer engage intensively, but the community is still active as a force and a centre of knowledge	Staying in touch, communicating, holding reunions, calling for advice
5	Memorable	The community is no longer central, but people still remember it as a significant part of their identity	Telling stories, preserving artefacts, collecting memorabilia

As people build connections, they coalesce into a community. Coalescing is important in getting a community to work, because it allows individuals to build not only relationships, but also trust and an awareness of common interests and needs. Once formed, a community often grows in both membership and the depth of knowledge the members share. Communities thrive when members receive the added value of participation.

When a CoP moves towards the maturity stage, it goes through cycles of high and low activity, like any other living things. During the maturity stage, the most important thing is to move from establishment to clarifying the focus of the community, its roles and boundaries. This is a very active stage for the community coordinators and support staff, who often break apart and rearrange the community when deemed appropriate.

At its peak, a CoP often takes active stewardship of the knowledge and practice the members share and consciously transforms itself. As time passes, a CoP can dissolve if the common interests among members disappear, for various reasons such as the change in context, and finally reaches its death. The radical transformation or death of a community is as natural a step in its lifecycle as any stage in a process of birth, growth and life. During this change, people leave the community if it is no longer useful (Saint-Onge and Wallace, 2003).

 **CASE STUDY** CoP lifecycle analysis in the case of Electric Cars – Now!

An analysis of the lifecycle stages of community development is presented by Pohjola and Puusa (2016), which focuses on the subject area of the development of 'electric cars' in Finland. The lifecycle is divided into three main stages: an early stage, a maturing stage and the end of the (active) community.

1 An early stage – motives and expectations

Pohjola and Puusa (2016) set out to identify how a community began forming: in particular, what motivated individuals to take part in the first place. Based on interview data, four motivational themes emerged:

- Joint target of interest: some interviewees said that the idea of an electric car appealed to them, depicting it as fresh, innovative and new. Here are a couple of quotes from the interviews: 'We started asking people to join the mailing list and to generate ideas there. It gathered people with similar interest, people who got excited about the idea of an electric car.' 'At the early stage, it was the reciprocal excitement and enthusiasm that was the driving force in the community as a whole. The passion for a cause, and the spirit was contagious.'

- Communality: meeting people and making friends, in other words, socializing. 'People were the fuel. Sure, the technology was there behind, but mainly I got a chance to meet a type of people I would not otherwise have ever met.'

- Interest in joint action and motivation to create networks: interviewees commented on the perceived opportunity to network with new people who shared their interest.

- The development of one's skills: the possibility of synergy and thus of learning complementary skills and developing their own competencies.

After the motives for joining the CoP had been identified, four groups of expectations regarding the future and achievements of the CoP were discovered among the participants:

- Ideological motivations: the objective was to contribute to something that would make the world a better place.

- Technical product: for some members, the driver for participation was an interest in being involved in building an innovative, tangible product – an electric car.
- Advisers: some people believed that they had something to offer, but for various reasons, chose to remain outsiders and adopted an advisory role.
- Hang-arounds: some members' primary goal was to observe the group and stay aware of its activities.

Pohjola and Puusa (2016) found that, at first, a common interest was enough to hold the group together. However, it soon became clear that people's participation was based on varying motives and their expectations were different. In consequence, the group, which at first had seemed cohesive, started dispersing and people began to divide into active or passive participants. Among the active participants, people became more familiar with each other's skills and competencies, and interpersonal relationships began to play a more pivotal role.

2 Maturing stage – role differentiation

When moving towards the maturity stage, the group started dividing into subgroups playing different roles. First, a core group met at a physical place and took shape, as members saw each other and communicated face-to-face. Those who were not able to take part in the meetings and the construction of the vehicle dropped to a peripheral group. They no longer actively participated in the group's activities but still followed the work of the community through virtual channels. Standing between the core group and the peripheral group were active members, who maintained their level of participation in the community work.

At the maturity stage, chemistry between individuals started playing a more significant role and affecting the dynamics within the group. As matters progressed, the dynamics changed, and intra-group criteria were developed as a new set of standards for the entire community. Subsequently, roles and responsibilities had to be delegated, which constituted a substantial change, because at the beginning of forming the community each member did pretty much whatever they felt best suited to, but now the roles and tasks were divided on a different basis. Within the core group in particular, people got to know each other and each other's strengths and limitations really well, while they also shared the idea of what the CoP was all about and what it aimed to achieve. Hence the development of the community's participation was based on 'new criteria'. At this stage, the group became more conscious of its own 'skills capital'; they learned what kind of expertise they lacked and then purposefully tried to recruit specialists to provide the skills missing from the community.

The core group members began to organize themselves so that the best expertise was channelled and pushed the electric car project forward. Although the CoP started acting in a more organized manner, it is noteworthy that no hierarchical management system was established, though the core group continued collectively and unofficially to lead the community.

In contrast to the early stage of the community's lifecycle, at this mature stage the participants' concerted efforts became more important from a group dynamics point of view. The openness and freely available information and knowledge started to change, such that it was no longer so open. A more distinct division emerged between openly shared information/knowledge and that given to only a few. Nevertheless, during the maturity stage, the participants came from all over Finland, and later, when awareness of the group spread through ICT, from all over the world. This generated the need for 'new forms of work', such as ICT and the use of virtuality. The interviewees who participated in Pohjola and Puusa's (2016) research commented that they felt excited that the community's work took place in different places, from over the internet to physical meeting places in garages. In fact, they were very proud of their open innovation platform on the internet, where community members were able to post all interesting and important things happening in the community.

3 The end of the (active) community

At some point in the later stages, one crucial decision from the group totally changed the dynamics of the community: the decision to seek external funding by involving external stakeholders. The participation of outside investors led to some unexpected outcomes: the expectations and demands to obtain results increased, and the need for monitoring and reporting emerged. This severely influenced the community's original motivation: the freedom and informality of the community in action. Transparency became even more selective; members of the community began wondering, consciously or sometimes unconsciously, what information and knowledge was worth in terms of money in the investors' eyes. At this point, information and knowledge were no longer available to everyone via the community network. While the increasing degree of fragmentation was recognized, there was a lot of suspicion, mutual competition and shortage of skills. Members of the core group tried to change this unwanted situation but without success.

After losing the group dynamics, the community no longer met at their physical meeting places, but turned to passive participation, often propped up by the members who had already became friends during the early and maturity stages of the community's development.

Even though the community still exists, its purpose and nature have changed. It is currently viewed as a forum for discussion by interested parties instead of as a community aiming at a concrete case. At this end stage, community members have become more equal again, as in the early stage of community development, because they are all participating in the community through virtual channels.

At the end of its lifecycle, ICT has played the role of a 'life support system', which created a platform through which people could stay in touch. It also helps to preserve the information gathered so far. The original purpose of the community was to produce a physical product (an electric car). At this point, the electric car conversion kit and product development have been discontinued, but the community continues to live virtually. The community's strengths lie in the fact that the people who were involved from the beginning have continued to maintain contact online. Their knowledge capital rose to the international level, and currently, the 'eCars – Now!' community is global.

Further details of the 'eCars – Now!' online community: http://ecars-now.wikidot.com/

Questions

1 What roles do you think ICT can play at each CoP lifecycle stage: the early stage, the maturing stage and the end of the (active) community?

2 Do you think the use of ICT has changed the lifecycle of the electric car community by avoiding the 'death' stage of the community?

7.2 Types of CoP

Many types of CoP can be distinguished, depending on the criteria used for classification. There have been a significant number of criteria, including level of formalization, size of CoP, geographical spread of the community members, means of interaction among CoP members, and the boundary. Table 7.2 provides an overview of different types of CoP based on these criteria.

In the early years of CoP concept development and its evolution (mainly the 1990s), it was believed that CoPs were largely formed voluntarily and operated informally, without formal controls or system support. Hence a CoP was not considered a new form of organization but a different point of view in the organization, which stressed how people were more involved in learning dynamics than the units they belonged to or the projects they worked on. However, as organizations gradually recognized the benefits and roles of CoPs, they began to link them to strategic business objectives by creating strategic communities or providing strategic support to those communities; subsequently, formal and strategic CoPs appeared and spread rapidly, especially in Eastern cultural contexts such as in Korea (Jeon, Kim and Koh, 2011).

According to Saint-Onge and Wallace (2003), CoPs can be divided into three categories: informal CoPs, supported CoPs and structured CoPs. Supported CoPs and structured CoPs, like strategic communities, are formally authorized and supported by firms. The role of informal CoPs is for

Table 7.2 Types of CoP and relevant criteria

Criteria	Types of CoP
Level of formalization	• Self-selected, voluntary basis • Initiated and facilitated by sponsored organizations and intentionally built
Size	• Small number of people • Hundreds and thousands of people
Geographical spread	• Everyone is co-located on one site • Globally dispersed, virtual and internet based
Means of interaction	• Face-to-face • Virtual/online
Boundary	• Within one single organization • Inter-organizational, spanning a whole industry/business sector

sharing knowledge among practitioners for the community's own sake, while the role of supported CoPs is building capacity for a given business or competency area, and the role of structured CoPs is providing a cross-functional platform for organizational problem solving. Members of an informal CoP are mainly self-selected or peer invited, but for a structured CoP members are usually invited by sponsors with strict selection criteria. With a supported CoP, members can be self-selected, be invited by peers or be included on managers' recommendations. Informal CoPs develop naturally and their work is predominantly voluntary. Supported CoPs are developed intentionally, mainly by sponsors and CoP members, while structured CoPs are developed organizationally and well aligned with business objectives.

While for large organizations it is possible to sponsor or even build structured, within-organization CoPs, for SMEs the construction of such a CoP can be problematic. It is unlikely that SMEs can spare the resources required for constructing a CoP. These resources can include time and the finance required for investment in a CoP, training for CoP leaders and IT tools to facilitate participation in a CoP. Given that SMEs have access to fewer resources than larger organizations, SMEs often engage in inter-organizational CoPs to acquire necessary knowledge to support their innovations (Pattinson and Preece, 2014).

The wide range of criteria to distinguish types of CoP can be organized into clusters. For example, two clusters are distinguished by Hislop, Bosua and Helms (2018). The first cluster is named 'proximity', which refers to the interaction between members and their geographical dispersion. The second cluster is named 'institutionalization', which refers to the level of formalization and support of the community within the organization.

The two clusters of criteria were used by Verburg and Andriessen (2011) in an attempt to classify CoPs using empirical data. They performed an analysis of 38 networks in large organizations and then suggested that the networks could be divided into four major groups, as summarized in Table 7.3.

The four groups are:

- **Informal networks:** characterized by high proximity and low institutionalization. Members of the network have much physical interaction because of their close proximity. However, owing to the low level of formalization and support from the organization, they can appear spontaneously from a need to share knowledge and learn.

Table 7.3 Types of networks based on proximity and institutionalization

		Institutionalization (level of formalization and support)	
		Low	**High**
Proximity	High (close)	**Informal networks** • High proximity, low institutionalization • Members share similar practice • Much physical interaction • Appear spontaneously	**Strategic networks** • High proximity, high institutionalization • Experts brought together to perform a strategic task for the organization • Supported with organization resources
	Low (far)	**Q&A networks** • Low proximity, low institutionalization • Loosely connected • Large networks of people with various backgrounds • Members post questions and answers online	**Online strategic networks** • Low proximity, high institutionalization • Interaction via electronic means, otherwise similar to strategic networks

- **Q&A networks**: characterized by low proximity and low institutionalization, loosely connected, large networks of people with various backgrounds. Members interact with each other by posting their questions and answers online, such as using online discussion forums.

- **Strategic networks**: characterized by high institutionalization and high proximity. This type of network is formed by bringing together experts with a clear purpose to perform a strategic task for the organization. The network can receive strong support from organization resources to ensure that the strategic purpose is achieved.

- **Online strategic networks**: characterized by high institutionalization and low proximity. This type of network is similar to the strategic network but because of the low proximity, members of the community interact through electronic means.

7.3 Can CoPs be managed?

The growing popularity of CoPs has brought about a sort of loss of identity of the concept itself and there is no agreed position about what a CoP should be and how this notion may be applied. Nevertheless, a dominant view in KM research is that a CoP, especially a formal CoP (ie supported and structured CoPs), can be a significant influence on knowledge-sharing and learning activities as well as on the performance of an organization or even a business sector, hence they should be cultivated and used to inform KM strategy where possible (Jeon, Kim and Koh, 2011). Understanding the concept of CoP and its key features is useful for detecting an existing CoP and for distinguishing one CoP from another.

However, CoPs initially emerged as self-organizing entities that management can encourage and support, gaining great advantages without owning or controlling them totally (Bolisani and Scarso, 2014). A challenge to managing CoPs at the organizational and managerial level is the extent to which management influence or intervention should be 'contained' in order not to stifle the dynamics of a CoP. One way to approach this challenge is, first, to understand what factors affect knowledge sharing and learning in a CoP, and second, to define the nature of relationships between the factors and knowledge sharing and learning.

Corso, Giacobbe and Martini (2009) investigated how to design and manage business CoPs from two dimensions: the combination of an organization's commitment and members' involvement. In this context, the community's boundary is within a single organization rather than spanning different organizations. Based on empirical evidence from seven case studies (primary data source) and the analysis of three best practices (secondary data source) covering a wide range of businesses, from more structured call centre operations to more complex new product development, the research identified three key factors to win organizational commitment and four key factors to win members' involvement. These key factors are summarized in Table 7.4. The research finds that a community can only be born when both organizational commitment and individual members' involvement and participation are present. It further concludes that a high level of commitment from the organization and a high level of individuals' involvement and participation are positively related to the effectiveness of the community in supporting organizational learning and KM processes.

From a motivational perspective, Jeon, Kim and Koh (2011) conducted a comprehensive study on three aspects: 1) identifying relevant intrinsic and extrinsic motivational factors affecting a CoP; 2) how the factors affect the members' attitude, intention and behaviour towards knowledge sharing; and 3) the moderating effect of CoP type on knowledge-sharing attitude. Based on empirical data collected from four Korean companies, with 282 valid responses, the research identifies both extrinsic and intrinsic motivational factors that potentially affect knowledge-sharing attitude, intention and behaviour in CoPs. Image and reciprocity are two important extrinsic motivational factors. Intrinsic motivational factors include enjoyment in helping others (altruism) and the need for affiliation. In terms of the relationships and moderating effects, the work developed 10 hypotheses which were tested with empirical data. The results (ie whether the hypotheses are supported or not supported) are summarized in Table 7.5.

As can be seen from Table 7.5, both extrinsic (image and reciprocity) and intrinsic (enjoyment in helping and the need for affiliation) motivational drivers have a positive effect on knowledge-sharing attitude, intention and behaviour. Different types of CoP have different degrees of effect, that is, extrinsic motivational drivers (image and reciprocity) have a stronger impact on knowledge sharing in a formal CoP than in an informal CoP, while intrinsic motivational drivers have a stronger impact on knowledge sharing in an informal CoP than in a formal CoP.

With respect to the relationships between CoPs and organizational performance, there has been some evidence in the literature, collected from empirical

Table 7.4 Factors to win organizational commitment and members' involvement

Category	Factors	Meanings
Winning organization's commitment	Increase a community's visibility	A community must be evident as a concrete and well-organized entity.
	Culture	A community has to have a cultural foundation that allows the organization to pursue its core values.
	Achievement of aims	A community must be able to deliver results in line with the organization's goals and, in particular, underline the impacts of its activities on business performance.
Winning members' involvement and participation	Improve individuals' involvement in terms of personal value and identification	If there is an overlap between individuals' own interests and a community's domain, individuals will participate in activities they perceive as useful.
	Enhance social relations	Individuals' involvement must occur through participation in a social context.
	Improve connectivity between members	Opportunities for members to come into contact with each other and build relations must be improved. This depends on the availability and quality of spaces for both physical and virtual interaction.
	Improve communality	The existence of common ground enables knowledge sharing among a community's members.

Table 7.5 Motivational factors and their effects on knowledge-sharing attitude, intention and behaviour

	Hypotheses	Results
H1	Image has a positive effect on CoP member's attitude towards knowledge sharing	Supported
H2	Reciprocity has a positive effect on CoP member's attitude towards knowledge sharing	Supported
H3	Enjoyment in helping has a positive effect on CoP member's attitude towards knowledge sharing	Supported
H4	The need for affiliation has a positive effect on CoP member's attitude towards knowledge sharing	Supported
H5	Attitude has a positive effect on CoP member's intention towards knowledge sharing	Supported
H6	Perceived behavioural control has a positive effect on CoP member's intention towards knowledge sharing	Supported
H7	Subjective norms have a positive effect on CoP member's intention towards knowledge sharing	Supported
H8	Intention has a positive effect on CoP member's knowledge-sharing behaviour	Supported
H9	Facilitating conditions have a positive effect on CoP member's knowledge-sharing behaviour	Supported
H10	The strength of relationships between motivational drivers and knowledge-sharing attitude differs by the type of CoP	Supported
H10-1	The impact of extrinsic motivational drivers (image and reciprocity) on knowledge-sharing attitude is stronger in formal CoPs than in informal CoPs	Supported
H10-2	The impact of intrinsic motivational drivers (enjoyment in helping and need for affiliation) on knowledge-sharing attitude is stronger in informal CoPs than in formal CoPs	Supported

studies. Based on qualitative and quantitative data from a case study of a multi-million-dollar construction project in the Swedish construction industry, a positive relationship between CoP activity and performance in terms of improvements on the community's learning curve was found (Schenkel and Teigland, 2008). The authors investigated the relationships between four identified CoPs within the project and one performance metric – the learning curve. The four CoPs were created through mutual engagement, narration, collaboration and social construction in the pursuit of a joint enterprise. A shared repertoire comprising a community's cumulative memory as well as a way of working was developed. The learning curves for the four CoPs were produced by calculating and plotting the cumulative total of deviations on a monthly basis, divided by the cumulative total of concrete produced. The results from the study provide some preliminary evidence of a positive relationship between CoPs and incremental improvement in their performance. Earlier work on the topic provided similar findings, revealing that in more formal CoPs or strategic communities, CoPs led to decreased learning curves for new employees, quicker responses for customers, reduced rework, avoidance of reinventing the wheel, and the development of new ideas for products and services (Lesser and Storck, 2001).

Although a CoP evidences the traits of a common community, it is associated with conflicts of interest within a company. Some CoP members perceive the risk of losing ownership of their unique knowledge (Jang and Ko, 2014). Such perceived risk can be rationally anticipated to hinder CoP activity. In their study, Jang and Ko distinguish online CoP from offline (ie more traditional face-to-face interaction) CoP. The research identified five factors that may have an impact on CoP activities: affirmative effect, social norm, perceived expectation (including perceived usefulness, image and reciprocity), perceived risk and organizational support. The relationships between CoP activities and members' commitment, and the relationships between members' commitment and individual performance, were also explored. Based on data from a survey with members from more than 100 Korean companies participating in online and offline CoPs, supported by 268 valid questionnaires, the research found that:

1 The affirmative effect of a CoP positively influences offline CoP activities, but influence on online activities is not evident.

2 Social norms positively influence online CoP activities, but influence on offline CoP activities is not evident.

3 Perceived expectation positively influences both offline and online CoP activities.

4 Perceived risk negatively influences online CoP activities, but the influence on offline CoP activities is not evident.

5 Organizational support positively influences both offline and online CoP activities.

6 Both offline and online CoP activities positively influence members' commitment.

7 Both offline and online CoP activities positively influence individual performance.

Recently, there have been a number of review papers on the role of CoP, for example in the business sector (Aljuwaiber, 2016) and in the public health sector (Barbour *et al*, 2018). These review papers provide a thorough analysis of the literature from the 1980s to the present time, with a comprehensive picture of the evolution of the concept. Important enablers of and barriers to the implementation of CoPs are classified, as shown in Table 7.6. As can be seen from the table, the structure of a CoP can be both an enabler of and a barrier to CoP implementation in practice. Hence it is important to provide a structure that can encourage knowledge sharing and learning in order to enable CoP implementation, while avoiding the elements that may negatively affect it.

Table 7.6 Classification of enablers of and barriers to CoP implementation

	Category	Key elements
Enablers	CoP structure	Network development, safe learning environment and structured time for reflection, clearly articulated learning plans for members, diversity among members
	Facilitation	Creating meaningful and enjoyable capacity-building opportunities, trusted relationship with the facilitator
	Activities	Frequent interactions, group problem solving, tailored knowledge transfer activities to meet the needs of sub-groups within the membership, consistently structured interactions with clear purpose and role descriptions
Barriers	CoP structure	Inadequate duration of the CoP, inadequate opportunity for discussion, inadequate facilitation

(continued)

Table 7.6 (Continued)

Category	Key elements
Insufficient interaction	Insufficient attention to understanding individual member needs, lack of prompt responses, density of networks whereby members have existing, longstanding relationships, limited interaction from fellow members, lack of time to interact

 Critical thinking and reflection
Managing CoPs

Many researchers have argued that management should try not to command and control CoPs but should nurture them. One way of facilitating CoPs is to allow employees to spend some of their work time in participating and taking on active roles in communities. What are your opinions on the 'right' level of management, and in what other ways can management nurture CoPs?

7.4 What a successful CoP looks like and how to build one

Not all CoPs are successful in terms of knowledge sharing and learning. What does a successful CoP look like? O'Dell and Hubert (2011) summarized 10 traits of successful communities:

1 a compelling, clear value proposition for all involved;

2 a dedicated, skilled facilitator or leader;

3 a coherent, comprehensive knowledge map for the core content of the community;

4 an outlined, easy-to-follow knowledge-sharing process;

5 an appropriate technology medium that facilitates knowledge exchange, retrieval and collaboration;

6 communication and training plans for members and interested stake-holders;

7 an up-to-date, dynamic roster of community members;

8 several key metrics of success to show results;

9 a recognition plan for participants;

10 an agenda of critical topics to cover for the first meeting and the next three to six months of existence.

In order to help create and maintain CoPs with these traits, 10 critical success factors for CoPs are proposed (O'Dell and Hubert, 2011). It should be noted that the following success factors are mainly associated with formal CoPs, such as the structured and sponsored CoPs that may form part of an organization's strategy in KM, rather than informal CoPs:

1 Create a consistent, enterprise approach and build on established networks where possible.

2 Ensure that communities align with organizational needs and fulfil explicit objectives. Distinguish between formal communities and ad hoc, short-term collaborations. Establish criteria and basic requirements for a formal community.

3 Secure and then maintain the support of managers, executives and subject-matter experts. Ensure that communities are seen as a legitimate way to spend time.

4 Focus on connecting employees across organizational lines, regions and business functions.

5 Leverage technology thoughtfully. New tools should provide enhanced connectivity and value.

6 Clearly articulate the roles and responsibilities of community leaders and make sure that they are backed by a distributed network of resources.

7 Ensure that each community has a coherent, comprehensive knowledge map for its core content as well as easy-to-follow knowledge-sharing processes.

8 Hold communities accountable for producing and stewarding critical knowledge.

9 Measure how the communities deliver value to your organization, and find meaningful ways to communicate that value organization-wide.

Depending on the objectives of a community, measures may include the investment and resources required to sustain communities, the level of activity and the degree to which knowledge and practices are transferred.

10 Ensure long-term success by removing competing priorities and continuing to align community objectives with ever-changing organizational needs.

Key learning points

- A community of practice is a group of individuals who share a common interest, a set of problems and seek to deepen their knowledge and expertise through ongoing interactions.
- A CoP consists of three key elements: a domain, a community and practice.
- Key features of CoPs include common activity, shared knowledge, shared identity, overlapping value, dynamic roles of leaders and learners, legitimate access and peripheral participation.
- A CoP has a lifecycle, which can consist of different stages such as potential, coalescing, active, dispersed and memorable.
- Participating in CoPs has benefits at multiple levels: individual, organizational and community.
- There are different types of CoPs, such as informal, structured and supported.
- Both intrinsic and extrinsic motivation factors can affect a member's attitude, intention and behaviour towards CoPs, hence affect the knowledge sharing and learning in a community.
- The structure of a CoP can be both an enabler of and a barrier to the implementation of the CoP.

Review questions

- Why is it important to understand CoP in knowledge management?
- How did Lave and Wenger's concept of CoP evolve from the beginning of the 1990s to the early 2000s? What might have caused their change of view on the concept?

- Is CoP mostly informal or just a formal form of organization?
- In a CoP, what are the differences between the core group, active group, peripheral group and outsiders?
- What are the key stages of the lifecycle of a CoP? During which stage(s) are knowledge activities taking place most actively?
- What are the main benefits to individuals of participating in CoPs?
- What are the main benefits to organizations of participating in CoPs?
- What are the key features of online CoPs?
- Why do some organizations invest in sponsoring or building CoPs?
- To what extent should CoPs be managed?
- What do you think are the top traits of a successful CoP?
- Why is it important to identify success factors for a CoP?

References

Adams, E C and Freeman, C (2000) Communities of practice: bridging technology and knowledge assessment, *Journal of Knowledge Management*, **4** (1), pp 38–44

Aljuwaiber, A (2016) Communities of practice as an initiative for knowledge sharing in business organizations: a literature review, *Journal of Knowledge Management*, **20**, pp 731–48

Barbour, L *et al* (2018) Communities of practice to improve public health outcomes: a systematic review, *Journal of Knowledge Management*, **22** (2), pp 326–43

Bolisani E and Scarso, E (2014) The place of communities of practice in knowledge management studies: a critical review, *Journal of Knowledge Management*, **18** (2), pp 366–81

Corso, M, Giacobbe, A and Martini, A (2009) Designing and managing business communities of practice, *Journal of Knowledge Management*, **13** (3), pp 73–89

Hislop, D, Bosua, R and Helms, R (2018) *Knowledge Management in Organizations: A critical introduction*, 4th edn, Oxford University Press, Oxford

Jang, H and Ko, I (2014) The factors influencing CoP activities and their impact on relationship commitment and individual performance, *Journal of Knowledge Management*, **18** (1), pp 75–91

Jashapara, A (2011) *Knowledge Management: An integrated approach*, 2nd edn, Pearson Education, Harlow

Jeon, S, Kim, Y G and Koh, J (2011) An integrative model for knowledge sharing in communities of practice, *Journal of Knowledge Management*, **15** (2), pp 251–69

Lave, J and Wenger, E (1991) *Situated Learning: Legitimate peripheral participation*, Cambridge University Press, Cambridge, MA

Lesser, E and Storck, J (2001) Communities of practice and organizational performance, *IBM System Journal*, **40**, pp 831–41

Mabery, M J, Gibbs-Scharf, L and Bara, D (2013) Communities of practice foster collaboration across public health, *Journal of Knowledge Management*, **17** (2), pp 226–36

O'Dell, C and Hubert, C (2011) *The New Edge in Knowledge: How knowledge management is changing the way we do business*, Wiley, Hoboken, NJ

Pattinson, S and Preece, D (2014) Communities of practice, knowledge acquisition and innovation: a case study of science-based SMEs, *Journal of Knowledge Management*, **18** (1), pp 107–20

Pohjola, I and Puusa, A (2016) Group dynamics and the role of ICT in the life cycle analysis of community of practice of practice-based product development: a case study, *Journal of Knowledge Management*, **20** (3), pp 465–83

Saint-Onge, H and Wallace, D (2003) *Leveraging Communities of Practice for Strategic Advantage*, Butterworth-Heinemann, Burlington, MA

Schenkel, A and Teigland, R (2008) Improved organizational performance through communities of practice, *Journal of Knowledge Management*, **12** (1), pp 106–18

Schiavone, F and Borzillo, B (2014) Creating technological knowledge in vintage communities of practice, *Journal of Knowledge Management*, **18** (5), pp 991–1003

Verburg, R M and Andriessen, E J H (2011) A typology of knowledge sharing networks in practice, *Knowledge and Process Management*, **18** (1), pp 34–44

Wenger, E (1998) Communities of practice: learning as a social system, *Systems Thinker*, **9** (5), pp 2–3

Wenger, E, McDermott, R and Snyder, W (2002), *Cultivating Communities of Practice*, Harvard Business School Press, Boston, MA

Knowledge boundaries and boundary-spanning mechanisms

08

Learning outcomes

After completing this chapter, the reader will be able to:

- distinguish different types of knowledge boundaries that may hinder knowledge mobilization and learning;
- compare different boundary-spanning mechanisms;
- identify knowledge boundaries and appreciate the use of boundary-spanning mechanisms in industrial contexts

A knowledge boundary is considered a major barrier to knowledge mobilization and learning. It is essential to understand the different types of knowledge boundaries that may exist, before seeking appropriate boundary-spanning mechanisms to address the issue. This chapter starts with an introduction to different types of knowledge boundaries, then looks at some specific boundary-spanning mechanisms in detail, and finishes with discussion of how knowledge boundaries can be identified and how boundary-spanning mechanisms can be used to facilitate knowledge mobilization and learning. The focus of this chapter is different from Chapter 7 on communities of practice. Within a CoP, even though it may cross organizational borders or geographic areas, people have a shared sense of identity, values and some common practice, hence knowledge process and learning in a CoP are within relatively homogeneous groups. In this chapter, knowledge mobilization and learning crossing boundaries involve people who are more diverse and heterogeneous, and may have divergent identities, knowledge bases and very limited common interest in knowledge, and sometimes even have conflicts. Generally speaking, the less common knowledge that exists and the greater the level of epistemic difference, the more complicated and difficult the knowledge mobilization and learning processes will be (Hislop, Bosua and Helms, 2018)

8.1 Knowledge boundaries

In general, a boundary can be defined as 'the line marking the limit of an area', according to the Oxford Dictionary (2005), and a demarcation that marks the limit of an area or a border that divides one group from another (Hislop, Bosua and Helms, 2018). Boundaries can be highly diverse, for example:

- Geographic boundaries: physically separate areas or groups of people.
- Social boundaries: separate groups with distinctive identities in terms of professional background, organizational position or social status.
- Cultural boundaries: distinguish between groups with fundamentally different systems of values and assumptions.
- Organization boundaries: define the border of an organization.
- Activity boundaries: divide different activities, such as procurement, design, manufacturing, production, distribution, retailing and after-sales service.

All types of boundaries could cause differences in people's knowledge base, hence they erect barriers to knowledge mobilization and learning activities; in other words, they create a form of knowledge boundary. However, knowledge boundaries are more than just geographic, social, cultural, organizational or activity boundaries. For example, how firms open up their boundaries of activity, by outsourcing part of their production to external parties, is a well-understood phenomenon. However, the opening of knowledge boundaries is less understood but deserves further investigation, as the integration of knowledge that stems from external parties often proves to be difficult, particularly when the knowledge differs from the existing knowledge domains of the firm (Wilhelm and Dolfsma, 2018).

Knowledge boundaries

A knowledge boundary represents the limit or border of an agent's knowledge base in relation to a different domain of knowledge. Knowledge boundaries are not static. They adjust through structured learning environments such as training programmes, and they fluctuate throughout a person's continuous social and material interactions (Hawkins and Rezazade, 2012). A person's knowledge base can heavily influence the structure of their interpretive framework. This interpretive framework then determines how people interpret information (from other people or shared) and view it as important or unimportant, subsequently deciding whether to integrate it into their existing knowledge base. Knowledge boundaries exist for many reasons, for example owing to the differences in their knowledge base, the way people work, share knowledge, expertise and different organizational cultures (Boshkoska, Liu and Chen, 2018). One of the most influential works on knowledge boundaries is probably from Paul Carlile, who developed a topology of knowledge boundaries according to the degree of novelty of the collective tasks being undertaken, varying from low to high. He distinguished three types of knowledge boundary that have been now widely cited by other scholars and researchers: syntactic boundaries, semantic boundaries and pragmatic boundaries (Carlile, 2002, 2004):

- Syntactic boundaries: this type of boundary is assumed to have a low level of novelty of the collective tasks being undertaken and is the easiest to work across, because in this context people share a common logic, a set of values and worldview (Jashapara, 2011; Hislop, Bosua and Helms, 2018). At a syntactic boundary, knowledge transfer processes between a sender and a receiver are observed. A common lexicon can be developed for knowledge transfer crossing a syntactic boundary. It is recognized that most traditional technology-based knowledge mobilization programmes are following such information-processing assumptions, where explicit knowledge is transferred (Filstad, Simeonova and Visser, 2018).

- Semantic boundaries: at this type of knowledge boundary, people do not have a shared logic or set of values. Instead, people may have different understandings and interpretations of the same knowledge. The level of novelty of the collective tasks being undertaken is higher than that at the syntactic boundary. In order to work across a semantic boundary, people will need to develop an understanding of, and sensitivity to, other people's understandings and interpretations (Jashapara, 2011; Hislop, Bosua and Helms, 2018). In crossing a semantic boundary, the emphasis is put on knowledge translation and the development of common meanings (to address interpretive differences). At this level, the differences in meaning and the importance of context-specific aspects of knowledge mobilization, especially in relation to tacit knowledge mobilization, are recognized (Filstad, Simeonova and Visser, 2018). However, technologies such as enterprise systems are still very important, because technology networks provide space for open discussions and help create shared meaning and enhance knowledge mobilization within and across functions, organizations and communities.

- Pragmatic boundaries: when the novelty level of the collective tasks increases even further, people not only have different interpretations and understandings of issues/events, they also have different interests, ultimately resulting in conflicts among different actors/parties (individual, groups/teams, organizations or communities). Consequently, pragmatic boundaries are the most complex and difficult to work across successfully. In order to resolve the different interests and conflicts (sometimes, dependencies need to be considered as well), different actors/parties need to be willing and prepared to negotiate their existing practice and to transform the existing knowledge, leading to development of a common interest (Jashapara, 2011; Filstad, Simeonova and Visser, 2018). Owing to the complexity and the extent to which individuals, groups/teams, organizations and communities develop a sense of investment in, and commitment to, their knowledge and practice, crossing this type of knowledge boundary is typically never straightforward (Hislop, Bosua and Helms, 2018). This perspective recognizes knowledge processes as 'creative abrasion' and focuses on the negotiation of the practice. It is argued that, at a pragmatic boundary, knowledge is shared through a process of transformation of diverse knowledge, where co-creation of common grounds and understanding occurs, which leads to new practice (Bechky, 2003).

The key characteristics of the three types of knowledge boundaries are summarized in Table 8.1.

As can be seen from the table, apart from the fact that the novelty level of the collective tasks increases from the syntactic boundary through the semantic boundary to the pragmatic boundary, it is argued that the type of knowledge dealt with may also differ. For example, explicit knowledge can be effectively shared when a syntactic boundary is successfully crossed, but tacit knowledge can only be shared effectively when semantic and pragmatic boundaries are successfully crossed. In terms of the facilities and protocols required to cross the boundaries, technology such as using documents and information systems

Table 8.1 Key characteristics of the three types of knowledge boundary

	Syntactic boundary	Semantic boundary	Pragmatic boundary
Level of novelty of collective tasks	Low	Middle	High
Knowledge approach	Transfer	Translation	Transformation
Type of knowledge crossing the boundary	Mainly explicit	Mainly tacit but also explicit	Mainly tacit but also explicit
Facilities/protocols	Technology (documents, information systems)	Social interaction (discussion and forums)	Social interaction (negotiation, co-creation of common grounds)
Main issues concerning knowledge mobilization	Quality of the information, technological issues (usefulness and ease of use)	Perceived value of the discussions, misinterpretations, language, own image, negative comments and preference to ask people for clarifications	Negotiation skills, willing to compromise
Frequency of knowledge mobilization	Sporadic	Rare	Rarest

would be sufficient for crossing a syntactic boundary, while social interaction is important for crossing semantic and pragmatic boundaries. Consequently, the main issues relating to crossing a syntactic boundary would be the quality of information contained in documents, and technological issues such as the usefulness and ease of use of the information systems. The main issues in connection with crossing semantic boundaries, issues such as the perceived value of discussion and the language used, are extremely critical, which could determine whether common understanding and interpretation will be developed. At pragmatic boundaries, major issues include negotiation skills and willingness to compromise, because resolving conflicts is the key to crossing the boundaries. Because of the different level of difficulties inherent within crossing different boundaries, crossing a syntactic boundary has been regarded as the easiest, hence it happens most often among the three. Crossing a pragmatic boundary is the most difficult and happens most rarely in reality.

These knowledge boundaries can erect great barriers to knowledge mobilization, and subsequently hinder coordination and problem solving among individuals, groups/teams, organizations and communities. However, managing knowledge across boundaries is a constant activity owing to the increasing reliance on assembling diverse individuals, groups/teams, organizations and even communities in modern businesses. The pressure from globalization requires business managers to respond and act quickly, which has intensified the need to develop strategies that rapidly overcome knowledge boundaries. Because knowledge is described as localized, embedded and invested in practice (Carlile, 2002, 2004), this specialization of 'knowledge in practice' makes working across boundaries and accommodating knowledge in another practice especially difficult. The next section will discuss boundary-spanning mechanisms to address the issue.

 Critical thinking and reflection
Knowledge boundaries in MNCs

In a multinational corporation (MNC), which type(s) of knowledge boundaries between its 'headquarters' and its 'subsidiaries' do you think would present major challenges to knowledge mobilization and learning processes, and why?

8.2 Boundary-spanning mechanisms

Despite the centrality of knowledge boundaries in business and open innovation, the assumption of permeable boundaries is sometimes taken for granted and yet remains ill understood. This section will look at four specific boundary-spanning mechanisms that can facilitate coordination and problem solving across individuals, groups/teams, organizations and communities. They are termed boundary spanners, boundary objects, boundary practice and boundary discourse. Boundary spanners and boundary objects are two well-established mechanisms, while boundary practice and boundary discourse are relatively new and less developed.

Boundary spanners

The concept of boundary spanners has been used in a variety of contexts with diverse meanings (Kusari *et al*, 2005; Levina and Vaast, 2005; Haas,

2015). The term 'boundary spanner' was first introduced by Michael Tushman in his article on special boundary roles in the innovation process (Tushman, 1977). In earlier years, boundary spanners were most frequently defined as interpreters of environmental conditions and providers of information to decision makers (Leifer and Huber, 1977). This primary focus on the information exchange role of boundary spanners is still in use today. However, the context to which the concept applies has been extended, so that it can be between groups/teams inside an organization, between an organization and its environment, and also between CoPs (Haas, 2015).

As the terminology 'boundary spanner' is generic, it can be used to describe different functions, both inside and outside an organization. A number of definitions are available. The following are representative of different times:

- Persons who operate at the periphery or boundary of an organization, performing organizational relevant tasks, relating the organization with elements outside it (Leifer and Delbecq, 1978).

- Individuals charged with the task of contacting people outside their own group (Friedman and Podolny, 1992).

- Firm members who serve as interfaces between a unit and its environment (Cross and Prusak, 2002; Cross and Parker, 2004).

- Links between a unit and its environment who can play several different functions, such as information exchange, access to resources and group representation (Haas, 2015).

- Individuals who operate at the periphery of an organization and act as exchange agents between the organization and its external environment (Keszey, 2018).

In essence, boundary spanners are human agents who frame and translate knowledge from one domain to another, in an effort to promote knowledge mobilization and learning, and further to facilitate coordination and problem solving among individuals, groups/teams, organizations and communities from different domains (Aldrich and Herker, 1977; Hawkins and Rezazade, 2012; Zhang *et al*, 2015). Boundary spanner studies focus on how human agents use languages and their cognitive power to mediate the movement of knowledge, hence this mechanism is believed to be most effective in moving explicit knowledge. The standing of the human agents and their social relationships in a community, organization or group/team is an important factor in this context.

A variety of terms have been used as alternatives for boundary spanners, including bridge, central connector, linking pin, gatekeeper, liaison role and knowledge broker (Haas, 2015). Based on the membership status of the spanners, the following types of boundary spanner have been differentiated:

- Boundary translators: individuals with membership in only *one* community, organization or group/team (Brown and Duguid, 1998).

- Boundary brokers or boundary crossers: Brown and Duguid (1998) labelled individuals who have membership in *two* communities, organizations or groups/teams involved in the knowledge mobilization process as knowledge brokers, while Hayes and Fitzgerald (2009) labelled them boundary crossers.

- Marginal people: individuals who have membership in *multiple* communities (Star and Griesemer, 1989).

Having membership status within a community, organization or group/team does not necessarily make the job of closing gaps among parties straightforward for boundary spanners. Because of the difference in membership status of different types of boundary spanners, it is argued that boundary translators can be tempted to bias knowledge translation in order to favour one community, organization or group/team over another; this is especially the case for boundary translators because they reside in only one community, organization or group/team (Nonaka, Toyama and Konno, 2000). For boundary brokers or crossers who have dual membership status, research found that working across organizational and occupational boundaries was difficult, demanding and, from a career perspective, potentially dangerous (Hayes and Fitzgerald, 2009). For marginal people, even though they have membership status in multiple communities, organizations and groups/teams, they may still feel unaccepted in all communities, organizations and groups/teams, as the term suggests. This is because membership can only give legitimacy and a certain level of trust; boundary spanners still need to possess the right traits, skills and capabilities, such as personality, political skills and cognitive capabilities, in order to successfully bridge the cognitive gaps between the parties involved (Hawkins and Rezazade, 2012).

This boundary-spanning mechanism is not adjusting an individual's knowledge base, but adjusting information to fit into an individual's knowledge base. Boundary spanners translate and reformulate knowledge from one domain to another. This knowledge mobilization process promotes learning in the parties through building on prior knowledge. The role of boundary spanners can be illustrated as in Figure 8.1. In this case, knowledge

Figure 8.1 Role of boundary spanners in knowledge mobilization

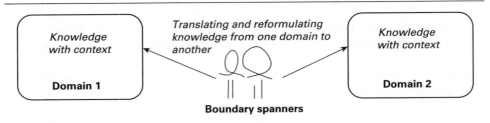

contextualized in Domain 1 and Domain 2 can be shared because the knowledge spanners are performing their roles as translators, and sometimes they reformulate the knowledge for different parties involved in the knowledge mobilization process.

 Critical thinking and reflection
Boundary spanners in MNC

To what extent do you think expatriates can act as boundary spanners in mobilizing knowledge within an MNC?

Boundary objects

The concept of boundary objects was developed by Leigh Star, who initially described boundary objects as being shared and sharable across different problem-solving contexts. In other words, these objects work to establish a shared context that sits in the middle (Star, 1989, 2010). The concept has since been further extended by many scholars. Subsequently, boundary objects came to refer to physical, abstract or mental entities/artefacts that are common to a number of domains and serve as a focal point in collaboration, enabling parties to represent, transform and share knowledge (Carlile, 2002, 2004; Hayes and Fitzgerald, 2009; Hawkins and Rezazade, 2012). A boundary object can be material/physical, digital or linguistic/symbolic in character. An example of a digital boundary object is a three-dimensional virtual workspace that facilitates the mobilization of knowledge in engineering design projects (Alin, Lorio and Taylor, 2013). An example of a linguistic/epistemic boundary object is one that is provided to transform genetics knowledge and science into medical practices that could be used to treat patients (McGivern and Dopson, 2010).

Figure 8.2 Boundary objects attach and transform de-contextualized knowledge

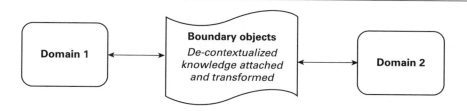

The boundary object concept has proven popular and has been used by an increasing number of analysts to understand various processes and the mobilization of domain-specific knowledge (Hislop, Bosua and Helms, 2018).

Boundary objects are used to de-contextualize and de-personalize knowledge so that it can be transformed from one domain to another. Figure 8.2 illustrates the role of boundary objects in facilitating knowledge mobilization crossing borders. Boundary objects are flexible enough to allow individuals, groups/teams, organizations and communities from different domains to attach localized meanings to the object. However, there is enough common, shared meaning across domains to enable the object to bridge the cognitive gap (Koskinen, 2005). Some examples of boundary objects are assembly drawings and software prototypes. Assembly drawings are among the artefacts in manufacturing industry widely used to facilitate knowledge mobilization between (design/manufacturing/production) engineers and workers on the assembly/testing lines. Similarly, software prototypes serve as artefacts to bridge the cognitive gaps between clients and software developers.

A more systematic analysis of the concept of boundary objects was undertaken by Carlile (2002, 2004). Based on his study to examine knowledge boundaries in new product development involving four business functions – sales/marketing, design engineering, manufacturing engineering and production, Carlile (2002) distinguished four types of boundary objects by adapting Star's work:

- Repositories: such as cost databases, CAD/CAM databases, and parts libraries. They supply a common *reference point* for data, measures or labels across functions that share definitions and values for solving problems.

- Standardized forms and methods: such as standards for reporting findings and engineering change forms. They provide a shared *format* for solving problems across different functional settings. When forms conforming to a mutually understood structure and language are used, defining and categorizing differences and potential consequences become more sharable and less problematic across different settings.

- Artefacts or models: such as sketches, assembly drawings, parts, prototype assemblies, mock-ups and computer simulations. These are simple or complex *representations* that can be observed and used across different functional settings. They depict or demonstrate the current or possible form, fit and function of the differences and dependencies identified at the boundary.
- Maps of boundaries: such as Gantt charts, process maps and workflow matrices. They represent *dependencies* and boundaries that exist between different groups or functions at a more systemic level. Maps help clarify the dependencies between different cross-functional problem-solving efforts that share resources, deliverables and deadlines.

The boundary-spanning knowledge process can be facilitated through the use of boundary objects. However, for boundary objects to be effective, the type of boundary object has to be appropriate to the type of boundary being crossed. Figure 8.3 illustrates the links between the four types of boundary objects (ie repositories, standardized forms and methods, artefacts or models, and maps of boundaries) with the three boundary types (ie syntactic boundary, semantic boundary and pragmatic boundary).

As can be seen from the diagram, repository-type boundary objects are sufficient for crossing syntactic boundaries, because when people have a shared

Figure 8.3 Links between boundary objects and boundary types

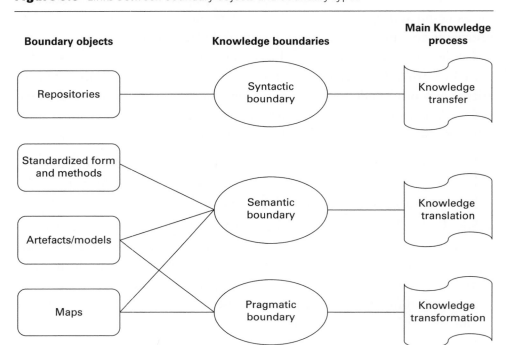

syntax and language in the form of common data and information provided by a repository, they can effectively work across the boundaries. The primary knowledge process involved in spanning syntactic boundaries is knowledge mobilization, where a repository is developed as a common knowledge base, agreed upon and understood by all parties, hence removing the barrier to knowledge transfer and sharing (Carlile, 2002, 2004; Hislop, Bosua and Helms, 2018).

At a semantic boundary, people do not have a shared syntax or language, and may have divergent interpretations and understandings. Working across a semantic boundary is more complex than a syntactic boundary; boundary objects that can facilitate the process of perspective making and taking will need to be developed and used; that is, people need to develop an increased understanding of the perspective of others (Hislop, Bosua and Helms, 2018). Carlile suggests that three types of boundary objects can be used to work across a semantic boundary: standardized forms and methods, artefacts or models, and maps. Standardized forms and methods provide shared means for understanding each other. Artefacts or models such as shared drawings provide a way in which people's differences in perspectives can be communicated and discussed. Maps outline the interdependencies between individuals, groups/teams, organizations or communities and allow the parties to understand how people's perspectives are shaped by their individual, group/team, organization and community interests and co-dependencies. In Carlile's opinion, with the spanning of semantic boundaries, the primary knowledge process is knowledge translation (Carlile, 2002, 2004).

Finally, at a pragmatic boundary, owing to the differences of interest that exist between the parties involved, working across these boundaries is the most complex and difficult. Carlile argues that both artefacts or models and maps are appropriate boundary objects in this context. First, the development and use of maps will allow people to better understand and appreciate the differences of interest in existence. Second, artefacts or models can provide a resource that not only allows people to develop a sense of shared interests and common endeavour, but also to transform their knowledge to achieve a collective goal. Thus, Carlile believes that knowledge transformation is the primary knowledge process at pragmatic boundaries.

In summary, boundary objects can remind parties of common themes, shared meaning of the object, the possibility of making sense of the object by different parties, and the impact of the physical characteristics of the object on cognitive processes.

Boundary practice

Boundary practice is defined as a boundary-spanning mechanism that overcomes a knowledge boundary by engaging agents from different knowledge groups/teams, organizations or communities in collective activities (Hawkins and Rezazade, 2012). The focal unit of analysis of this mechanism is practice. By engaging in collective activities, new knowledge will be generated. Knowledge-spanning functions in boundary practice will not only help share knowledge at the boundary, but also improve one, two or all parties' understanding of the knowledge. Besides the knowledge itself, participating in collective practice may also facilitate understanding of other parties' interpretive framework. All these may spark insightful knowledge connections and thus bridge cognitive gaps. Boundary practice has the capability of engaging knowers from different domains in a shared site of knowing. Engaging in collective practice at the boundary of different knowledge areas creates a situation that facilitates the development of new knowing, in other words, co-generating new knowledge. As already discussed in Chapter 2, Ba theory recognizes the importance of the provision of knowledge space (ie 'Ba') in knowledge creation (Nonaka, Toyama and Konno, 2000). The role of boundary practice in boundary spanning for knowledge mobilization and learning is illustrated in Figure 8.4.

Boundary practice is most effective in addressing knowledge boundaries involving tacit knowledge through learning by doing. However, what makes

Figure 8.4 Role of boundary practice in boundary spanning for knowledge mobilization and learning

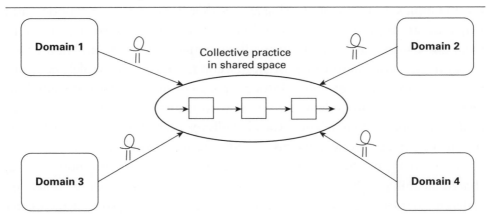

a practice a boundary practice? Two important aspects need to be taken into account in order to answer this question:

- First, compared with boundary work, which is established and routine practice, boundary practice has significant novelties for experts from different domains. Through engagement in a situated series of activities with different knowers, boundary practice provides a zone of possibilities for creating new knowledge and will likely lead to innovation. Of course, boundary work also involves cross-boundary interactions, such as bringing organization or community members into contact with non-members. For example, lawyers and frontline employees often engage in boundary work when talking to clients and customers, respectively. Boundary practice involves an overlap of activities from different agents, but the practice itself is not specialized to a particular individual, group/team, organization or community, because the particular boundary practice emerges out of the context and the participating agents' collective activities (Hawkins and Rezazade, 2012).

- Second, compared with specialized practice, boundary practice should be unassignable or unable to be separated into sub-tasks that can be delegated to experts in each specialized domain. The collective activities should be performed together within a flexible space between the domains of expertise (Nicolini, 2011).

Boundary practice as a boundary-spanning mechanism is a relatively new concept, and research in this area is still in its early stage. In many situations, it is explored in conjunction with other boundary-spanning mechanisms such as boundary objects, because people need to use certain forms of objects in order to perform practice, and vice versa. For example, Star and Griesemer, the originators of the boundary object concept, recognized that individuals using boundary objects sometimes needed to learn how to use them correctly, for example through practice (Star and Griesemer, 1989).

The boundary practice concept, designed to close gaps, is linked to the structural hole bridging metaphor promoted by network theory (Burt, 2004). Structural hole theory will be discussed in detail in Chapter 9, where we will look at knowledge networks.

Boundary discourse

Boundary discourse refers to the *content* of knowledge that shapes the *dialogue* among the experts from distinct domains (Hawkins and Rezazade,

2012). In other words, the primary attention is paid to what is communicated between individuals, groups/teams, organizations or communities that will build knowledge to ultimately allow the parties to close the cognitive gap. This type of boundary-spanning mechanism is most effective with explicit knowledge. In order for participating parties to engage experts from different domains in a dialogue effectively and acquire the needed knowledge, the content, such as the ideas and issues of a dialogue, should have a certain level of conceptual overlap (in-between-ness) with the cognitive schemas of the experts involved, thus they are properly distinct from the dominant discourse within each domain. Thus, when implementing the boundary discourse mechanism, it is highly important to address the issue of how to use languages and lexicons, building on syntactic and semantic knowledge similarities to help the parties to overcome the knowledge boundary.

Similar to boundary practice, boundary discourse is often related to other boundary-spanning mechanisms, in particular boundary spanners and boundary objects, as they all can involve languages (verbal or written) and they are all effective with explicit knowledge. However, the three mechanisms have distinctive differences. Boundary spanners can use verbal or written languages as well as lexicons to translate and reformulate knowledge, so that the other party/parties in the knowledge mobilization and learning process can understand the meaning. The primary interest to boundary spanners is adjusting information to fit into an individual's knowledge base. Boundary objects can be in written form, such as narratives and slogans, which serve as a focal point to attach and transform knowledge among parties so that they can understand each other. The key here is objectifying the knowledge. Boundary discourse used in a dialogue is focused on identifying and adjusting a participating agent's knowledge base, but not objectifying the knowledge as boundary objects do, while knowledge spanners are not focused on adjusting an individual's knowledge base. Boundary objects are used by each party in their own practice, but boundary discourse derives from communal knowledge, which is similar to boundary practice in this regard.

The comparisons among the four boundary-spanning mechanisms are summarized in Table 8.2. The comparisons are conducted from five perspectives:

- Unit of analysis: human agents are the unit of analysis for boundary spanners, artefacts for boundary objects, practice (ie collective activities) for boundary practice, and content of knowledge for boundary discourse. Content of knowledge can be conveyed through both artefacts and human agents, and both human agents and artefacts can participate in practice.

- Important attributes of the units: for human agents as boundary spanners to be effective in bridging gaps between parties, important attributes include membership status, personalities, skills, cognitive capabilities, and various types of relations, such as their social, political and power relations. For boundary objects, important attributes include shared meaning, materiality, physicality, abstraction and mental presence. Engaging and collective activities are crucial for boundary practice. Boundary discourse needs ideas, domains of knowledge and cognitive proximity.

- Type of knowledge that mobilizes at the boundary: among the four boundary-spanning mechanisms, boundary practice is most effective, primarily with tacit knowledge, while the other three mechanisms (boundary spanners, boundary objects and boundary discourse) are most effective mainly with explicit knowledge.

- Knowledge-spanning functions: boundary spanners translate and frame/reformulate knowledge from one domain to another; however, the individual remains contextualized and thus their status and social legitimacy (if it exists) can facilitate or hinder the knowledge-spanning process. In comparison, the main knowledge function of boundary objects is transforming knowledge that can remind parties of common themes, by objectifying, de-contextualizing and de-personalizing concepts that otherwise might have been difficult to notice in the absence of those objects. Boundary practice fills knowledge gaps by the creation of new knowledge between distinct domains of knowing through joint activities. Unlike boundary objects, boundary practice contextualizes the problem and knowledge in a specific context of knowing, hence it allows parties to learn and better understand knowledge. By linking back to the SECI model (Nonaka and Takeuchi, 1995) discussed in Chapter 2, boundary practice is likely to involve knowledge internalization, that is, the 'I' in the SECI model. Finally, boundary discourse enhances the opportunities for knowledge building by sensitizing the parties involved to ideas and themes, selecting and situating the dialogue on specific themes, and articulating and clarifying the knowledge of one side to be transferred to the other side.

- Likelihood of changes to participating party's knowledge base: boundary spanners and boundary objects do not change an individual's knowledge base, but boundary spanners change information to fit into the individual's knowledge base while boundary objects make cognitive gaps disappear or close by objectifying knowledge. Both boundary practice and boundary discourse create new knowledge, hence increase an individual's knowledge base.

Table 8.2 Comparisons between the four types of boundary-spanning mechanisms

	Boundary spanners	Boundary objects	Boundary practice	Boundary discourse
Unit of analysis	Human agents	Presence of artefacts	Practice	Content of knowledge
Important attributes of the unit	Cognitive capabilities and social/political/power relations, skills and personalities, membership status, trust	Shared meaning, materiality, physicality, abstraction or mental presence	Engaging, collective activities	Knowledge, ideas, domains of knowledge, cognitive proximity
Type of knowledge work most effective	Explicit	Explicit	Tacit	Explicit
Knowledge-spanning functions	Translating Framing/reformulating Legitimization	Transforming Objectifying Reminding De-contextualization, De-personalization	Co-creation Learning Understanding Internalization Contextualization	Building Sensitizing Articulation Clarification
Change to individual knowledge base	Not adjusting individual's knowledge base, but adjusting information to fit into it	Objectifying knowledge without changing individual's knowledge base	Co-generating new knowledge to increase knowledge base	Building knowledge to increase knowledge base

To conclude the section, among the four boundary-spanning mechanisms, theories about boundary spanners and boundary objects are well established, while boundary practice and boundary discourse are relatively new. They are all mutually interdependent yet sufficiently distinct from each other. In a knowledge-spanning process, several boundary-spanning mechanisms are usually integrated and utilized by organization experts over time; in other words, a combination of the boundary-spanning mechanisms is often used in knowledge mobilization and learning processes at boundaries. Research has revealed that an individual mechanism can benefit from the compounding effect of being linked together with other mechanisms. In fact, it can be considered that the four boundary-spanning mechanisms provide four complementary perspectives of a boundary-spanning knowledge process, as shown in Figure 8.5. They are the *actor perspective* provided by boundary spanners, the *artefact perspective* provided by boundary objects, the *activity perspective* provided by boundary practice, and the *content perspective* provided by boundary discourse. Boundary spanners represent human agents, who organize, facilitate and coordinate the collective activities inherent within boundary practice. Both boundary spanners and boundary practice may need to use appropriate boundary objects in facilitating knowledge mobilization and learning activities. In any boundary-spanning knowledge process, the content of knowledge provided through knowledge discourse is of paramount importance to both boundary spanners and boundary practice in terms of what is actually communicated or what is actually done. That is why we can confidently conclude that when a number of the boundary-spanning mechanisms are used together in harmony, the boundary-spanning knowledge process will be likely to be more effective and complete.

Figure 8.5 Complementary elements of boundary-spanning knowledge process

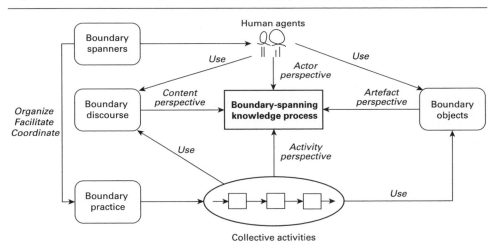

 Critical thinking and reflection
Boundary-spanning mechanisms

If a new project is commissioned to develop a new piece of software for business clients and you are appointed as the project leader, what major barriers do you envisage that may hinder knowledge mobilization within the project team and collaboration with external parties? What type(s) of boundary-spanning mechanisms would you consider using to facilitate the knowledge mobilization process?.

8.3 Boundary-spanning knowledge activities in industrial applications

Based on the foundations of the previous sections discussing the types of knowledge boundaries and various boundary-spanning mechanisms, this section looks at their application in real industrial contexts. Knowledge boundaries can be identified at different levels: individual level, group/team level, organization level or network level; boundary-spanning knowledge activities can take place at those levels as well. This section will present three case studies to illustrate how knowledge boundaries at different levels can be identified and crossed in three application contexts: the automotive, defence and agricultural industries.

Managing an organizational knowledge boundary for open innovation in the automotive industry

An extensive body of literature posits that successful firms thrive because of their ability to manage their innovation effectively, and open innovation has been recognized as a key strategy to achieve higher business performance in an increasingly competitive and turbulent market (Keszey, 2018). There are two types of open innovation: inbound and outbound. Inbound open innovation is when a firm enriches its own knowledge base by accessing external knowledge, for example through technology licensing or acquisition (West and Bogers, 2017). Outbound open innovation is often referred to as commercializing innovation, when the firm's existing knowledge can be exploited outside its boundaries by licensing intellectual property (IP) or by cross-industry innovation (West *et al*, 2014). This case study focuses on inbound open innovation and examines knowledge boundaries at organizational level with major car manufacturers based in Germany (Wilhelm and Dolfsma, 2018).

The automotive industry is a mature, large-scale and knowledge-intensive sector. The process of opening knowledge boundaries can be particularly challenging for firms in this industry as they have been more rigid in changing their well-established internal processes than many other emerging industries, such as the service industry. However, because of customer requirements and the desire for new product features, such as the growing demand from consumers for lighter and fuel-efficient cars with reduced emissions, creating all innovations internally is less viable, in terms not only of financing but also of knowledge provision. Carmakers have reacted to these trends by intensifying collaboration with their first-tier suppliers. Suppliers can be a primary source of product and process innovation in bringing environmental improvements to the firm, and play a critical role in electric vehicle development and assembly, as these activities require a significant amount of special capabilities and specialized knowledge. While the automotive industry can be considered as advanced in managing boundaries with automotive part suppliers, experience in integrating with other external actors outside the industry is at a very nascent stage. This might be problematic, as functional innovations increasingly require the integration of knowledge from distant domains that the established suppliers do not offer. Open innovation does not mean that knowledge boundaries between an organization and its environment will easily disappear. On the contrary, increased openness implies that new boundaries may emerge and need to be bridged for knowledge mobilization across boundaries to be effective (Bengtesson *et al*, 2016).

All three types of knowledge boundaries (the syntactic boundary, semantic boundary and pragmatic boundary) defined by Carlile (2002, 2004) were investigated in this case study, but they were termed slightly differently: information-processing boundaries (corresponding to syntactic boundaries), interpretive boundaries (corresponding to semantic boundaries) and political boundaries (corresponding to pragmatic boundaries). Wilhelm and Dolfsma (2018) believe that information-processing boundaries need to be established first in order to develop shared and stable syntax. Only when a knowledge sender and a knowledge receiver have a shared syntax can they start to recognize knowledge as relevant and potentially valuable, and proceed to exchange it. However, even when a common syntax is present, interpretive differences can still occur between people from different domains. The second type of boundaries, interpretive boundaries, emphasizes the importance of a common meaning of the knowledge shared among actors that come from different domains. The third type, pragmatic or political boundaries, exists because different actors have different interests and preferences in developing electronic vehicles. For example, some actors may simply not be aware of others in the supply chain being in need of certain knowledge. The more distant and novel the knowledge is, the more difficult it would be to mobilize the knowledge across boundaries.

The case study examines the use of gatekeepers as boundary spanners and their role in open innovation, which advocates the importance of networking beyond organizational boundaries. The gatekeepers undertake three tasks in terms of the boundary-spanning knowledge process: external knowledge acquisition, external knowledge translation and internal knowledge dissemination (Whelan *et al*, 2010). First, the gatekeepers scan the outside world for relevant knowledge that is needed by the organization, and when they find it, they acquire the knowledge as necessary. Subsequently, they translate this external knowledge into terms that are meaningful and useful to their more locally oriented colleagues. The translation task includes more than just framing and reformulating the elements of one party's worldview in terms of the worldview of another party; it also involves evaluating and explaining the relevance and significance of the knowledge to the recipient's work practice (Pawlowski and Robey, 2004). Finally, gatekeepers disseminate external knowledge to targeted work colleagues whom they know would be able to use the knowledge they have acquired. Gatekeepers can be dedicated staff or employees who have other roles in the organization already. Within the case study, the gatekeepers' role was performed by the carmakers' innovation managers.

The unique case selected for the study was an open innovation initiative in the German automotive industry that is embedded in a wider, project-based network, termed the automotive innovation network (AIN). The AIN has over 60 official member firms and a large coverage of the German automotive industry with manufacturers like BMW, Porsche and Daimler being active, as well as their first-tier suppliers, engineering service firms, consultants and research institutes. The case study used three methods for data collection: archival data, interviews and field observations. The longitudinal case study continued for five years from 2006 to 2011, which was a significant period for a piece of research work. The case study results reveal some interesting insights into managing knowledge boundaries for open innovation.

Managing information-processing boundaries (syntactic boundaries)

The case study found that the information-processing boundaries were not sufficiently permeable to ideas from small innovators, as private innovators and start-ups were struggling to find the right contact person within a carmaker's organization. Communication channels existed only between carmakers and established suppliers. Identifying the right contact person within a technical development function was difficult, if not impossible, for outsider innovators. Moreover, even if inventors managed to get in touch with the right department, they were often unable to present their ideas to the original equipment manufacturer (OEM) in an attractive way.

In order to overcome the barriers, the AIN set up an innovation competition in January 2007, targeting existing ideas that were used in foreign industries such as medical, pharmaceutical, health, telecommunications, entertainment, aviation and aerospace. The competition designed a standardized format which required a maximum of two-page submissions, including a short description of an innovation, its maturity level, its previous use, a picture or drawing and an explanation of its potential use in the automotive industry. The competition aimed for a broad search scope, hence an innovation could be a product, solution or prototype already in use in other industries that had substantial transfer potential for the automotive industry, or could create substantial added value for the end customer, or could change the use of the vehicle, such as for energy saving. A jury of 20 innovation experts evaluated 150 submissions in the first year and selected the 30 best innovative ideas, which were presented to the public at the annual automobile summit where AIN members and other representatives of the German automotive industry met.

The open competition with a standardized submission format and direct interactions with inventors at the annual automobile event helped the innovation managers of carmakers, as gatekeepers, to identify promising ideas and follow up on them after the competition. It can thus be said that information-processing boundaries were successfully crossed.

Managing interpretive boundaries (semantic boundaries)

Even though innovation managers, as gatekeepers, were successful in helping to overcome information-processing boundaries, interpretive boundaries persisted, as private inventors and carmakers often used the same terminology but attached different meanings to them. Some of the innovation managers did not have the necessary expertise to perform the translation function. The innovation managers had to rely on the jury to evaluate the submissions and select ideas for them. Even the experts on the jury, despite their broad technical expertise, sometimes had difficulties in evaluating the submissions when they were not able to interpret the meanings in the original submission. The lack of a translation of external knowledge that was often passed on internally in 'raw' form was particularly problematic, as it could raise the question whether external knowledge was meaningfully interpreted and whether the evaluation was actually performed fairly and well, or whether the overall evaluation results from the jury were sufficiently consistent.

Most jurors experienced the inflow of diverse ideas in the first year of the competition as overwhelming, so the carmakers decided to concentrate more on targeting new knowledge from within the automotive industry and formulate theme clusters. Despite coming up with the theme clusters (more conventionally represent the current innovation focus of the automotive industry), the competition ended up in the automotive sector again, with submissions mainly from familiar 'faces', and as a result the number of submissions drastically reduced. To tackle the problem, the carmakers decided to introduce an additional cluster in the following year that led to almost doubling the submissions, but did not generate the type of knowledge that carmakers were actually looking for. The introduction of clusters in the innovation competition was successful in raising the quantity, but less so in motivating the right type of submissions. Thus, it seemed that the interpretive boundaries were not overcome by innovation managers who were supposed to perform the 'translation' function in their gatekeepers' role. Rather than seeking direct interaction with outside industrial actors to establish a common meaning to cross the knowledge boundaries, carmakers retreated to the familiar knowledge domains of the automotive industry.

Managing political boundaries (pragmatic boundaries)

Political boundaries are the most persistent knowledge boundaries, and this was reflected in the German carmakers' case. The traditional organization of the carmakers' technical development departments, with a high degree of specialization around traditional technological domains, such as platform, chassis, drivetrain and electric, did not facilitate the adoption of new ideas. Even though innovation managers were active in their gatekeeper's role to disseminate promising ideas to their internal networks with different technical development departments, it was hard to actually convince their colleagues to follow up on the selected ideas. After six years of conducting the innovation competition, with no innovation ideas that actually materialized in a vehicle, the carmaker representatives jointly decided to stop their engagement in the innovation competition. It is fair to say that the innovation managers, as gatekeepers, were not able to overcome political boundaries within their firms.

To conclude the case, Table 8.3 summarizes the three types of knowledge boundaries and the status as to whether they were managed successfully or not. It is evident from the case study that the information-processing boundaries or syntactic boundaries existing between the carmakers and outside inventors, especially small private inventors and start-ups that were not inside the automotive chains, were bridged successfully. By using a standard template, outside inventors were able to submit their innovations and the expert jury were able to evaluate and select promising ideas.

The interpretive boundaries or semantic boundaries between the inventors and carmakers were not successfully crossed. Even though innovations from inventors were submitted, innovation managers could not understand the meaning of the ideas because of the technical terms used in the submissions, and had to rely on technical experts' judgement on the submissions. The jury experts also experienced difficulties in comprehending some of the innovations and were not able to fully understand and appreciate the ideas received. Hence, it raised a question about the fairness and consistency of the overall evaluation process. Furthermore, the innovation managers were not able to translate the innovations selected into ideas that their technical colleagues could understand, and therefore it was not possible to convince the technical departments to follow up on any of the selected innovations from external inventors. Besides the boundary spanners (innovation managers and experts within the firms) and the boundary objects (standardized submission forms), there were plenty of dialogues centred on the innovative ideas going on all the time, hence boundary discourse was also used during the gatekeepers' efforts in closing the interpretive boundaries.

To make things worse, different technical development departments within a firm had very different domain knowledge. These departments were not really interested in the innovations selected by the jury and recommended by the innovation managers, especially if an innovation would require colleagues to obtain a great deal of new knowledge to adapt the innovation for their vehicle, which would put them out of their comfort zone. Even though a combination of boundary-spanning mechanisms was used, the political boundaries were not crossed.

This case study provides insights into identification of the three types of knowledge boundaries and how gatekeepers (such as the innovation managers from different carmakers who were active in the open innovation initiative) strived to cross these knowledge boundaries. The case showed that the information-processing boundary existed in different carmakers' organizations prior to the innovation competition. Outside industry actors chose the wrong presentation format when they submitted their ideas, and did not use

Table 8.3 How three types of knowledge boundary were managed in the German carmakers' case

Boundary type	Parties at the boundary	Status of the gaps	Boundary mechanisms used
Information processing boundary (syntactic)	Between carmakers and outside inventors	Successfully closed	Boundary spanners (innovation managers, experts on competition jury), boundary objects (standardized form for innovation submission)
Interpretive boundaries (semantic)	Between inventors and carmakers, between innovation management team and technical development departments	Not successfully closed	Boundary spanners (innovation managers, experts on competition jury), boundary objects (standardized form for innovation submission), boundary discourse (dialogue between innovation managers, experts and technical development colleagues)
Political boundaries (pragmatic)	Between traditionally organized technical departments	Not successfully closed	Boundary spanners (innovation managers), boundary objects (standardized form for innovation submission), boundary discourse (dialogue between innovation managers and technical development colleagues)

the terminology that was requested by the carmakers. The main findings of the case study led to three propositions (Wilhelm and Dolfsma, 2018):

- When gatekeepers fulfil their external knowledge acquisition role, for example by inviting ideas submitted in a standardized format, a common syntax between actors within and outside the organization is created, and the permeability of information-processing boundaries increases.

- Despite the presence of a common syntax, outside knowledge is not meaningfully interpreted when gatekeepers fail to fulfil their external knowledge translation role, resulting in the impermeability of interpretive boundaries.

- Once interpretive boundaries remain intact, political boundaries are likely to remain impermeable too, even though gatekeepers managed to build up external legitimacy for new knowledge.

Crossing knowledge boundaries in the case of networked projects in the defence industry

Big projects span boundaries, bringing together multiple organizations that enable cross-boundary teams to contribute their collective knowledge assets. This case study demonstrates how knowledge boundaries can be identified and knowledge gaps can be closed in cross-boundary projects at organizational and individual levels (Swart and Harvey, 2011).

Project teams are temporary organizations formed of individuals who have, presumably, been chosen for their skills, knowledge and networks they can bring to the project. Members of a project team can be divided into groups: visible members and invisible members. Invisible members are indirect members such as subcontractors or suppliers in a project even though they are not direct members. This means that a project team's knowledge is not just that held by visible members, but includes that available to the team through its invisible members or through the network of contacts the team members have and the project sponsors are willing to use for the project (Swart and Harvey, 2011).

Project team members may lack mutual social awareness, commitment to a common goal, shared performance norms and equal liability for the outcomes (Ajmal, Helo and Kekale, 2010). Because project teams are typically transient in nature, knowledge boundaries between member groups and between organizations are not static but highly dynamic, and they lack well-defined mechanisms for knowledge mobilization and learning. However, knowledge must flow within project teams if the essence of teamwork is to be established. This is of particular importance in a cross-boundary team as no single organization holds all the assets or specialities required to deliver the knowledge alone.

Swart and Harvey (2011) presented a case study of networked projects spanning the UK Ministry of Defence (MoD) and defence industry boundary. The research used a combination of focus group, semi-structured interview, survey and cross-sector comparators to collect data from individuals, primarily project leaders and consultants, and groups.

The main findings from the case study include:

- Project knowledge is interconnected and dynamic: a knowledge typology is developed with links between different types of knowledge found in the case. Many types of direct links and some hidden links are observed. The links are needed for the whole knowledge set to develop and deliver effective projects. Lack of awareness of the links is likely to be a barrier to knowledge development where the types are considered in isolation while a holistic view is required.

- Knowledge levels differ: different levels of knowledge were found on each side of every cross-boundary team. This should be seen as a positive attribute, because each party needed enough knowledge from right across the typology to engage effectively with the whole team. Furthermore, knowledge levels vary along the project cycle – with the relative weight of the different types of knowledge needed varying in different phases.

- Knowledge shapes differ across boundaries at organizational level: the concept of T-shaped knowledge was used to help understand the knowledge required in the case study (Hansen and Oetinger, 2001). A T-shaped knowledge model is a two-dimensional model developed with visuals depicting the relative depth and breadth of an organization's knowledge. Knowledge depth represents the specialist knowledge and is shown as the downward stroke of the T-shape, while knowledge breadth represents the general knowledge across different areas and is shown in the horizontal stroke of the T-shape. Drawing T-shaped knowledge models allowed organizations to see the knowledge dependencies and level of overlap. The model creates a conversation that builds new understanding within an organization. If there is little overlap between two T-shaped models of two organizations, a knowledge intermediary is needed to add value by translating, interpreting and connecting people and their knowledge for the consumption of others.

- Knowledge at individual level: The case study further drilled down into the location of the knowledge on which a team relies, from the organization level to the individual level. The shape of an individual's knowledge model and distribution of knowledge types were different for each part of the team. In the case of networked projects, a design engineer's T-shaped model is much thinner but taller than that of a project manager, because a design engineer's knowledge breadth is not as good as a project manager's but engineers have in-depth knowledge in technology, design history and design process which are comparably big parts of their holdings. If their T-shaped models have no overlap it will be difficult for people to interact; in other words, there are bigger knowledge gaps between them. People with very different T-shapes are likely to find it difficult to work across a boundary, because their different knowledge holdings mean that they will approach problems in very different ways and they want different knowledge to compensate for their own knowledge gaps. Understanding the differences in individuals' knowledge shapes and what underpins them is a critical first step towards a successful interface. If individuals' T-shaped knowledge models are very different or the boundary fractious, an interfacing layer may be required. Individuals who are aware of their personal knowledge shape and how it interlocks with those around them are more able to manage communication and knowledge flow.

- A cross-boundary project team develops new knowledge: knowledge was found to be developed through unconstrained usage and interaction. Interacting with people holding the same type of knowledge and those with a different set of knowledge were both seen to be valuable, but sufficient overlap of knowledge was required in order for people to have the same language and desire to engage. In general, knowledge is perceived as slow to develop, with the barriers far outweighing the enablers. However, a cross-boundary team will develop new knowledge much faster than its traditional counterparts because of the knowledge activities taking place at the boundaries, where people can hold and access more knowledge with far less effort because the interconnected knowledge types are managed as a holistic whole and held within context. The diversity of background, networks and experience inherent in a cross-boundary team are connected to form a valuable, wide knowledge pool.

To summarize, the case study demonstrates that identifying knowledge boundaries and developing knowledge shapes at both organizational level and individual level are critical, as the very nature of success in a networked project is to integrate the various shapes and forms of knowledge to deliver practical results.

Defining ontologies for crossing knowledge boundaries in agricultural value chains

This case study examines knowledge boundaries in the context of agricultural value chains. First, the research identifies potential knowledge boundaries that exist between different stages of a value chain in the agri-food production system (Boshkoska, Liu and Chen, 2018). Then, an ontology is created using software tool OntoGen. Finally, based on the ontology, a decision support system is proposed for the evaluation of the level to which the boundaries may be crossed.

One of the difficulties in offering decision support for value chain management results from the knowledge boundaries that exist between the different stages of a value chain, or even between people within the same stage but with different levels of knowledge, such as between novices and experienced practitioners (Carlile, 2002). In a value chain, knowledge needs to flow and mobilize along two dimensions: one is the vertical dimension, that is, among different value chain stages; in other words, from farm/producers, through food processors, distributors/wholesalers, retailers to fork (consumption). The other dimension is horizontal, that is, different organizations at the same stage of the value chain, for example a cluster of farmers as food producers. Subsequently, knowledge boundaries potentially exist on both of these dimensions. Vertically, organizations situated at different value chain stages have different knowledge domains, for example farmers, cooperatives, food processors, distributors/wholesalers, retailers and consumers sit in their own knowledge domain (Chen, Liu and Oderanti, 2017). Horizontally, organizations may set up knowledge boundaries on purpose, such as through regulations, in order to protect their knowledge assets (Lee, Min and Lee, 2017). Knowledge mobilization and learning activities have been generally accepted as positive means to opening a boundary; it has been argued that regulations are just the other side of the coin of a boundary, that is, to close a boundary, so that an organization's knowledge can be protected or at least shared with measured/controlled risk level.

Besides the three types of knowledge boundaries (syntactic, semantic and pragmatic) proposed by Carlile (2002, 2004), Tell *et al* (2017) classified knowledge boundaries in five categories: individual, domain specific, task oriented, spatial and temporal. Based on the understanding of relevant knowledge boundary concepts, the case study analysed over 60 articles discussing knowledge boundaries, and constructed a knowledge boundary ontology for agricultural value chains. Figure 8.6 is a representation of the ontology, with categories of boundary-spanning mechanisms (in rectangle) and some examples of each category (on the outer layer).

The five categories of boundary-spanning mechanisms most often used in agricultural value chains, based on the analysis of the article samples, are: cross-boundary education, organization and technology, knowledge sharing and teams, innovation and boundary objects, and learning and joint development. Examples of organization and technology are community of communities and technological tools. Other examples recommended in other categories include knowledge-sharing incentives, cross-boundary teams, open innovation

Figure 8.6 An ontology of knowledge boundaries and boundary-spanning mechanisms

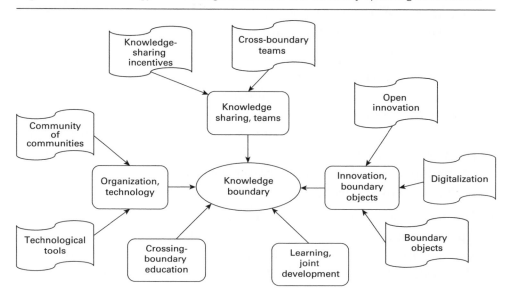

strategy, digitalization, and boundary objects. Compared with the studies from Carlile (2002, 2004) and Tell *et al* (2017), this case study reveals a number of new boundary-spanning mechanisms, hence it extends existing knowledge in the literature.

Based on the above ontology, a decision support system has been developed to help decision makers in the agricultural value chains to make concerted decisions. The ontology and the decision system were further evaluated using three different types of agri-food chains: a tomato value chain, a Chinese leaf value chain and a cauliflower value chain (Boshkoska *et al*, 2019).

Key learning points

- A knowledge boundary represents the limit or border of an agent's knowledge base in relation to a different domain of knowledge. Knowledge boundaries are usually considered as barriers to knowledge mobilization and learning.

- Three types of knowledge boundaries proposed by Paul Carlile are widely accepted: syntactic boundary, semantic boundary and pragmatic boundary.

- A syntactic boundary is assumed to have a low level of novelty of the collective tasks being undertaken and is the easiest to work across. At a syntactic boundary, people share a common logic and a set of values. A common lexicon can be developed for knowledge mobilization crossing syntactic boundaries. A syntactic boundary is also referred to as an information-processing boundary.

- At a semantic boundary, people do not have shared logic or a shared set of values. Instead, people may have different understandings and interpretations of the same knowledge. In order to cross a semantic boundary, people will need to develop an understanding of and sensitivity to other people's understandings and interpretations. The emphasis is on knowledge translation and common meaning development. A semantic boundary is also known as an interpretive boundary.

- The pragmatic boundary is also referred to as a political boundary. At this type of boundary, the novelty level of the collective tasks is at its highest, where people not only have different interpretations and understandings of issues/events, they also have different interests, which ultimately may result in conflicts among different parties and actors participating in the activities and events.

- This chapter discussed four boundary-spanning mechanisms: boundary spanners, boundary objects, boundary practice and boundary discourse. Among the four mechanisms, boundary practice is most effective in dealing with tacit knowledge, and the other three mechanisms are more effective in dealing with explicit knowledge. Different mechanisms are often used in combination in reality.

- Boundary spanners are human agents who frame/reframe and translate knowledge from one domain to another, in an effort to promote knowledge mobilization and learning, further to facilitate coordination and problem solving. This boundary-spanning mechanism does not adjust an individual's knowledge base, but adjusts information to fit into an individual's knowledge base.

- Boundary objects are entities/artefacts that are common to a number of domains or communities and serve as a focal point in collaboration, enabling parties to present, transform and share knowledge. The objects can be physical, abstract or mental. Four types of boundary objects defined by Paul Carlile by adapting Leigh Star's work are: repositories, standard forms and methods, artefacts or models, and maps.

- Boundary practice overcomes a knowledge boundary by engaging agents from different domains in collective activities in a shared site of knowing, during which new knowledge is co-created. Boundary practice as a boundary-spanning mechanism is a relatively new concept, compared with boundary spanners and boundary objects.

- Boundary discourse refers to the content of knowledge that shapes the dialogue among experts from distinct domains. The primary attention is paid to what is communicated between parties that will build knowledge to ultimately allow them to close the cognitive gap.

- Knowledge boundaries can be observed in various application areas and industries. Different boundary-spanning mechanisms should be carefully selected to help cross different boundaries.

Review questions

- What do you think are the main reasons for knowledge boundaries to exist? Can you think of any situations where knowledge boundaries are created by people without realizing they are doing it, and boundaries are created on purpose? Use examples that you are familiar with, such as the organizations you have worked for or studied with, to support your answers.

- About the three types of knowledge boundaries: syntactic, semantic and pragmatic, do you think they can be clearly isolated or they are mixed with each other in practice?

- Why is a pragmatic boundary more difficult to work across than semantic or syntactic boundaries?

- How important do you think membership status is in implementing boundary spanners as a mechanism to cross knowledge boundaries? By having membership status within an organization or a community, is it enough to make the boundary-crossing process straightforward?

- Is an individual's knowledge base changed during a boundary-spanning process using boundary spanners?

- Can you give some examples of boundary objects that are not in a physical form?

- Why are standardized forms and templates often used at work as an effective boundary object to facilitate knowledge mobilization?

- Why is boundary practice most effective in closing boundaries where tacit knowledge rather than explicit knowledge is involved?

- What links can you see between boundary practice and 'Ba' theory?

- What makes a practice a boundary practice? Compare a boundary practice with an organization's established, routine practice. Also compare a boundary practice with specialized practice.

- Do you think boundary discourse can be implemented on its own as a boundary-spanning mechanism without being used in conjunction with other mechanisms?

- What do you think are the main knowledge-spanning functions taking place using boundary spanners, boundary objects, boundary practice and boundary discourse?

- What have you learned from the automotive case study presented in Section 8.3 in terms of crossing knowledge boundaries using the boundary-spanning mechanisms?

- Why is a T-shaped knowledge model useful in crossing knowledge boundaries?

References

Ajmal, M, Helo, P and Kekale, T (2010) Critical factors for knowledge management in project business, *Journal of Knowledge Management*, **14** (1), pp 156–68

Aldrich, H and Herker, D (1977) Boundary spanning roles and organization structure, *Academy of Management Review*, **2** (2), pp 217–30

Alin, P, Lorio, J and Taylor, J (2013) Digital boundary objects as negotiation facilitators: spanning boundaries in virtual engineering project networks, *Project Management Journal*, **44** (3), pp 48–63

Bechky, B A (2003) Sharing meaning across occupational communities: the transformation of understanding on a production floor, *Organization Science*, **14** (3), pp 312–30

Bengtsson, L *et al* (2016) Open innovation: managing knowledge integration across multiple boundaries, in *Managing Knowledge Integration Across Boundaries*, ed F Tell *et al*, pp 87–105, Oxford University Press, Oxford

Boshkoska, B M, Liu, S and Chen, H (2018) Towards a knowledge management framework for crossing knowledge boundaries in agricultural value chain, *Journal of Decision Systems*, **27** (s1), pp 88–97

Boshkoska, B M *et al* (2019, in review) A Decision support system for evaluation of the knowledge sharing crossing boundaries in agri-food value chains, *Computers in Industry*

Brown, J S and Duguid, P (1998) Organizing knowledge, *California Management Review*, **40** (3), pp 90–111

Burt, R S (2004) Structural holes and good ideas, *American Journal of Sociology*, **110** (2), pp 349–99

Carlile, P (2002) A pragmatic view of knowledge and boundaries: boundary objects in new product development, *Organization Science*, 14 (4), pp 442–55

Carlile, P (2004) Transferring, translating and transforming: an integrative framework for managing knowledge across boundaries, *Organization Science*, 15 (5), pp 555–68

Chen, H, Liu, S and Oderanti, F (2017) A knowledge network and mobilization framework for lean supply chain decisions in agri-food industry, *International Journal of Decision Support System Technology*, 9 (4), pp 37–48

Cross, R L and Parker, A (2004) *The Hidden Power of Social Networks: Understanding how work really gets done in organizations*, Harvard Business School Press, Boston, MA

Cross, R and Prusak, L (2002) The people who make organizations go or stop, *Harvard Business Review*, 80 (6), pp 5–12

Filstad, C, Simeonova, B and Visser, M (2018) Crossing power and knowledge boundaries in learning and knowledge sharing: The role of ESM, *The Learning Organization*, 25 (3), pp 159–68

Friedman, R A and Podolny, J (1992) Differentiation of boundary spanning roles: labour negotiations and implications for role conflict, *Administrative Science Quarterly*, 37 (1), pp 28–47

Haas, A (2015) Crowding at the frontier: boundary spanners, gatekeepers and knowledge brokers, *Journal of Knowledge Management*, 19 (5), pp 1029–47

Hansen, M and Oetinger, B (2001) Introducing T-shaped managers: knowledge management's next generation, *Harvard Business Review*, 79 (3), pp 106–16

Hawkins, M A and Rezazade, M H (2012) Knowledge boundary spanning process: synthesizing four spanning mechanisms, *Management Decisions*, 50 (10), pp 1800–15

Hayes, K and Fitzgerald, J (2009) Managing occupational boundaries to improve innovation outcomes in industry-research organizations, *Journal of Management and Organization*, 15 (4), pp 423–37

Hislop, D, Bosua, R and Helms, R (2018) *Knowledge Management in Organizations: A critical introduction*, 4th edn, Oxford University Press, Oxford

Jashapara, A (2011) *Knowledge Management: An integrated approach*, 2nd edn, Pearson Education, Harlow

Keszey, T (2018) Boundary spanners' knowledge sharing for innovation success in turbulent times, *Journal of Knowledge Management*, 22 (5), pp 1061–81

Koskinen, K U (2005) Metaphoric boundary objects as co-ordinating mechanisms in the knowledge sharing of innovation processes, *European Journal of Innovation Management*, 8 (3), p 323

Kusari, S *et al* (2005) Trust and control mechanisms in organizational boundary spanners' cognitions and behaviours, Academy of Management Best Conference Paper

Lee, J, Min, J and Lee, H (2017) Setting a knowledge boundary across teams: knowledge protection regulation for inter-team co-ordination and team performance, *Journal of Knowledge Management*, 21 (2), pp 254–74

Leifer, R and Delbecq, A (1978) Organizational/environmental interchange: a model for boundary spanning activity, *Academy of Management Review*, 3 (1), pp 40–51

Leifer, R and Huber, G P (1977) Relations among perceived environmental uncertainty, organization structure and boundary-spanning behaviour, *Administrative Science Quarterly*, **22** (2), pp 235–47

Levina, N and Vaast, E (2005) The emergence of boundary spanning competence in practice: implications for implementation and use of information systems, *MIS Quarterly*, **29** (2), pp 335–63

McGivern, G and Dopson, S (2010) Inter-epistemic power and transforming knowledge objects in a biomedical network, *Organization Studies*, **31** (12), pp 1667–86

Nicolini, D (2011) Practice as the site of knowing: insights from the field of telemedicine, *Organization Science*, **22** (3), pp 602–20

Nonaka, I and Takeuchi, H (1995) *The Knowledge Creating Company*, Oxford University Press, New York

Nonaka, I, Toyama, R and Konno, N (2000) SECI, Ba and leadership: a unified model of dynamic knowledge creation, *Long Range Planning*, **33**, pp 5–34

Oxford Dictionary (2005) *The Oxford Dictionary*, Oxford University Press, Oxford

Pawlowski, S D and Robey, D (2004) Bridging user organizations: knowledge brokering and the work of information technology professional, *MIS Quarterly*, **28** (4), pp 645–72

Star, S L (1989) The structure of ill-structured solutions: boundary objects and heterogeneous distributed problem solving, in *Reading in Distributed Artificial Intelligence*, ed M Huhns and L Gasser, Morgan Kaufman, Menlo Park, CA

Star, S L (2010) This is not a boundary object: reflections on the origin of a concept, *Science, Technology and Human Values*, **35** (5), pp 601–17

Star, S L and Griesemer, J (1989) Institutional ecology, translations and boundary objects: amateurs and professionals in Berkeley's Museum of Vertebrate Zoology, *Social Studies of Science*, **19** (3), pp 387–420

Swart, J and Harvey, P (2011) Identifying knowledge boundaries: the case of networked projects, *Journal of Knowledge Management*, **15** (5), pp 703–21

Tell, F *et al* (2017) *Managing Knowledge Integration Across Boundaries*, Oxford University Press, Oxford

Tushman, M (1977) Special boundary roles in the innovation process, *Administrative Science Quarterly*, **22** (4), pp 587–605

West, J and Bogers, M (2017) Open innovation: current status and research opportunities, *Innovation*, **19** (1), pp 43–50

West, J *et al* (2014) Open innovation: the next decade, *Research Policy*, **43** (5), pp 805–11

Whelan, E *et al* (2010) How Internet technologies impact information flows in R&D: reconsidering the technological gatekeeper, *R&D Management*, **40** (4), pp 400–13

Wilhelm, M and Dolfsma, W (2018) Managing knowledge boundaries for open innovation: lessons from the automotive industry, *International Journal of Operations and Production Management*, **38** (1), pp 230–48

Zhang, C, Wu, F and Henke, J W (2015) Leveraging boundary spanning capabilities to encourage supplier investment: a comparative study, *Industrial Marketing and Management*, **49** (8), pp 84–94

Knowledge networks

09

Learning outcomes

After completing this chapter, the reader will be able to:

- define knowledge networks;
- explain key properties of knowledge networks;
- appreciate the effect of knowledge network properties on knowledge sharing and learning.

Based on discussion from previous chapters, we know that explicit knowledge can be transferred/shared indirectly through various technologies; for example, explicit knowledge travels over computer networks, while tacit knowledge requires direct interaction and sharing of experience between two or more individuals, groups, organization units or organizations. Both technological and social networks are important to knowledge sharing crossing boundaries. This chapter will introduce the concept of knowledge networks and examines the main properties of knowledge networks from a social relations point of view. Knowledge networks from a technology point of view will be discussed in Chapter 10.

9.1 Introduction

A knowledge network can be defined as a set of nodes that serve as heterogeneously distributed repositories of knowledge and agents that search for, adopt, transmit and create knowledge (Phelps, Heidl and Wadhwa, 2012). Nodes may be individuals or higher-level collectives, such as groups, teams, organizational units, organizations, communities or even nation states. Most knowledge nodes have double roles: they can be simultaneously sources and recipients of knowledge. A second important element in the knowledge network composition is social relationships between nodes. The relationships are the linkages among nodes, representing not only knowledge combination possibilities and capabilities but also knowledge-flow channels, that is, these relationships constitute a means by which nodes can search for knowledge, a medium through which knowledge diffuses and flows, and a lens through which nodes evaluate each other (Podolny, 2001). Ideally, one actor in the network sets off a chain reaction, then every node can be reached quickly with the least burden on any specific nodes. Knowledge networks have traditionally considered face-to-face interactions. The concept has expanded to include the use of electronic platforms such as the DBLP citation network, the GitHub collaboration network and LinkedIn (Shi, Yang and Weninger, 2017). Knowledge networks can be interpersonal, intra-organizational or inter-organizational.

Knowledge networks are related to social networks, because knowledge creation and sharing is often seen as a social process (Saifi, Dillon and McQueen, 2016), as the SECI model, for example, advocated. However, knowledge networks and social networks are not isomorphic but rather de-coupled, in the sense that they have their own unique structural features and content flows (Brennecke and Rank, 2017). The basic building blocks or 'nodes' of a knowledge network are knowledge elements, such as technological knowledge, which are the fundamental components of an invention. Explicit knowledge elements are often embodied in discrete artefacts such as patents, products, processes or scientific publications. The connections or ties between knowledge elements result from their combination in the process of knowledge creation and invention. Ties in a knowledge network thus indicate the degree of relatedness in the subject matters of individual knowledge elements, with elements that have been combined in inventions more often being more closely related. The position of each knowledge element in a knowledge network reflects its combinatorial history or potential.

Based on this knowledge network definition, this chapter examines three categories of knowledge network properties in the following three sections: network structural properties, relational properties and nodal properties. Integrated in each section is discussion of how knowledge network properties affect knowledge sharing and learning (including knowledge properties), as well as knowledge creation and innovation. Figure 9.1 illustrates the main knowledge network properties covered in this chapter.

Figure 9.1 Knowledge network properties

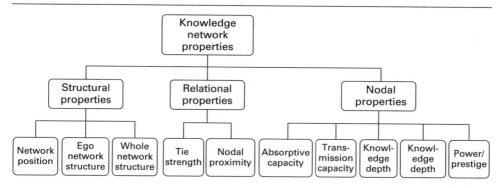

As shown in the diagram, the next section discusses the structural properties of knowledge networks, including network position, ego network structure and whole network structure. Relational properties are presented in Section 9.3, including the strength of ties and nodal proximity (such as similarity between nodes in terms of competitiveness, expertise, status and personality, as well as geographic distance between ties). Finally, Section 9.4 examines nodal properties characterized by a node's absorptive capacity, transmission capacity, depth of knowledge and diversity of knowledge of contacts, and the power or prestige the nodes possess. As a whole, this chapter provides an overall picture of knowledge network properties and how they impact on knowledge activities at different levels, that is, from interpersonal to intra-organizational to inter-organizational levels.

9.2 Network structural properties

Three structural features of knowledge networks have been distinguished: network position – the location of a node relative to others, ego network structure – the pattern of ties within a focal node's immediate set of contacts, and whole network structure – the pattern of ties among all nodes in a network. These features can be studied at different levels, that is, with regard to the interpersonal knowledge network, intra-organizational knowledge network, inter-organizational network, and cross-level analysis.

Network position

An **individual's** network position captures a person's social proximity to other individuals in a network. This proximity can be interpreted from two perspectives: social cohesion and structural equivalence. Social cohesion refers to the number, length and strength of the paths that connect individuals. Structural equivalence is about the similarity of their profiles of network relations.

The cohesion perspective views ties as pipes through which knowledge flows and characterizes network position in terms of centrality, which is the extent to which an individual is well connected to others in the network, both directly and indirectly. Broadly, centrality refers to the number of ties that an actor has with others in a network. These ties can provide structurally advantageous positions that support enhanced learning and improved knowledge acquisition. Centrality positions in knowledge networks have been associated with influence and power. Network centrality can be a legitimate indicator of knowledge acquisition capability. However, most often it is implicitly assumed that all actors within a network possess the same level of domain knowledge. That is, knowledge ties are interpreted as binary (either present or not) to determine centrality. In this case, centrality reflects the breadth of knowledge acquisition but not its intensity or frequency (Sasidharan, 2019).

It is believed that centrality provides individuals with timelier access to more, richer and more diverse knowledge, increasing the extent to which they learn from their network and their potential to synthesize and integrate this knowledge into novel ideas (Burt, 2004). Besides accessing knowledge, central individuals have more power to influence other people, which can increase their ability and motivation to adopt and implement innovations (Audia and Goncalo, 2007). However, this last point has been contradicted by other research. For example, McFadyen and Cannella (2004) conclude that the costs of more ties can ultimately exceed their benefits. Furthermore, it is suggested that the influence of network position may depend on whether an individual's ties span organizational boundaries (Phelps, Heidl and Wadhwa, 2012). It is the boundary-spanning ties that provide access to diverse knowledge, because peripheral players can act on diverse knowledge free from the constraining influence of others resulting from intra-organizational ties.

In contrast to cohesion perspective, structural equivalence defines social proximity as the similarity of two nodes' profiles of network relations. Equivalent nodes occupy substitutable social roles and compete for resources provided by others to which they are jointly connected, increasing their incentives to imitate each other to ensure that no one has an advantage (Burt, 2004).

While interpersonal knowledge network study focuses on the relationships among individual members of a collective within an organization unit, such as a team or division, **intra-organizational** knowledge network study focuses on the relationships these collectives have with each other. At the intra-organizational level, units that are more central have more and shorter paths to other knowledge sources in their intra-organizational networks. They are able to access and obtain more knowledge of greater fidelity. In other words, an organizational unit's network centrality enhances its knowledge activity. Furthermore, if an organizational unit maintains organizational boundary-crossing ties, other units in the same organization will consider it an important source of diverse knowledge and increase their motivation to share knowledge with, and learn from, the unit. It should be noted that maintaining direct ties consumes resources, especially for units with little absorptive capacity, so the costs of maintaining numerous relationships can exceed their knowledge benefits. Research further reveals that the costs of maintaining direct ties to transfer codified, explicit knowledge typically exceed their benefits, because such types of knowledge can be effectively transmitted and absorbed without such social ties; however, direct ties increase the efficiency of sharing tacit knowledge (Tsai, 2001; Hansen, Mors and Lovas, 2005).

At the **inter-organizational level**, centrality can be defined as the closeness of a firm's position to the centre of the network (Dong and Yang, 2016). Generally speaking, the closer a firm is to the centre of a network, the more opportunities it has to contact its partners in the network, hence enabling it to acquire more knowledge from multiple sources (Wang, Chen and Fang, 2018). Occupying positions near the centre of the network, a firm tends to strengthen its knowledge integration and application capabilities in its effort to absorb, incorporate and utilize newly acquired knowledge to secure its competitive advantages.

However, there is no agreement on whether having a greater number of direct ties contributes to the positive impact on a firm's knowledge sharing and innovation performance. On the one hand, having a greater number of partners may imply greater access to knowledge sources. On the other, it can be argued that an increasing reliance on partners for knowledge can have a negative effect on knowledge creation. Also, maintaining an increasing number of inter-organizational ties can be costly (Phelps, Heidl and Wadhwa, 2012).

However, there seems to be agreement on the extent to which the depth and diversity of knowledge to which an organization has access via its partnerships is beneficial. When indirect ties are incorporated into a network's centrality, organizations whose direct ties connect them to a larger number of indirect ties have timelier access to more diverse knowledge, which should increase the organization's knowledge sharing and organizational learning. An organization's network position also affects how strongly it can influence the decisions of others. For example, greater centrality is usually associated with higher social status, and higher social status organizations tend to be more influential on others' decisions.

Ego network structure

Ego refers to the focal nodes in a network. This network structural feature is about whether a focal node's direct contacts have ties to each other or not: in other words, triadic closure. When two of the ego's direct contacts do not share a tie, it is said that a 'structural hole' exists between them. When all three nodes (the ego and its two direct contacts) maintain ties with one another, it is said that the triad is closed ('network closure'). Ego network density captures the extent to which triads in an ego network are closed, while measures of structural holes capture the extent to which triads are open. Both closure theory and structural holes theory have claimed to be the source of social capital. The closure theory argues that networks where every node is connected, ie dense networks or strong ties, are a primary source of social capital, because closure can facilitate trust, strong relations and reliable communication channels. On the other hand, structural holes theory argues that weak ties separate non-redundant sources of knowledge and are thus an opportunity to broker the flow of knowledge between nodes (Rangachari, 2009; Kim et al, 2014).

In terms of the impact of the ego network structure on knowledge sharing at **interpersonal level**, there have been consistent results and explanations. Some studies show that network density increases knowledge sharing among network contacts and enhances learning. Other studies found a positive effect of structural holes on individual knowledge creation. This positive effect increases with the strength of the ego's ties (McFadyen, Semadeni and Cannella, 2009). Because tie strength and network density tend to be mutually reinforcing and strongly correlated, a trade-off exists between social cohesion in an ego network and its structural diversity (characterized by structural holes). While social cohesion from tie strength and network closure promote greater knowledge flows, structurally diverse ego networks with structural holes reduce knowledge flows. On a network boundary, density among the ego's contacts can enhance knowledge sharing and learning, and contacts that span structural holes beyond the network can facilitate knowledge creation and learning by ensuring that novel knowledge flows into the network. Greater ego network density combined with contacts having more diverse expertise or more collaborative ties themselves can increase an individual's knowledge production, because network density facilitates trust and reciprocity among network members, which increases their willingness to share their diverse knowledge with the ego (Fleming, Mingo and Chen, 2007).

At the **intra-organizational level** where organizational units (ie groups and divisions) are the analysis units, groups combining high internal density with more compositionally diverse members exhibit greater knowledge creation and greater knowledge flows. This is because diverse group members (in terms of their demographic characteristics or expertise or proxies for structural holes) may have different sets of extramural contacts and knowledge sources, hence are more likely able to span organizational boundaries during their knowledge-sharing and learning processes (Brennecke and Rank, 2017). Greater internal density increases internal knowledge flows and shared understanding of who knows what in a group, which allows the diverse external knowledge inflows to be utilized more effectively in knowledge creation (Hulsheger, Anderson and Salgado, 2009).

At **inter-organizational level**, two competing perspectives exist about the influence of ego network structure on an actor's knowledge activities. Earlier research found that structural holes in a network enhance an organization's knowledge creation (Baum, Calabrese and Silverman, 2000). However, later research suggests that network closure enhances the diffusion of novel practices, especially in tacit knowledge sharing (Schilling and Phelps, 2007).

Whole network structure

At **individual level**, the whole network's density and average path length have an important impact on network members' knowledge sharing and learning, and subsequently on their innovation performance. Network density (connectivity) increases the rate, extent and fidelity of knowledge diffusion in a network, hence it can increase network members' innovativeness (Singh, 2005). Path length means the average geodesic distance in the mean number of links that any two members of the network have to traverse to be connected (Kim *et al*, 2014). The shorter the distance, the faster and easier the knowledge transfer. Subsequently, a decrease in a network's average path length should increase the network's density, hence improve members' knowledge sharing and innovation performance. In other words, concentration of ties and shorter path length should improve the sharing of complex knowledge between network segments and members, hence an improved innovation performance.

At **intra-organizational level**, network concentration is the extent to which organizational units are connected only to a central unit such as corporate headquarters. High network concentration impedes intra-organizational knowledge transfer because it reduces the discretion and willingness of organizational units to share their knowledge with each other (Tsai, 2002).

At **inter-organizational level**, whole networks in which groups of organizations are densely interconnected yet maintain some ties across clusters, and hence reduce the network's average path length, subsequently should improve organizational innovation (Schilling and Phelps, 2007). Local clustering promotes social cohesion and knowledge sharing, and a short path length allows diverse knowledge from different clusters to diffuse crossing cluster boundaries. However, excessive clustering may reduce organizational innovation by creating levels of social cohesion and reducing the availability of diverse knowledge within clusters (Phelps, Heidl and Wadhwa, 2012).

9.3 Relational properties

Relational properties are among the most studied aspects of knowledge networks at interpersonal, intra-organizational and inter-organizational levels. Two key factors of relational properties affecting knowledge processes are the strength of the ties and the proximity or similarity of the nodes.

Tie strength

At **interpersonal level**, it is widely accepted that there is a need to build strong relationships to facilitate knowledge-sharing activities (Saifi, Dillon and McQueen, 2016). This is because strong ties can help establish trust and reciprocity norms between individuals, which reduces concerns about opportunistic behaviour and increases expectations of cooperation, thereby increasing individuals' awareness of and access to each other's knowledge and their willingness to invest in transferring, receiving and absorbing knowledge (Kachra and White, 2008). In general, stronger interpersonal ties imply higher communication frequency, longer duration and more affective attachments. In particular, tie strength increases the ease and efficacy of sharing complex, private tacit knowledge and improves exploratory learning (Centola and Macy, 2007). Furthermore, individuals having strong ties to others with dissimilar competencies to others separated by structural holes are more innovative. This suggests that the social cohesion provided by strong ties enhances individuals' ability to create knowledge from collaborating with partners possessing diverse knowledge (McFadyen, Semadeni and Cannella, 2009).

At **intra-organizational level**, strong ties between organizational units also provide a number of benefits for a unit's knowledge activities. Strong ties indicate high levels of social interaction or frequent communication and affective closeness. Increasing tie strength within and between units leads to more effective knowledge sharing and promotes knowledge creation. Increasing tie strength can promote knowledge sharing by mitigating the negative influence of geographical distance, technological differences and competition between units. Similar to the interpersonal level, strong ties can particularly improve the sharing of complex, tacit knowledge at intra-organizational level (Hansen, Mors and Lovas, 2005).

At both interpersonal and intra-organizational levels, there are costs attached to strong ties. Increasing tie strength among the individuals of an organizational unit tends to encourage members to search for knowledge within the group and reduces their motivation to search beyond it. Similarly, an increase in the strength of a unit's inter-unit ties reduces its autonomy and access to diverse knowledge. At high levels of inter-unit tie strength, the cost of maintaining such ties can outweigh their knowledge-sharing benefits and reduce unit performance (Hoegl and Wagner, 2005).

At **inter-organizational level**, strong ties are characterized by a number of indicators, including long duration of relationship, frequent and intense collaboration and repeated partnership over time. In terms of the impact of inter-organizational tie strength on organizational knowledge activities, the majority of research has shown that strong ties increase knowledge sharing, knowledge creation and innovation adoption (Capaldo, 2007; Tiwana, 2008; Williams, 2007). This effect can be explained from a number of viewpoints. First, strong ties provide social cohesion (trust, reciprocity and social identity), which increases the motivation of organizations to share knowledge. This is because increasing relationship duration can increase the recipient organization's understanding of a source's knowledge, improving the organization's ability to adapt the source's knowledge to its local operations and context. Second, development of relational capital and longer duration of the relationship can have a positive effect on inter-organizational knowledge sharing and learning (Williams, 2007). Third, an increase in the scope and depth of inter-organizational interactions can help diffuse practice, hence improves knowledge sharing of complex and private knowledge that is embedded in practices, namely, tacit knowledge. However, there has been disagreement from a minority of researchers, arguing that prior alliances with the same partner, an indicator of tie strength, can reduce an organization's innovativeness, because an increasing level of trust between partners could lock them into the same relationships at the expense of gaining access to diverse knowledge from new partners (Molina-Morales and Martinez-Fernandez, 2009).

Based on the above discussion, tie strength is a double-edged sword. Table 9.1 summarizes the cross-level analysis of the benefits and costs of having strong ties. There are common benefits of having strong ties to all three levels, including higher levels of trust and willingness to share knowledge, better communication, more frequent collaboration and increasing knowledge sharing, in particular the sharing of complex, private tacit knowledge. However, too high a level of tie strength also has some drawbacks (ie costs), such as reducing an individual's, organizational unit's or organization's autonomy and preventing access to diverse knowledge, which could compromise innovativeness and new product/service development.

Table 9.1 Double-edged effect of having strong ties on knowledge sharing and learning

	Key benefits	Key costs/drawbacks
Interpersonal level	Common to all three levels: • Higher level of trust and willingness of knowledge sharing • Better communication • More frequent collaboration • Increases knowledge sharing, in particular the sharing of complex, private tacit knowledge	Searches for knowledge within the group and reduces motivation to search beyond the group
Intra-organizational level		Reduces organizational unit's autonomy and access to diverse knowledge
Inter-organizational level		Locks organizations into the same partnership without gaining access to diverse knowledge from new partners

Nodal proximity

Another relational property is nodal proximity, including a node's geographic distance and its similarities in competitiveness concerns, expertise, status and personality.

At **interpersonal level**, when two individuals maintain a direct tie, they are socially proximate. Within an organization, direct ties reduce competitive concerns and increase individuals' willingness to share and absorb knowledge if they belong to the same competitive group. When individuals are involved in ties crossing group boundaries within an organization or crossing organization boundaries, their competitiveness concerns can diminish their motivation to share knowledge (Kachra and White, 2008).

Geographic distance between members of a tie influences their knowledge activities. Geographic proximity can increase the efficiency and efficacy of communication and knowledge sharing. In a knowledge management case study carried out with a large information technology service company, it was found that face-to-face social networks (least geographic distance) lead to clear improvement of knowledge-sharing performance (Saifi, Dillon and McQueen, 2016). Furthermore, research has concluded that face-to-face social interaction forms an effective channel of communication, which makes the sharing of tacit knowledge, in particular, easier (Noorderhaven and Harzing, 2009). However, the knowledge shared tends to be less novel, thus less useful, because the knowledge shared between geographically proximate people tends to be more homogeneous, while knowledge shared across geographic regions tends to be more diverse and heterogeneous, hence is potentially more novel and more valuable for learning (Bell and Zaheer, 2007).

The similarity of dyad members' expertise, status and personality can also affect their knowledge sharing and learning. First, knowledge proximity as a dimension of knowledge refers to the similarity of dyad members' expertise in a knowledge network that might influence the transfer of knowledge both ways. Proximity between individuals has been one of the most important drivers of tie creation (Kleinbaum, Stuart and Tushman, 2013). Being connected to similar knowledge elements within a knowledge network should facilitate interactions among individuals, as it provides them with a shared foundation and a common understanding of the world surrounding them, hence the actors can communicate and exchange ideas more efficiently. In addition, similar others seem more approachable and show a higher responsiveness to knowledge requests. Thus, the costs for approaching knowledge sources are smaller, thus increasing their motivations to share knowledge and learn from each other, which can be a precondition to absorb knowledge and generate new knowledge (Brennecke and Rank, 2017). However, organizations might encourage individuals to actively seek knowledge from colleagues possessing dissimilar knowledge in order to complement their own knowledge stock. In particular, accessing heterogeneous knowledge decreases the risk of inventive lock-in and is beneficial for innovative performance.

Social status similarity can increase mutual identification, trust and respect, hence increases individuals' motivation to share knowledge and learn. In contrast, social status difference may increase the motivation of lower-status individuals to share knowledge with those of higher status, but higher-status individuals tend to reject such efforts (Black, Carlile and Repenning, 2004).

At **intra-organizational level,** the closeness of organizational units in competitive and geographic space also affects knowledge sharing between them. The extent to which organizational units compete for organizational resources reduces their motivation, as a knowledge source, to share knowledge. Geographic proximity between units increases the efficacy of knowledge sharing between them, because co-location of organizational units increases communication. This is similar to that at interpersonal level. Another observation from research is that if some units have had successful collaboration in the past, the negative effect of geographical distance on knowledge sharing can be mitigated (Salomon and Martin, 2008).

At **inter-organizational level,** the effect of partner organizations' similarity on knowledge activities should also be seen from two complementary aspects. On the one hand, a low level of knowledge similarity will reduce partner organizations' ability to communicate and share knowledge, which may cause difficulties in learning from each other. On the other, partners with a high level of knowledge overlap will have little to share and learn between them. A moderate level of knowledge similarity/dissimilarity seems to be best for knowledge sharing and organizational learning. In contrast to knowledge similarities/differences, research consistently shows that similarities in partner organizations' product markets can impede inter-organizational knowledge sharing and knowledge creation, because partners tend to become highly protective of their knowledge when they are market rivals (Lee, Min and Lee, 2017).

It can be concluded that, at all three levels, neither too low nor too high a level of knowledge overlap between nodes in a knowledge network is ideal. On the one hand, too little or nothing in common could cause problems for knowledge activities, for example too difficult to communicate with each other. On the other, when two nodes have too much overlap in knowledge, there would be very little worth sharing or learning between them. This effect is illustrated in Figure 9.2.

Figure 9.2 Different levels of knowledge similarity between two nodes

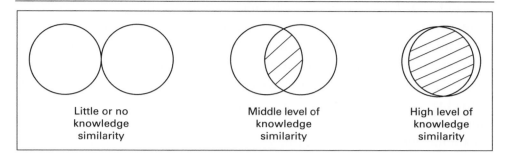

Little or no
knowledge
similarity

Middle level of
knowledge
similarity

High level of
knowledge
similarity

9.4 Nodal properties

Important nodal properties are characterized by a node's power/prestige, absorptive capacity, transmission capacity, knowledge depth and diversity of knowledge. In a knowledge network, an actor, labelled as a focal node as shown in Figure 9.3, can be a knowledge source and a knowledge recipient at the same time. Figure 9.3 can help us to understand how nodal properties affect knowledge activities and learning.

Figure 9.3 Nodal properties in a knowledge network

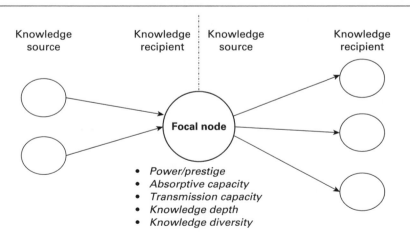

Knowledge
source

Knowledge
recipient

Knowledge
source

Knowledge
recipient

Focal node

- *Power/prestige*
- *Absorptive capacity*
- *Transmission capacity*
- *Knowledge depth*
- *Knowledge diversity*

At **interpersonal level,** individuals with more power derived from their organizational role are able to challenge the status quo and effect change, hence are more willing to share knowledge and more effective in adopting and implementing innovations. Similarly, individuals possessing higher absorptive and transfer capacity can communicate better with others and learn from others, especially when conveying complex ideas to diverse audiences, hence increasing the ease with which they can transfer knowledge to others.

In terms of the impact of the diversity of knowledge contacts on knowledge sharing and learning, there have been consistent findings from research. Individuals learn more when their contacts work in different organizational units, because such contacts can provide more diverse knowledge, which is consistent with the 'structural holes' theory. The positive effect of an ego network's knowledge diversity on individuals' knowledge creation can be enhanced by the increased knowledge flow generated by social cohesion, through either network density or tie strength (Kim *et al*, 2014).

Critical thinking and reflection
Knowledge diversity

Knowledge diversity can be studied from different perspectives. In Section 9.3, about relational properties, when nodal proximity in terms of expertise is low, it suggests that two nodes may have quite different knowledge. In Section 9.4, about nodal properties, if a focal node is connected to a variety of nodes that have different skills or knowledge sets, then the focal node may have an advantage of accessing more diversified knowledge. Do you think these two different perspectives of knowledge diversity have fundamentally the same or completely different effects on knowledge-sharing and learning activities, and why?

An individual with critical and unique knowledge has greater expertise power. Uniqueness as a dimension of knowledge refers to a node being knowledgeable in an area where other nodes are not. Those powerful individuals with unique knowledge tend to attract more colleagues to call for their knowledge and expertise; in this case, the focal node's role is as a knowledge source. Theories of social networks have long emphasized the idea that access to unique knowledge sources can be of great value for individuals and organizations (Saifi, Dillon and McQueen, 2016). However, individuals with unique knowledge might be preoccupied with its exploitation and thus less active in seeking new inputs from colleagues. In addition, uniqueness could be a sign of knowledge being of little importance or use to the firm's innovative activities. Other individuals might thus not be interested in exploiting this knowledge further, which could negatively influence the possessing node's popularity in the network, and its expertise power may be reduced. The knowledge uniqueness property really has a double-edged effect. In order to profit from the unique knowledge that individuals possess, they should strive to informally connect with others to promote the recombination and thus exploitation of their knowledge elements (Brennecke and Rank, 2017).

At **intra-organizational level,** the nodal properties also affect organizational units' knowledge sharing and learning performance. As can be seen from Figure 9.3, one organizational unit is also a node in an intra-organizational knowledge network. From a knowledge recipient point of view, a node with higher absorptive capacity will have a positive impact on knowledge sharing. This is mainly because higher absorptive capacity will help a node to understand and digest the knowledge received. A node with more knowledge depth can better identify and call for the right knowledge (Kim *et al*, 2014). The depth of knowledge available from knowledge sources to a recipient in the network provides more opportunities for the recipient to combine or integrate knowledge in a novel way, and use the new knowledge in their innovation activities.

From an outward knowledge-flow point of view, a node's knowledge-sending ability is dependent on its disseminative or transmission capacity (knowledge-sending capacity) (Lichtenthaler and Lichtenthaler, 2009). Disseminative or transmission capacity is not just about the amount of knowledge being sent out, but also the efficiency and effectiveness of the knowledge disseminated. The concept is defined as the ability of knowledge holders to efficiently, effectively and convincingly frame knowledge in a way that other people can understand accurately and put their learning into practice (Tang, 2011). Based on case studies from multinational corporations (MNCs), research confirms that three capability dimensions are crucial for becoming a successful knowledge-sending unit within an MNC: cultural, structural and human capabilities are generally higher at plants that have already engaged in significant knowledge-sending activities. Human capabilities, that is, frequent social interactions between different plants, have been highlighted by several case studies as having the potential to compensate for the lack of other disseminative capabilities (Szasz *et al*, 2019).

Knowledge diversity refers to the variety in knowledge elements possessed by the network nodes. Based on an organization's structure, especially the hierarchical, function-based structure, such as in a traditional car manufacturing firm, one tends to find organizational units responsible for the vehicle's platform, chassis, drivetrain and electrics. These organizational units have developed highly specialized, narrow knowledge. In a knowledge network, some units are connected to few knowledge elements within the firm's knowledge network. However, other organizational units may have ties with many more knowledge elements; then they are able to relate knowledge from different areas, make more informed choices with respect to knowledge combination, and integrate knowledge with their own ideas for new knowledge creation and innovation (Brennecke and Rank, 2017).

At **inter-organizational level**, research has shown consistent results in terms of absorptive and transmission capacity. Similar to that at interpersonal and intra-organizational levels, an organization with higher absorptive capacity increases its ability to leverage the diverse expertise of the innovation supplier and adapt the innovation to its own needs (Weigelt and Sarkar, 2009). While an organization's absorptive capacity affects its ability to receive and use knowledge, its transmission capacity affects its ability to transfer knowledge to other organizations. Higher transmission capacity facilitates knowledge transfer and potentially increases an organization's influence on their partners. Partner organizations can develop a collaborative capability based on their collaborative experience. A collaborative capability can enhance an organization's ability to benefit from partnerships equipped with effective and efficient routines to search for new knowledge within existing partnerships.

The prestige (ie status) of a knowledge source organization is likely to increase the adoption of innovation at the recipient organization, because the prestige can increase its influence on the adoption decisions of partners. Similarly, the extent to which scientific collaborations involve prestigious research institutes and companies can increase the frequency with which their publications are cited (Gittelman, 2007).

Finally, the depth and diversity of the innovation capability of source organizations positively influence a recipient organization's knowledge activities and learning. Accessing heterogeneous knowledge provides opportunities for a firm to construct its innovative advantages because it can create and develop novel products and services (Wang, Chen and Fang, 2018). An increase in the depth of an organization's innovative capabilities reduces potential recipients' uncertainty about the quality of its knowledge, making it more attractive as a knowledge source, especially for recipients located far away, because they may lack other means to evaluate the knowledge from a potential source. Consequently, the depth of a source's innovative capabilities reduces the negative impact of geographic and cultural distances on knowledge activities and learning (Tallman and Phene, 2007).

To summarize the chapter, a knowledge network is a network of nodes, where nodes are seen as knowledge providers/owners/senders/sources, knowledge receivers/recipients and knowledge brokers. The nodes can be individuals, groups, organizational units or organizations. This view sees knowledge networks from an actor's perspective. When seen from the knowledge property's perspective, that is, what actually flows through the network, a knowledge network is a network of explicit and tacit knowledge (Chatti, 2012). The main purpose of studying knowledge networks is to understand how and where knowledge flows or stops among organizational members, organizational units, and crossing organizational boundaries, so that managers can effectively support knowledge sharing and learning within and across organizations.

Key learning points

- Knowledge networks are networks of knowledge nodes (repositories and agents) that search for, adopt, transmit and create knowledge. Nodes can be individuals or higher-level collectives such as groups, teams, organizational units, organizations, communities or even nation states. Subsequently, there are different types of knowledge networks, including interpersonal knowledge networks, intra-organizational knowledge networks and inter-organizational networks.

- Besides nodes, a second important element in knowledge network composition is social relationships between nodes. The relationships are the linkages among nodes, representing not only knowledge combination possibilities and capabilities but also knowledge-flow channels.

- Knowledge networks and social networks are related to each other because knowledge activities such as creation and sharing are often seen as a social process. However, they are not isomorphic but rather decoupled in the sense that they have their own unique properties and content flows. The basic building blocks or nodes of a knowledge network are knowledge elements, such as the technological knowledge that is a fundamental component for innovation.

- Network structural properties, relational properties and nodal properties are three important properties for a knowledge network. Key aspects of network structural properties are network position, ego network structure and whole network structure. Relational properties are characterized by tie strength and nodal proximity. Typical nodal properties are absorptive capacity, transmission capacity, knowledge depth, knowledge diversity and power/prestige.

- In a knowledge network, social cohesion refers to the number, length and strength of the paths that connect individual nodes. This cohesion perspective views ties as pipes through which knowledge flows and characterizes network position in terms of centrality.

- The ego network structural feature is about whether a focal node's direct contacts have ties to each other; in other words, triadic closure. When two of the ego's direct contacts do not share a tie, a 'structural hole' exists between them. When all three nodes (the ego and its two direct contacts) maintain ties with each other, it is a 'network closure'.

Review questions

- What is the impact of centrality on knowledge sharing at individual, intra-organizational and inter-organizational levels?

- How do knowledge depth and knowledge diversity affect knowledge sharing in interpersonal, intra-organizational and inter-organizational knowledge networks? Use examples to support your answer.

- Would you support the statement 'structural holes are bad and network closure is good for knowledge sharing and learning in knowledge networks', and why?

- Does network density always have a positive impact on knowledge sharing? Compare the effect at three different levels: interpersonal, intra-organizational and inter-organizational levels.

- Is it always a good thing to have strong ties in a knowledge network?

- What are the advantages and disadvantages of having geographically close nodes in a knowledge network?

- How do a node's absorptive capacity and transmission capacity affect its knowledge-sharing performance?

- What do you think of knowledge uniqueness in a knowledge network?

References

Audia, P G and Goncalo, J A (2007) Past success and creativity over time: a study of inventors in the hard disc drive industry, *Management Science*, **53**, pp 1–15

Baum, J A C, Calabrese, T and Silverman, B S (2000) Don't get in alone: alliance network composition and start-ups' performance in Canadian biotechnology, *Strategic Management Journal*, **21**, pp 267–94

Bell, G G and Zaheer, A (2007) Geography, networks and knowledge flow, *Organization Science*, **18**, pp 955–72

Black, L J, Carlile, P R and Repenning, N P (2004) A dynamic theory of expertise and occupational boundaries in new technology implementation: building on Barley's study of CT scanning, *Administrative Science Quarterly*, **49**, pp 572–607

Brennecke, J and Rank, O (2017) The firm's knowledge network and the transfer of advice among corporate inventors: a multilevel network study, *Research Policy*, **46**, pp 768–83

Burt, R S (2004) Structural holes and good ideas, *American Journal of Sociology*, **110**, pp 349–99

Capaldo, A (2007) Network structure and innovation: the leveraging of a dual network as a distinctive relational capability, *Strategic Management Journal*, **28**, pp 585–68

Centola, D and Macy, M (2007) Complex contagions and the weakness of long ties, *American Journal of Sociology*, **113**, pp 702–34

Chatti, M A (2012) Knowledge management: a personal knowledge network perspective, *Journal of Knowledge Management*, **16** (5), pp 829–44

Dong, J Q and Yang, C H (2016) Being central is a double-edged sword: knowledge network centrality and new product development in U.S. pharmaceutical industry, *Technological Forecasting and Social Change*, **113** (Part B), pp 379–85

Fleming, L, Mingo, S and Chen, D (2007) Collaborative brokerage, generative creativity and creative success, *Administrative Science Quarterly*, **52**, pp 443–75

Gittelman, M (2007) Does geography matter for science-based firms: epistemic communities and the geography of research and patenting in biotechnology, *Organization Science*, **18**, pp 724–41

Hansen, M T, Mors, M L and Lovas, B (2005) Knowledge sharing in organizations: multiple networks, multiple phases, *Academy of Management Journal*, **48**, pp 776–93

Hoegl, M and Wagner, S M (2005) Buyer–supplier collaboration in product development projects, *Journal of Management*, **31**, pp 539–48

Hulsheger, U R, Anderson, N and Salgado, J F (2009) Team level predictors of innovation at work: a comprehensive meta-analysis spanning three decades, *Journal of Applied Psychology*, **94**, pp 1128–45

Kachra, A and White, R E (2008) Know-how transfer: the role of social, economic/competitive and firm boundary factors, *Strategic Management Journal*, **29**, pp 425–45

Kim, Y G et al (2014) Trailing organizational knowledge paths through social network lens: integrating the multiple industry cases, *Journal of Knowledge Management*, **18** (1), pp 38–51

Kleinbaum, A M, Stuart, T E and Tushman, M L (2013) Discretion within constraint: homophily and structure in a formal organization, *Organization Science*, **24**, pp 1316–36

Lee, J, Min, J and Lee, H (2017) Setting a knowledge boundary across teams: knowledge protection regulation for inter-team co-ordination and team performance, *Journal of Knowledge Management*, **21** (2), pp 254–74

Lichtenthaler, U and Lichtenthaler, E (2009) A capability-based framework for open innovation: complementing absorptive capacity, *Journal of Management Studies*, **46** (8), pp 1315–38

McFadyen, M A and Cannella, A A (2004) Social capital and knowledge creation: diminishing returns of the number and strength of exchange, *Academy of Management Journal*, **47**, pp 735–46

McFadyen, M A, Semadeni, M and Cannella, A A (2009) Value of strong ties to disconnected others: examining knowledge creation in biomedicine, *Organization Science*, **20** (3), pp 552–64

Molina-Morales, F X and Martinez-Fernandez, M T (2009) Too much love in the neighbourhood can hurt: how an excess of intensity and trust in relationships may produce negative effects on firms, *Strategic Management Journal*, **30**, pp 1013–23

Noorderhaven, N and Harzing, A (2009) Knowledge sharing and social interaction within MNEs, *Journal of International Business Studies*, **40** (5), pp 719–41

Phelps, C, Heidl, R and Wadhwa, A (2012) Knowledge, networks and knowledge networks: a review and research agenda, *Journal of Management*, **38** (4), pp 1115–66

Podolny, J M (2001) Networks as the pipes and prisms of the market, *American Journal of Sociology*, **107**, pp 33–60

Rangachari, P (2009) Knowledge sharing networks in professional complex systems, *Journal of Knowledge Management*, **13** (3), pp 132–45

Saifi, S A, Dillon, S and McQueen, R (2016) The relationship between face to face social networks and knowledge sharing: an exploratory study of manufacturing firms, *Journal of Knowledge Management*, **20** (2), pp 308–26

Salomon, R and Martin, X (2008) Learning, knowledge transfer and technology implementation performance: a study of time-to-build in the global semiconductor industry, *Management Science*, **54**, pp 1266–80

Sasidharan, S (2019) Reconceptualising knowledge networks for enterprise systems implementation: incorporating domain expertise of knowledge sources and knowledge flow intensity, *Information and Management*, **56**, pp 364–476

Schilling, M A and Phelps, C C (2007) Inter-firm collaboration networks: the impact of large-scale network structure on firm innovation, *Management Science*, **53**, pp 1113–26

Shi, B, Yang, L and Weninger, T (2017) Forward backward similarity search in knowledge networks, *Knowledge-Based Systems*, **119**, pp 20–31

Singh, J (2005) Collaborative networks as determinants of knowledge diffusion patterns, *Management Science*, **51**, pp 756–70

Szasz, L *et al* (2019) Disseminative capabilities and manufacturing plant roles in the knowledge network of MNCs, *International Journal of Production Economics*, **208**, pp 294–304

Tallman, S and Phene, A (2007) Leveraging knowledge across geographic boundaries, *Organization Science*, **18**, pp 252–60

Tang, F (2011) Knowledge transfer in intra-organization networks, *Systems Research and Behavioural Science*, **28** (3), pp 270–82

Tiwana, A (2008) Do bridging ties complement strong ties: an empirical examination of alliance ambidexterity, *Strategic Management Journal*, **29**, pp 251–72

Tsai, W (2001) Knowledge transfer in intra-organizational networks: effects of network position and absorptive capacity on business unit innovation and performance, *Academy of Management Journal*, **44**, pp 996–1004

Tsai, W (2002) Social structure of co-opetition within a multiunit organization: co-ordination, competition and intra-organizational knowledge sharing, *Organization Science*, **13**, pp 179–90

Wang, M C, Chen, P C and Fang, S C (2018) A critical view of knowledge networks and innovation performance: the mediation role of firm's knowledge integration capability, *Journal of Business Research*, **88**, pp 222–33

Weigelt, C and Sarkar, M B (2009) Learning from supply-side agents: the impact of technology solution providers' experiential diversity on client's innovation adoption, *Academy of Management Journal*, **52**, pp 37–60

Williams, C (2007) Transfer in context: replication and adaptation in knowledge transfer relationship, *Strategic Management Journal*, **28**, pp 867–89

ICT-enabled knowledge management: Internet of Things and big data analytics

10

Learning outcomes

After completing this chapter, the reader will be able to:

- understand the links between knowledge management and ICT;
- explain the role of contemporary ICT technologies such as the Internet of Things in knowledge management within and crossing knowledge boundaries;
- appreciate the effect of big data and big data analytics on knowledge management.

While Chapter 9 has discussed knowledge networks mainly from a social interaction perspective, this chapter focuses on the role of Information and Communication Technology (ICT) in KM, that is, it examines knowledge activities within and crossing boundaries from a technology perspective. ICT has been seen as crucial in removing the boundaries of communication and knowledge flows, hence is considered as an enabler of KM. As the literature, including plenty of textbooks, has extensively described how ICT has transformed KM from many different angles, this chapter will focus on the challenges and opportunities brought by disruptive, emerging technologies. It will discuss two such interrelated technologies: the Internet of Things (IoT) and big data analytics (BDA). IoT technology will allow the use of cross-platform communication to collect real-time data/information about all aspects of business, and BDA will provide approaches to analysing the collected data/information to generate new knowledge and business intelligence for smart business decisions.

10.1 Linking knowledge management and ICT

There is no doubt that ICT has played a crucial role in KM and will continue to revolutionize KM processes in the future. During every stage of the whole KM lifecycle (from knowledge building, knowledge holding and knowledge mobilization to knowledge utilization; refer to Chapter 3 for details), ICT has been an integral part of KM systems, not only to manage explicit knowledge but also to facilitate tacit knowledge creation and sharing.

One of the success stories of ICT is in helping to build knowledge management systems (KMS). KMS refers to information systems that focus on managing organizational knowledge and improving the creation, storage, mobilization and utilization of knowledge. According to Santoro *et al* (2018), an effective KMS is mainly comprised of three components:

- ICT infrastructures: physical technology that helps to manage knowledge, such as hardware and software components, intranet, extranet and local area network (LAN).

- Collaborative technologies, including discussion forums, shared databases, document repositories and workflows.

- The use of ICT to integrate different collaborative technologies and their orientations has three primary implementation aims: informative orientation, communicative orientation and workflow orientation (Imran and Gregor, 2019). Informative orientation aims at providing commercial information to various stakeholders across organizational and functional boundaries. Communicative orientation allows cost reduction and interaction with business agents within and outside an organization. Workflow orientation facilitates the execution of business processes within an organization crossing business units or collaborative processes crossing organizational boundaries.

Hislop, Bosua and Helms (2018) classified the approaches of ICT to KM into six categories:

1 repository-based approach: using ICT to help with the storage and retrieval of knowledge (Jashapara, 2011);

2 process and domain-based approach: creating knowledge bases to facilitate KM processes in different domains (Becerra-Fernandez and Sabherwal, 2015);

3 collaboration tools to facilitate communication and knowledge sharing (Dalkir, 2017);

4 crowd-based approach: using ICT technology to get in touch with the wisdom of crowds, such as partners, customers, suppliers and wider stakeholders (Mladenow, 2014);

5 network-based approach: such as knowledge sharing in online communities crossing hierarchical and geographic boundaries (Pohjola and Puusa, 2016);

6 sensor-based approach: use of the IoT and BDA by including real-time data and big data to enhance the effectiveness of KM (Santoro *et al*, 2018).

The first four categories – using ICT for knowledge base storage, facilitating KM processes and building domain systems, using ICT as collaboration tools and to get in touch with the crowd – have been widely discussed in the literature already. Category 5 is about using ICT as a technology platform to communicate with people and communities, discussed in Chapters 7 (communities of practice) and 9 (knowledge networks). Category 6, the sensor-based approach, will be discussed in this chapter. The following two sections will discuss the IoT and BDA, respectively.

10.2 Internet of Things and knowledge management

Internet of Things

The IoT refers to an emerging paradigm consisting of a continuum of uniquely addressable objects communicating with each other to form a worldwide dynamic network (Borgia, 2014). This interconnected network uses disruptive digital technologies, influencing daily business operations as well as long-term strategies (Kim and Kim, 2016). Besides the great excitement generated by IoT, businesses today, characterized by trends such as globalization and technological and industrial convergence, also face great challenges in developing, adopting and adapting disruptive technologies in order to increase their efficiency and innovativeness in the current knowledge- and technology-driven economy. How to utilize IoT to better manage knowledge and smooth knowledge flow within an organization and the crossing of knowledge boundaries has become an increasingly hot topic, because organizations have now realized that leveraging the firm's collective knowledge can provide competitiveness to improve innovativeness and responsiveness to the changing environment, further to achieve the business's sustainability in the longer term.

The term 'Internet of Things' was coined by Kevin Ashton, one of the founders of the original Auto-ID Center in Massachusetts Institute of Technology (MIT), in 1999 during a presentation given at Proctor & Gamble (Ashton, 2009). The MIT Auto-ID Center is the development community of Radio Frequency Identification (RFID). In Ashton's presentation, IoT represents an architecture for globally emerging internet-based information services. He visualizes that the physical world can be connected to the internet via sensors and actuators that are capable of providing real-time data and information (feedback) that have huge potential to enhance the comfort, security and control of our lives. Following Ashton's inspiration, a great number of definitions have been proposed by different authors with different foci in connection with their different backgrounds and interest in the concept. Table 10.1 provides an overview of some of the well-known definitions.

It can be seen that besides individuals' contributions, there are a number of influential groups which have enriched the meanings and interpretations of IoT, most notably the RFID group (at MIT), the International Telecommunications Union (ITU) and the Cluster of European Research Projects (CERP). Initially, the 'things' in IoT were associated with the use of RFID. The MIT Auto-ID Center's idea was visionary: they aimed at discovering information about a tagged object by browsing an internet address or a database entry corresponding to a particular RFID (Borgia, 2014). Today, the concept of 'things' is more general and not limited to RFID. It has expanded to include any real, physical object (such as RFID sensors, actuators, smart items), 'spime' data objects and any virtual or digital system capable of moving in time and space (Mishra *et al*, 2016). When these entities are connected to the internet and assigned a unique identification such as a number, name and/or address, they can be read, recognized, located and controlled via the internet.

Table 10.1 An overview of IoT definitions

Source	Definitions	Key points
(Brock, 2001)	An intelligent infrastructure linking objects, information and people through computer networks where RFID technology found the basis for its realization.	Infrastructure, computer networks, RFID
(ITU, 2005)	IoT will connect the world's objects in both a sensory and intelligent manner through combining technological developments in item identification (ie tagging things), sensors and wireless sensor networks (ie feeling things), embedded systems (ie thinking things) and nanotechnology (ie shrinking things).	Not only RFIDs, but also high number of different objects, univocally addressable
(Atzori, Lera and Morabito, 2010)	IoT is the result of the convergence of three different visions: things oriented (sensors), internet oriented (middleware, networking paradigm) and semantic oriented (knowledge).	Convergence, things oriented, internet oriented, semantic oriented
(Weber, 2010)	An emerging global, internet-based information service architecture facilitating the exchange of goods in global supply chain networks on the technical basis of the present Domain Name System (DNS)	Information service architecture, exchange of goods, DNS
(Uckelmann, Harrison and Michahelles, 2011)	The future Internet of Things links uniquely identifiable things to their virtual representations in the internet containing or linking to additional information on their identity, status, location, or any other business, social or privately relevant information at a financial or non-financial pay-off that exceeds the efforts of information provisioning and offers information access to non-predefined participants. The provided accurate and appropriate information may be accessed in the right quantity and condition, at the right time, in the right place and at the right price.	Web 2.0 technology, simple and instinctive interfaces, interaction between 'things' and users, Web of 'things'

(continued)

Table 10.1 (Continued)

Source	Definitions	Key points
(Vermesan *et al*, 2011)	CERP define IoT as a dynamic global network infrastructure with self-capabilities based on standard and interoperable communication protocols where physical and virtual 'things' have identities, physical attributes, virtual personalities and use intelligent interfaces, and are seamlessly integrated into the information network.	Global network, standard and interoperable communication protocols, intelligent interfaces, seamless integration
(Gama, Touseaui and Donse, 2012)	MIT Auto-ID Center developed Electronic Product Code that serves as a universal identifier such as RFID, for any specific item, hence defines IoT as the worldwide network of interconnected objects uniquely addressable based on standard communication protocols.	Worldwide network, interconnected objects, standard communication protocols
(Gubbi *et al*, 2013)	Interconnection of sensing and actuating devices providing the ability to share information across platforms through a unified framework, developing a common operating picture for enabling innovative applications. This is achieved by seamless ubiquitous sensing, data analytics and information representation with cloud computing as the unifying framework.	Sharing information across platforms, data analytics, cloud computing
(Borgia, 2014)	A complete concept of IoT can be observed via 6As, that is, Anytime – Anywhere, Anyone – Anything, and Any path/network – Any service.	People and 'things' to be connected not only anytime, anywhere with anyone and anything, but also via any network and any service available

In addition, the RFID group's focus on identification technology is fundamental in order to overcome the first hurdle in the realization of IoT: recognizing objects connected to the internet. This focus on identification has been criticized on the grounds of passivity (ie being *passively* recognized). The CERP group expects 'things' to become *active* (rather than being passively recognized) participants in business, information and social processes, and the IoT enables 'things' to interact and communicate among themselves and with the environment, by exchanging data and information sensed about each other and about the environment. The 'things' should be able to react autonomously to the real/physical world's events and influence the world by running processes that trigger actions and create services with or without direct human intervention. The ITU group complements other groups' work, with great emphasis on a series of issues involved in implementing the IoT, from tagging things, feeling things, thinking things to shrinking things (for a greater level of integration). It means that the new generation of devices is *smart*, thanks to the embedded electronics that allow them to sense, compute, communicate and integrate seamlessly.

A review of IoT by Atzori, Lera and Morabito (2010) concluded that the IoT is the result of the convergence of three constructs: 1) *things oriented*, where the focus is on the 'objects' and on finding a paradigm that is able to identify and integrate 'objects'. 2) *internet oriented*, where the emphasis is on the networking paradigm and on exploiting the Internet Protocol (IP) to establish an efficient connection between devices, while simplifying the IP so that it can be used on devices with very limited capacity; and 3) *semantic oriented*, aiming to use semantic technologies describing objects and managing data to represent, store, interconnect and manage the huge amount of information provided by the increasing number of IoT objects. IoT is rapidly gaining momentum, bringing millions of devices and objects into the connected world. The integration of sensors, actuators, RFID tags and communication technologies serves as the foundation of IoT, and the various physical objects and devices can be connected through the internet to communicate and cooperate with each other in order to reach common goals (He and Xu, 2014). The adoption of IoT has been accelerated by a number of technological factors, including a fast decline in the costs of sensors and actuators, an increasing ability to connect the sensors and actuators, often wirelessly, and the ability to analyse the huge amount of data generated (Uden and He, 2017).

Illustration
IoT applications in agriculture and breeding

There is growing interest in using IoT technologies in various industries and areas. Borgia (2014) reviewed IoT applications in many areas, including agriculture and breeding, logistics and product lifetime management, industrial processes, smart mobility and smart tourism, smart grid, smart homes and buildings, public safety and environmental monitoring, medical and healthcare, and independent living. This illustration will focus on the application of IoT to help with the management of agriculture and breeding in five different respects, specifically:

1   For monitoring animals in order to meet regulations for animal traceability: using IoT identification systems such as RFID and sensors can help identify animals with any diseases, report promptly to the relevant authorities, and isolate infected animals from healthy ones, thus avoiding the spread of contagious disease.

2   For preventing animal fraud: through the use of microchips, IoT can help to collect and store data and information about an animal's demographic information, veterinary checks, contracted diseases, vaccines given, body temperature and health status, and then use the information to streamline animal health certification and control trade and imports, to avoid fraud. By analysing the collected data, the authorities can also verify the actual number of livestock reported by local breeders, and provide the right amount of subsidies accordingly.

3   For monitoring and controlling production and feed: using IoT, advanced sensor systems can detect the presence of genetically modified organisms (GMO) and additives, further to ensure the health of plants and products that are suitable for both human and animal consumption.

4   For the management of the registration, modification or closure of farms: IoT can be used not only to support farm registration, modification and closure, but also to monitor and ensure the health of organizations.

5   For farms to have direct relationships with consumers: IoT has been widely used by farmers to reach consumers directly by cutting out the middleman in the supply chain. For example, IoT can provide farms with a public forum, communicating with consumers about farms and the products they offer, so that consumers can place orders directly with farms without the need to go through the long chain of retailers, wholesalers, distributors and processors to reach the producers.

Questions

1 Can you think of any other aspects of agriculture and breeding in which IoT has been or could be used?

2 Compare your aspects with the five aspects discussed above. How different or similar are they in terms of the ways IoT is used, for example the scale of technology usage and the focus of IoT use (*things* orientation, *internet* orientation or *semantic* orientation)? Refer to Atzori, Lera and Morabito (2010) for information about the three orientations, if needed.

Direct and indirect impacts of IoT on KM

IoT allows for greater connectivity among individuals, groups, organization units, organizations and communities, and thus presents opportunities to leverage knowledge via mobilization within and crossing boundaries. Five key business benefits of using IoT have been observed (Diffey, 2014):

- IoT can refine, integrate, optimize and automate business processes across an organization.

- IoT can promote innovation and new product development, enabling businesses to move to a service-based proposition, generating recurring revenues and servicing new markets that initiate new revenue streams.

- IoT can enhance customer relationship management. It can be used to increase the number of customer touchpoints for a business, and allow businesses to strengthen their relationships with end users.

- IoT can promote safety and security, which helps businesses to keep their staff and customers safe through monitoring things such as fire alarms' functionality and escape route access.

- IoT can enable asset management by creating more touchpoints for assets, monitoring the status of assets and providing necessary maintenance in time.

The specific impact of IoT on KM can be examined from two angles. One is the direct impact and the other is the indirect impact through business performance. The direct impact exists because IoT provides technologies and means for accessing real-time and big data by all stakeholders, subsequently converting the data and information into real-time knowledge as well as sharing knowledge among the stakeholders; hence KM approaches have to

Figure 10.1 Direct and indirect impact of IoT on KM

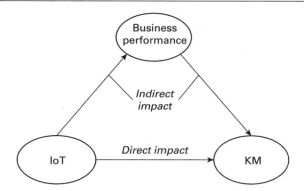

adapt to reflect the IoT impact. In terms of the indirect impact, it is a fact that IoT has revolutionized the business world, from value creation and value delivery to value capture. It is also understood that the ultimate aim of KM is to achieve competitive advantages for an organization and improve its business performance. Subsequently, KM has to improve and change to better support decision making in the revolutionized business world. This double effect from IoT on KM is illustrated in Figure 10.1.

In essence, IoT provides a technological network platform that can facilitate all stages of KM processes, including:

- allowing the creation of new knowledge facilitated by the data and information collected from a wide range of sources, whether via physical sensors and devices or virtual entities;
- allowing the storage of knowledge using the cloud and other systems;
- allowing knowledge mobilization among all stakeholders and the wider environment, within an organization or crossing boundaries that are connected through any paths/networks;
- allowing the utilization of knowledge through any services enabled by IoT.

Section 10.1 has described the key components of a traditional KMS supported by conventional ICT technologies. In the IoT era, a new generation of KMS should offer additional capabilities, which should be able to (Uden and He, 2017):

- create personalized experience and tackle multiple sources;
- move and reposition data and information from different sources and channels;

- optimize data, information and knowledge for different uses;
- provide real-time on-demand data, information and knowledge for both rational and emergent decision making;
- collect instructional data and machine data; and
- enable the KMS to be seamless and interoperable, and to have realistic connectivity that reduces costs, improves quality and drives greater productivity.

It should be pointed out that the relationship between IoT and KM is not one-directional but bi-directional. KM plays an important role in strategic decisions for the design of an effective IoT network. For example, to make the right decisions in terms of the 'things' and the 'network (internet)', it is essential to know what data to focus on and how to allocate analytical resources. To find out the answers to these questions, there are bigger issues regarding businesses to address first, as IoT technology will be worth investing in and will be able to gain support only if IoT strategy is aligned with business objectives. Therefore, it is important to ask relevant business questions. For example:

- What are the core business processes that IoT aims to support?
- What key decisions in the processes will benefit from analytical insights?
- What data, information and knowledge really matter to the business?
- What are the knowledge leverage points of business performance?

Apart from strategic decisions, KM can play a crucial part in the implementation of IoT, because the realization of IoT requires a combination of skills and knowledge from, among others, computer science (internet and network), engineering (infrastructure and devices) and management (project planning and monitoring, requirements analysis). Not even the most advanced technological software packages can obviate the need for a high degree of human skills and experience in the successful analysis and development of IoT platforms (Uden and He, 2017). A deep understanding of how data can be collected, travel along the network, be analysed, be transformed into actionable information and knowledge, and be used to transform businesses often comes from personal experience. Much of this knowledge is tacit. The whole process of implementing IoT systems, from requirements analysis, design and development to realization, requires support from effective KM throughout knowledge creation, holding, mobilization, utilization and learning, let alone all the contextual knowledge required for the adoption of IoT in the first place. KM will help to make sure that the adoption and implementation of IoT will be able to support the collection of the right data, the analysis of those data, and the transformation of data and information into actionable knowledge on which business decisions can be based.

 Critical thinking and reflection
IoT and knowledge management

Do you think the impact of IoT on knowledge management in a business context is mainly positive or negative, and why? Use examples to back up your arguments.

10.3 Big data analytics and knowledge management

IoT and big data are closely related because the huge number of internet-connected 'things' in the IoT will generate a massive amount of data available for analysis. Data do not equal information, and information does not equal knowledge. However, by analysing raw data, information can be extracted. When more information is gathered and validated, new knowledge may be created. The real value of collecting data comes through data analysis and aggregation on a large scale, where new knowledge is discovered or revealed. IoT allows massive data to be collected from myriad sensors and devices. These data need to be classified, mined, organized and used to generate new knowledge and business intelligence to support better business decisions. In short, the links between big data and KM are through BDA, which can help in understanding and extracting valuable knowledge from huge amounts of data, and the new knowledge generated from BDA can then be used to enhance business performance.

In the current highly dynamic and competitive business environment, a big challenge for organizations is to possess 'dynamic capability' in sensing and adapting to new trends, as well as learning and creating new knowledge for achieving sustainable competitive advantage (Fuchs, Hopken and Lexhagen, 2014). Business leaders and executives want decisions to be made faster, in real time if possible, for example in emergent decision-making situations or in the case of disruption, such as an earthquake, an epidemic, a political disaster or an unexpected competitor. In KM based on big data, it is possible to take many more factors into account, including knowledge about competitors, trends in the market discerned from customer feedback, and *force majeure* (epidemics, earthquakes and so on). The valuable knowledge gained from big data and BDA can provide answers and advantages (Sumbal, Tsui and See-to, 2017).

Big data

The term 'big data' was first used by Doug Laney, an analyst from META (now Gartner). Despite the huge interest from academics and practitioners since then, its authoritative definition remains a work in progress. Davenport (2014) predicted that the term would have a relatively short life span, and other scholars concurred that there was no rigorous definition of big data (Mayer-Schonberger and Cukier, 2013). At its most basic, earlier research described big data with a 3V model, including volume, variety and velocity (McAfee *et al*, 2012); later a fourth V was added: veracity (Buhl *et al*, 2013). Today, the big data model also has a fifth V: value (Fosso Wamba *et al*, 2015):

- Volume refers to the large amount of data (too much), that is, their enormous size (measured in terabytes and exabytes) (McNeely and Hahm, 2014). With never-ending technological innovation, the quantity of data created every day grows exponentially. Today, in every second on the internet the amount of data generated is more than the capability of the entire internet of 20 years ago (Ferraris *et al*, 2019).

- Variety means that data exist in various forms (structured, semi-structured and unstructured), mostly not structured in a usable way. It also means the complexity of data content, that is, data can be generated through various means, emanating not only from the usual business and government sources but also from sensors and social media connected to IoT (Uden and He, 2017).

- Velocity is about the huge pace (moving too fast) at which big data are generated and flow, which could be well beyond the analytical capacities of most traditional database software tools (Davenport, 2014). Today, data are obtainable in real time or nearly real time. This makes it possible for organizations to be much more agile and faster in making decisions.

- Veracity refers to the fact that data may contain noise or be incomplete and out of date, which could affect the quality and usefulness of the data captured. The data collected must have quality, and the original source must have a certain level of trust (Sumbal, Tsui and See-to, 2017).

- Value is a source of competitive advantage, which highlights the meaning and importance of big data, and how to extract the hidden value from large data sets (Chen, Mao and Liu, 2014; Chang, Wang and Hawamdeh, 2019). Fosso Wamba *et al* (2015) provided a comprehensive review of the literature, with different types and examples of value. Value is often linked to an organization's ability to make better decisions.

Without being able to reach an authoritative definition, researchers have sought ways to understand big data from different dimensions: mainly the technology dimension, the organizational dimension and the social dimension.

In terms of **technology**, to enable big data to live up to the claims currently being made for it, there is still a long way to go. However, a significant number of technologies central to the future of big data have been developed, such as the Hadoop open source framework, NoSQL databases and massively parallel analytic databases (Tian, 2017). In terms of uptake, two broad knowledge trends are cloud computing and social media.

The cloud, where the internet is used as a platform to collect, store and process data (as well as share information and knowledge), allows businesses to lease computing power when they need it, rather than having to buy expensive equipment. Because of the volume, variety and velocity, computing with big data requires clusters of servers and tools to support the process, which can be expensive. Thus, organizations are increasingly looking at cloud computing as the infrastructure to support their big data projects. They can choose to keep their most sensitive data in-house, such as prices and costs, but a high volume of other data, such as those from social media, may be located externally on the cloud. Major drivers for linking big data to the cloud include cost reduction, overhead reduction, rapid provision of products and services, faster time to market, and flexibility and scalability (Tian, 2017).

Social media are a technological and social phenomenon where, by using platforms ranging from websites to 'apps', people from around the world are engaged in sharing views and information, which generates a high quantity of complex data. Facebook, Twitter and hundreds of other social network systems are providing enormous amount of information about customer demographics, their likes and dislikes about products, services, lifestyles and much else (Liu, Wang and Lin, 2017). Social media have been successfully used by many organizations for various business activities, such as direct-to-customer marketing, omnichannel retailing to increase sales both in-store and online, customer participation in design and personalized service. The sheer scale and complexity of such transactions mandates a role for big data.

Although these are positive examples of the combination of social media and big data technologies to obtain better business outcomes, too much emphasis on the role of technology should be avoided. This technology dimension is perhaps best viewed as a platform with tools that support the online community and its activities, a perspective that views technology, action and roles as emergent, inseparable and co-evolving. An overly technological perspective focuses on what technology is and does, rather than on the ways in which it becomes mutually constituted within its organizational context to influence behaviours (Tian, 2017). Limiting an overly technological perspective can be addressed in conjunction with the organizational dimension.

Obstacles to successful big data projects do not solely lie in technologies. Analytics-driven insights must be closely linked to business strategy, easy for end users to understand, and embedded into organizational processes to enable business users to make intelligent decisions based on the collaborative leveraging of organization-wide knowledge. Such strategic significance is emphasized by Elbashir *et al* (2013), who recognized the critical importance of collaborative knowledge synergies between senior management, chief knowledge officers (CKOs) and IT managers in facilitating improved decision making across an organization's value chain. The availability of big data alone does not equate to value creation. Processing data requires not only the technologies and analytical tools/techniques but also the consideration of the wider **organizational** dimension. Along with recent technological advances in IoT, data availability is not so much an issue anymore but often there is too much data. This is especially true when a vast amount of data is generated both from internal business transactions and shared through the open data movement. There has been a growing awareness of 'data rich, knowledge poor' problems (Houston and Clarke, 2008).

What is often missing is the knowledge to extract wisdom from the data and to use the knowledge and wisdom to support the right decisions. For example, how to decide what data to keep and what to discard, as well as what are kept reliably with the right metadata. When more data and information is available, there is a greater need for human judgement in decision making, which can only be supported effectively when big data activities are well aligned with the organizational business knowledge. It is an advantage when data are treated as an organizational asset. On the other hand, big data can become a threat when data are poorly managed over time, which could result in organizational knowledge asset loss (Chang, Wang and Hawamdeh, 2019). The wide spectrum of big data and the increasing demand for knowledge discovery have heightened the importance of the transformation of data into actionable knowledge for organizations' business decisions.

> ## 💡 Critical thinking and reflection
> Concept of big data
>
> A colleague tells you that big data equal big datasets. You know that this is a misconception and you want to help your colleague to understand the big data concept properly. How would you explain to your colleague the real meaning of big data?

Big data analytics (BDA)

In the current IoT era, as the number of mobile devices connected to the internet continues to grow, the problem resulting from the amount of data generated from these devices will continue to magnify. Smart cars, smart homes, smart learning devices and smart cities are some examples of IoT applications that have the capability to monitor, capture, compute, collaborate and transmit real-time data. Data collected from these applications can be made up of structured or unstructured data in various forms, such as text, images, audio and video (Sivarajan *et al*, 2017). The value of big data is not in the data themselves but rather in the knowledge discovered through BDA.

Data science and data analytics are becoming increasingly popular and seen as essential to the success of big data. Data science and data analytics are related but have different foci. Data science refers to the empirical synthesis of actionable knowledge from raw data through the complete data lifecycle process, which requires a systematic methodology to extract meaningful information and knowledge from data (Provost and Fawcett, 2013). Data analytics is an indispensable skill in the understanding of how to apply analytical tools in advancing data science (Bumblauskas *et al*, 2017). While data analytics might be dealing with data at a higher business analysis level, data science handles raw data with more complexity and uncertainty. Analysing the massive, continuous stream of mobile, location-aware, person-centred and context-relevant data from IoT-enabled devices represents a still under-explored area of BDA (Chen, Chiang and Storey 2012).

BDA is the process needed to comprehend the conglomeration of data in order to extract useful information and generate new knowledge (Chen *et al*, 2012). Thus, managers can use big data to know more about their businesses and to transform the knowledge generated into efficient decisions (Gupta and George, 2016). Fosso Wamba *et al* (2015) defined BDA as a holistic approach to managing, processing and analysing the five Vs data-related dimensions (volume, variety, velocity, veracity and value) in order to create actionable insights for sustained value delivery, measuring performance and establishing competitive advantages. A review of BDA in e-commerce reveals the business value in organizations using BDA. The review not only shows that BDA has been widely used, for example for service personalization, improved customer service and predictive analytics to demonstrate new business functions, but it also finds great potential in the use and application of BDA in various areas of organizations (Akter and Fosso Wamba, 2016). Most notably, nearly 50 per cent of supply chain professionals were already using BDA or had plans to use it in the near future (Schoenherr and Spier-Pero, 2015). Organizations consider time to be one of the most valuable resources, hence time-to-decision, with proper mitigation of risks via predictive analytics (accurate forecasting for sales, revenues and production of goods and services), is an important element within BDA. With large volumes of data virtually untapped in almost all organizations, those that can succeed in creating time-effective actionable knowledge can gain a distinct advantage over their competitors (Bumblauskas *et al*, 2017).

Many challenges exist for BDA. Industry analysts frequently observe that the volume of data is not the only challenge, but also the variety and velocity of the data. Focusing on volume alone could lead to the underutilization of the data's value. Generating value from big data is a multi-step process, consisting of data acquisition, information extraction and cleaning, data integration, modelling and analysis, and interpretation and deployment (Jagadish *et al*, 2014).

One of the issues identified in BDA is a lack of vision concerning what 'questions' need to be answered by the data. This leads to data collection without analysis. Therefore, it is extremely important for organizations to put business objectives at the centre of big data activities and programmes. Bumblauskas *et al* (2017) proposed five specific elements for consideration in any BDA activities or projects:

- the optimization of revenue and gross profit;
- the optimization of working capital and the investment in tangible and intangible capital or assets;
- the optimization of the expense structure, or the expense side of the profit model;
- the possible opportunities or costs associated with the activity or project; and
- the associated risk in terms of both new risks and the mitigation/modification of existing internal controls.

It is even more challenging for organizations to implement BDA projects successfully because of the continuous addition of new data generated throughout the organization and supply chain. Furthermore, these additional data are generated in a recursive manner. As soon as new data are generated, previous knowledge gained from previous data may become obsolete, which means that existing knowledge needs to change or be updated, and organizational decisions and actions may need to change accordingly. With the volume, variety, velocity and veracity inherent in big data, the possibilities of continually reanalysing the data, making decisions and taking actions based on new knowledge from the new data are endless. In order to provide value to business and management, data must be continuously re-evaluated from new perspectives in the changing business world (Bumblauskas *et al*, 2017).

Figure 10.2 shows how BDA should take feedback from the changing business environment. In essence, BDA is a transformation process, during which data are transformed into new knowledge and usable information. In an organizational context, the generated knowledge and information have relatively marginal value if they are not used to support business decisions. Business decisions aim to improve business performance. New knowledge could lead to new business decisions, and new business decisions could lead to new business performance. When actual business performance deviates from defined business objectives, new (hopefully improved) decisions will usually be triggered. New decisions may require support from new knowledge, hence impact on the BDA process and data inputs. The chain influence in both forward and backward directions, as shown in the Figure 10.2, is crucial for BDA projects; that is, to constantly link BDA with business decisions and business objectives, rather than to look at them in an isolated manner. Part Four of this book will provide details on business decision making.

Figure 10.2 BDA and knowledge support for business decisions

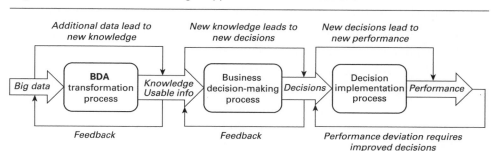

Relationship of knowledge and KM with big data and BDA

It has been established that BDA will generate new knowledge from the vast amount of data. But, what exactly would the rising and growing influence of big data and BDA mean for KM? One thing is certain: KM plays a fundamental role in the management and application of big data and BDA. Without knowledge and KM, big data and BDA do not exist, because it is human knowledge that has developed the capabilities of big data and BDA (Pauleen and Wang, 2017). If we zoom into the BDA part of the Figure 10.2 and examine knowledge and KM in BDA, we can create Figure 10.3 to provide a detailed representation of the role of knowledge and KM that are entangled with BDA.

As shown in Figure 10.3, the critical role that KM plays in BDA comes from two main threads: management of the content of new knowledge generated from BDA and management of contextual knowledge for the whole BDA transformation process.

Figure 10.3   Relationship between KM and BDA

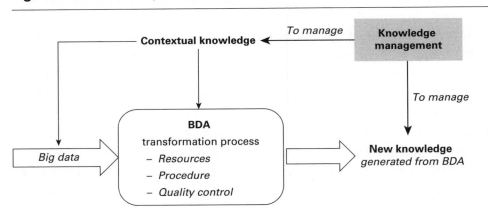

First, the main output from BDA is new knowledge, and this new knowledge has to be managed purposefully (ie to be stored, transferred, mobilized and used properly) for the benefit of organizational business decisions and performance. In other words, it is human knowledge that will decide how the new knowledge generated from big data and BDA will be stored, mobilized and used (Erickson and Rothberg, 2014). How to integrate and combine the new knowledge generated from BDA with organizational knowledge for more effective use has been a continuous research topic (Ferraris *et al*, 2019). Second, all aspects of BDA – its inputs and the transformation process itself, including the resources required for BDA, the actual procedure taken for BDA, and quality control – need contextual knowledge to take place.

Contextual knowledge refers to how knowledge is situated in organizational contexts (Aspers, 2006). Contextual knowledge is usually tacit or implicit, including the implicit knowledge contained in organizational processes and activities, embedded within an organization's outputs such as products and services, and the tacit knowledge of employees and stakeholders throughout the supply chain, including the intended markets. Specifically:

- In terms of the inputs to the BDA transformation process, human knowledge and experience are solely responsible for the decisions on what data to collect, where to collect the data and how to collect them. Even at the inception stage of BDA projects, it is contextual, organizational knowledge that defines the goals and problems and provides the motivation for initiating big data and BDA projects. Therefore, it is impossible to negate the influence of knowledge and KM when discussing the influences on and the impact of big data and BDA.

- Contextual knowledge is required in order to decide on the resources needed to support the BDA process, such as what BDA tools to purchase, which employees should take on the work, and what training to provide. These decisions, of course, will depend on what the organization wants to get out of big data projects. Is it to support routine operational transactions or to enable drastic business process reform? If it is the latter, more financial and human investment is likely to be needed to purchase and use more advanced BDA tools at larger scale.

- In an organizational environment, managers and professionals need to set up procedures and steps for data collection and analysis based on the contextual knowledge at the operational level. This is commonly seen, for example, in enterprise systems environments where certain operations or steps have to be completed before other transactions and steps can occur. In this case, contextual knowledge guides the BDA process through a combination of parallel or sequential activities.

- Finally, the quality of the new knowledge generated has to be ensured via quality control mechanisms. Because of the veracity inherent in big data, that is, the inputs into the BDA transformation process, appropriate standards or regulations interpreted through contextual knowledge have to be complied with. Knowledge that is of low quality (such as outdated, imprecise, vague, partial, contradictory knowledge) can only bring negative effects to business decisions.

To conclude, with the above understanding of the function of knowledge and KM in the design, implementation and use of big data and BDA, it becomes clear that KM should assume a leading role in the management and governance of big data and BDA projects in organizational settings. KM has the theoretical base and practical experience to decide what data are needed for the organization to run efficiently and effectively, how those data should be analysed to provide the information and knowledge most useful for organizational processes and decision making, and how to develop knowledge-based feedback loops. It is important that changes can be made to data collection and analysis in response to changes in the business environment, both internally and externally (Pauleen and Wang, 2017). It is also important that contextual knowledge and the new knowledge generated from big data and BDA should be integrated in the virtual, cross-boundary context, such as cross-functional units within an organization or inter-organizational settings (Alavi and Tiwana, 2002). Research findings have shown that organizations that develop more BDA capabilities than others, both technological and managerial, increase their performance and that KM orientation plays a significant role in amplifying the effect of BDA capabilities (Ferraris *et al*, 2019).

In order to explore the benefits of big data and BDA to their full potential, it is crucial that managers can embrace technologies within the existing organizational culture. It has been emphasized that a key challenge for using big data and BDA is to make big data trustworthy and understandable to all employees (Barton and Court, 2012). For example, frontline employees in a retail industry may be reluctant to use big data, because they do not have to rely on big data to make decisions or are not capable of understanding how big data work. In many organizations, business analytics skills are still confined to the 'expert' level and are not disseminated to all employees in an organization. However, in order to add value from using big data and BDA, it is essential that employees at all levels are equipped with the right skills through, for example, training and learning programmes. More importantly, employees should be encouraged and motivated to use big data and BDA wherever evidence shows that the business can benefit. The right organizational culture for knowledge mobilization and learning is just as critical as technologies themselves in promoting and improving the use of big data and BDA in businesses (Ferraris *et al*, 2019).

> **Critical thinking and reflection**
> links between BDA, KM and business decisions
>
> If you were a member of your organization's top management team, would you advocate for a holistic approach to BDA, KM and business decisions, or would you rather treat them as isolated programmes, and why?

Chapter summary

The key topics discussed in this chapter are interrelated, and form a closed circle as shown in Figure 10.4. As a technological network platform connecting 'things' (sensors, actuators, people, systems, devices etc), IoT enables the collection of a huge amount of data from various sources in various formats. IoT is a platform where big data can be sourced. The big data are then analysed through advanced BDA, where data are transformed into new knowledge. The valuable new knowledge generated from BDA, through appropriate KM and learning activities, can then be used to guide business decisions. Finally, the decisions are implemented, monitored, evaluated and improved through the 'things' on the IoT. This closed circle suggests that IoT, big data and BDA, KM and business decisions need to be considered in a holistic

Figure 10.4 Links among IoT, big data, BDA, KM and business decisions

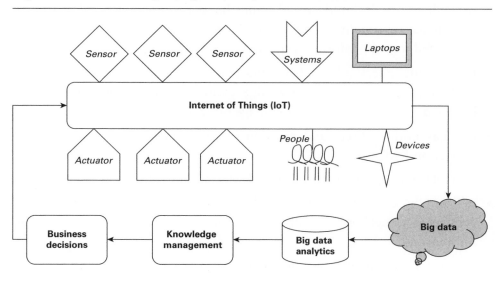

manner. In other words, modern business managers need to be able to integrate all these areas, including technologies, organization theories, KM, decision making and businesses, in order to make better decisions to achieve excellent business performance.

Key learning points

- The 'Internet of Things' refers to an emerging paradigm consisting of a continuum of uniquely addressable 'things' communicating with each other to form a worldwide dynamic network. There are many different definitions of IoT.

- The MIT Group developed an electronic product code that serves as a universal identifier, such as RFID, for any specific item; hence it defines IoT as the worldwide network of interconnected objects uniquely addressable based on standard communication protocols.

- In the ITU Group's vision, IoT connects the world's objects in both a sensory and intelligent manner through combining technological developments in item identification (ie tagging things), sensors and wireless sensor networks (ie feeling things), embedded systems (ie thinking things) and nanotechnology (ie shrinking things).

- CERP define IoT as a dynamic global network infrastructure with self-capabilities based on standard and interoperable communication protocols where physical and virtual things have identities, physical attributes and virtual personalities and use intelligent interfaces, and are seamlessly integrated into the information network.

- IoT provides a technological network platform that can facilitate all stages of KM processes, from knowledge creation, knowledge holding and knowledge mobilization to knowledge utilization.

- IoT has both a direct and an indirect (through business performance) impact on KM.

- The relationships between IoT and KM are bi-directional.

- IoT and big data are closely related because the huge number of internet-connected 'things' on IoT will generate massive amounts of data available for analysis.

- The five Vs of big data are volume, variety, velocity, veracity and value.

- BDA is the process needed to comprehend the conglomeration of data in order to extract useful information and generate new knowledge.

- In the current fast-moving business world, new data are generated at high speed (represented by the velocity of big data) and in a recurring manner. When additional data are available, new knowledge may be created through BDA, which may require earlier business decisions based on previous data and old knowledge to be adjusted or changed. It is challenging for organizations to implement BDA projects successfully because of the constant changes in the business environment.

- KM is influenced by big data from both the knowledge content created by BDA and the contextual knowledge of BDA.

Review questions

- What role does ICT play in KM?
- What are the 'things' in IoT?
- What are the main differences among the IoT definitions from MIT, ITU and CERP?
- How are IoT and big data connected?
- What is the major impact of IoT on KM?
- Is 'big data' the same as big datasets?
- What are the differences between the variety and velocity of big data?
- What are the management implications from the 'veracity' of big data?
- What does 'value' mean in big data's five V model? What are the different types of value?
- Why should big data be understood from multiple dimensions rather than from the technology dimension alone?
- Search the literature for a number of definitions or explanations of BDA, compare them and identify some common features that you think are key to BDA.
- If BDA is a transformation process, what are the main inputs and outputs of the process? What are the main constraints of the process? What are the resources required to enable the transformation process?
- Why is contextual knowledge for the BDA transformation process important?
- Why is KM greatly influenced by big data and BDA?

References

Akter, S and Fosso Wamba, S (2016) Big data analytics in e-commerce: a systematic review and agenda for future research, *Electronic Markets*, **26** (2), pp 173–94

Alavi, M and Tiwana, A (2002) Knowledge integration in virtual teams: the potential role of KMS, *Journal of the American Society for Information Science and Technology*, **53** (12), pp 1029–37

Ashton, K (2009) That 'Internet of Things' thing, *RFID Journal*, **22**, pp 97–114

Aspers, P (2006) Contextual knowledge, *Current Sociology*, **54** (5), pp 745–63

Atzori, L, Lera, A and Morabito, G (2010) The Internet of Things: a survey, *Computer Networks*, **54** (15), pp 2787–805

Barton, D and Court, D (2012) Making advanced analytics work for you, *Harvard Business Review*, **90** (10), pp 78–83

Becerra-Fernandez, I and Sabherwal, R (2015) *Knowledge Management: Systems and processes*, 2nd edn, Routledge, Abingdon

Borgia, E (2014) The Internet of Things vision: key features, applications and open issues, *Computer Communications*, **54** (1), pp 1–31

Brock, D L (2001) The Electronic Product Code (EPC) – a naming scheme for physical objects, MIT White Paper, January

Buhl, H U *et al* (2013) Big data, *Business and Information Systems Engineering*, **5** (2), pp 65–69

Bumblauskas, D *et al* (2017) Big data analytics: transforming data to action, *Business Process Management Journal*, **23** (3), pp 703–20

Chang, H C, Wang, C Y and Hawamdeh, S (2019) Emerging trends in data analytics and knowledge management job market: extending KSA framework, *Journal of Knowledge Management*, **23** (4), pp 664–86

Chen, H, Chiang, R H and Storey, V C (2012) Business intelligence and analytics: from big data to big impact, *MIS Quarterly*, **36** (4), pp 1165–88

Chen, M, Mao, S and Liu, Y (2014) Big data: a survey, *Mobile Networks and Applications*, **19** (2), pp 171–209

Dalkir, K (2017) *Knowledge Management in Theory and Practice*, 3rd edn, MIT Press, Cambridge, MA

Davenport, T A (2014) *Big data: Dispelling the myths, uncovering the opportunities*, Harvard Business School Press, Cambridge, MA

Diffey, M (2014) [accessed 3 September 2019] The Internet of Things Is More Than a Fashion Statement, *Business Spectator on The Australian Business Review* [Online] www.theaustralian.com.au/business/business-spectator/news-story/the-Internet-of-things-is-more-than-a-fashion-statement/9328343d108e54ef4fecc1b6d17b6746 (archived at https://perma.cc/CP89-LQCV)

Elbashir, M Z *et al* (2013) Enhancing the business value of business intelligence: the role of shared knowledge and assimilation, *Journal of Information Systems*, **27** (2), pp 87–105

Erickson, S and Rothberg, H (2014) Big data and knowledge management: establishing a conceptual foundation, *The Electronic Journal of Knowledge Management*, **12** (2), pp 83–154

Ferraris, A *et al* (2019) [accessed 3 September 2019] Big data analytics capabilities and knowledge management: impact on firm performance, *Management Decision*, [Online] https://doi.org/10.1108/MD-07-2018-0825 (archived at https://perma.cc/TW2S-7EHW)

Fosso Wamba, S *et al* (2015) How big data can make big impact: findings from a systematic review and a longitudinal case study, *International Journal of Production Economics*, **165**, pp 234–46

Fuchs, M, Hopken, W and Lexhagen, M (2014) Big data analytics for knowledge generation in tourism destinations: a case from Sweden, *Journal of Destination Marketing and Management*, **3**, pp 198–209

Gama, K, Touseaui, L and Donsez, D (2012) Combining heterogeneous service technologies for building an Internet of Things middleware, *Computer Communications*, **35** (4), pp 405–17.

Gubbi, J *et al* (2013) Internet of Things (IoT): a vision, architectural elements and future directions, *Future Generation Computer Systems*, **29** (7), pp 1645–60

Gupta, M and George, J F (2016) Toward the development of a big data analytics capability, *Information and Management*, **53** (8), pp 1049–64

He, W and Xu, L (2014) Integration of distributed enterprise applications: a survey, *IEEE Transactions on Industrial Informatics*, **10** (1), pp 35–42

Hislop, D, Bosua, R and Helms, R (2018) *Knowledge Management in Organizations: A critical introduction*, 4th edn, Oxford University Press, Oxford

Houston, J and Clarke, R (2008) *Moving beyond 'Data Rich – Knowledge Poor' in Human Resources*, Deloitte Consulting, New York, NY

Imran, A and Gregor, S (2019) Conceptualizing an IT mind-set and its relationship to IT knowledge and intention to explore in the workplace, *Information Technology and People*, doi.org/10.1108/ITP-04-2017-0115

ITU (2005) *ITU Internet Reports – Internet of Things*, International Telecommunications Union, Geneva

Jagadish, H V *et al* (2014) Big data and its technical challenges, *Communications of ACM*, **57** (7), pp 86–94

Jashapara, A (2011) *Knowledge Management: An integrated approach*, 2nd edn, Pearson Education, Harlow

Kim, S and Kim, S (2016) A multi-criteria approach toward discovering killer IoT application in Korea, *Technological Forecasting and Social Change*, **102**, pp 143–55

Liu, C H, Wang, S and Lin, C W (2017) The concepts of big data applied in personal knowledge management, *Journal of Knowledge Management*, **21** (1), pp 213–30

Mayer-Schonberger, V and Cukier, K (2013) *Big Data: A revolution that will transform how we live, work and think*, Houghton Mifflin Harcourt, New York

McAfee, A *et al* (2012) Big data: the management revolution, *Harvard Business Review*, **90** (10), pp 61–67

McNeely, C L and Hahm, J (2014) The big data bang: policy, prospects and challenges, *Review of Policy Research*, **31** (4), pp 304–10

Mishra, D *et al* (2016) Visions, applications and future challenges of Internet of Things: a bibliometric study of the recent literature, *Industrial Management and Data Systems*, **116** (7), pp 1331–55

Mladenow, A (2014) Crowd logistics: the contribution of social crowds in logistics, *International Journal of Web Information Systems*, **12** (3), pp 379–96

Pauleen, D J and Wang, Y C (2017) Does big data mean big knowledge? KM perspectives on big data and analytics, *Journal of Knowledge Management*, **21** (1), pp 1–6

Pohjola, I and Puusa, A (2016) Group dynamics and the role of ICT in the life cycle analysis of community of practice of practice-based product development: a case study, *Journal of Knowledge Management*, **20** (3), pp 465–83

Provost, F and Fawcett, T (2013) Data science and its relationship to big data and data-driven decision making, *Big Data*, **1** (1), pp 51–59

Santoro, G *et al* (2018) The Internet of Things: building a knowledge management system for open innovation and knowledge management capacity, *Technological Forecasting and Social Change*, **136**, pp 347–54

Schoenherr, T and Spier-Pero, C (2015) Data science, predictively analytics, and big data in supply chain management: current state and future potential, *Journal of Business Logistics*, **36** (1), pp 120–32

Sivarajan, U *et al* (2017) Critical analysis of big data challenges and analytical methods, *Journal of Business Research*, **70**, pp 263–86

Sumbal, M S, Tsui, E T and See-to, E W K (2017) Interrelationship between big data and knowledge management: an exploratory study in the oil and gas sector, *Journal of Knowledge Management*, **21** (1), pp 180–96

Tian, X (2017) Big data and knowledge management: a case of déjà vu or back to the future, *Journal of Knowledge Management*, **21** (1), pp 113–31

Uckelmann, D, Harrison, M and Michahelles, F (Eds) (2011) *Architecting the Internet of Things*, vol 1, Springer Verlag, Berlin

Uden, L and He, W (2017) How the Internet of Things can help knowledge management: a case study from the automotive domain, *Journal of Knowledge Management*, **21** (1), pp 57–70

Vermesan, O *et al* (2011) *Internet of Things strategic research roadmap: Cluster of European Research Projects (CERP) on the Internet of Things*, CERP-IoT, Brussels

Weber, R H (2010) Internet of Things new security and privacy challenges, *Computer Law and Security Review*, **26** (1), pp 23–30

PART FOUR
Knowledge support for business decision making

This part of the book is dedicated to the utilization of knowledge and knowledge management approaches for business decision support. It consists of three chapters.

Chapter 11 presents an overview of the business decision context. First, the changing nature of business environments is discussed from a number of perspectives, including the value, network and globalization perspectives. Then, four core aspects of business and the links among these aspects are explained, in order for decision makers to comprehend relevant decisions that need to be made corresponding to the business aspects. Examples are given for decisions about operations management and supply chain management, decisions about marketing and sales, decisions about accounting and finance, and decisions about human resource management and leadership. Finally, the chapter maps out business decisions along two dimensions: time and breadth of participation. In terms of time, business decisions can be made at the strategic, middle or operational level. In terms of the breadth of participation, decisions can be distinguished as individual, group and organizational decisions.

Chapter 12 focuses on human decision-making processes and the need for knowledge support. This chapter starts with definitions of decision making. A typology of the structure of decisions is provided. Various decision process models ranging from three to six stages are discussed, followed by a detailed critique of rational decision making. Then, knowledge requirements for decision making are described, with illustration of the types of knowledge that may be applied at different stages of a decision-making process.

Chapter 13 discusses knowledge-based decision support systems. An evolution from classic decision support systems to knowledge-based decision support systems is presented first. Then the chapter emphasizes two types of technology for knowledge-based decision support systems: knowledge modelling/representation and knowledge reasoning/inferencing. Ontology and clustering have been selected as the illustration of knowledge modelling technologies for detailed discussion in the chapter. For knowledge reasoning technologies, rule-based and case-based reasoning are discussed. Lastly, the chapter demonstrates the application of knowledge-based decision support systems in three industries/sectors: healthcare, construction and agriculture.

The business decision context

Learning outcomes

After completing this chapter, the reader will be able to

- appreciate the changing nature of the business world in which business decisions are situated;
- understand the links between different aspects of business that influence decision making;
- explain the key features of different types of decision in business.

Business decision making is challenging because the business world is changing constantly, no matter whether decision makers see it or not. Classical decision models presented in the literature do not always provide the best help to business leaders, because the decision approaches are often used out of context. This chapter introduces some key characteristics of business, in order to provide readers with some useful context and help them to apply appropriate decision models for better business decisions. First, the chapter will discuss the changing nature of the current business world where business decisions are situated. Then the links between different aspects of business (ie functional areas) and different types of business decision will be described. Lastly, decisions at different levels of business, from strategic to operational, from individual to organizational, will be explained. As a whole, this chapter aims to join the dots and provide a holistic, overall picture of the business decision context.

11.1 Business environments that challenge business decisions

The modern business environment, with its emphasis on competition and cooperation, building larger markets, strategic planning, teamworking, performance appraisal and so on, has created the need for a range of new business thinking and decision-making strategies. In particular, the business world has been changing faster than ever since the last part of the 20th century, because of the invention of advanced technologies such as the internet, web and social networks. As a result, e-business has thrived. E-business is the organized effort of individuals and organizations to produce and sell products and services that satisfy consumers' and society's needs through the internet, for a profit (Pride, Hughes and Kapoor, 2012). However, starting in late 2007, the world witnessed an economic crisis, which resulted in a series of severe problems, including high unemployment rates, reduced consumer spending, slowdowns in construction and many other industries, a large number of troubled banks and financial institutions, depressed stock markets and numerous shocking business failures. Not surprisingly, the first decade of the 21st century was characterized by many economic experts as the best and worst of times rolled into one package (Pride, Hughes and Kapoor, 2012). Looking from the positive side, advanced ICT technology such as internet and web became available at an affordable price, and businesses could create and sell products and manage business transactions online with unprecedented efficiency. Many pioneers in e-business and e-commerce have embraced new commercial means such as omnichannel retailing (Melacini *et al*, 2018). Today, we are again in a new business world, in which technology advances, such as the Internet of Things, have opened up commercial opportunities at an unforeseen pace. For example, we now have a situation where the world's largest bookseller does not own a single brick-and-mortar bookstore (Amazon), the world's largest telecommunications provider does not own any network infrastructure (Skype), the world's largest hotel business does not own bedrooms (Airbnb) and the world's biggest taxi company does not own cars (Uber). The unexpected emergence and fast growth of these e-businesses are pushing other businesses into shrinking market shares and changing the rules of game-play in the industry. Of course, these examples are only a drop in the ocean, but they vividly illustrate the fast-changing nature of the business world. Being able to use change to advantage is key to business success, which requires business decision makers to truly under-stand the nature of the business decision context. The nature of the change in the business world can be interpreted from a number of perspectives.

Globalization perspective

Business globalization is one of the biggest changes happening in the busi-ness world in the 21st century. Plenty of successful businesses have expanded from their home country to international trade and production (in foreign countries). Business globalization has had an immense impact on how busi-ness operates as well as on its strategy. Compared with business within the home country only, global business has two main advantages: access to global markets and the use of global resources (including knowledge, exper-tise, technologies and skills) (Mohamed, 2007). Along with the advantages, there are many extra factors that need to be taken into account when busi-ness leaders and managers make decisions. First, in association with access to global markets, that is, selling products and services in foreign countries, a number of issues need considering. For example, trade tariffs may affect deci-sions on pricing, currency exchange rates may change or fluctuate from time to time, cultural and spatial distance could influence how consumers perceive the value of product/service offering and the ways in which products/services are advertised and communicated to potential customers. Second, access to global resources also needs to take account of more factors for production decisions, such as whether the product/service functions need modification to meet the host country's consumer needs. A typical example of this functional modification is the different layout of a computer keyboard for different language users in different countries. Sourcing materials from host countries may need extra quality checks because of different quality standards used in home and host countries. Usually, one of the reasons for setting up produc-tion operations in host countries is to use cheap labour, which could help reduce costs. If relevant knowledge, expertise and skills of the workforce in host countries are not up to scratch, extra training programmes may need to be put in place, which unavoidably will incur extra cost. Global business decisions can also be affected by the political and economic instability in host countries, as international markets tend to be more uncertain, which could imply more risks (Needle, 2015). In essence, in global business decision making, there are more decision variables and decision constraints that need to be considered.

From a human resource development perspective, global business decision making requires decision makers to have certain abilities. A global decision-making model developed by Harvey *et al* classifies decision makers' capabilities in three groups: analytical intelligence, creative intelligence and practice intelligence (Harvey *et al*, 2009). Analytical intelligence involves the planning, implementation and evaluation of problem-solving processes and knowledge acquisition. Creative intelligence is the individual's ability to develop innovative solutions to new problems encountered in novel environments. Practice intelligence refers to individual tacit knowledge that draws on common sense, intuition and 'street-smart' knowledge to adapt to an environment or to shape the environment to the problem at hand. Figure 11.1 illustrates the classification scheme for the key capabilities.

Figure 11.1 Classification scheme for decision maker's key capabilities

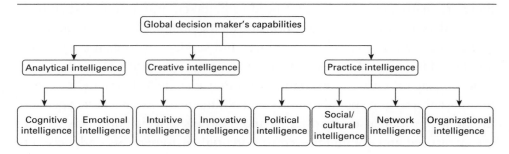

As can be seen from Figure 11.1, analytical intelligence includes cognitive intelligence and emotional intelligence, creative intelligence consists of intuitive intelligence and innovative intelligence, while practice intelligence comprises political intelligence, social/cultural intelligence, network intelligence and organizational intelligence. The meanings of the eight capabilities are explained in Table 11.1.

The network perspective

Since the 1980s, companies have experienced a paradigm shift, from a world consisting of individual companies competing against each other to supply chains competing against supply chains, in order to meet the ever-more-stringent demands of customers (Crandall, Crandall and Chen, 2010). Today, businesses are in an even more complex situation, in which a business is often sitting as part of a supply network that could comprise multiple chains, each of them supporting a mixed flow of materials/goods, information/knowledge, finance and people.

Table 11.1 Meanings of the eight global decision maker's capabilities

Capability groups	Capabilities	Meanings
Analytical intelligence	Cognitive intelligence	The ability to reason, learn and think analytically – the traditional measure of intellectual ability.
	Emotional intelligence	The ability to use one's own effective state to tap the effective state of others to accomplish tasks and achieve objectives, that is, the ability to display an appropriate emotional state and respond to others' emotions in an effective manner.
Creative intelligence	Intuitive intelligence	The ability to have quick insights without processing information actively or formally (ie being street-smart).
	Innovative intelligence	The ability to diverge/innovate in thinking to create fresh and novel ideas and solutions to problems.
Practice intelligence	Political intelligence	The ability to use formal and informal power in the organization to accomplish tasks and achieve objectives.
	Social/cultural intelligence	The extent to which one is socialized adequately in a society, an organization or a group. Recognition and understanding of roles, norms, values and taboos in various configurations (eg groups, organizations).
	Network intelligence	The ability to accomplish tasks when working with unique organizational subunits by effectively understanding and managing inter/intra-organizational relations.
	Organizational intelligence	Understanding and insights as to how the organization operates functionally and the time that is needed to accomplish goals. In-depth knowledge of how to get things done in an organization.

This means that a business is operating in the context of a web of other businesses with which it interacts, influences or is impacted by. Many of the supply chains and networks have extended beyond country borders and become true global supply chains and networks (Koberg and Longoni, 2019). There are a number of reasons why supply chains and networks have flourished in the past few decades. First, the development of a complex supply network is driven by pressure from consumers. Consumers have expressed increasing demand for products and services with more functions, higher quality standards, faster delivery and lower price. The pressure from consumers forced businesses to rethink their strategy and reconfigure resources in order to be able to deliver products and services that can meet and satisfy the consumer's needs. If their own capacity, either knowledge/expertise or physical resources, cannot meet the requirements alone, businesses have to seek partnerships with other businesses and form supply chains and networks, so that the supply chain and network together can provide the collective power to meet the consumer's needs. Second, all businesses in a supply chain and network as a whole can share risks, especially under uncertainty, for example when launching innovative products and services at a larger scale, entering new unknown markets or involving big investments. Third, technology advances have enabled and eased collaboration and cooperation among a high number of partners, for example ICT technology has made communication and mobilizing information/knowledge so much easier today than 30 years ago. Collaborative innovation teams today can work through virtual platforms to achieve an overall common goal of the whole supply chain and network (Wang and Hu, 2017).

Understandably, supply chain and network complexity has brought great difficulty to business decision making because of a number of challenges (Liu *et al*, 2013; Carvajal, Sarache and Costa, 2019):

- Decision making in a supply chain and network needs to engage a wide range of stakeholders with different roles, from material providers, designers and manufacturers to distributors, retailers and end customers. They can have very different or even conflicting interests and preferences in the decisions. The status of each stakeholder or business in a supply chain and network can be very different as well. Some players can be dominant and others can be weak partners. Indeed, decision makers might be positioned in complex social networks, which could further influence their decision-making behaviours (Capo-Vicedo, Mula and Capo, 2011).

- Owing to the nature of a supply chain and network (in terms of its complexity, dynamics and diversity), various types of decision need to be made at different times in distributed locations. Hence, different decision-making processes or even multi-process models may be used (Liu *et al*, 2010).

- The decision propagation paths within a supply chain and network can be in multiple directions (vertical, horizontal, or hub-and-spoke). As a consequence, management of decision changes in the supply chain and network environment is not easy (Kainuma and Tawara 2006).

- The decisions at supply chain and network level will require greater support from information and knowledge mobilization crossing different stages of a supply chain and network. Gathering and processing supply-network-wide information may not be a difficult task anymore by using appropriate technologies such as the Internet of Things and big data analytics; however, knowledge mobilization barriers are likely to exist at various boundaries (Boshkoska *et al*, 2019). For details on how to cross knowledge boundaries, refer to Part Three of the book, in particular Chapters 8 and 9.

The value perspective

The business world revolves around markets and consumers. In the past, the number one priority of business value was to create products that customers would be willing to pay for. Subsequently, organizations were competing against each other based on physical materials and facilities they owned. Companies owning unique facilities such as production lines or machines could produce successful products and processes, hence their competitive advantage, and they could generally rely on economy of scale to deter competitors from entering their market. Over the years, consumers' value perception has shifted and businesses are focusing more and more on services and knowledge rather than on products alone. In other words, business is dematerializing (Haslam and Shenoy, 2018).

The growing importance of service and knowledge has changed the way organizations compete and do business in the 21st century, which has resulted in the emergence of new terms such as the service economy and the knowledge economy. The knowledge economy was discussed in Chapter 1. This section discusses the service economy. In many developed countries today, such as the United States and the UK, service businesses employ a bigger workforce than manufacturing, and their major source of income is the money paid by customers to consume services rather than purchase goods, hence it is said that these nations have a service economy (Lai and Luo, 2019). In a service economy, more effort is devoted to the provision of services than to the production of goods. Typical service businesses include banking, education, healthcare, insurance, transportation, hospitality, festive entertainment, television programmes, security, dry cleaning and consultancy.

From a business management point of view, products (ie goods) and services cannot be strictly separated in a business. Most businesses in fact provide a combination of products and services, but with a different degree of each component. Generally, manufacturing organizations predominantly produce and sell goods. For example, the most important product of a car manufacturer is cars. However, there is usually also a service component included in the car sale's package, such as a 10-year guarantee. Service businesses provide service as their main offering to customers, but can also provide certain physical products as a minor component. For example, the main offering of the banking business is financial services; however, banks also provide bank cards and ATM machines for customers to better use the banking service. A more appropriate interpretation would be that some businesses, such as in manufacturing industry, are product dominant, and in the service industry they are service dominant, but most businesses provide customers with a whole package of both products and service.

Consumers' perception of value has also been extended from the classical economic value to include social and environmental value, which without a doubt is affecting how business operates. Of course, the products and services that customers will pay for will need to have their economic value. For example, a customer is willing to pay £10,000 to purchase a family car because the car can provide them with the convenience of going to their desired places at their chosen time, which public transport cannot provide. Another customer may be willing to pay £30,000 to purchase a luxurious car, because the luxurious car can provide more space, more comfort and more entertainment, such as high-quality music, as well as the image conjured up by the luxury brand, which may be important to the customer's social status. Generally, consumers are paying more and more attention to social value. Often, we see many colleagues and friends buy and drink certified fair-trade coffee, which indicates compliance with a code of conduct including labour conditions, wage standards and so on. Many businesses, such as some big brand names in the clothing industry, have been forced to demonstrate their corporate social responsibility in their business practice, by not using child labour or illegal workers in the production of cheap clothes (Oliveira, Zanella and Camanho, 2019). Otherwise, these businesses would not only break the law and breach relevant regulations but, once exposed, they could also easily lose those socially responsible and socially conscious consumers.

Besides economic and social values, more and more consumers these days are increasingly aware of environmental issues such as global warming and climate change (Koberg and Longoni, 2019). Many consumers are willing to pay for green products, that is, buying and using environmentally friendly products and services that do not cause risks for human health and natural ecosystems. Green consumerism comes from the desire to protect resources for future generations and to increase quality of life. Subsequently, sensitive business leaders have detected this consumer behaviour and adopted the concept of 'green business' in their business strategy and operations. As a result, in recent years, a combination of forces, including economic factors, growth in population, increased energy use and concerns for the environment, is changing the way business operates and individuals as consumers live (Pride, Hughes and Kapoor, 2012).

The change in consumers' perception of business value no doubt has a profound impact on business decisions, in particular in terms of the decision criteria and decision variables to be considered for both strategic and operational decisions.

Critical thinking and reflection

The changing business environment

Apart from the globalization, network and value perspectives presented in this section, what other perspectives can you think of to highlight the nature of changes in the current business world, and how would the perspectives affect business decision making?

11.2 Links between different aspects of business and associated decisions

In order to make good business decisions, it is important to understand the key aspects of business and the links among them. Most businesses have four fundamental aspects (Pride, Hughes and Kapoor, 2012; Needle, 2015):

- Operations management and supply chain management: operations management is the core of all businesses, which is about the creation and delivery of products and service to customers. Without good products or services, it is unlikely that customers would be willing to pay and the business could not be sustained over time. Innovation is extremely important for product and service development as part of operations management. Innovation in a business can take many forms, including product and service innovation, process innovation, technology innovation and business model innovation. When the whole lifecycle of a product/service is considered, a focal operation will have its suppliers, customers, suppliers of suppliers and customers of customers, together forming a supply chain which can include both a forward chain and a reverse chain. A forward chain starts from material purchasing, design and manufacturing and moves towards distribution, retailing and consumption, while a reverse chain is concerned with product recovery, recycling, reuse or remanufacturing. Forward and reverse chains together make up a closed loop and potentially a sustainable supply chain (Koberg and Longoni, 2019).

- Marketing and sales: this is the business function that is most directly concerned with satisfying customers' needs by establishing effective communication with customers in order to understand the markets, customers' requirements and customers' buying behaviour. The four crucial elements of a marketing mix include product, price, promotion and position (the 4Ps). Important activities of marketing include developing integrated marketing communications, building and maintaining customer relationships, pricing products reasonably so that customers can afford them and are willing to pay, and selling products/services via a series of activities (such as wholesaling, retailing and physical distribution) using various channels (eg physical store, online, multi-channel and omnichannel). This is the business aspect that captures the value of the products/services a business offers.

- Human resource (HR) management and leadership: this aspect of business is concerned with the most important and least predictable of all resources – people or talent management, such as hiring, training and developing employees. Other important activities include attracting and retaining the best employees, motivating and satisfying employees and teams, and enhancing union and management relations.

- Accounting and finance: accounting and finance look after the money side of the business. Accounting and finance traditionally have interrelated but slightly different focus. Accounting is more about satisfying financial regulations through book-keeping to provide an overall picture of the financial status of a business. For example, a business is required by government to provide ongoing financial statements such as cash flow statements (cash movements), profit and loss account (wealth generated) and balance sheets (accumulated wealth). Finance is more about funding and investing in business, including understanding the functions and characteristics of money, identifying the services provided by banks and financial institutions, understanding the importance of credit and credit management, and appreciating how the government reserve system regulates the money to maintain a healthy economy.

These four different aspects of a business are closely related to each other. Figure 11.2 shows the interrelationships among them. Examples of the nature of the interrelationships are labelled on relevant connecting lines. For example, operations and supply chain management needs to provide HR with hiring needs and personnel requirement information, so that HR will be able to help recruit people with the right knowledge, expertise, skills and qualifications in order to fulfil the job vacancies in the operations and supply chain management. HR will provide advice on legal requirements, such as working hours, working conditions and salary scales, as well as checking that the recruited employees have the right to work and their entitlement to

Figure 11.2 Links among the four key aspects of business

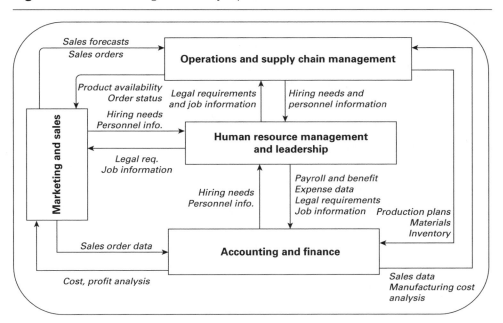

benefits and so on. Similarly, the interrelationships exist between any two of the business aspects. In order to make the right decisions for any one aspect of business, the interrelationships have to be taken into consideration.

Examples of decisions on the four aspects of a business are (Anderson *et al*, 2016):

- In operations and supply chain management, product-mix decisions need to be made by most businesses, for example how many of each model of mobile phone to produce for the next three months for different markets? How many boys' bikes and girls' bikes should be produced per month in order to maximize profit based on the resource constraints within the company? Other examples of decisions concerning operations and supply chain management include inventory planning and control decisions, facility layout decisions, transportation route decisions, distribution planning decisions, fleet configuration decisions and supply network coordination decisions.

- In marketing and sales, typical decisions include how to best allocate a fixed advertising budget among alternative advertising media. What price should be given to a specific product/service in order to stimulate sales (that is, a price customers would be happy to pay), while maximizing profit as much as possible in the meantime? Important decisions in marketing and sales can also be new product sales analysis, market-mix analysis, media planning decisions and retail promotion decisions.

- Human resource decisions need to answer some basic questions, such as how many people to employ to run the business and what selection criteria should be used in recruiting the right people. Other decisions that need to be made regularly include work shift scheduling decisions, labour-management negotiation decisions, personnel evaluation and appraisal decisions, and employee training and promotion decisions.

- In accounting and finance, examples of decisions can be how much revenue a business has generated over a month and how much is the total cost to produce and deliver 500,000 units of the product. A business may also need to make finance decisions on investment, for example to select among a variety of investment alternatives all of which have different levels of risks associated. Other examples of financial decisions could be pension fund management, cash management, portfolio management and financial planning and control.

Apart from the example decisions on generic issues in the above business areas, there are also decisions associated with specific industries or sectors. For example, education and healthcare could be included in the broad area of service operations management, but they have obtained their stand-alone status because of their high importance in people's quality of life and a nation's overall living standards (Johansen and O'Brien, 2016). Typical decisions in education can be concerned with library management, teaching scheduling, classroom assignment and the selection of MBA students. Regular healthcare decisions include nurse scheduling, inward bed allocation, diagnosis and therapy, and blood distribution. In the natural resources sector, example decisions might be about hydroelectric system management, mining project evaluation and water pollution control. This section is not aiming to provide an exhaustive list of examples, but to offer some examples so that readers can get an impression of the different types of business decision.

Critical thinking and reflection
Links among business aspects

What would be the potential consequences if the links among different aspects of a business are ignored when making organizational decisions? Is it possible to make some business decisions without taking the links into account?

11.3 Business decisions at different levels

Business decisions need to be made on various levels, which can be seen from two dimensions. First, depending on the time period associated with decisions, business decisions can be made at strategic level, middle level or operational level. Second, depending on the breadth of participation, business decisions can be made at individual level, group level or organizational level. Figure 11.3 illustrates the different levels at which business decisions have to be made. On the time dimension, everyday, short-term, operational decision problems are relatively routine, predictable and well structured, hence operational decisions can be made relatively easily. On the dimension of the breadth of participation, individual decision making involves one person only, hence this tends to be the simplest, compared with decisions at group and organizational levels. At group and organizational levels, decision makers

Figure 11.3 Business decisions at different levels along two dimensions

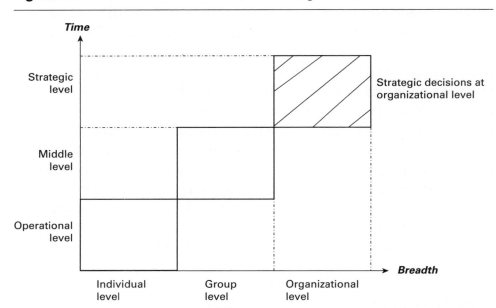

may have diversified or even conflicting interests, hence it can be difficult to achieve consensus at these levels. The most complex decisions would be strategic decisions at organizational level, because they have the broadest participation and are associated with the longest time span. Strategic decisions at organizational level (the shaded area in Figure 11.3) are concerned with the business's long-term directions and are extremely important to the organization's survival and prosperity, hence they are often called 'high-impact decisions' (Guillemette, Laroche and Cadieux, 2014). Examples of high-impact decisions include the decision to implement a new disruptive technology, the decision to invest in the development of a new product or to abandon the production of an existing one, and the decision regarding the termination of a marketing campaign. Strategic decisions at organizational level are also considered as 'wicked problems', because these decision problems are mostly tough to define, ill-structured and complex, have multiple causes and often do not have a right answer. This section will focus on strategic decisions at the organizational level.

Scholars recognize that today's business environment (such as fast changes, uncertainty and globalization) and lack of the right expertise and knowledge are conspiring to create wicked problems (Haslam and Shenoy, 2018). At organizational level, when a strategic decision needs to be made, decision makers often know very little about the situation but there are a lot of unknowns (both known unknowns and unknown unknowns). It is usually the case that people make the biggest decisions (ie strategic decisions) about an endeavour when they know the least, learn more about the situation over time, and then business leaders and managers are surprised when things do not turn out as they have anticipated. To improve decision making to avoid surprises, decision makers need to speed up their acquisition of knowledge, expertise and skills by emphasizing the importance of learning in decision-making processes. That is why this book advocates a holistic approach to decision making, knowledge management and organizational learning, rather than treating these topics in an isolated manner.

Strategic decisions at organizational level are usually substantial, sometimes dramatic and can be game-changers, because these decisions affect the organization's direction, vision, mission and goals. For example, a UK sports clothing company, which was formed over 100 years ago, decided one day to shift to designing and making clothes in fabrics other than the one upon which the business's reputation had been founded, and to move manufacturing offshore. This was a strategic decision made at the top level which dramatically changed the direction and purpose of the business (Pride, Hughes and Kapoor, 2012).

Strategic decisions at organizational level are often made top-down; however, there are a number of challenges to this top-down approach, including (Haslam and Shenoy, 2018):

- Top-down decisions can provide both focus and blinkers. A clear sense of organizational purpose from the top can be recognized as restrictive and dampen an organization's ability to adapt and be creative, and could even make managers at middle and operational levels afraid of questioning the direction from the top.

- The decisions will be closely dependent on the top team's strategic competence and capacity. In a top-down approach, strategic decisions rest in the hands of the few, that is, the top team's ability to make appropriate strategic choices. It requires the top team to have the quality of strategic thinking and to consider different perspectives in order to make good strategic decisions. The perspectives can be organizational (for example, the chief financial officer's view compared with that of the executive vice-president of operations), demographic (eg embracing gender and age distinctions) or cultural.

- There is a danger of unfettered power. When decision power is in the hands of a very small number of people, or one person sitting at the very top of an organization, there could be a risk of autocracy and dictatorship, where no one else is able to challenge the strategic decisions or contribute perspectives, and then alarm bells ring. Defence against the risks of unfettered power can be made even more difficult by the reputation that a leader might have built and the impact of that reputation down the line.

- Can top-down decisions truly engage people? There is often a difference between individuals and organizations (ie collections of individuals) when it comes to motivation and desire. A strategic decision from top management, however, needs support from all levels in an organization to be successfully implemented. As a first step, can top-down strategic decisions cross the bridge between top management and individual personnel to ensure their engagement and desire? If, and perhaps only if, yes, can organizations actually derive any benefits? The central facet of top-down decision making is clarity of intent; most often, top decisions can be translated into strategic executions through the allocation of resources, changing the organizational structure and processes, and measured by targets and relevant metrics. So, the challenge during this translation is around whether individual people genuinely engage with a vision that they did not create themselves, and especially if it is not for them.

> **Critical thinking and reflection**
> Top-down approach for strategic decision making
>
> Despite much criticism of the top-down approach to strategic decision making, why do you think the approach is still adopted in many organizations?

Key learning points

- The business environment has changed significantly, especially since the late 20th century. The changes can be interpreted from many different perspectives, such as the globalization perspective, network perspective and value perspective.

- It is important to understand all aspects of a business and the links among them in order to make holistic business decisions. The main aspects of business include operations management and supply chain management, marketing and sales, accounting and finance, and human resource management and leadership.

- Strategic decisions at organizational level made through a top-down approach have been criticized on many fronts, for example the danger of unfettered power, insufficient engagement from employees and the potential for autocracy and dictatorship.

Review questions

- What main links do you think should be considered among the four main aspects of business (ie operations and supply chain management, marketing and sales, accounting and finance, and human resource management and leadership) when making decisions at strategic level in an organization?
- What are the main differences among individual, group and organizational decision making?
- What are the main challenges you can envisage in making supply-chain-wide strategic decisions?
- Would you prefer a top-down or bottom-up approach for making organizational strategic decisions, and why?

References

Anderson, D R *et al* (2016) *An Introduction to Management Science: Quantitative approaches to decision making*, 14th edn, Cengage Learning, Boston, MA

Boshkoska, B M *et al* (2019) A decision support system for evaluation of the knowledge sharing crossing boundaries in agri-food value chains, *Computers in Industry*, **110**, pp 64–80

Capo-Vicedo, J, Mula, J, and Capo, J (2011) A social network-based organizational model for improving knowledge management in supply chains, *Supply Chain Management – An International Journal*, **16** (4), pp 284–93

Carvajal, J, Sarache, W and Costa, Y (2019) Addressing a robust decision in the sugarcane supply chain: introduction of a new agricultural investment project in Colombia, *Computers and Electronics in Agriculture*, **157**, pp 77–89

Crandall, R E, Crandall, W R and Chen, C C (2010) *Principles of Supply Chain Management*, CRC Press, Taylor and Francis, London

Guillemette, M G, Laroche, M and Cadieux, J (2014) Defining decision making process performance: conceptualization and validation of an index, *Information and Management*, **51**, pp 618–26

Harvey, H *et al* (2009) Globalization and its impact on global managers' decision processes, *Human Resource Development International*, **12** (4), 353–70

Haslam, S and Shenoy, B (2018) *Strategic Decision Making: A discovery-led approach to critical choices in turbulent times*, Kogan Page, London

Johansen, M L and O'Brien, J L (2016) Decision making in nursing practice: a concept analysis, *Nursing Forum*, **51** (1), pp 40–48

Kainuma, Y and Tawara, N (2006) A multiple attribute utility theory approach to lean and green supply chain management, *International Journal of Production Economics*, **101** (1), pp 99–108

Koberg, E and Longoni, A (2019) A systematic review of sustainable supply chain management in global supply chains, *Journal of Cleaner Production*, **207**, pp 1084–98

Lai, F and Luo, X (2019) Social commerce and social media: behaviours in the new service economy (Guest Editorial), *Information and Management*, **56**, pp 141–42

Liu, S *et al* (2010) Integration of decision support systems to improve decision support performance, *Knowledge and Information Systems – An International Journal*, **22** (3), pp 261–86

Liu, S *et al* (2013) A decision-focused knowledge management framework to support collaborative decision making for lean supply chain management, *International Journal of Production Research*, **51** (7), pp 2123–37

Melacini, M *et al* (2018) E-fulfilment and distribution in omni-channel retailing: a systematic literature review, *International Journal of Physical Distribution and Logistics Management*, **48** (4), pp 391–414

Mohamed, M S (2007) The triad of paradigms in globalization, ICT and knowledge management interplay, *VINE – the Journal of Information and Knowledge Management Systems*, **37** (2), pp 100–02

Needle, D (2015) *Business in Context*, 6th edn, Cengage Learning EMEA, Andover

Oliveira, R, Zanella, A and Camanho, A S (2019) The assessment of corporate social responsibility: the construction of an industry ranking and identification of potential for improvement, *European Journal of Operational Research*, **278**, pp 498–513

Pride, W M, Hughes, R J and Kapoor, J R (2012) *Introduction to Business*, 11th edn, South-Western Cengage Learning, Boston, MA

Wang, C and Hu, Q (2017) [accessed 3 September 2019] Knowledge Sharing in Supply Chain Networks: Effects of Collaborative Innovation Activities and Capability on Innovation Performance, *Technovation* [Online] https://doi.org/10.1016/j.technovation.2017.12.002 (archived at https://perma.cc/P649-MZPZ)

Human decision- 12
making processes
and knowledge
requirements

Learning outcomes

After completing this chapter, the reader will be able to:

- understand the concepts of decision making and decision support;
- explain human decision-making processes and compare different decision process models;
- identify knowledge requirements for decision support.

The previous chapter on the business decision context has provided us with knowledge about *what* types of decisions are made and *where* the decisions are made (ie at different levels of organizations). This chapter will continue the discussion on business decision making but will focus on *how* the decisions are made and how they can be supported by knowledge management. After an introduction to the concepts of decision making and decision support, this chapter will present decision-making processes by comparing different process models. Then the chapter will discuss the limitations of human decision making and identify requirements for knowledge support.

12.1 Concepts of decision making

Definitions

Decision making is a well-established research area. The origin of the decision-making concept can be traced back to two primary sources:

management and psychology. The management origin is represented by the theoretical study of organizational decision making undertaken by Herbert Simon at the Carnegie Institute of Technology during the late 1950s and early 1960s (Simon, 1960). Psychologist Egon Brunswick posited that an individual utilized fallible 'cues' from the environment while trying to be as empirically accurate as possible in making judgements about objects and events (Brunswick, 1979). Since then, a great many definitions have been proposed. Table 12.1 provides some definitions from different times.

Table 12.1 Definitions of decision making

Source	Definition
(Simon, 1960)	Making a choice among alternatives.
(Shull, Delbecq and Cummings, 1970)	A conscious and human process, involving both individual and social phenomena, based upon factual and value premises, which includes a choice of one behavioural activity from one or more alternatives with the intention of moving towards some desired state of affairs.
(Brunswick, 1979)	Making judgements about objects and events using fallible 'cues'.
(Ackoff, 1981)	A decision-making individual or group has alternative courses of action available. The choice made can have a significant effect.
(Mintzberg, 1983)	A commitment to action.
(Nolan, 1989)	Making the best choice from the known options.
(Harrison, 1999)	A moment, in an ongoing process of evaluating alternatives for meeting an objective, at which expectations about a particular course of action impel the decision maker to select that course of action most likely to result in attaining the objective.
(Anderson et al, 2016)	Decision making is generally associated with the problem-solving process. The first step of decision making is to identify and define the problem. Decision making ends with the choosing of an alternative, which is the act of making the decision.

As can be seen from Table 12.1, one of the difficulties with defining decision making lies in the fact that it is a concept that, when operationalized, takes many forms. In other words, decision making can be varied and multifaceted. It may be possible to identify elements of a decision that are common to other decisions, but it is not possible for all decisions to be of the same nature. To summarize the observations from the literature on the concept of decision making:

- Two different decision-making styles exist following the two sources of origin of decision making, which complement each other very well.

Decision makers do not always behave rationally based on analysis (management science), but also use intuitive judgement of the situation (psychology), especially under uncertainty (Fitzgerald, Mohammed and Kremer, 2017). Scholars later rejected the view that analytical and intuitive thinking were dichotomous modes of thought, but were poles on a continuum as decision making is neither purely analytical nor purely intuitive, but lies somewhere in between on the continuum (Johansen and O'Brien, 2016).

- Following from the previous point (ie both analytical and intuitive judgement are important), it can be deduced that the evaluation of alternatives for a choice can be undertaken using either qualitative or quantitative analysis. Qualitative analysis is primarily based on the decision maker's experience and judgement, which could include a business manager's intuitive feel for the problem and is more an art than a science. If a decision maker has had experience with similar problems, or if the problem is relatively simple, well structured and programmed, qualitative analysis may play a dominant part in the decision making. However, for a novice decision maker or a business manager who has had little experience with similar problems, or if the decision is sufficiently complex, unstructured and non-programmed, a quantitative analysis of the decision alternatives can be an especially important consideration in the manager's final decision (Anderson *et al*, 2016).

- Two different decision-making behaviours exist. Some decision makers seek the best possible result, mainly maximum profit. This type of decision maker is referred to as a 'maximizer'. Other decision makers opt for a good enough choice that meets some criteria, hence the term 'satisficers'. When faced with a decision situation, maximizers search for more information and knowledge and browse more intensively. They actively seek to identify a large number of alternatives and consider a large number of criteria. Their behaviour is characterized by going forward and backward between choices, and engaging in intensive comparison activities. Satisficers engage in 'satisfying' behaviour by searching for alternatives that are good enough, rather than attempting to reach some kind of optimal outcome. They are highly selective in using and processing information and knowledge, which reduces their search effort in terms of cycles and time, and decreases their analysis and evaluation effort in terms of alternatives and criteria (Karimi, Papamichail and Holland, 2015).

- Complex business decisions often need to consider multiple criteria such as to pursue economic and social values, meet product/service quality and safety standards, deliver the product/service to customers on time and satisfy environmental regulations. In such decision situations, multi-criteria decision analysis (MCDA) methods should be used to support complex business decisions (Hafezalkotob *et al*, 2019).

A typology concerning the structure of decisions

Despite the content of a decision (eg is it related to operations and supply chain management, human resource management and leadership, accounting and finance, or marketing and sales?), all business decisions can be classified into meaningful categories according to the key attributes of the decisions. Figure 12.1 provides a typology concerning the structure of decisions. This includes: structured or unstructured decisions, programmed or non-programmed decisions, strategic or operational decisions, and individual, group or organizational decisions (Teale *et al*, 2003; Anderson *et al*, 2016):

- Structured and unstructured decisions: structured decisions are considered to be clear, unambiguous and easily definable. On the contrary, unstructured decisions are unclear, ambiguous and difficult to define.

Figure 12.1 A typology concerning the structure of decisions

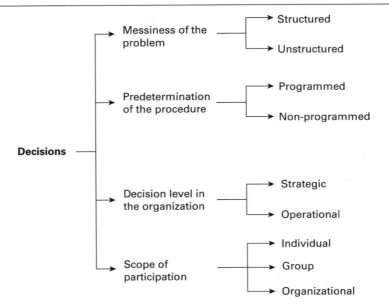

- Programmed and non-programmed decisions: decisions are programmed to the extent that they are repetitive and routine, and a definitive procedure has been worked out for handling them. Programmed decisions rely on some form of predetermined organizational apparatus or routine, for example an administrative procedure that is invoked when a particular problem occurs. Non-programmed decisions are novel, unstructured and consequential. There is no cut-and-dried method for handling the problem, either because it has not arisen before, or because its precise nature and structure are elusive or complex, or because it is so important that it deserves a custom-tailored treatment. In essence, no procedural guidelines exist.

- Strategic decisions and operational decisions: strategic decisions are long term and involve fundamental changes in ideology and/or authority, and therefore the direction of an organization. Operational decisions concern the short term and the day-to-day running of the business, such as maximizing efficiency for resource allocation.

- Individual, group and organizational decisions: compared with individual decisions, group decisions involve a number of people, hence they may need to negotiate to resolve conflicts and achieve consensus. Organizational decisions are the most complex and most important, hence the decision-making process requires the highest level of coordination and integration of decisions at different levels (Abubakar *et al*, 2019). The impact of organizational decisions is organization-wide, so organizational decisions require support from individuals and groups.

Elements of decision making

Because of the complexity of decision making and the varied attributes of business decisions, it is sensible to decompose decision making into its individual elements to better understand the what (what decision needs to be made), who (who will make the decision), how (how can/should such a decision be made) and why (why is the decision made in this/that way) (Anderson *et al*, 2016). Figure 12.2 illustrates the various elements comprising decision making, which are organized into four groups around the core element of the decision-making process. The four groups represent the inputs (on the left-hand side), outputs (on the right-hand side), constraints (on the top) and mechanisms (at the bottom).

Figure 12.2 Decision elements organized in inputs, outputs, controls and mechanisms

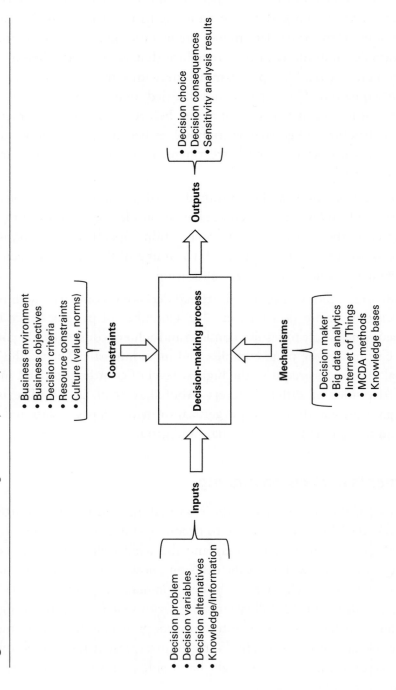

Decision making is the transformation process sitting in the middle of Figure 12.2, which should consist of a number of phases or steps. The next section will be dedicated to the discussion of the decision-making process and comparison of various process models. This section looks in detail at the four groups of decision elements in a decision-making process.

- **Inputs**: these are the elements involved in the decision-making process that must be transformed into decision outputs. Examples of inputs are decision problems, decision variables, decision alternatives and any known data, information or knowledge associated with the decision problem.

- **Outputs**: these are the outcomes of the decision-making process. The most important outcome is, of course, the decision choice. Ideally, the decision process will also generate the evaluation of the decision choice, that is, the possible consequences of taking a particular decision choice. In most decision-making situations, especially for high-level strategic decisions involving many uncertainties, a series of alternatives is available, but each alternative has consequences depending on the occurrence or non-occurrence of some future variables or conditions. These future variables or conditions (states of nature) can be anything, for example the action of a competitor, the state of the economy, the stability of the political system or a technological advance. These states of nature or condition or events are beyond a business leader's or manager's control. In such a situation, a decision maker should assess the probability of occurrence of each variable, based on the assessment criteria. Sensitivity analysis is sometimes called 'what if' analysis. Sensitivity analysis, as a technique, attempts to make business managers more aware of the 'states of nature' (ie different variables as indicated above) and of their impacts on business situations.

- **Constraints**: business decisions are made under many constraints. The constraints are often derived from the business environment (for example, globalization and the supply network as discussed in Chapter 11) and business objectives (profit or non-profit driven). There are various decision criteria, such as product/service quality, delivery speed, cost target, and the flexibility of delivering a variety of products and service to customers. Businesses also have resource constraints, such as limited production facilities, availability of knowledge and skills, time and funding constraints. Another source of constraints can be organizational culture; for example, the fundamental values, assumptions and norms within an organization may impose constraints on decision makers to choose certain alternatives or to change the decision makers' preferences in choosing decision criteria.

- **Mechanisms:** these are the enablers or facilitators that can support the decision-making process. The most important and intelligent mechanism is undoubtedly the decision makers. Who makes decisions? In business, people often think that managers make decisions. However, managers are not the only people who make decisions. You could even argue that everyone has the potential to make decisions. Doctors, lawyers, teachers, architects, shop assistants, librarians and so on all make decisions of some kind. Other often-used mechanisms include decision models (such as the profit model and linear programming model), analytical methods (for example big data analytics and multi-criteria decision analysis), ICT platforms (such as the Internet of Things and all sorts of company intra-networks), software packages and knowledge bases.

💡 Critical thinking and reflection
Classification of decision elements

To what extent do you agree or disagree with the classification of decision elements into the four groups of inputs, outputs, constraints and mechanisms? Research the topic and devise your own classification for decision elements, and see how many groups there would be in your classification. Compare the element groups in your classification with the four groups of inputs, outputs, constraints and mechanisms, and discuss the main differences between the two classifications.

12.2 Different decision process models

It is generally believed that a well-defined decision-making process can help leaders, managers and other business professionals to more thoroughly examine decision alternatives and more confidently select the optimal or most appropriate choice. Reflecting on the rational–intuitive judgement continuum for decision making, past research has indicated that in the context of a crisis, such as when a fire breaks out or the organization is facing a natural disaster, decision makers tend to adopt a more straightforward approach, mainly relying on intuitive judgement. However, high-impact decisions, such as strategic decisions, are usually approached more systematically. With a more systematic yet flexible decision process, decision makers are better able to see the potential advantages and disadvantages when applying it elsewhere, but a one-off, ad hoc, trial-and-error solution seldom provides any guidance on how to approach the next new decision situation that comes along. For example, in planning a new strategic initiative, decision makers tend to evaluate and re-evaluate their implementation plans carefully, guided by a well-structured decision process (Guillemette, Laroche and Cadieux, 2014). In such cases, decision makers will take a more rational and less intuitive or political path by following a structured decision-making process. Indeed, the positive impact of high-quality analysis with a well-defined decision process on the performance of decision making is well documented in the literature (Cabantous and Gond, 2011). A significant number of decision process models have been developed, varying in the number of stages and the sequence of the stages in action. This section has chosen some of the widely adopted, generic decision-making process models. These decision process models need to be systematic enough to enable people to be trained to be confident decision makers. They also need to be flexible enough to enable users to adapt them to various applications (Hicks, 2004).

Simon's three- and four-stage models

One of the earliest and most influential decision-making process models is probably Herbert Simon's three-stage model, which includes intelligence, design and choice (Simon, 1960). Stage one, the intelligence stage, is about problem identification, problem structuring and problem statement. It is important to gather intelligence and understand the nature of the problem. For example, is the problem with the concept of the product or service, the package offered to customers, the process to deliver the product/service, or a combination of these? What is the scope of the problem? What are the main contributing factors? How can the problem be broken down, if needed, such as when facing complex issues? The second stage, the design stage, focuses on setting decision criteria, searching for alternatives and formulating decision models. Finally, the choice stage will involve solving the decision models, including weighting, ranking and prioritization of the decision alternatives. This stage may also be concerned with conflict resolution.

Simon later extended his three-stage decision model by adding a fourth 'review' stage, which involves implementing the decision choice and then monitoring and evaluating the decision performance (Simon, 1997). If the implementation of the decision choice solves the problem and achieves the expected business performance, the decision is considered a success.

Otherwise, the decision choice is not a successful one, and it should be fed back to previous stages for revision. On some occasions, decision makers can intervene in the decision process by adjusting inputs or outputs based on their tacit or explicit knowledge of the business (Kaki, Kemppainen and Liesio, 2019). It should be noted that a decision model, like any other model, is only an abstraction of reality. A model is not an exact description of reality, but it should reflect the key features of it. A decision model needs to solve problems in reality. Even at the early stage of a decision-making process, it is important to examine the reality closely to make sure that intelligence re-flects the real-world problems. When a decision model is created, it should be validated through testing it against e reality. Similarly, when a choice is made, the solution should be tested in reality. Figure 12.3 illustrates Simon's deci-sion model, with feed-forward and feedback links between the different stages of the decision-making process, as well as the links between the reality and a decision process model.

Figure 12.3 Annotation of Simon's decision-making process model

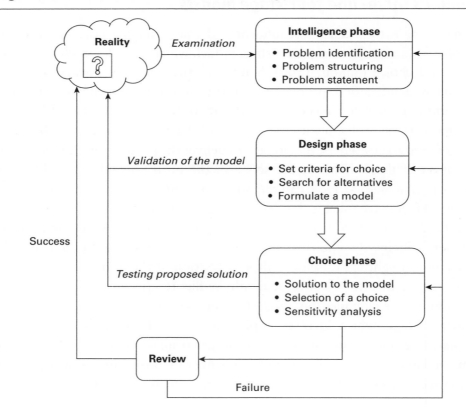

> **Illustration**
> Concept of the decision-making process

Let us consider the following example of the decision-making process. Imagine that you are the decision maker for a high-tech British company which needs to expand its business and is looking into entering the Chinese market. One effective way to access foreign markets would be to find a new production site and open a new factory – manufacturing and selling products there. The question is: where to open the new factory in China? Suppose your initial search for locations has resulted in three alternatives: Location A, Beijing (capital city of China, North); Location B, a rural area in Yunnan province (West); and Location C, Shenzhen (a special commercial area, next to Hong Kong, South of China). Which location would be the 'best' one in which to open the new factory?

In this case, the first decision step, intelligence, is straightforward. Things are pretty clear. Your company needs to access the Chinese market, so finding a location would be the preceding step to opening a new factory so that new products could be manufactured in China and sold in the Chinese market. The decision problem can be stated as 'to decide the best location for the new factory'.

You already know that there are three alternatives: Locations A, B and C. In the design stage, you need to be clear about what criteria you are going to use to assess them. Obviously, the cost of the site would be an important factor in the decision. If 'cost of site' were the only criterion of importance to your decision, the alternative selected as the 'best location' would be the one with the lowest 'cost of site'. Problems in which the objective is to find the best solution with respect to one criterion only are referred to as **single-criterion decision** problems. Suppose that you identify two other important factors to consider when deciding the location, 'skills availability' (your new factory would need to employ people with the right expertise and skills) and 'access to airport' (for business travel and logistics purposes). Thus, you have three decision criteria in total: 1) cost of site, 2) skills availability and 3) access to airport. Problems that involve more than one criterion are referred to as **multi-criteria decision** problems.

Now you have three alternatives and three decision criteria. What you need to do next is to define a decision model to solve the decision problem. You could use a five-point scale from 1 to 5 and evaluate each location against all three criteria; that is, if a location satisfies a criterion in a really 'poor' way, you give it 1 point, then 2 means 'fair', 3 for 'average', 4 for 'good' and finally, 5 for 'excellent'.

Once you have established this decision model, you can make your judgement, based on your research on the three locations, by using the three criteria. If you record your judgement scores in a table like the one below, for example, it will give you an overall view of all decision alternatives in terms of how well they satisfy each of the chosen criteria.

	Cost of site	Skills availability	Access to airport
Location A	Good (3)	Good (4)	Good (5)
Location B	Excellent (5)	Good (3)	Fair (2)
Location C	Average (3)	Excellent (5)	Excellent (5)

Suppose that you want to go for the location that has achieved the highest overall score. Based on your judgement, you are now ready to make a choice from the three alternatives; alternative C – Shenzhen (very expensive to obtain land but with a lot of university graduates concentrated in the area, so easy to recruit people with skills, and well linked to Hong Kong Airport and Baiyun Airport in Guangzhou) with a total of 13 points (3+5+5) would be your decision.

Questions

This example illustrates one of the most critical points in a decision-making process: no alternative is the 'best' with regard to all criteria, which is often the case in many business decision situations. Also, all criteria are probably not all equally important.

1 How do you think you can take into account the different degrees of importance of the different criteria in your decision making?

2 Will your decision on the location change after considering the degrees of importance of the decision criteria in your decision-making process?

3 If you add a fourth criterion, the potential of the site for future expansion, would your decision change, and why?

Anderson et al's five-stage model

Some scholars have argued that the fourth step Simon added to his decision-making process model, 'review', is not really within the scope of decision making, but rather within the scope of problem solving. Typically, Anderson *et al* (2016) clearly distinguish decision making and problem solving. They argue that a decision-making process ends as soon as a choice is made from the alternatives. Implementing the decision and evaluating the results should be part of the problem-solving process. Hence, decision making is only part of problem solving, which can be illustrated in Figure 12.4.

Figure 12.4 Difference between decision making and problem solving

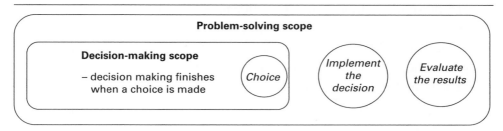

Following this argument, Anderson *et al* proposed a five-stage decision-making process model:

- Stage 1: define the problem.
- Stage 2: identify the alternatives.
- Stage 3: determine the criteria.
- Stage 4: evaluate the alternatives.
- Stage 5: choose an alternative.

The first three stages are about structuring the problem, and the last two stages are about analysing the problem (Anderson *et al*, 2016).

Badke-Schaub and Gehrlicher's six-stage model

Badke-Schaub and Gehrlicher (2003) defined a decision-making process with six stages: goal clarification, solution search, solution analysis, solution evaluation, decision and control. This decision process model was defined in the context of engineering design, which places a lot of attention to finding solutions to design problems, hence words such as 'solution' are used in three out of the six stages. Badke-Schaub and Gehrlicher (2003) further identified five patterns to reveal the key characteristics of the decision-making process. The five patterns are leaps, loops, cycles, sequences and meta-processes:

- Leaps: describe a fragmented decision process with jumps back and forth, resulting in unfinished and failed decisions, characterized by being fast processes.
- Loops: iterations of sequences of steps with the same content, resulting in stagnating information accumulation and vague, long and failed decision processes.

- Cycles: similar to loops but consist of sequences of steps with different content, resulting in accumulated information but long decision processes. There are different types of cycle, for example comprehension cycles where the decision makers gradually understand complex issues and failure cycles where decision makers start all over again (Jensen and Ahmed-Kristensen, 2010).

- Sequences: decision processes that follow the rational decision model, with structured iterations, resulting in fast processes and progress in the problem-solving process.

- Meta-processes: guided by an individual as a moderator, resulting in both long and fast decision processes and problem solving.

 Critical thinking and reflection
Decision process models

Research decision process models in the literature, to see whether you can find any decision processes that include fewer than three stages or more than six stages. If you find some, compare the stages in the decision process models with the three-, four-, five- and six-stage models described in this section, and explain the differences and the possible reasons for the differences.

Critique on rational decision making

Theoretically, decision-making processes provide a disciplined structure for managers and other business professionals to exercise consistent judgement in their search for the 'best' or 'optimal' decisions, which is extremely helpful, especially with highly complex decisions (Busari *et al*, 2017). Rational decision making incorporates a structured process and critical evaluation of evidence that requires time and conscious effort; in other words, rational procedures help decision makers to establish relevant decision criteria, identify a comprehensive set of alternatives, and evaluate their individual objectivity, hence they encompass cautious and methodical thoughtfulness of all conceivable decision choices (Fitzgerald, Mohammed and Kremer, 2017). Rational decision making is largely free from ridiculousness and predispositions, thus it results in enhanced decisions. However, the rational view is heavily criticized for a number of reasons (Hicks, 2004):

- Rational decision making is done on the basis that an exhaustive set of alternatives are readily available, which is not always true.

- It is assumed that full knowledge of the consequences of each of the alternatives is available, which is not the case in most decision situations. In fact, only one alternative (ie the chosen one) will be implemented and its consequence will be known. All other alternatives will not materialize, hence their consequences will be unknown.

- It may be impossible to measure the extent to which the consequences of each alternative would achieve the desired objectives.

In addition, the rational model is difficult to apply in practice, because of:

- difficulties encountered in devising alternatives;

- difficulties in deciding or reaching a consensus about what the evaluation criteria would be, resulting from multiple and often conflicting business objectives;

- difficulties in getting reliable and relevant information;

- difficulties in getting sufficient knowledge and expertise;

- the personality and prejudice of the decision maker; and

- the politics of the situation.

The above critical thinking implies that decision-making process can lead only to a 'partial solution' rather than the 'best' or 'optimal' decision. The decision process may be repeated endlessly as conditions and aspirations change, and as new information and knowledge are available. Thus, decision making has been perceived as a cyclical, incremental learning process. Despite the wide use of decision-making process models, it does not guarantee that decision makers will not overlook potentially excellent options in their limited search for courses of action, nor can it ensure that all relevant criteria will be used in their comparative evaluation of alternatives. Strictly speaking, the decision-making process appears to be heuristic (guided by trial and error, based on past experience and knowledge) and stochastic rather than rational. No matter how good a decision process is, good decisions depend on good judgement, while good judgement depends on the right knowledge and expertise. This is why the next section will focus on knowledge support for decision making.

> **Critical thinking and reflection**
> Rational decision-making process
>
> What is your critical view of rational decision making by using pre-defined, structured decision processes? How often do you follow rational decision-making processes? Give an example, and explain whether or not the rational decision model you used actually helped you to reach the final choice in the decision case.

12.3 Calling for knowledge support in decision making

Bounded rationality

As human beings, decision makers have limited capacity in many aspects that could affect decision-making capability, for example limited usable information on a complex decision problem, limited knowledge to make the right judgement and limited analytical capability to evaluate the alternatives. Refer back to Figure 11.1 about the global decision maker's capabilities; it is a lot to ask for any decision maker to have intelligence in all eight capabilities (Harvey *et al*, 2009). The essential ingredients of the rational model, in reality, are often compromised out of sheer necessity, resulting in an oversimplification of the whole process. In other words, the capacity of the human brain is not up to handling the magnitude of the task of making a truly rational decision on complex real-world problems. This phenomenon is described as 'bounded rationality' (Teale *et al*, 2003; Hicks, 2004).

With the rapid advancement in technologies such as ICT and big data analytics, human decision makers' limitations in information processing have been eased. The development of various decision analysis methods and approaches, especially multi-criteria decision analysis, has empowered human decision makers in terms of overcoming their analytical limitations. There are plenty of books and references available on big data and decision analysis. However, because of its tacit nature and its contextualization, knowledge is much more difficult for decision makers to learn and adapt to a specific decision context. This section will focus on knowledge requirements for decision support.

Knowledge requirements in decision making

Knowledge support in decision making has been recognized as essential from both analytical and intuitive judgement perspectives. There are many different forms of knowledge that are important for decision making. One classification of the knowledge can be experiential knowledge, factual knowledge and relationship knowledge according to the level of connectedness:

- Experiential knowledge: intuitive judgement is the decision to act on a sudden awareness of knowledge that is related to previous experience, perceived as a whole, and difficult to articulate. This reflects the 'tacitness' of experiential knowledge that was emphasized by Nonaka (1994). Experience and knowledge increase the cognitive resources available for the interpretation of the decision problem and relevant data, which usually results in more accurate judgement and a more informed decision. Experiential knowledge is built upon learning that occurs during the normal process of accumulating and ageing of experience (Abubakar *et al*, 2019).

- Factual knowledge: of course, experiential knowledge is necessary but alone it cannot suffice in practice, especially in emergent decision making. For example in the situations such as the Accident and Emergency Department in a hospital and a call centre of firefighting services, factual knowledge can be just as important as years of experience in decision accuracy (Johansen and O'Brien, 2016).

- Relationship knowledge: decision makers might sense patterns, feelings and objects in seemingly unconnected facts. Intuition can also provide decision makers with relationships without understanding why such relationships exist. When decision makers' understanding of a situation increases, disorganized facts and information become more and more organized until some kind of threshold is reached; then patterns emerge and unconscious thought can be transformed into conscious relationship knowledge, which would be really valuable in supporting decision makers' judgement (Abubakar *et al*, 2019). Focused learning is effective for building relationship knowledge, during which learning originates from deliberate efforts to cultivate habits and attain intuitive responses (Patton, 2003).

Based on a case study in new product development (NPD), Jensen and Ahmed-Kristensen (2010) classified important knowledge in NPD decisions into five categories, termed embodied, embrained, encultured, embedded and encoded, according to the level of tacitness of the knowledge. Linking back to the tacit–explicit continuum discussed in Chapter 2 (Figure 2.2), these five types of knowledge can be placed on the continuum, from the tacit end to the explicit end:

- Embodied knowledge: primarily tacit, related to practical experience and physical interaction between individuals.

- Embrained knowledge: based upon a person's ability to understand abstract knowledge and often based on experience. New knowledge is obtained from abstract thinking and understanding complex causations, for example ability to propose specific requirements on the basis of insights.

- Encultured knowledge: socially constructed, and related to both tacit and explicit shared understanding between individuals. It can be analysed from social structures and describes cultural understandings that affect social interactions in and between groups of individuals.

- Embedded knowledge: closely related to encultured knowledge but can be easily analysed from formal routines and procedures.

- Encoded knowledge: documented as text, audio or video, primarily explicit.

If the knowledge is mapped onto the tacit–explicit continuum and Simon's three-stage decision process, there are some overlaps, but, in general, knowledge with a high level of tacitness, such as experiential knowledge, embodied knowledge and embrained knowledge, dominates the early phase of the decision-making process – the intelligence phase. Knowledge with a high level of explicitness, such as factual knowledge, embedded knowledge and encoded knowledge, dominates the later stage of the decision-making process – choice. Relationship knowledge and encultured knowledge are most used in the middle stage of the decision process – design. Figure 12.5 shows this mapping between knowledge types and the decision-making process, which demonstrates the importance of knowledge support in every stage of a decision-making process.

When the types of knowledge used in different stages of decision making are identified, it is important to understand how knowledge is used in the decision process. A study by McKenzie *et al* (2014) investigated the use of

Figure 12.5 Mapping knowledge types to the decision process

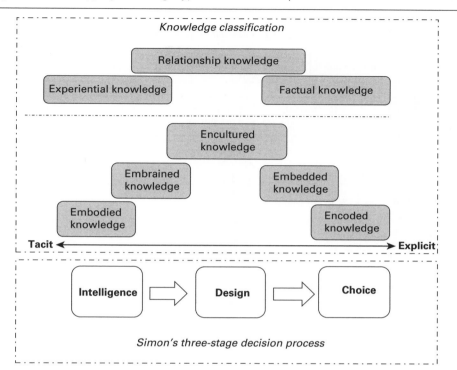

ecosystem service knowledge in spatial planning decision making. The research revealed three modes of using knowledge for decision making:

- Instrumental mode: in this mode of use, knowledge flows linearly from scientists to decision makers who make observable decisions on technical grounds.

- Conceptual mode: knowledge broadens and deepens understanding, shapes thinking and enables people to develop new beliefs and values.

- Strategic mode: knowledge is used to support and promote a specific intervention or policy option, or to justify previously held beliefs and values.

The modes of using knowledge provide concrete bridges between knowledge types and decision making, as shown in Figure 12.6. Again, here we use Simon's three-stage decision model to illustrate a decision process. Both tacit and explicit knowledge can support the decision making via strategic use, conceptual use and instrumental use.

Figure 12.6 Modes of use to link knowledge with decision process

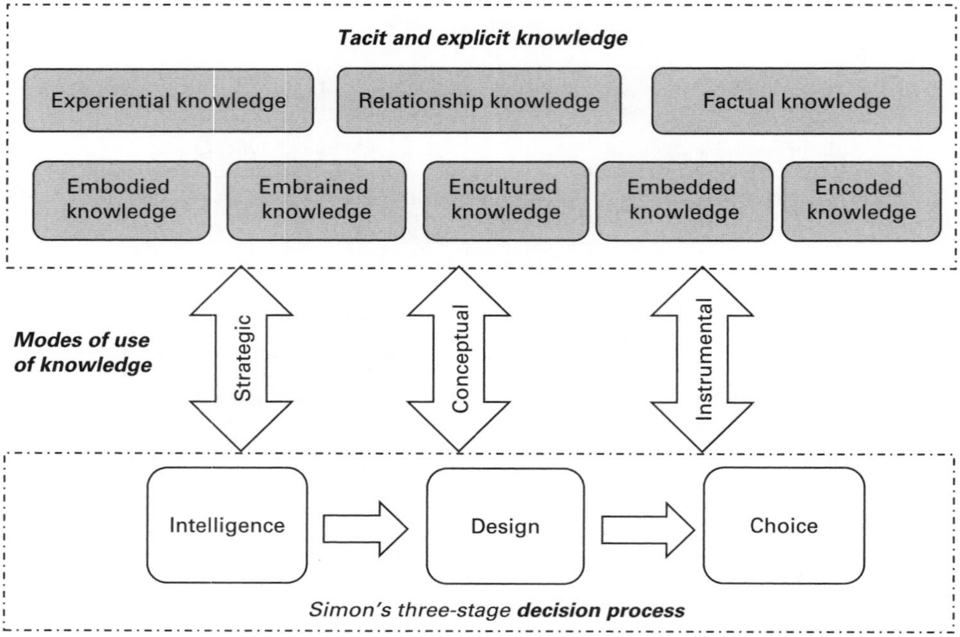

Key learning points

- Many definitions of decision making are available in the literature. An early and concise definition by Herbert Simon is 'making a choice among alternatives'.

- Decisions can be classified as structured or unstructured, programmed or non-programmed, strategic or operational, and individual, group or organizational.

- Decision elements involved in a decision-making process can be organized into four categories: inputs, outputs, constraints and mechanisms. The main inputs of a decision process include decision problem, decision variables, decision alternatives and known knowledge/information. The main outputs include decision choice, decision consequences and sensitivity analysis results.

- The decision-making process has been one of the most researched topic areas and many decision process models have been proposed in the literature. One of the most widely cited decision process models is Herbert Simon's three-stage model, including intelligence, design and choice.

- Many scholars use 'decision making' and 'problem solving' interchangeably; however, some distinguish between them, arguing that a decision-making process ends as soon as a choice is made from the alternatives and that implementing the decision and monitoring the results should be part of a problem-solving process rather than a decision-making process.

- Rational decision making incorporates a disciplined, structured process which is considered helpful in handling complex decision problems. However, it has also received much criticism in terms of assumptions made about the exhaustiveness of the alternatives, selection of decision criteria, availability of knowledge and information, and the possibility of the evaluation of decision consequences.

- Knowledge support has been recognized as an important aspect in decision making. Different forms of knowledge for decision support have been identified, including experiential knowledge, factual knowledge and relationship knowledge.

Review questions

- What is your favourite definition of decision making, and why?

- What do you think are the main benefits of structuring a decision process's elements into different groups, such as inputs, outputs, constraints and mechanisms?

- What do you think are the main factors to be considered in each stage of Simon's three-stage decision process model?

- Do you think decision making and problem solving are the same, or should they be distinguished as different, and why?

- Would you prefer a rational approach to decision making, and why?

- What are the main differences between embodied knowledge and embedded knowledge?

References

Abubakar, A M *et al* (2019) Knowledge management, decision making style and organizational performance, *Journal of Innovation and Knowledge*, **4**, pp 104–14

Ackoff, R (1981) *The art and science of mess management*, Interfaces, **11** (1), The Institute of Management Science, pp 20–26

Anderson, D R *et al* (2016) *An Introduction to Management Science: Quantitative approaches to decision making*, 14th edn, Cengage Learning, Boston, MA

Badke-Schaub, P and Gehrlicher, A (2003) Patterns of decisions in design: leaps, loops, cycles, sequences and meta-processes, *International Conference on Engineering Design (ICED 03)*, Stockholm, 18–19 August

Brunswick, E (1979) *The Conceptual Framework of Psychology*, University of Chicago Press, Chicago

Busari, A H *et al* (2017) Analytical cognitive style moderation on promotion and turnover intention, *Journal of Management Development*, **36** (3), pp 438–64

Cabantous, L and Gond, J P (2011) Rational decision making as performative praxis: explaining rationality's Eternel Retour, *Organizational Science*, **22**, pp 573–86

Fitzgerald, D R, Mohammed, S and Kremer, G O (2017) Differences in the way we decide: the effect of decision style diversity on process conflict in design teams, *Personality and Individual Differences*, **104**, pp 339–44

Guillemette, M G, Laroche, M and Cadieux, J (2014) Defining decision making process performance: conceptualization and validation of an index, *Information and Management*, **51**, pp 618–26

Hafezalkotob, A *et al* (2019) An overview of MULTIMOORA for multi-criteria decision making: theory, developments, applications and challenges, *Information Fusion*, **51**, pp 145–77

Harrison, E F (1999) *The Managerial Decision-Making Process*, 5th edn, Houghton Mifflin, Boston, MA

Harvey, H *et al* (2009) Globalisation and its impact on global managers' decision processes, *Human Resource Development International*, **12** (4), pp 353–70

Hicks, M J (2004) *Problem Solving and Decision Making: Hard, soft and creative approaches*, 2nd edn, South-Western Cengage Learning, London

Jensen, A R V and Ahmed-Kristensen, S (2010) Identifying knowledge in decision making process: a case study, *International Design Conference – Design 2010*, Dubrovnik, Croatia, 17–20 May

Johansen, M L and O'Brien, J L (2016) Decision making in nursing practice: a concept analysis, *Nursing Forum*, **51** (1), pp 40–48

Kaki, A, Kemppainen, K and Liesio, J (2019) What to do when decision makers deviate from model recommendations? Empirical evidence from hydropower industry, *European Journal of Operational Research*, **278**, pp 869–82

Karimi, S, Papamichail, K N and Holland, C P (2015) The effect of prior knowledge and decision making style on the online purchase decision making process: a typology of consumer shopping behaviour, *Decision Support Systems*, **77**, pp 137–47

McKenzie, E *et al* (2014) Understanding the use of ecosystem service knowledge in decision making: lessons from international experiences of spatial planning, *Environment and Planning C: Government and Policy*, **32**, pp 320–40

Mintzberg, H (1983) *Power in and around Organizations*, Prentice Hall, Englewood Cliffs, NJ

Nolan, V (1989) *The Innovator's Handbook: The skills of innovative management – problem solving, communication and teamwork*, Sphere Books, London

Nonaka, I (1994) A dynamic theory of organizational knowledge creation, *Organizational Science*, 5 (1), pp 14–37

Patton, J R (2003) Intuition in decisions, *Management Decision*, **41** (10), pp 989–96

Shull, F A, Delbecq, A L and Cummings, L L (1970) *Organizational Decision Making*, McGraw-Hill, New York

Simon, H A (1960) *The New Science of Management Decision*, Harper Brothers, New York

Simon, H A (1997) *Administrative Behaviour*, 4th edn, The Free Press, New York

Teale, M *et al* (2003) *Management Decision-Making: Towards an integrative approach*, Pearson Education, Harlow

Knowledge-based decision support systems   13

Learning outcomes

After completing this chapter, the reader will be able to:

- understand the concept of knowledge-based decision support systems;
- critically analyse key technologies for knowledge modelling and knowledge reasoning;
- explain the main application areas of knowledge-based decision support systems.

Intelligent decision support systems (DSS) and knowledge management-based DSS have been identified as two out of the eight important sub-fields in DSS by Arnott and Pervan, based on the content analysis of over one thousand DSS articles published in 14 major journals from 1990 to 2004 (Arnott and Pervan, 2008). This revelation has highlighted the importance of knowledge, KM and learning in supporting decision making. In order to demonstrate the value of knowledge, KM and learning activities in business decisions, this chapter discusses the integration of knowledge, KM and learning theories that have been learned from earlier chapters in this book, together with artificial intelligence (AI), into business decision making. The concept of knowledge-based decision support systems (KB-DSS) will be introduced first, then the chapter will present some key technologies for knowledge modelling/representation and knowledge reasoning/inference for the development of a KB-DSS. Finally the application of KB-DSS in various industrial areas will be examined.

13.1 From DSS to KB-DSS

DSS is a well-established research and development area that has existed since the 1960s. Fundamentally, DSS is an information system that has the function of supporting decision making. A widely adopted definition for DSS is 'an interactive computer-based information system that is designed to support solutions on decision problems' (Bhatt and Zaveri, 2002; Shim *et al*, 2002). DSS research and its applications evolved significantly during the 1970s. By the early 1980s, the first DSS architecture had been proposed by Sprague and Carlsson (1982); it consisted of three components: a database management subsystem, a model-base management subsystem, and a human–computer interface. DSS was considered one of the most popular areas in information systems during the 1980s. A wide variety of DSS were developed to support business decisions at all levels in an organization, from supporting problem structuring, operations optimization, production simulation and financial management to strategic decision making (Liu *et al*, 2010). Many enhanced and more powerful DSS have been developed and used in business practice, including:

- Group decision support system (GDSS): DSS that is designed to support group decision making rather than individual decision making. GDSS can take inputs from a number of decision makers simultaneously, allowing them to interact and negotiate to arrive at a consensus. Such systems can provide brainstorming, idea evaluation and communication facilities to support team problem solving (Limayem, Banerjee and Ma, 2006).

- Executive information systems (EIS): DSS that is designed to support senior executives in a decision-making process. It extends the scope of DSS from personal or small-group use to the corporate level. EIS can provide a wide variety of information, such as an executive summary of the business, critical success metrics, key information indicators, reports with the ability to drill down to underlying details of budget information, plans and objectives, competitive information, news, and more (Elam and Leidner, 1995).

However, in the 1990s, interest in traditional problem-solving DSS was in decline because of new challenges and opportunities coming from a number of directions. First, new technologies, especially ICT such as internet/web technologies, have revolutionized the domain of information management and information systems. Traditional database management has shifted to data warehousing and online analysis processing (OLAP). The emergence of the internet and web has allowed management to share information and knowledge from anywhere in the world. Second, the business environment has shifted from local to global, and the increasing expansion of supply chains has made business decision making a far more complex, uncertain and risky task. Subsequently, many other types of information systems have been developed to compete with DSS. Typically, enterprise resource planning (ERP) systems, supply chain management (SCM) systems and customer relationship management (CRM) systems have been very successful in overtaking the DSS market. Third, an increasing level of complexity, uncertainty and risk of business decision making has put enormous cognitive load on decision makers and business leaders, who need to digest and interpret the information received from all sources and in diversified forms, in order to make the right decisions faster and more consistently. Most often, this high level of cognitive load exceeds human decision makers' analysis and inference capabilities. Finally, decisions on complex and more dynamic business situations require a huge amount of business knowledge and expertise, from global market knowledge and resource knowledge to supply network configuration and coordination knowledge, which has constantly challenged decision makers. Evidence has shown that a high level of knowledge leads to better decisions, and lack of knowledge hinders decision making (Bolukbas and Guneri, 2018).

To cope with the complexity, uncertainty and associated risks of business decision making, decision makers need substantial support in order to overcome their own limitations, in particular in terms of timely access to useful data and information, analytical and inference capabilities, and the availability of expert knowledge. Accordingly, classic DSS has to be enriched to revive its old glory. One of the key solutions is by the utilization of new technologies. The incorporation of KM and AI technologies in traditional DSS has resulted in the emergence of KB-DSS (Zarate and Liu, 2016). Technically, a KB-DSS is the integration of a classic DSS and an expert system (Hwang, Shan and Looi, 2018).

Two key components from an expert system would greatly enhance a DSS with extra power. One is a knowledge base that contains expert knowledge for a particular domain. The other is a reasoning mechanism that can generate inferences over the knowledge base. Hence, an expert system can emulate the decision-making ability of a human expert (Liao, 2005). Clearly, an expert system can complement the functions of a DSS by contributing its knowledge base and inference mechanism, providing the potential for intelligent decision making. Figure 13.1 shows the complementary nature of a DSS and an expert system.

Figure 13.1 Complementary nature of a DSS and an expert system

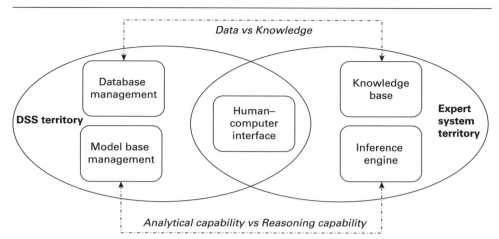

As can be clearly seen from Figure 13.1, the left-hand side is the territory of a DSS and the right-hand side an expert system. The only common component of a DSS and an expert system is a human–computer interface. The special components of a DSS are its database management, providing the right information, and its model-base management, providing 'what-if' analysis for decision making. Comparatively, an expert system provides knowledge through its knowledge base and reasoning capability through an inference engine. By combining a DSS and an expert system to form a KB-DSS, the enhanced system can provide not only required information and knowledge, but also analytical and reasoning capabilities to better support decision making. Thus, a KB-DSS would be well suited for complex and ill-structured problem domains such as business decision making in dynamic, uncertain and risky situations. Because of its clear merits, KB-DSS has been widely used in many industrial areas and sectors, such as healthcare, construction and agriculture. Section 13.3 will discuss details of KB-DSS applications. Section 13.2 will discuss some key technologies for KB-DSS.

13.2 Key technologies for knowledge modelling and knowledge reasoning

Many technologies have contributed to the realization of KB-DSS. For example, the ICT technologies discussed in Chapter 10, such as the Internet of Things and cloud computing, have no doubt made a great impact on KB-DSS.

Figure 13.2 Technologies for knowledge modelling and knowledge reasoning

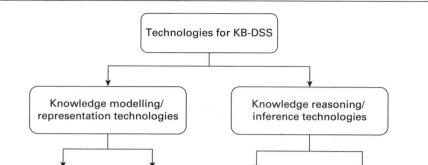

This section focuses on two types of technologies rooted in KM and AI, namely, technologies for knowledge modelling and representation, and technologies for knowledge reasoning and inference. Figure 13.2 illustrates the scope of the technologies detailed in this section.

Technologies for knowledge modelling and representation

Knowledge modelling refers to the creation of machine-interpretable models of knowledge that can be used to stimulate intelligence. Knowledge modelling is a cross-disciplinary area that is concerned with approaches to acquiring, refining, analysing, capturing and describing knowledge in a way that facilitates its preservation and ensuring that it can be aggregated, substituted, improved, mobilized, applied and reapplied (Dutta and Madalli, 2015). The knowledge being modelled can be varied, either general knowledge describing general notions (for instance, space, time, events, matter, material and process), domain knowledge (for instance, food, biomedicine, music and disaster management) describing the domain in terms of classes and properties, or application knowledge describing tasks in terms of ordering the execution, reasoning and inferencing knowledge.

Knowledge modelling needs to satisfy a set of quality requirements (Pigott and Hobbs, 2011), for example:

- order: representing the natural sequence of recording facts/information;
- accuracy: representing the scale, accuracy and precision of a relation;

- likelihood: representing a probability-valued relation;

- evidentiality: representing issues of trust, experience and consistency for a relation;

- conjecture: representing whether a relation is known, conjecture, or one of a set of alternative conjectures.

Various modelling technologies and frameworks have been developed and evolved over time. Two widely used technologies for knowledge modelling are ontology and clustering, hence they have been chosen as representatives for discussion in this section.

Ontology

Ontology is a formal, explicit specification of a shared conceptualization which provides a means for knowledge representation, hence facilitating knowledge capture and sharing (Dutta, Chatterjee and Madali, 2015). An early definition by Gruber (1995) defined ontology as 'a specification of a representational *conceptualization* for a *shared domain* of discourse – definitions of classes, relations, functions and other objects'. Later, Noy and McGuinness (2001) defined ontology as 'a formal *explicit* description of *shared conceptualization* in a domain of discourse, with properties (roles or slots) of each concept describing various features and attributes of the concepts, as well as the relationships among the concepts and classes'. In both definitions, a *domain* is a specific area of knowledge or field of study that is of interest, for example construction, healthcare and new product development. A *conceptualization* is an abstract model of facts in the world identifying the relevant concepts of the phenomenon. The word '*shared*' reflects the notion that an ontology captures consensual knowledge, that is, it is not private to an individual, but accepted by a group. In Noy and McGuinness (2001), 'explicit' means that the type of concepts used and the constraints on their use are defined without ambiguity (Fensel, 2002; Sureephong *et al*, 2008). Based on both definitions, an ontology can be thought of as a specification of how the knowledge of a particular domain can be modelled (represented, described or structured) and shared with representative primitives (eg classes, attributes and relationships) (Kamsu-Foguem *et al*, 2019). Fundamentally, the role of ontology in a KM process is to facilitate the construction of a domain model. It provides a vocabulary of terms and relations in a specific domain (Park and Ramaprasad, 2018).

Constructing an ontology generally consists of two phases: analysis and synthesis (Xu and Zlatanova, 2007). During the analysis phase, compound and complex concepts are first broken down into fundamental ideas, then the concepts/ideas are analysed according to their characteristics, and are grouped based on their features. During the synthesis phase, relationships between concepts are established. Built upon the two phases, a 10-step process for ontology construction was proposed recently, including preparation for analysis and post-synthesis activities (Dutta, Chatterjee and Madali, 2015). The 10 steps can be classified into four main stages: preparation for analysis, analysis, synthesis, and post-synthesis formalization and evaluation. Table 13.1 provides a summary of the main activities during each step and the classification of the steps in relevant stages. Based on the 10 steps, a food ontology has been developed with a focus on restaurant catering.

Table 13.1 Summary of a 10-step ontology construction process and its main stages

No	Step name	Main activities
	Stage: Preparation	
1	Domain identification	Recognize a domain surrounding which an ontology will be built. In general, domain identification is guided by user requirements, application needs and project goals.
2	Domain footprint	Define the purpose and intention of building an ontology, outline more specific use case scenarios and applications of the ontology for end users.
3	Knowledge acquisition	Gather knowledge/information from different resources (eg brainstorming to gather domain-related ideas, terms, concepts and their features), leading to broadening the spectrum of domain knowledge.
	Stage: Analysis	
4	Knowledge formulation	Analyse domain-related compound and complex ideas and break them into their elemental ideas. Each of the ideas is analysed based on its characteristics and then they are grouped together depending on their commonness.
	Stage: Synthesis	
5	Knowledge production	Synthesize the domain knowledge, which leads to arranging the domain knowledge, consisting of multiple facets, by establishing relationships between the concepts.

(continued)

Table 13.1 (Continued)

No	Step name	Main activities
6	Term standardization	Standardize the terms denoting the domain concepts. When more than one candidate term exists, a preferred term should be selected from synonymous terms following its use by domain experts in their written and verbal communication.
7	Knowledge ordering	Order the terms within an array, for instance, alphabetical order, increasing and decreasing intension, increasing and decreasing complexity, canonical order. The knowledge-ordering criteria are led by the purpose, scope and intention of the ontology as defined in Step 2.
8	Knowledge structuring	Structuring the various facets of domain knowledge that were developed in the preceding steps. It depicts the entity, entity relationships and their properties unambiguously, and allows preservation of knowledge, which further ensures the aggregation, substitution, improvement, sharing and reapplication of the ontology.
Stage: Post-synthesis formalization and evaluation		
9	Knowledge formalization	Formalize the domain knowledge for automating the process of knowledge extraction. It involves expressing domain concepts unambiguously and formally following formal logic languages.
10	Evaluation	Measure the quality, standard and specification of the ontology to verify how far the ontology has met the purpose for which it was built.

In an earlier study, Sureephong *et al* (2008) developed a five-stage ontology model for industry clustering, including:

- Phase 1 – feasibility study: the main purpose of this phase is to select the most promising focus area and target solution. This phase identifies problems, opportunities and potential solutions for the organization and environment, including the analysis of corresponding critical success factors for a knowledge system. Feasibility judgement may also include process breakdown and knowledge assets.

- Phase 2 – ontology kick-off: to model the requirements specification for the knowledge management system in the organization. Guides should be provided concerning inclusion and exclusion of concepts/relations and the hierarchical structure of the ontology. The guides contain useful information, such as the domain and goal of the ontology, design guidelines, knowledge sources, user and usage scenario, competency questions and application support provided by the ontology.

- Phase 3 – refinement: to produce a mature and application-oriented target ontology according to the specification given by the kick-off phase. The main tasks in this phase are knowledge elicitation and formalization. The knowledge elicitation process is performed with domain experts, based on the initial inputs from the kick-off phase. Knowledge formalization is the transformation of knowledge into formal ontology representation languages depending on the application (Boshkoska *et al*, 2019).

- Phase 4 – evaluation: to check whether the target ontology meets the ontology requirements and whether the ontology-based knowledge management system supports or answers the competency questions that were analysed in the feasibility and kick-off phases of the project. Thus, the ontology should be tested in the target application environment. A prototype should already show core functionalities of the target system. Feedback from users of the prototype provides valuable inputs for further refinement of the ontology.

- Phase 5 – maintenance and evolution: to update and maintain the knowledge and ontology in the organization. In this phase, an ontology editor may be developed to help knowledge engineers undertaking maintenance tasks. Maintenance should be a continuous process to enable improvement in evolution.

By comparing the two ontology development processes illustrated in Figure 13.3, we can see that the first four phases are agreed in both models. From both the analysis and ontology kick-off phases, an initial ontology is developed. A mature ontology is developed after either synthesis or the refinement phase. After the post-analysis and evaluation phases, an ontology is considered to have been tested in application. Even though different terms are used in the two models, essentially the four phases represent similar activities and tasks in both models. The only difference is that the model by Sureephong *et al* (2008) has an extra phase 5 of maintenance

Figure 13.3 Comparisons between the two ontology development processes

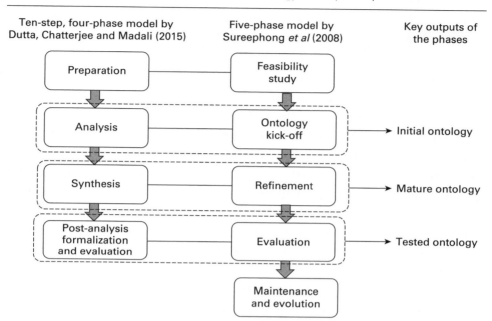

and evolution, which has been omitted in the model by Dutta, Chatterjee and Madali (2015).

Domain knowledge can be modelled using ontology markup languages and various ontology tools. Some well-known markup languages include RDF (Resource Description Framework), OIL (Ontology Inference Layer), DAML (DARPA Agent Markup Language) + OIL, and OWL (Ontology Web Language). Examples of ontology tools are Protégé and OILed (Gayathri and Uma, 2018).

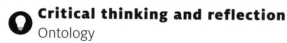 **Critical thinking and reflection**
Ontology

Two hypotheses are usually made about ontology: 1) knowledge can be described by a limited number of attributes; 2) attributes to describe knowledge are assured. What are your critical views on these two hypotheses?

Clustering

Cluster analysis is an effective tool in scientific and managerial inquiry that has also been used in KM. In a knowledge modelling and representation context, clustering technology is about dividing knowledge into distinctive, homogeneous, meaningful categories or classes according to some principles, so that knowledge in the same class has maximum common features (Huang, 1989; Tasoulis and Vrahatis, 2007). Within the same cluster, similar rules are used. Distinct clusters of rules are formed using representatives. When new knowledge needs to be stored in a knowledge base, the knowledge is assigned to a particular cluster. Similarly, when knowledge needs to be retrieved, the search engine will search through the most relevant clusters first rather than aimlessly scanning through the whole knowledge base (Pan, Wang and Liu, 2007). By clustering, some disadvantages produced by the centralized storage of knowledge can be overcome and the working efficiency of a knowledge base can be vastly improved, especially when the size of a knowledge base is very large (Zarate and Liu, 2016).

Clustering algorithms can be roughly divided into two groups: hierarchy based and partitioning based. Compared with hierarchy-based clustering algorithms, partitioning-based clustering algorithms can find all the clusters simultaneously, and can update and refine corresponding cluster centres iteratively (Ma, Zhong and Zhang, 2015). Partitioning clustering can be further divided into exclusive and overlapping methods, depending on which set theory the algorithms are built. Exclusive clustering (eg k-means, self-organizing maps) is built on classic set theory where an element is an exclusive member of a set. Overlapping clustering (eg fuzzy c-means) is based on fuzzy set theory where an element can be a member of one or more sets (Hanafizadeh and Mirzazadeh, 2011).

K-means clustering is one of the earliest and probably most well-known clustering methods (Jain, Murty and Flynn, 1999). It is a type of unsupervised learning which is used for unlabelled data, that is, data without defined groups or categories. The goal of k-means is to find groups for all data, with the number of groups represented by the variable k. The process starts with an initially selected centroid of the groups, then the distances between each data point and all centroids of the k groups are calculated. Based on the distance results, all data can be assigned to a group from which the distance is the shortest. After the first-round assignment of all data, the centroids of each group are recalculated. Then the distance from all data points to all centroids are recalculated. This process will be repeated until the grouping results become stable (without any more changes). An advantage of k-means is that the grouping process can start with any randomly selected points as centroids of the groups. Instead of defining groups before looking at the data, k-means allows finding and analysing the groups that have formed organically. Each centroid of a cluster is a collection of feature values that define the resulting groups. However, the accuracy of the k-means procedure (ie how fast the final clusters are found) depends on the choice of initial seeds, which often falls into a local optimum. Some research has used genetic algorithms to optimize the selection of initial seeds in order to speed up the k-means process (Kim and Ahn, 2008). Using a pre-defined cluster number also becomes a major disadvantage for many business decision cases; for example, for post-hoc market segmentation, it means that the accurate designation of market clusters is not possible for market managers (Hanafizadeh and Mirzazadeh, 2011). In addition, k-means clustering has poor visualization, which makes it a comparatively ineffective method for supporting many business decisions, such as market segmentation.

Fuzzy c-means is another widely known clustering method, integrating fuzzy set theory with c-means (Tang *et al*, 2019). Powered by fuzzy set theory, each data point is assigned membership of a cluster centre. Hence fuzzy c-means clustering is more flexible because it recognizes those objects that have some overlapping interface with more than one cluster. Thus, fuzzy c-means clustering has the advantage over k-means clustering, because k-means clustering is pretty rigid in that one object is assigned to one cluster according to its shortest distance from the centroid of the closest group. However, fuzzy c-means clustering still shares the same shortcomings as k-means clustering in terms of poor visualization and by requiring a pre-defined number of clusters.

There are many more clustering methods that have been created based on different algorithms, such as distance, similarity measurement and evaluation indicators, and each has its strengths and weaknesses (Franzoni and Milani, 2016). The resulting clusters have been widely used in logistic regression, classification and regression trees, neural networks and random forests (Arumugam and Christy, 2018). A comprehensive review of clustering analysis is provided by Xu and Tian (2015).

Because all individual clustering technology has its limitations, a clustering ensemble is proposed. A clustering ensemble combines different clustering partitions of a dataset into a final one. The result of a clustering ensemble is superior to a single-clustering algorithm. The single-clustering algorithm has its own weakness, so it leads to one algorithm being suitable only for a specific dataset. A clustering ensemble combines these clustering algorithms to avoid the shortcomings of a single-clustering algorithm. It fits more datasets into the clustering and it is also robust against noise and outliers (Wu *et al*, 2018).

Essentially, clustering methods are based on the application of similarity (or density) measures, defined over a fixed set of attributes of the domain knowledge, with the goal of creating classes, namely homogeneous knowledge subgroups. Classes of knowledge are taken as collections that exhibit low interclass similarity (density) and high intra-class similarity (density) (Fanizzi and d'Amato, 2007).

Technologies for knowledge reasoning and inference

Knowledge reasoning is an important technology for knowledge retrieval and mapping for knowledge use and reuse. Knowledge retrieval essentially uses the semantic information in knowledge bases to find useful matches. It not only exploits contextual information but also conducts reasoning on relevant concepts (Peng *et al*, 2019). Inference and reasoning ability is a main feature of a knowledge-based decision support system. Over the years, a significant number of reasoning methods have been developed, for example rule-based reasoning, case-based reasoning, common-sense reasoning, fuzzy reasoning, non-monotonic reasoning, model-based reasoning, probabilistic reasoning, causal reasoning, qualitative reasoning, spatial reasoning and temporal reasoning (Gayathri and Uma, 2018). This section will focus on two main types of knowledge reasoning that are widely used in the development of DSS for business and management, namely, rule-based reasoning (RBR) and case-based reasoning (CBR). As the terms indicate, RBR encodes knowledge as rules and CBR as cases. For a comprehensive review of knowledge reasoning technologies and their application in KB-DSS, refer to Zarate and Liu (2016) or to dedicated AI textbooks.

Rule-based reasoning (RBR)

RBR is one of the earliest reasoning methods used for knowledge retrieval and reuse in the development of expert systems. As early as the mid-1970s, MYCIN – an expert system designed to diagnose and recommend treatment for certain blood infections – was developed by Ted Shortliffe and colleagues at Stanford University, in which clinical knowledge was represented as a set of rules with certainty factors attached to diagnosis (Buchanan and Shortliffe, 1984). MYCIN is among the most famous early expert systems, described by Mark Musen as being 'the first convincing demonstration of the power of rule-based approaches in the development of robust clinical decision support systems' (Musen, 2002).

RBR is a mechanism to get conclusions based on formal descriptions of expert experience and knowledge encoded as rules. Rules are patterns, hence an RBR engine can search for patterns in the rules that match patterns in the data. The knowledge most often appears as IF–THEN production rules. This IF–THEN representation of knowledge enables transformation from expert experience to rules (Song, Yan and Zhang, 2019). Rules and an inference engine are necessary conditions to realize RBR. An inference engine is a software program that refers to existing knowledge, manipulates the knowledge according to needs, and makes recommendations about actions to be taken. It generally utilizes pattern matching and searching techniques to draw its conclusions (Akerkar and Sajja, 2010). An inference engine is the core part of RBR, which enables the process of reasoning from existing facts according to certain rules. New rules are added when possible. In other words, an inference engine not only refers to knowledge available within a knowledge base, but also infers new knowledge as needed. During the RBR process, rule-matching and rule-conflicting resolutions may be required to get reasoning conclusions (Thike *et al*, 2019). In RBR, the emphasis is on the mechanism of reasoning and the form of knowledge, with less emphasis on knowledge content (Saraiva *et al*, 2016).

There are two strategies that RBR can use to chain together an appropriate set of rules from a knowledge base. They are forward chaining and backward chaining (Ahmed *et al*, 2015). In forward chaining, environmental inputs and data are stored in a working memory (ie a database of derived facts and data). The arrival of new data in the working memory triggers a searching process. The inference engine, using forward chaining, searches rules until it finds one where an 'IF' clause is known to be true. When found, it can conclude, or infer, the 'THEN' clause, which results in the addition of new information to its dataset. On the other hand, backward chaining starts with the desired conclusions and works backward to find supporting facts. That is, it needs to know the value of a piece of data or a hypothesis. The system searches for rules whose conclusions mention the data. Before a rule can be used, the system must test all conditions. Backward chaining is also called goal-driven or hypothesis-driven, because inferences are not performed until a particular goal is proven (Kumar, Singh and Sanyal, 2009). The comparisons between forward chaining and backward chaining are summarized in Table 13.2.

Table 13.2 Comparisons between forward chaining and backward chaining

	Forward chaining	Backward chaining
Starting point	Some facts (environmental inputs and data)	Value of a piece of data or a hypothesis
Checking focus	Matching conditions	Goal matching
Main purpose	Uses rules to derive new facts from an initial set of data	Uses rules to answer questions about whether a goal clause is true or false
Advantage	Fast process, can provide quick identification and response to problems	Focused because only relevant rules are processed; inferencing is directed, hence information can be requested from the user when needed
Applicability	• There exists sufficient information about an environment to conclude a final decision • There is a single initial state • When a goal state is unpredictable or unimportant or it is difficult to form a goal to verify	• A goal is given or obvious • Environmental constraints or data are not clear • Relevant data must be acquired during the inference process • A large number of applicable rules exist
Example	Real-time monitoring and diagnostic systems	Advisory systems where users ask questions and get asked leading questions to find an answer

In RBR, using either forward chaining or backward chaining, a key issue is conflict resolution, because both forward and backward chaining work in cycles by managing and updating the facts or hypotheses of goals in a working memory. Based on the content of the working memory, appropriate rules from the knowledge base are selected and triggered. Most often, there is more than one single rule to be selected. The collection of triggered rules is known as a conflict set. Conflict resolution is the process whereby the inference engine selects one rule out of all rules in the conflict set, based on some pre-defined criteria (Akerkar and Sajja, 2010). In general, there are three commonly used strategies to resolve a conflict:

• Simply select the first rule from the conflict set. In this case, the order in which rules are stored in the conflict set is very important.

• Select a rule randomly. The function that generates the random rule identifier may be based on a formula learned through references.

- Set priorities for the rules and select the rule with the highest priority. For example, one may consider a heuristic approach by managing a simple pointer referencing how frequently a rule is fired. Then, the rule fired most often is given the highest priority and is selected. An alternative is to select the rule with more details or constraints. Another alternative is to select the rule that was most recently updated.

RBR's main limitations lie in its inability to learn, its inflexibility and the fact that it is time consuming. First, RBR systems do not inherently learn, that is, given the same problem situation, the system will go through exactly the same amount of work to come up with the same solution (Ahmed *et al*, 2015). Second, given a problem that is outside the system's original scope, the system often cannot render any assistance. Finally, RBR systems are very time consuming to build and maintain, because RBR requires explicit knowledge of the details of each domain to be expressed as rules. Rule extraction from experts is labour-intensive; it could take years to build a knowledge base if the domain area is complex, such as in an intensive care unit (ICU) in healthcare. As there are so many specific and specialized sub-domains inside the healthcare service, for example cardiology, poisoning, neurotrauma, cancer and accidents, to which an ICU is related, the knowledge base structure will be very complex, with many levels and branches forming a hierarchy or network, so rules are inherently dependent on each other. The problem with this complexity in the knowledge structure is that it will impose strict constraints on how a knowledge base can be accessed and how it should be maintained (making the addition of new knowledge to the system a complex debugging task). Also, the maintenance of the knowledge base for each domain is a demanding task, hence it will be very difficult to extend it from one domain to another (Kumar, Singh and Sanyal, 2009).

 Critical thinking and reflection
Rule-based reasoning

Considering the two chaining mechanisms, forward chaining and backward chaining, in a clinical decision support system, which chaining mechanism do you think would be most suitable for prognosis, monitoring and control, and which chaining mechanism would be most suitable for diagnosis?

Case-based reasoning (CBR)

CBR has proven a popular technology for acquiring and retrieving knowledge through reusing experience with old cases and past solutions. CBR relies on past, similar cases to find solutions to new problems, critique old solutions and explain anomalous situations (Ahmed *et al*, 2015). Cases may be kept as concrete experience, or a set of similar cases may form a generalized case. Cases may be stored as separate knowledge units or split into subunits and distributed within the knowledge structure. Cases can be indexed by a prefixed or open vocabulary and within a flat or hierarchical structure. The solution from a past case may be directly applied to a new problem, or modified according to the differences between the two cases. CBR works particularly well for repetitive problems such as those found at help desks and call centres. CBR is useful in many situations in providing quick answers to new problems as long as sufficient numbers of previously solved cases are available. CBR is suitable for the following situations (Akerkar and Sajja, 2010):

- when it is difficult to formulate domain rules but cases are available;
- when rules can be formulated but require more information than is typically available because of incomplete problem specifications or because the knowledge needed is simply not available at the time;
- when general knowledge is not sufficient because of too many exceptions, or when new solutions can be derived from old solutions more easily than from scratch.

In CBR, a whole practice case is expressed in a set of features. The feature set of a case in CBR systems includes two main parts: a problem feature subset and a solution feature subset (Jashapara, 2011). Sometimes, a case may have a third part: outcomes. The key to CBR is similarity measurement. When a new case arises, the problem features of the new case are interpreted and compared with those of past cases stored in a knowledge base. Based on all or some of the problem features, similar cases will be retrieved as candidates for further evaluation. If the similarity between the new case and a past case matches well, the solution features of the past case that has the greatest similarity with the new case is taken as the result of the knowledge reasoning (Guo *et al*, 2019). However, if the similarity between the problem features of the new case and the past case is low, the solution features of the past case may be modified as the solution for the new case. The new solutions will be retained in the knowledge base for future use. This process of CBR can be summarized into five key steps, as shown in Figure 13.4.

Figure 13.4 Five key steps in a CBR process

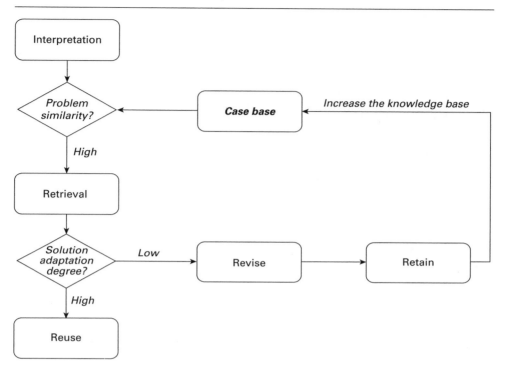

This means of knowledge reasoning has obvious advantages over other AI techniques such as RBR and model-based reasoning (Ifenthaler, 2015), because CBR is based on the way in which human beings solve problems, and it processes existing problems through the reuse or modification of solutions to previous similar problems. Thus, CBR only needs to obtain past cases and does not need to build the whole set of rules or an explicit model. Many domains are so complex that it is impossible or impractical to specify all the rules as in RBR, or build a model as in model-based reasoning. Furthermore, CBR is an incremental approach. This means that each time a problem is solved, the new experience is retained, making it immediately available for future problems. Hence the knowledge base (case library) is being expanded while being used. Its maintenance is relatively easy compared with the RBR system and can be carried out by domain experts. Research has also shown that cases better support knowledge transfer and explanation than other AI techniques (Saraiva *et al*, 2016).

However, CBR has its own limitations. First, CBR lacks deep knowledge and has poor explanations, which could result in the misapplication of cases.

Second, knowledge engineering can still be difficult in designing and selecting problem features, solution features and similarity-matching algorithms. In recent years, along with the emergence of big data, the size of the data in the cases (ie past cases and new cases) in a knowledge base can increase rapidly, which causes huge computing tasks in similarity measurement. Furthermore, data types become very complex, which adds more difficulties for similarity measurement (Guo *et al*, 2019). In order to improve CBR efficiency within a big data context, researchers have proposed the integration of CBR with other AI techniques, for example the Bayesian Network (BN) for case retrieval (Madsen, Jensen and Salmeron, 2016). BN reasoning uses a joint probability distribution function of all problem features of all past cases rather than traditional similarity measurement of each case, hence integration of BN into CBR can vastly improve the knowledge reasoning capability when dealing with big data sizes and complex data types. Another criticism of CBR is the 'similarity assumption' adopted, that is, the most similar past case is considered the most relevant to the new problem to be solved. However, it has been argued that, in reality, a retrieved most similar case cannot always be easily modified to fit a new case (Wan *et al*, 2019). Hence what really matters is actually the adaptation of knowledge, that is, the retrieved case should have the highest degree of adaptation as the basis for generating solutions to the new case.

 Critical thinking and reflection
Case-based reasoning

1   What do you think are the main strengths and limitations of CBR?

2   Irrespective of AI and computer-based knowledge systems, most of us use past experience and lessons learned to support decision making. How often do you use past experience to solve new problems? What would you consider to be an appropriate time limit, if any, of past experience for it to be sufficiently useful?

Hybrid reasoning mechanisms

RBR and CBR are alternative knowledge reasoning mechanisms. However, there are many researchers combining multiple mechanisms to make use of the strengths of various mechanisms. For example, RBR and CBR is one of the most popular combinations because rules and cases offer complementary capabilities. In the literature, there are four different approaches to combine cases and rules:

- a hybrid RBR-first and CBR-last approach, using RBR as the main reasoning process (Rossille, Laurent and Burgun, 2005);

- a CBR-first and RBR-last approach, using CBR as the main reasoning process (Saraiva *et al*, 2016);

- both RBR and CBR are used in parallel, while both outcomes are simply presented (Evans-Romaine and Marling, 2003);

- both RBR and CBR are used in parallel, while the best outcome is calculated according to given criteria (Bichindaritz, 2003).

A second direction to form a hybrid approach is to enrich the reasoning landscape by integrating other technologies into individual reasoning mechanisms. Fuzzy logic has been widely explored together with RBR and CBR (Soufi *et al*, 2018). Fuzzy logic has provided an alternative to Boolean logic-based systems. Unlike Boolean logic, which has only two states, true or false, fuzzy logic deals with truth values, which range continuously from 0 to 1. Thus, it provides a means to distinguish between something that is half true (0.5), very likely true (0.9) or probably not true (0.1). Clauses in fuzzy logic are real-value functions called membership functions. The membership functions allow mapping the fuzzy set for the example 'hot' onto the domain of the fuzzy variable 'temperature' to produce a truth value that ranges from 0.0 to 1.0, which is a continuous output value, much like neural networks (Ahmed *et al*, 2015).

 Critical thinking and reflection
Integration of RBR and CBR

When integrating RBR with CBR, how would you decide which order to use, that is, RBR first or CBR first?

13.3 KB-DSS applications

KB-DSS are now widely used for decision support in businesses covering most industries and sectors, from medicine and healthcare, construction, manufacturing and engineering, to agriculture and sustainability. A review of KB-DSS application in the service industry is provided by Zarate and Liu (2016), including healthcare service, public service, IT service, customer service and other service areas. This section chooses three case studies from different industries to demonstrate the application of KB-DSS to support decision making from a business and management perspective.

KB-DSS application to support triage management decisions in healthcare service

Owing to the great need of expert knowledge, experience and guidance in the healthcare service, KB-DSS has been widely used to support all sorts of decision making, for example using KB-DSS in clinical diagnosis and clinical pathways (Canovas-Segura *et al*, 2019), clinical risk assessment, medication review, preventive care, home care assistance and multi-morbidity patients (Zarate and Liu, 2016). This section discusses a decision support system using a knowledge base and an inference engine for triage management, reported by Soufi *et al* (2018).

Triage is a quick initial clinical assessment in an emergency department, usually performed by emergency nurses. Based on triage assessment, patients are sorted into different triage levels according to the severity of their clinical condition, so that urgent healthcare can be provided for the patients for whom it is most needed, that is, those who have been classified as priority groups. Fast and accurate patient triage is critical to save people's lives, while making the best use of scarce resources in hospitals. However, triage assessment and making fast decisions is challenging for a number of reasons. First, patients often turn up at the emergency department quite suddenly, which gives triage assessment professionals no warning of their medical history. For example, casualties from serious accidents may be unconscious and not able to tell nurses anything. Second, a large number of patients could turn up at an emergency department at the same time, which puts medical professionals under great pressure physically, mentally and emotionally on some occasions. Third, patients turning up at an emergency department could present a wide range of medical conditions. These conditions are highly unpredictable, which means that it is never known beforehand when a patient with a particular condition might come through the front door. Guidance from a KB-DSS would be immensely valuable for nurses/medical professionals to quickly assess patients and ensure the accuracy of triage assessment.

The KB-DSS presented by Soufi *et al* (2018) used a combination of RBR and a fuzzy logic classifier (FLC) to predict the triage level of patients based on knowledge collected from triage specialists and emergency severity index

(ESI) guidelines. The ESI encompasses four decision points on assigning patients into five triage levels, considering the patients' acuity, pain and resource needs. Patients whose conditions are life threatening require immediate life-saving intervention, hence will be assigned to the top priority level, level 1. Patients whose conditions are least severe would be assigned to level 5. Patients' data regarding vital signs such as heart rate and respiratory rate can be used as inputs to feed into the FLC and trigger production rules for reasoning. The inference engine then searches the knowledge base (populated with rules) and analyses initial facts and past patterns in order to match applicable rules.

Knowledge representation in the triage KB-DSS uses typical production rules in the form of 'IF conditions, THEN conclusions'. Conditions specify the level of consciousness, patient acuity, required resources, and parameters of vital signs (using the FLC). The outcome state consists of triage levels as the final suggestion (conclusion) of a triage nurse. All guideline recommendations and specialist opinions at the four decision points are expressed in IF–THEN format, which makes up a decision tree with all parameters strictly defined using routinely collected triage data. In the system, variables regarding a patient's vital signs are fuzzified as linguistic variables, and other decision points are modelled in the form of qualitative rules.

The knowledge/inference system used to predict the triage levels has four main components:

- a fuzzier: translates a crisp input (ie classical numbers) into fuzzy values;
- an inference engine: applies a fuzzy reasoning mechanism to obtain a fuzzy output;
- a knowledge base: contains fuzzy rules and membership functions representing the fuzzy sets of linguistic variables;
- a defuzzier: translates the fuzzy output into crisp values.

The KB-DSS was evaluated with clinical professionals. The results show that the accuracy of triage assessment is significantly improved when supported by the guidance provided by the knowledge base and inference system. The hybrid approach of RBR and FLC can reduce triage misdiagnosis in a highly accurate manner. The KB-DSS has been proven to provide helpful guidance to nurses as they make decisions with improved quality measures for accuracy in the triage process.

KB-DSS application to support project management decisions in construction

Hwang, Shan and Looi (2018) reported a KB-DSS for a project team to assess the feasibility of using off-site construction, PPVC, for a given project. PPVC stands for prefabricated prefinished volumetric construction, which is a process where building elements, components and modules are manufactured and assembled in off-site factories and then transported to the installation site. Compared with traditional on-site construction, PPVC has many advantages, for example being innovative and clean, improving productivity and workflow, minimizing construction waste, reducing the number of on-site contractors and reducing construction project lead-time. Construction projects are often big investments. The decision on whether or not to use innovative approaches such as PPVC has a significant impact on an organization's business performance.

The KB-DSS developed for the feasibility assessment of adopting PPVC has a dedicated knowledge base, which is a repository of the knowledge and experience of experts about the PPVC method. The knowledge base includes sets of decision-making factors affecting the adoption of PPVC, and recommended action plans for the implementation of PPVC if the feasibility assessment produces a positive recommendation. The knowledge stored in the knowledge base is based on a number of sources: comprehensive literature review, pilot interviews with experts and a subsequent system validation exercise.

The decision support component inside the KB-DSS has a number of functions. First, it can score the decision-making factors retrieved from the knowledge base for each project in terms of PPVC adoption. Then it computes an overall PPVC score by taking account of a decision maker's inputs and preferences for the given project. Based on the computed PPVC score, the system can make recommendations by the combinatorial use of two types of knowledge reasoning mechanisms: RBR and CBR. The reasoning process is as follows:

- If the overall PPVC score is less than 60, adopting PPVC for the project is not feasible; the system recommends the project to use conventional on-site construction methods instead of the PPVC method.

- If the overall PPVC score is greater than 80, the feasibility assessment is positive and the KB-DSS recommends some actions that can facilitate the implementation of the PPVC method, for example ensuring active participation by and commitment of various project stakeholders, arranging manufacturing plant tours and site visits, and appointing PPVC specialists.

- If the overall PPVC score is between 60 and 80, the feasibility assessment shows potential but requires improvement. The KB-DSS would recommend the project team to refer to similar past projects using the PPVC method, to revisit and modify the building design to make it more suitable for PPVC, and to appoint PPVC specialists to help with design improvement and then with the implementation of PPVC.

The KB-DSS has been evaluated through interviews and questionnaire surveys with experts from 41 organizations in Singapore. For its main strengths and limitations, refer to the original publication (Hwang, Shan and Looi, 2018).

KB-DSS application to support quality management decisions in the agri-food sector

Food quality management is a complex task because food quality has to meet a range of characteristics and a set of standards in order to be acceptable to customers. Food quality includes both internal factors (eg chemical, physical, microbial) and external factors such as appearance (size, shape, colour, gloss and consistency), texture and flavour. Food quality management decisions include detecting food defects (ie food characteristics that are not acceptable to customers) and deciding appropriate actions to take. Food quality management requires substantial expertise, experience and knowledge. The application of KB-DSS in food quality management has attracted a lot of attention in recent years. Buche *et al* (2019) presented an expertise-based decision support system for managing food quality in agri-food companies.

The KB-DSS provides two main functions to help control the quality and defects of food manufacturing: 1) the system can recommend appropriate technical actions to take at process and operations level when a food defect is detected; 2) the system can determine the impact of the actions taken on other food quality factors and food defects, to make sure that the actions taken to correct one defect will not have adverse effects on other quality factors or defects. A seven-step iterative process is discussed for the development of the food quality management KB-DSS, including important knowledge aspects related to the knowledge base and inference engine, such as knowledge collection, knowledge structuring (modelling) and knowledge reasoning to retrieve the right recommendations. The seven steps and the main activities at each step are:

- Step 1: define the scope of the study – the food manufacturing process and food quality standards or defects of interest.

- Step 2: break the manufacturing process down into a set of unit operations and associated controllable parameters.

- Step 3: a systematic questionnaire is derived from the description of the process in order to collect expert knowledge on the potential impact that each unit operation may have on the product in terms of defects and quality standards.

- Step 4: collect expert knowledge through two types of interview – individual interviews and group interviews. Group collective interviews are useful to resolve potential contradictions detected when pooling knowledge from individual interviews in order to obtain consensus.

- Step 5: knowledge representation as a tree structure using mind mapping.

- Step 6: translate the knowledge in mind maps into conceptual graph formalism (Chein and Mugnier, 2009), which allows the terminology, facts, rules and constraints of an application domain in a knowledge base to be managed and inferred (accessed, queried, updated, reasoned etc). The mind-mapping approach is well suited to quickly capturing experts' knowledge of a process; however, it is not sufficient for ensuring the consistency of a large dataset, as it lacks a formal representation model to ensure data consistency. That is why conceptual graph formalism is used to complement mind mapping.

- Step 7: provide an end-user interface, ensuring that end users of the application can use it easily without knowing anything about conceptual graph formalism.

What lies behind the KB-DSS that is not explicitly discussed in the seven-step process is the domain ontology implemented to support knowledge reasoning. The ontology provides a powerful reasoning mechanism for exploiting the knowledge and managing changes in the knowledge base (Buche *et al*, 2019). The food quality domain ontology provides unambiguous reasoning by following causal relationships between technical actions that can be taken and food defects that have been detected.

Key learning points

- A classic decision support system has three key components: a database management subsystem, a model-base management subsystem, and a human–computer interface.

- Compared with a classic decision support system, the extra components that a knowledge-based decision support system has are a knowledge base and an inference engine.

- Group decision support systems are designed to support group decision making rather than individual decision making. Such systems can offer extra functions such as brainstorming, communication, interaction and negotiation.

- Ontology can be defined as a formal explicit description of shared conceptualization in a domain of discourse, with the properties of each concept describing various features and attributes of the concepts, as well as the relationships among concepts and classes.

- A number of ontology development processes are available in the literature. A five-stage process proposed by Sureephong *et al* (2008) includes a feasibility study, ontology kick-off, refinement, evaluation, and maintenance and evolution.

- Clustering technology is about dividing knowledge into distinctive, homogeneous, meaningful categories. Within the same clusters, similar rules are used.

- K-means and fuzzy c-means are two widely known clustering algorithms. Both can divide knowledge into a pre-defined number of groups. The main difference between the two algorithms is that the k-means algorithm groups knowledge into mutually exclusive categories, that is, each knowledge point is assigned to one group only. But fuzzy c-means can recognize the overlapping knowledge points, which can be grouped in more than one category.

- RBR and CBR are two very important knowledge reasoning mechanisms. In RBR, knowledge is represented in rules; in CBR knowledge is represented in cases.

- Forward chaining and backward chaining take opposite directions when inferring about knowledge. Forward chaining starts by checking condition clauses and then finds conclusions. Backward chaining starts from a hypothesis and then proves the hypothesis to be true by finding supporting evidence.

Review questions

- What do you think are the key differences between a decision support system and an information system?

- What are the main differences between a knowledge management system, an expert system and a knowledge-based decision support system?

- If you were asked to lead a feasibility study for an ontology development in a specific domain, you would want first to identify a list of tasks for the feasibility study, so that you can allocate the tasks to your project team. What would be on your tasks list? Choose a domain that you are familiar with for this exercise, if it helps.

- In order to evaluate an ontology that has been developed, you will need to know what criteria to use for the evaluation. What would you put on the criteria list for an ontology evaluation?

- Why is knowledge clustering important when the size of the knowledge base is extremely large?

- What is the main advantage of fuzzy c-means clustering compared with k-means clustering?

- What are the main differences between RBR and CBR?

References

Ahmed, I M *et al* (2015) Reasoning techniques for diabetes expert systems, *Procedia Computer Science*, **65**, pp 813–20

Akerkar, R A and Sajja, P S (2010) *Knowledge-Based Systems*, Jones and Bartlett, Burlington, MA

Arnott, D and Pervan, G (2008) Eight key issues for the decision support systems discipline, *Decision Support Systems*, **44**, pp 657–72

Arumugam, P and Christy, V (2018) Analysis of clustering and classification methods for actionable knowledge, *Materials Today: Proceedings*, **5**, pp 1839–45

Bhatt, G D and Zaveri, J (2002) The enabling role of decision support systems in organizational learning, *Decision Support Systems*, **32** (3), pp 297–309

Bichindaritz, I (2003) Solving safety implications in a case based decision support system in medicine, in *Proceedings of the Fifth International Conference on Case-Based Reasoning: Workshop on case-based reasoning in the health sciences*, pp 178–83

Bolukbas, U and Guneri, A F (2018) Knowledge-based decision making for the technology competency analysis of manufacturing enterprises, *Applied Soft Computing*, **67**, pp 781–99

Boshkoska, B M *et al* (2019) A decision support system for evaluation of the knowledge sharing crossing boundaries in agri-food value chains, *Computers in Industry*, **110**, pp 64–80

Buchanan, B G and Shortliffe, E H (1984) *Rule-Based Expert Systems: The MYCIN experiments of the Stanford Heuristic Programming Project*, Addison-Wesley, Reading, MA

Buche, P *et al* (2019) Expertise-based decision support for managing food quality in agri-food, *Computers and Electronics in Agriculture*, **163**, 104843

Canovas-Segura, B *et al* (2019) A lightweight acquisition of expert rules for interoperable clinical decision support systems, *Knowledge-Based Systems*, **167**, pp 98–113

Chein, M and Mugnier, M I (2009) Graph based knowledge representation and reasoning, in *Computational Foundations of Conceptual Graphs*, Springer, London

Dutta, B, Chatterjee, U and Madali, D P (2015) YAMO: Yet Another Methodology for large-scale faceted Ontology construction, *Journal of Knowledge Management*, **9** (1), pp 6–24

Dutta, B and Madalli, D P (2015) Trends in knowledge modelling and knowledge management: an editorial, *Journal of Knowledge Management*, **19** (1), pp i–iii

Elam, J J and Leidner, D G (1995) EIS Adoption, use and impact: the executive perspective, *Decision Support Systems*, **14** (2), pp 89–103

Evans-Romaine, K and Marling, C (2003) Prescribing exercise regimens for cardiac and pulmonary disease patients with CBR, in *Workshop on CBR in the Health Sciences*, Fifth International Conference on Case-Based Reasoning (ICCBR-03), pp 45–62

Fanizzi, N and d'Amato, C (2007) A hierarchical clustering method for semantic knowledge bases, in *Knowledge-Based Intelligent Information and Engineering Systems*, ed B Apolloni, R J Howlett and L C Jain, pp 653–60, Springer, Berlin

Fensel, D (2002) Ontology-based knowledge management, *Computers*, **35** (11), pp 56–59

Franzoni, V and Milani, A (2016) A semantic comparison of clustering algorithms for the evaluation of web-based similarity measures, in *Computational Science and Its Applications – ICCSA 2016*, ed O Gervasi *et al*, pp 438–52, Springer, Cham, Switzerland

Gayathri, R and Uma, V (2018) Ontology based knowledge representation technique, domain modelling languages and planners for robotic path planning: a survey, *ICT Express*, **4**, pp 69–74

Gruber, T R (1995) Towards principles for the design of ontologies used for knowledge sharing, *International Journal of Human–Computer Studies*, **43** (5–6), pp 907–928

Guo, Y *et al* (2019) Research on the integrated system of case-based reasoning and Bayesian network, *ISA Transactions*, **90**, pp 213–25

Hanafizadeh, P and Mirzazadeh, M (2011) Visualizing market segmentation using self-organizing maps and fuzzy Delphi method: ADSL market of a telecommunication company, *Expert systems with Applications*, **38** (1), pp 198–205

Huang, Y J (1989) A clustering method of knowledge acquisition in a real-time control system, *Annual Review in Automatic Programming*, **15** (2), pp 49–51

Hwang, B G, Shan, M and Looi, K Y (2018) Knowledge-based decision support system for prefabricated prefinished volumetric construction, *Automation in Construction*, **94**, pp 169–78

Ifenthaler, D (2015) Effects of experimentally induced emotions on model-based reasoning, *Learning and Individual Differences*, **43**, pp 191–98

Jain, A K, Murty, M N and Flynn, P J (1999) Data clustering: a review, *ACM Computing Surveys*, **31** (3), pp 264–323

Jashapara, A (2011) *Knowledge Management: An integrated approach*, 2nd edn, Pearson Education, Harlow

Kamsu-Foguem, B *et al* (2019) Graph-based ontology reasoning for formal verification of MREEAM rules, *Cognitive Systems Research*, **55**, pp 14–33

Kim, K and Ahn, H (2008) A recommender system using GA k-means clustering in an online shopping market, *Expert Systems With Applications*, **34**, pp 1200–09

Kumar, K A, Singh, Y and Sanyal, S (2009) Hybrid approach using case-based reasoning and rule-based reasoning for domain independent clinical decision support in ICU, *Expert Systems With Applications*, **36**, pp 65–71

Liao, S H (2005) Expert system methodologies and applications – a decade review from 1995 to 2004, *Expert Systems with Applications*, **28** (1), pp 93–103

Limayem, M, Banerjee, P and Ma, L (2006) The impact of GDSS: opening the black box, *Decision Support Systems*, **42**, pp 945–57

Liu, S *et al* (2010) Integration of decision support systems to improve decision support performance, *Knowledge and Information Systems – an International Journal*, **22** (3), pp 261–86

Ma, A, Zhong, Y and Zhang, L (2015) Adaptive multi-objective memetic fuzzy clustering algorithm for remote sensing imagery, *IEEE Transactions on Geoscience and Remote Sensing*, **53** (8), pp 4202–17

Madsen, L A, Jensen, F and Salmeron, A (2016) A parallel algorithm for Bayesian network structure learning from large data sets, *Knowledge-Based Systems*, **117** (1), pp 46–55

Musen, M A (2002) Medical informatics: searching for underlying components, *Methods of Information in Medicine*, **41** (1), pp 12–19

Noy, N F and McGuinness, D L (2001) Ontology development 101: a guide to creating your first Ontology, Stanford Knowledge Systems Laboratory Technical Report KSL-01-05 and Stanford Medical Informatics Technical Report SMI-2001-0880, Stanford, CA

Pan, X, Wang, J and Liu, L (2007) Knowledge sharing model based on concept clustering, *Systems Engineering – Theory and Practice*, **27** (2), pp 126–32

Park, J and Ramaprasad, A (2018) Toward ontology of designer-user interaction in the design process: a knowledge management foundation, *Journal of Knowledge Management*, **22** (1), pp 201–18

Peng, G *et al* (2019) A hypernetwork-based approach to collaborative retrieval and reasoning of engineering design knowledge, *Advanced Engineering Informatics*, **42**, 100956

Pigott, D J and Hobbs, V J (2011) Complex knowledge modelling with functional entity relationship diagrams, *VINE – the Journal of Information and Knowledge Management Systems*, **41** (2), pp 192–211

Rossille, D, Laurent, J F and Burgun, A (2005) Modelling a decision support system for oncology using rule-based and case-based reasoning methodologies, *International Journal of Medical Informatics*, **74** (2), pp 299–306

Saraiva, R *et al* (2016) Early diagnosis of gastrointestinal cancer by using case-based and rule-based reasoning, *Expert Systems with Applications*, **61**, pp 192–202

Shim, J P *et al* (2002) Past, present and future of decision support technology, *Decision Support Systems*, **33**, pp 111–26

Song, B, Yan, W and Zhang, T (2019) Cross-border e-commerce commodity risk assessment using text mining and fuzzy rule-based reasoning, *Advanced Engineering Informatics,* **40**, pp. 69–80

Soufi, M D *et al* (2018) Decision support system for triage management: a hybrid approach using rule-based reasoning and fuzzy logic, *International Journal of Medical Informatics*, **114**, 35–44

Sprague, R H and Carlsson, E D (1982) *Building Effective Decision Support Systems*, Prentice-Hall, Englewood Cliffs, NJ

Sureephong, P *et al* (2008) An ontology-based knowledge management systems for industry clustering, in *Global Design to Gain a Competitive Edge*, ed X T Yan, W J Ion and B Eynard, pp 333–342, Springer, London

Tang, J *et al* (2019) A hierarchical prediction model for lane-changes based on combination of fuzzy c-means and adaptive neural network, *Expert Systems With Applications*, **130**, pp 265–75

Tasoulis D K and Vrahatis, M N (2007) Generalizing the k-windows clustering algorithm in metric spaces, *Mathematical and Computer Modelling*, **46**, pp 268–77

Thike, P H *et al* (2019) Materials failure analysis utilizing rule-case hybrid reasoning method, *Engineering Failure Analysis*, **95**, pp 300–11

Wan, S *et al* (2019) A knowledge based machine tool maintenance planning system using case-based reasoning techniques, *Robotics and Computer Integrated Manufacturing*, **58**, pp 80–96

Wu, X *et al* (2018) A comparative study of clustering ensemble algorithms, *Computers and Electrical Engineering*, **68**, pp 603–15

Xu, D and Tian, Y (2015) A comprehensive survey of clustering algorithms, *Annals of Data Science*, **2** (2), pp 165–93

Xu, W and Zlatanova, S (2007) Ontologies for disaster management response, in *Geomatics Solutions for Disaster Management*, ed J Li, S Zlatanova and A G Fabbri, pp 185–200, Springer, Berlin

Zarate, P and Liu, S (2016) A new trend for knowledge-based decision support system design, *International Journal of Information and Decision Sciences*, **8** (3), pp 305–24

INDEX